FACT AND FICTION

EDITED BY CHRISTINE LEHLEITER

Fact and Fiction

Literary and Scientific Cultures in Germany and Britain

UNIVERSITY OF TORONTO PRESS
Toronto Buffalo London

Toronto Buffalo London
www.utppublishing.com

ISBN 978-1-4426-4598-1 (cloth)

Library and Archives Canada Cataloguing in Publication

Fact and fiction : literary and scientific cultures in Germany and Britain / edited by Christine Lehleiter.

Includes bibliographical references and index.
ISBN 978-1-4426-4598-1 (cloth)

1. German literature – 18th century – History and criticism. 2. English literature – 18th century – History and criticism. 3. Literature and science – Germany – History – 18th century. 4. Literature and science – Great Britain – History – 18th century. 5. Science in literature. 6. Knowledge, Theory of, in literature. I. Lehleiter, Christine, editor II. Title.

PT148.S3F32 2016 830.9'36 C2015-905663-2

University of Toronto Press acknowledges the financial assistance to its publishing program of the Canada Council for the Arts and the Ontario Arts Council, an agency of the Government of Ontario.

Canada Council for the Arts Conseil des Arts du Canada

Funded by the Government of Canada Financé par le gouvernement du Canada

Contents

Illustrations

Acknowledgments

This volume emerged from a symposium, "Fact and Fiction: Literature and Science in the German and European Context," which took place at the University of Toronto in spring 2011. The workshop was generously sponsored and supported by the Department of Germanic Languages and Literatures and the Faculty of Arts and Sciences at the University of Toronto, the Social Sciences and Humanities Research Council (SSHRC), the German Academic Exchange Service (DAAD), the Munk School of Global Affairs, Joint Initiative in German and European Studies (JIGES), and the Centre for European, Russian, and Eurasian Studies (CERES). We gratefully acknowledge the support of these institutions. A thank you to those who helped mount the symposium and guaranteed its smooth running, especially Yasmin Aly, Dale Gebhardt, Gayle Grisdale, Monika Lang, Nicole Perry, Markus Stock, and John Zilcosky. Financial support for the publication of this volume was provided by a SSHRC Aid to Research Workshops Grant.

Thanks go also to the Jackman Humanities Institute (JHI) at the University of Toronto for its support of a working group on the relationship between "Science and Culture," initiated by Cannon Schmitt in 2008 and co-organized by Marga Vicedo and Christine Lehleiter in 2010–11. The discussions in this working group inspired the preparations for the symposium and it has been gratifying to see that several of its members have become contributors.

I wish to acknowledge my gratitude to all contributors for their outstanding engagement with this project and for their patience during the editorial process. We owe special thanks to the two anonymous peer-reviewers for their extremely insightful suggestions and comments. For her copy-editing work in the early stages of the volume's production

I thank Marlo Burks, for the professional copy-editing John St James, and for help with finishing the indexing Teresa Sudenis. Finally, a deeply felt "thank you" goes to Richard Ratzlaff, our editor at the University of Toronto Press, who supported this project from the moment of its inception and was there with help and advice at every step of the process.

Introduction

Fact and Fiction: Literary and Scientific Cultures in Germany and Britain – Thoughts on a Contentious Relationship

CHRISTINE LEHLEITER

The title of this volume alludes to the paradigm of "The Two Cultures," which became popular through Charles Percy Snow's *Rede* lectures delivered in 1959. In these lectures, Snow lamented the divide of the two knowledge-producing systems of the humanities and the sciences.[1] Despite the reference to Snow, however, it is not the volume's aim to represent and solidify an antagonistic formulation of the relationship between scientific and literary cultures. Rather, the articles assembled here investigate Snow's division between science and the humanities as a historically conditioned and complex phenomenon. When the title refers to literary and scientific cultures, it is with the acknowledgment of this historical complexity and, at the same time, with the recognition that the terminological pair of "literature and science" has become a practical reference for an area of study that is still in its development.[2]

Towards a Field?

Since Snow's lamentation about the split between scientific and literary worlds and – even more – about the unwillingness of the participants of these cultures to engage with each other's fields of knowledge, much work has been undertaken in disciplines such as the history of science and literary studies with the goal to develop a clearer picture of the relationship between science and literature and of its historical development. Indeed, there was much excitement two decades ago about the establishment of a new field under the heading of *Literature and Science*. In their 1989 publication, Christie and Shuttleworth expressed the hope that this field would become comparable to research areas such as Gender Studies or Postcolonial Theory.[3] Similarly, Bruce and Purdy, in their volume *Literature and*

Science (1994), announced the emergence of an "exciting new field" under the name "Literary and Science Studies."[4] However, despite initial excitement and optimism, little has materialized in the last decades in terms of an institutional anchoring of such a field. There are few programs in North America that have found promising ways to bring together under one roof scholars trained in distinct disciplines (York University is an example) or to unite them in the context of a scholarly association (the Society for Literature, Science, and the Arts, SLSA, is an exception). These attempts at institutionalizing have remained far and few between.

The hesitations and delays in establishing and institutionalizing the field are connected to the realization that it is difficult to formulate a stringent set of questions which this area of study might address. Even before formulating such questions, we would need to ask: how are the terms defined within the field's name? When we say "literature" and "science," do we mean a specific historical and disciplinary constellation which became possible once scientific and literary methodologies were defined as separate from each other? Or do we assume a much more generous definition of the terms – running the risk that the title's distinction, if not the opposition that it claims, becomes void? These questions are difficult to answer.

Notwithstanding the difficulties, there is a rich body of work that has tried to address questions such as these. Gillian Beer in particular has been instrumental in establishing and conceptualizing a field of research that focuses on the relationship between literature and science. In "Translation or Transformation," Beer considers the question of whether the distinction between the disciplines is justified at all. To discuss the relationship between the disciplines, Beer employs the terms "translation" and "transformation." She dismisses what she calls "translation" as inadequate, because it assumes a primacy of one field which is then translated into another. Instead of delineating clearly defined boundaries between disciplines, Beer highlights the unstable nature of the relationship between literature and science. She stresses "interchange rather than origins and transformation rather than translation" and notes that "neither literature nor science is an entity, and what constitutes literature or science is a matter for agreement in a particular historical period or place."[5] Instead of assuming a hierarchy or split between disciplines, Beer turns her attention to the shared language of literary and scientific texts. Using the Victorian period as a case study, she examines how in texts of scientists such as Charles Darwin (1809–82) and Charles Lyell (1797–1875) narrative models and myths are reused in order to tell the story of evolution.[6]

Following the lead of literary scholars such as Beer and theoreticians such as Michel Foucault, significant work has been done in recent years in the history of science to shift the attention from individual discoveries and experiments to the discursive, textual production of these moments. This "linguistic turn"[7] is perhaps most clearly marked in James Secord's Halifax keynote address, in which he proposes that historians of science should approach "science as a form of communication."[8] Suggestions such as Secord's have helped to raise the status of textual expertise within the history of science, where this new attention to language has proved extremely productive. One recent exploration of this work is the excellent *Focus* section of the leading history of science journal *ISIS* on the topic "History of Science and Literature and Science" (September 2010). Colin Milburn observes there that historians have become more aware of what he calls "literary technologies" in the sciences, but he notes that the contribution of science fiction "and even literature as such" to the sciences has not been adequately studied yet.[9] In the same *ISIS* issue, Henry S. Turner encourages readers to learn from literary scholarship and to consider "form" as a category for the study of the history of science. Laura Dassow Walls's contribution stresses the "rootedness of all texts in lived experience" and suggests that "both literary and scientific texts may be approached as performances that weave together discursive and material elements."[10] Two observations regarding the *ISIS* issue stand out in connection to the subject of our volume: first, the focus on the interrelatedness of literature and science and, second, the conviction that literary tools help historians of science to understand better their objects of study. Consequently, James Bono states in the issue's introduction that the essays assembled in this *ISIS* edition demonstrate "that history of science and literature and science are, in fact, interdependent fields" and that the field of "literature and science shares with the history of science a concern to understand the making of science."[11]

The focus on language and on shared discourses has proved to be a fruitful path towards an understanding of how scientific innovation takes place and how scientific paradigms emerge. However, it has also made it difficult to pay attention to specific disciplinary questions and to the specific contribution of literary cultures to knowledge.[12] Although numerous studies have shown by now that the emergence of knowledge cannot be confined within disciplinary boundaries, it is also a fact that disciplines remain a shaping structure of knowledge production and academic life. As Katherine Hayles has noted, disciplinary formation is so strong that we often don't even notice any longer the disciplinary "lenses" that we wear.

"They are crafted through long years of apprenticeship as we absorb, often unconsciously, attitudes and ways of speaking that determine not only the answers we accept, but the questions we ask and the rhetoric we use to ask them."[13] It seems likely that the challenges in establishing an interdisciplinary field of Literature and Science Studies have not only to do with a yet to be formulated set of questions, but also with the fact that institutionalized disciplines remain today the place whence interdisciplinary inquiries are launched. Even more, disciplinary training, as Donald T. Campbell argues, is a necessary precondition for research as we understand it today.[14] Accepting disciplinary division, Campbell suggests a "Fish-Scale Model of Omniscience" that promises access to truth by means of partially intersecting expert knowledge.

This volume is rooted in disciplinary traditions, but it is also indebted to the historical sensibility that scholars such as Beer bring to the disciplines' definition and development. The aim here is less a search for omniscience than an exploration of the historical condition and relation of disciplines and methods whose continued existence (and necessity) the volume acknowledges. By examining individual cases of disciplinary relations, *Fact and Fiction* does not promise to formulate a binding and abstract definition of Literature and Science Studies. It pursues a more confined but hopefully no less productive agenda. Starting from the premise that the eighteenth century is shaped by a differentiation of disciplines, this volume asks how authors from the eighteenth century onwards have assessed the relationship between literary and scientific cultures. In engaging with this question, the scholars that contribute to this volume are indebted to specific disciplinary traditions and tools. However, by using these tools they aim to look beyond their disciplines.

In undertaking interdisciplinary work, the papers in this volume remind us that interdisciplinarity is in no way "more natural" than the disciplinarity that we have exercised for so many years. Interdisciplinarity is understood here as an effect of disciplinary divisions, not as their abolition. Mindful of its own historical condition, the volume testifies that if there will be a place for Literary and Science Studies, it will be as much an expression of an interest in interdisciplinarity as it will be an expression of a historical and political moment in which literature feels under pressure from the sciences. What Tim Lenoir has stated regarding disciplines – "It is at best an interested abstraction formed in the service of a disciplinary program"[15] – could also be said about interdisciplinarity. Despite these difficulties and hesitations regarding an institutionalization of Literature and Science Studies, the papers in this volume are witnesses to how productive it can be to think beyond disciplinary boundaries.

Science and Poetry

And yet, the distinction of the two areas of knowledge production is justified and their study legitimated not only by the current disciplinary wars, but by the fact that authors have referred to the division from the eighteenth century onwards. In an often quoted passage, the German polymath Johann Wolfgang Goethe (1749–1832) acknowledges and regrets the existence of the division: "Nowhere would anyone grant that science and poetry can be united. People forgot that science had developed from poetry and they failed to take into consideration that a swing of the pendulum might beneficently reunite the two, at a higher level and to mutual advantage."[16] The German term "Wissenschaft" (science) that Goethe uses in this quote encompasses a broader spectrum of meaning than its English translation into "science" would suggest. While science is often understood as "natural sciences," the German "Wissenschaft" refers more broadly to scholarly inquiry, which includes not only "Natur*wissenschaft*" (natural sciences), but also "Geistes*wissenschaft*" (humanities) and disciplines such as "Literatur*wissenschaft*" (literary studies). The term "Wissenschaft" refers to a methodology rather than to a specific object of study.[17] Thinking about Snow's suggestion regarding the two cultures, David Knight has highlighted the new significance of scientific inquiry that emerges in Goethe's times. He observes that in Romanticism "the real division was between the realm of science, governed by reason, and that of practice, or rule of thumb."[18] Knight's observation brings to our attention the growing awareness for scientific methods which informs Goethe's statement, but it also overlooks how closely scientific inquiry was shaped in Goethe's times by the practical and the quotidian. Botany – the field of study to which Goethe refers – is a particularly relevant example. Its study around 1800 relied heavily on the contribution of individuals with no specific training or schooling.[19] Goethe's statement suggests that it was not only the opposition to the practical but even more the opposition to the imaginary and poetic which was crucial for the development of a modern understanding of the sciences.

While noting the split between scientific and poetic methodologies, Goethe assumes that they are genealogically linked. He is not alone in this assumption, nor is he the first to formulate it. His statement that science has developed from poetry resonates with the work of philosopher and theologian Johann Gottfried Herder (1744–1803) from the mid-1760s – published only a few years before Goethe got in close contact with Herder and his thinking when befriending him in Strasbourg during his study years. Herder had argued that conceptual language developed from poetry and, as John Noyes formulates in this volume, that "there is something about the poetic that resides at the heart of factuality."[20] Much as Herder observed a historical development from poetic to conceptual language, Goethe understood the split between science and poetry *not* as an ontological condition, but attributed it to historical circumstances which, when changed, could reconfigure this relationship ("nach einem Umschwung von Zeiten" [after a change of times]).

Despite Goethe's hope for a potential reconciliation of the two ways of creating knowledge, it is important to note that Goethe does not regret so much the existence of the differentiation of the methodologies as the assumption that they could not talk to each other in a meaningful way. In his contribution to this volume ("Elective Affinities / *Wahlverwandtschaften*: The Career of a Metaphor"), Christian Weber examines the ways in which poetic language and scientific inquiry relate to each other in Goethe's work. He demonstrates that in Goethe's texts the imaginative potential of poetic language can *both* surpass the empirical exploration of the world *and* fall short in grasping its reality. In order to be successful it is necessary according to Weber's reading of Goethe that imagination constantly "renegotiates the abstract symbolic meaning of words with the more concrete images of natural things."[21]

Goethe discusses the relationship between science and poetry in the context of his poem on plant morphology and the hesitation of his publisher as well as his audience to accept it as a valid contribution to botany. He attributes this hesitation to his readers' expectation that a writer known to them as an author of literary pieces will, and should, stay within the limits of his expertise. For expertise, Goethe uses the German terms "Feld" (field) and "Fach" (subject).[22] Both terms refer to a defined space, a field of research (Feld) or a subject area (Fach).[23] Parallel to the methodological split between scientific and poetic approaches, there is then also a disciplinary context in which Goethe's statement has to be read. His lamentation regarding the unwillingness of his audiences to see the complementarity of poetic and scientific approaches can be read as witness to the increasing disciplinary differentiation, in which the natural sciences become defined as fundamentally different from, or even the opposite of, literature.

While it is certainly true that Snow's paradigm of the two cultures needs to be understood as an expression of his own historical moment,[24] Goethe's engagement with his readers' reaction to his scientific work demonstrates that it is no less true that the long eighteenth century knew already of potential tensions between scientific and literary accounts of the world. The unity that Goethe envisions does not negate the existence of disciplinary differentiation; rather, it considers disciplines as complementary forces which need to cooperate in the attempt to understand the world in which we live. David Knight's statement that "around 1800 'science' was not opposed to 'arts'; there was nothing like the 'Two Cultures' of C.P. Snow's famous essay"[25] seems, therefore, overstated. Goethe's plea for an overcoming of the gap is not an expression of his ignorance of the differences, but a proof of the experience of their existence.

Certain and Probable

There have been a number of attempts to understand the prehistory of the split between the arts and the sciences. In one of these accounts the Enlightenment provided decisive foundations for later disciplinary divisions.[26] Enlightenment physicists who believed in the potential of their mathematical tools to access reality are pitted against philosophers who continued to search for epistemological clarity.[27] Margaret Osler observes that "whereas the physicists believed themselves to be approaching the position of Laplace's omniscient intelligence, the philosophers came to abandon the hope that scientific methods can lead to certainty or even penetrate the veil of appearances."[28] Osler concludes: "Where the physicists sought a science known with certainty, the philosophers saw at best the possibility of probable knowledge."[29]

The appeal of probabilistic thinking went across whatever divide might have existed between philosophical and mathematical approaches to reality. While Laplace (1749–1827) formulated the belief in the obtainability of omniscience, he was at the same time deeply involved in contributing to the mathematical theory of probability.[30] Laplace's example is significant because it illustrates that even if we can observe disciplinary splits, individuals engage simultaneously with a number of different methodologies. We have to be careful not to confuse the divide between approaches to knowledge with the divide between individuals. These individuals often lived "in a variety of conflicted epistemologies."[31]

The split between those approaches to knowledge that were based on the assumption of certainty and those approaches that continued to explore epistemological questions anticipates later formulations of disciplinary divisions. It is important to note, however, that in this Enlightenment articulation of the division the uniting principle is rationality: both approaches assume that truth finding needs to be conducted by rational means. In contrast to later thinkers, these philosophers neither rely on faith nor do they want to employ *Poesie* – as Goethe would later suggest – in order to come closer to the truth or in order to sketch probable scenarios.

Probabilistic thinking became a powerful tool that was used well beyond its Enlightenment origins to elaborate on the likeliness of events of which the particular occurrence could not be known with certainty. Tina Young Choi's contribution to this volume ("Probabilistic Knowledge in the Works of James Clerk Maxwell and George Eliot") attests to the fact that nineteenth-century scientists such as Maxwell (1831–79) and writers such as Eliot (1819–80) took recourse to probabilistic thinking in order to elaborate where certainty was missing. By the late nineteenth century, however, how certainty about reality was defined had changed significantly compared to the Enlightenment understanding. As Choi shows, by the time Maxwell published his thoughts on molecules and thermodynamic laws in his1873 *Nature* article, such certainty had become defined as that which can be accessed by the senses.[32] While the physicists' optimistic belief in "Laplace's omniscient intelligence"[33] relied unapologetically on mathematical approaches to reality, Maxwell felt it necessary to admit to his readers that "no one has ever seen or handled a single molecule" and that they "cannot be subjected to direct experiment."[34]

A second decisive change had occurred around 1800: once certainty had become defined by the empirical and experimental, the imaginary became its opposite. Maxwell found it justified and necessary to "extrapolate from limited data by engaging the 'constructive imagination.'"[35] In a way that might have pleased Goethe, Maxwell connected to Lord Tennyson's (1809–92) poetic imagination of the atom in his 1868 poem "Lucretius" in order to overcome factual limitations. Maxwell's text witnesses two important phenomena. First, it highlights the options that probabilistic thinking offered in moments of missing certainty, now defined as empirical truth. And, second, it witnesses the closeness that Maxwell saw between probabilistic and poetic-imaginative thinking when certainty became defined via the empirical. Once philosophers had highlighted the epistemological limits of knowledge, probabilistic thinking became one way to deal with them. However, once the criteria for scientific certainty had become defined by the empirical and experimental, there was also a second alternative opened, the imaginary.

Factual and Imaginable

Many scholars have noted that the study of Romanticism played a crucial role in the understanding of how disciplines emerged and became institutionalized. In *Romanticism and the Sciences* (1990), Cunningham and Jardin suggest reading Romanticism as a counter-movement to the Enlightenment and its mechanical and dividing tendency.[36] With this assessment they confirm the core of Hans Eichner's argument in "The Rise of Modern Science and the Genesis of Romanticism" (1982). Building on work by René Wellek and Morse Peckham, Eichner, in an essay that is impressive in both its comprehensiveness and clarity, argues that Romanticism can be understood as "a desperate rearguard action against the spirit and the implications of modern science."[37] Eichner ultimately reads the split between humanities and natural sciences as a split between physics and ethics and locates its beginning at that point when the sciences, starting with Galileo, did not engage any longer with the question of final causes.[38] In the new mathematical and mechanical world the space for God, transcendental hope, and the possibility of free will had shrunk if not altogether vanished.[39] According to Eichner, Romanticism tried to overcome the shortcomings of mechanical philosophy by rejecting the material existence of the world and by positing instead a cosmos that is a product of the mind.[40] In order to attain truth Romantic thinkers "relied on the irrational faculties of the mind – unmediated insight, 'enthusiasm,' 'intellectual intuition,' and the imagination."[41] Eichner goes one step further yet by assigning a specific genre to this approach to truth finding: poetry becomes the place where imagination reigns and it is considered "the supreme tool of cognition."[42]

Assuming a split between imagination and empirical science, it seems difficult in this approach to account for the decisive contributions that Romantic scientists have made in fields indebted to empiricism such as medicine and physics. Eichner concedes such advances, but he reads them as the result of a compromise. Romantic scientists obtained their scientific discoveries not as a result of their speculative methodologies, but because they had interiorized the empirical paradigm long before they encountered the thought of Romantic philosophers such as Schelling.[43] Eichner's insights are decisive, but his strict division between the empirical and the imaginary makes it difficult to acknowledge the genuine contributions of Romanticism to modern sciences except as a compromise between different methodologies.[44]

The relationship of Romantic thinkers to the heritage of Enlightenment might be more complex. In connecting to what Eichner calls "empirical paradigms" of the Enlightenment, Romantic thinkers fundamentally transformed them. In her contribution here ("Constructing the *Faktum* in the Enlightenment and Early German Romanticism"), Jocelyn Holland zeroes in on the status of the "fact" in Romantic thought. Holland traces the term through a rich etymological and conceptual history which exposes its temporal quality. She demonstrates how Romantic writers such as Novalis and Friedrich Schlegel (1772–1829) became interested in exploring this temporal quality of the fact "by connecting it to an open-ended process which, ideally, would facilitate the emergence of new facts." For these Romantic thinkers the fact is not defined as a verifiable observation but as "potential conveyer of intellectual activity."[45] For Schlegel, as Holland observes, even aesthetic statements can become a fact. Such close readings of how Romantic thinkers engaged with the heritage of the Enlightenment shed new light on the Romantic contribution to the sciences. Contrary to the assumption that Romantic scientists retained empiricist methodologies because they were trained in them and compromised when they used them, Holland's article demonstrates that Romantic authors embraced facts by fundamentally redefining them. This redefinition made it possible to think beyond the split between natural sciences and aesthetics because both were understood as products and origins of intellectual activity. If Romanticism has been read as a poetic reaction against mechanical philosophy, Holland's paper challenges the division between the mechanic and poetic, since the mechanical itself becomes a productive tool which cannot be distinguished in its epistemological status from aesthetics. Romantic thinkers dissolved disciplinary boundaries not because they could not accept that they rely on different objects and methodologies of studies, but because they saw similar epistemological questions at work in both areas.

If the beginning of the nineteenth century experienced an unprecedented interest in the accumulation of empirical data obtained by means of experiment, the "facts" collected also gained a new status as both epistemologically uncertain and rich. In this context, aesthetics was not providing the meaning that the mechanical data collection could not provide: rather, both fact and aesthetic object rely on the subject who reads and posits the data. In her chapter on the invention of homeopathy, Alice Kuzniar shows the extent to which the work of the physician Samuel Hahnemann (1755–1843) was shaped by an uncertainty regarding the status of the fact. While his research efforts are devoted to the collection of huge data sets, there is no attempt to find general rules or approach the large numbers statistically. This lack of interest in generalization is not the result of a capitulation, but expression of the conviction that facts cannot be distinguished from the act of reading. The data that Hahnemann collects becomes intrinsically tied to individual engagements with it. Drawing connections between Hahnemann's and Novalis's (1772–1801) work, Kuzniar observes that both experimental research and literature of the time searched for affinity and analogy between unique and disparate facts. Despite the reliance on the fact, this search was, as Kuzniar demonstrates, "conducted intuitively and idiosyncratically" and, therefore, relied heavily on an act of reading.[46] While Goethe strove for an objectivity which was still guaranteed by the object itself, thinkers such as Hahnemann and Novalis put a greater stress on the perceiving entity of the subject which can only guarantee the sense-making process.

Subjective and Objective

For a short time, then, in Romanticism, the subject-object distinction was virtually dissolved. However, in the history of disciplinary differentiation a new definition of the opposition between "objective" and "subjective," which also emerges around 1800, marks a crucial point. As Lorraine Daston and Peter Galison show, from the fourteenth century, when this opposition was introduced by scholastic philosophers such as Duns Scotus (c. 1266–1308) and William of Ockham (c. 1287–1347), until the nineteenth century, objective denoted objects "as they are presented to consciousness," while subjective denoted the objects themselves.[47] Daston and Galison credit Immanuel Kant (1724–1804) with redefining the terms. But, as they point out, even Kant's "objective validity" was not directly linked to external objects. Instead, it referred to the "forms of sensibility" – time, space, causality – which for Kant make experience possible. Kant's introduction of subjective as an approximate equivalent for "merely empirical sensations" shares with the later usage a pejorative connotation.[48] Daston and Galison observe further that in the first third of the nineteenth century, dictionaries in Germany, Britain, and France started to explain the terms "objective" and "subjective" similarly to today's usage: as fact and fiction.[49] Objective is from now on defined as referring to external objects, while subjective is connected to feelings and thoughts inside a person. It is this new definition of subjective and objective that starts to be associated with certain disciplines. While natural scientists increasingly strove to exclude subjectivity from their work, subject-based approaches to the world gained value in literary cultures. Daston and Galison observe: "In notable contrast to earlier views held from the Renaissance through the Enlightenment about the close analogies between artistic and scientific work, the public personas of artist and scientist polarized during this period. Artists were exhorted to express, even flaunt, their subjectivity, at the same time that scientists were admonished to restrain theirs."[50]

While one can witness some resistance to this differentiation, particularly in those countries in which Romantic epistemology had a significant influence, such as Germany,[51] the subject-object division increasingly became equated with the division between science and the humanities. At the same time, one can also observe decisive attempts to dissolve the distinction within a positivistic paradigm, namely, by reinterpreting a number of disciplines, like history, as natural sciences.[52] Tobias Wilke's contribution in this volume examines how empirical approaches in the late nineteenth century kindled a paradigmatic shift in the understanding of aesthetics, which started to engage in empirical methodologies to establish the psychological phenomena behind aesthetic experiences.

Under the pressure of the dominating natural sciences, new attempts were made to define what the unique contribution of the humanities could possibly be. Wilhelm Dilthey's (1833–1911) texts from the late nineteenth century can be interpreted as an expression of this "crisis" of the humanities. Dilthey's immensely influential work moves along a similar axis as that of Daston and Galison. Dilthey defines the kind of research undertaken in the natural sciences as geared towards finding universal laws, while the research undertaken in the humanities is shaped by a historicist perspective and is interested in individual approaches to the world. In his work, the sciences are defined as explaining the factual world, while the humanities are given the task of understanding the world from the centre of the hermeneutic circle, the subject.[53]

In light of empirical methodologies emerging in the sciences, literature more than any other discipline became the space for subjectivity and imagination. Faced with disciplinary fragmentation, it also became that discipline in which meta-disciplinary discussion could be held. This is an interesting development, because it somehow defines literature both as the place where the non-factual resides and as that place where a higher factuality is searched for. While imagination remains epistemologically suspect, it is at the same time privileged as the place where a truth might be found.

Disciplines and Institutions

Although Daston and Galison can locate the differentiation of the terms "subjective" and "objective" along disciplinary lines in the first third of the nineteenth century, disciplinary differentiation was far from being completed. Even when disciplines have been institutionalized, they are, as Hayles has pointed out, "far from being monolithic,"[54] and we can observe intricate links between disciplines well into the twentieth century and beyond. How complex the picture of the emergence of disciplines remains even, or, rather precisely when paying close attention to historical conditions is pointed out by Gowan Dawson and Bernard Lightman. Focusing on the developments in Great Britain, they observe that for the British Royal Literary Fund in the early nineteenth century science was considered one of literature's branches. At the same time, the term literature "was also being used, by members of the very same charitable organization, in a newer, much narrower sense to signify merely imaginative or fictional writing."[55] Dawson and Lightman highlight that different notions of literature existed simultaneously in the early nineteenth century. Much as Daston and Galison, they note that the understanding of literature as "imaginative fictional writing" was the one that became defining for the later nineteenth century.[56] Parallel to a new understanding of literature as fiction, science came to be defined in Britain as natural science. Dawson and Lightman locate the emergence of this more restrictive understanding of the word "science," which focuses on "experimental method and the investigation of the natural world," with the formation of the British Association for the Advancement of Science in 1831.[57] Fulford, Lee, and Kitson assume a slower solidification, but they also place disciplinary differentiation in nineteenth-century institutional history. They locate the professionalization of disciplines in the later nineteenth century and observe: "There were institutional parameters, and bodies concerned with enforcing them, ensuring that intellectuals could, in practice, define what was, and was not, acceptable as a proper scientific discourse. The sanction of the Royal Society and the Royal College of Physicians was important, and both these bodies preferred work that followed inductive method and used an empiricist and realistic style."[58]

In their introduction to *Nature Transfigured: Science and Literature, 1700–1900* (1989), Christie and Shuttleworth observe that the split between science and literature is often based not on different underlying methodologies but on the tendency to understand disciplines as products of different human faculties. They state that while we tend to align rationality with the natural sciences, we align literature with emotional faculties.[59] Departing from this quasi-anthropological paradigm, Christie and Shuttleworth suggest tracing the split between scientific and literary cultures neither to epistemologies nor to human faculties but to institutional decisions in the seventeenth and eighteenth centuries.[60] By doing so, they open the inquiry into the relationship between the two areas of knowledge production to questions regarding specific local and national cultures. Instead of a uniform historical – or even natural – development towards ever greater disciplinary stratification, they describe the dependency of disciplinary differentiation on specific geographical, political, and national conditions. For example, they note the great difference between the institutionalization of disciplines in France and Britain, thereby offering readers a new framework to understand the division between French and British scientific cultures. To follow Christie and Shuttleworth's approach, the greater openness of British scientific cultures to popular occupations and representations in fields such as botany and physics can be traced back to the less pronounced institutional divisions between disciplines in Britain compared to France.[61]

Germany and Britain

Christie and Shuttleworth's work points to the necessity of looking at national developments in order to understand the relationship between literature and science and its historical origins. The authors have formulated first insights into the French and the British contexts and conditions of the emergence of disciplines. Without being able to provide a comprehensive picture – nor having the ambition to do so – *Fact and Fiction* offers an opportunity to compare and contrast German and British disciplinary developments.

Germany and Britain offer a rich field for such studies because of the significance of their scientific cultures for furthering disciplinary developments and their crucial role in shaping modern sciences. In the history of the sciences, as David Knight has pointed out, precisely those countries in which Romantic natural science was strongest turn out to have had decisive impact on the development of modern science culture. Knight observes: "The theory of the conservation of energy and evolutionary theory in the mid-nineteenth century developed in Germany and Britain, where romantic natural science had been strongest, and not in France." Knight goes so far as to claim that "this was a factor in the relative decline of French science in the course of the nineteenth century."[62]

Regarding the comparison of German and British traditions of scientific inquiry, two statements have been made traditionally. Knight mentions the first one, namely, the indebtedness of British scientists to empirical methodologies compared to the continued devotion of German scientists to metaphysics.[63] The second one is – as Christie and Shuttleworth note – the greater openness of British scientific cultures to popular occupations and representations.[64] Ann Shteir's contribution to this volume, "'She comes! – the GODDESS!' Narrating Nature in Erasmus Darwin's *The Botanic Garden*," bears witness to the willingness of British authors to engage with a wider public. As Shteir shows, Erasmus Darwin (1731–1802) uses literary imagination and mythology to make scientific knowledge accessible to the layperson. In discussing Darwin's *The Botanic Garden*, Shteir not only pays attention to Darwin's use of poetic language for the purpose of making scientific context accessible to larger audiences, she also examines the role of poetic language in making sense of the scientific data. Shteir argues that by drawing on mythology, Darwin is able to project a holistic understanding of nature, which would not be possible by the presentation of botanical nomenclature alone. Here, we observe a thinker who is indebted to an Enlightenment epistemology of empirical observation, while at the same time acknowledging that the data alone can provide neither meaning nor the ability to communicate knowledge. For both activities, Erasmus Darwin relies on literary cultures.

It might seem that Darwin's attempts to popularization confirm the long-standing conviction that attributes greater openness regarding larger audiences to British scientists. However, singling out British scientists as more open to popularizing their science risks overlooking the extent to which communication and cross-fertilization between British and Continental scientific communities were vivid and ongoing. Erasmus Darwin drew significantly on the work of Swiss polymath Albrecht von Haller (1708–77) and Darwin's own poem *Loves of the Plants* was highly influential in Germany in general and for Goethe in particular. As Shteir points out, while Goethe might have dismissed Darwin's "pile-up of textual features,"[65] he nevertheless acknowledged Darwin's influence. Goethe's own botanical poem *Metamorphose der Pflanzen* (Metamorphosis of Plants) is driven by a very similar pedagogic-didactic impetus.

While German intellectuals around 1800 might have made attempts to distinguish their work from any form of trivialization – as Goethe did when he rejected Darwin's poem as a "fashionable" piece of writing in a letter to his friend Friedrich Schiller[66] – their texts nevertheless took shape in similar paradigms as those of their British counterparts. It is indeed interesting that Goethe and Schiller sketched pieces such as *Über den Dilettantismus* (On Dilettantism) in which they erected barriers against the work of women and other less educated groups, while Goethe himself was deeply involved in dilettantish attempts at painting and, as some would argue to his dismay, botany and optics. In fact, Goethe and Schiller might have been aware of the discrepancy between their theoretical attempts and their writing practice: the *Dilettantismus* sketch was never published during their lifetimes.[67] Goethe's remark on Darwin's poem and the sketch on dilettantism suggest that there is an attempt in German intellectual circles around 1800 to distinguish "high" from "low" forms of literary and scientific engagement which has no equivalent in British circles. However, as Shteir's article makes visible, ultimately German and British writers, scientists, and "dilettantes" in the late eighteenth and early nineteenth century engaged in surprisingly similar forms of scientific and poetic explorations.

In light of the close interaction between empirical and imaginary, scientific and popular cultures that we can observe in both German and British science communities, this volume encourages us to reconsider the conviction that British cultures were more indebted to empirical work and to popularization than their German counterparts. As in the case of the openness of British culture to popular forms of learning which were rejected by Goethe and Schiller, the attention to the work of authors such as Erasmus Darwin, Hahnemann, and Novalis highlights the fact that such preferences might have been more declaration and rhetoric than actual practice. Knight suggests as much, when he adds that the British were indebted to empirical work "at least in public."[68] Why these public declarations were felt to be necessary needs further examination from the perspective of fields such as the sociology of science and the history of science.

Attention to the relationship between literature and science also sheds new light on one of the most influential theories of modernity that emerged in the twentieth century, Niklas Luhmann's systems theory. In Luhmann's model, modernity is marked by a differentiation of value spheres, such as art, religion, or love.[69] Each of these spheres is ultimately a self-referential system with no access to (and interest in) the questions asked or the knowledge produced in other systems. Daniel Fulda and Thomas Prüfer have noted that Luhmann's model seems too schematic in light of the permeability of forms of knowledge and the fundamental significance of convergence for autonomous disciplines.[70] The contributors to this volume observe both interdependence between knowledge fields and the conviction of the authors of the time that such distinct knowledge fields exist.

The Volume's Organization

Fact and Fiction is organized into five parts, with each of the parts devoted to one activity that relates literary and scientific cultures in Germany and

Britain. In the first, "Reading: Electricity, Medicine," Holland and Kuzniar investigate the fragility of the "fact" in literary and scientific texts from the Enlightenment to Romanticism. Discussing examples and language taken from the fields of electricity and medicine, both authors point out that in the cases they study the fact is not considered something empirically given, but rather produced in an act of reading. Holland opens the section with the fundamental question of how the fact is defined in texts around 1800. She traces the eighteenth-century history of the term "fact" and observes that at the end of the century the term did not yet encompass notions like "objectively known" or "scientifically proven," with which we associate it today. Instead, for Romantic authors the "'primal' factum is in essence the one which we are ourselves, posited in the original activity of the subject." Focusing on this temporal and processual quality, authors like Novalis and Schlegel begin to see the fact as a conveyor of intellectual productivity. Drawing on vocabulary and concepts used in contemporary research on electricity, Romantic authors redefine the fact as "conductor" (Leiter), an instrument for the facilitation and creation of new facts. If the difficulty to establish facts haunts scientific endeavours around 1800, Romantic authors explore the epistemological potential of such uncertainty in their literary and philosophical texts. Perhaps ironically, these explorations become possible precisely because of new conceptual frameworks which the sciences provide.

Kuzniar, in the second chapter of this part, starts her investigation with a focus on Hahnemann's medical writings, to discover that these writings share important features with literary theories which emerge simultaneously in early Romanticism. Kuzniar demonstrates that the discovery of similarities between symptoms which forms the basis of Hahnemann's homeopathic theory of healing (the Law of Similars: "like cures like") is only possible in a moment of nonsensical intuition. While Hahnemann's infinite listing and cataloguing of symptoms follows an eighteenth-century methodology of taxonomical observation, his law of similars follows the principle of the absurd, which aligns it closely with Romantic notions of the chaotic and fragmentary. Rejecting any attempt of systematization or generalization, Hahnemann's theory of medicine does not allow for the establishment of a stable set of symptom–remedy relations. Instead, it relies on individual and idiosyncratic acts of reading symptoms and establishing similarities between them, thereby connecting it strongly to the productive acts of reading propagated in Romantic literature and philosophy, which Holland negotiates in the first chapter of this section. What both chapters witness in the late eighteenth century is a heightened awareness of the instability, or even absence, of "reality" and a growing acknowledgment that our perception of the world is a process which produces the fact that it studies. Here fiction does not differ from fact: the distinction has become obsolete.

While Holland and Kuzniar discover the instability of the fact in Romantic thought, in the next part, "Imagining: Botany, Chemistry, Thermodynamics," Shteir, Christian Weber, and Choi explore the place of imagination vis-à-vis empirical studies in the production of knowledge. Shteir investigates the many ways in which physician and poet Erasmus Darwin employs imagination in order to both arrive at a more comprehensive understanding of nature and to mediate this understanding to new audiences, in particular women. Shteir points to the tensions in Darwin's expository poem *The Botanic Garden* between, on one side, taxonomy built on empirical observation and differentiation and, on the other, Darwin's multiple use of analogies, which establish "the vastness of relations within nature."[71] In his poem, Darwin goes beyond mimetic presentation of the Linnaean nomenclatura and empirical classification and by combining prose and poetry, Shteir argues, leaves Enlightenment taxonomy behind to propagate what Pierre Hadot in *The Veil of Isis* has called an "Orphic" idea of nature.

By discussing *The Botanic Garden* as a generic hybrid, which mixes poetry and prose, scientific information and mythology in the tradition of Albrecht von Haller's "Die Alpen" (The Alps), Shteir joins Kuzniar and Michael House (see part 3) in highlighting the extent to which epistemological questions have an impact on genre. The epistemological aporia finds its generic expression in Ernst Platner's (1744–1818) aphoristic writing style and in Hahnemann's practice of simply jotting down symptoms which do not add up to a given set of sicknesses, but require – much like Romantic fragments – individual acts of reading to become meaningful. Erasmus Darwin's *Botanic Garden* is shaped by a similar tension between an (Enlightenment) taxonomic understanding of nature and a (Romantic) search for analogies, which Kuzniar observes also in Hahnemann's homeopathy.

Shteir observes that for Erasmus Darwin "imagination underlies science as much as poetry, and is as important for him as information." In the opening lines of the poem, Darwin declares the goal "to inlist Imagination under the banner of Science." The quote suggests that imagination is for Darwin both resource and tool in the production of knowledge. However, it also alludes, it seems, to the fact that imagination has a dangerous potential which threatens to get out of control and thereby endanger the scientific inquiry. It is this last aspect which is taken up by the second chapter in this part, in which Christian Weber discusses the relationship between empiricism and imagination in Goethe's work.

Weber opens his chapter with the observation that although we have come to understand literature and science as two mutually exclusive fields – one thriving on subjectivity and imagination, the other shunning them – they ultimately depend on each other. While literature receives inspiration from the sciences, each scientific inquiry will experience at some point the limits of factual analysis and will, at this point, be forced to leave the area which can be approached by the senses and use imagination and figurative language to newly conceptualize the problem at hand. Weber takes the term *Elective Affinities* as a case study for this figurative use of language. He traces it from its origin in eighteenth-century chemistry to its use in Goethe's novel of the same title. Weber demonstrates not only how poetics supplies the sciences with metaphors for their inquiries, but how the novel itself becomes a virtual experiment. It has the potential to take on a meta-discursive function, stimulating and assessing the formative potential of metaphors and scientific models.

Much as in Goethe's *Elective Affinities*, in Eliot's *Daniel Deronda*, which is the focus of Choi's contribution, science is less the novel's topic than its informing model. Choi explores how Eliot draws on probability theory used in nineteenth-century thermodynamics to articulate the characters' speculations on what lies beyond empirical observation. When the characters in *Daniel Deronda* speculate about the feelings and actions of other people, they can articulate general observations and probable outcomes, but they fail to predict actions and decisions of the individual. Where Eliot shows how much the scientific model that she employs fails to predict the individual case, she closely follows probability theory, which, as Eliot's contemporary Maxwell laments in the context of thermodynamics, can predict behaviour of all, but not the behaviour of individual, particles. Both Goethe and Eliot describe the necessity of imagination in the moment of the failure of empirical observation and both transfer scientific models into literature. However, while Goethe considers this transfer from science to literature, and ultimately life, problematic because the model cannot grasp the far more complex reality for which it is taken, Eliot embraces the scientific model at hand precisely because it does not offer a conclusive reading of reality, but expresses an epistemological aporia.

Eliot and Goethe grapple with the question of what happens, as Maxwell had put it, when the scientific inquiry turns to "things invisible and imperceptible by our senses." The urgency of this question was never clearer than at the point in history when the sciences started to define themselves as a field of inquiry based on the method of empirical study and experiment, and in opposition to subjective imagination. The third part in this volume, entitled "Sensing: Anthropology, Psychology, Aesthetics," connects to the previous in that it asks how to account for something which is not easily graspable by logical deduction: feelings, in both their sensory and psychological interpretation. At the centre of this part, which presents papers by Noyes, House, and Wilke, stands the question of how to account for feelings in a science of the human and how to distinguish "true" from "false" or merely "simulated" (fictitious) feelings within a field of inquiry which, methodologically, is increasingly committed to the factual. Opening this part, Noyes traces Herder's philosophical project from Kant's lectures on metaphysics via Alexander Gottlieb Baumgarten's (1714–62) and Johann Georg Hamann's (1730–88) aesthetics to the advent of anthropology as a science. Noyes describes the extent to which Herder's anthropological turn is indebted to Kant, with whom he shares the conviction that "Being is a concept that cannot be further analyzed." Against the backdrop of the crisis of rationalism and in the wake of the empiricism which Locke and Hume had promoted, Herder's aim is to establish a philosophy that accounts for both rational and sensory capacities of the human being.

Noyes's chapter on Herder marks an important point in the narrative to which this volume contributes, since it illustrates the enormous changes that happened in the course of the eighteenth and nineteenth centuries in the assessment of sensual experience for a scientific understanding of the world. While for philosophers like Leibniz, Wolff, and Kant sensory information was suspicious because it was considered blurred and therefore provided only imprecise information, Herder rehabilitates sensory experience as a necessary correlation to a rational approach to the world; but only the nineteenth century turns to observation and experience as the major tool of a scientific methodology, thereby redefining the empirically obtained information as the more factual and precise one, undistorted by subjective and fictitious accounts of the world.[72] It is precisely at this point that House's chapter continues the discussion.

Much as in Noyes's contribution, one of the main concerns that House discerns in the authors that he discusses – in particular Salomon Maimon (1754–1800) and Karl Philipp Moritz (1756–93) – is how to conceptualize the relationship between universal and particular. However, while for Herder this terminological pair was analogue to, and defined by, the terms rational and sensory, House demonstrates that it could also be interpreted as empirical versus fictitious. For Enlightenment thinkers, it was the rational mind that reflected and abstracted the information transmitted by the senses. Maimon, however, doubts the conviction that such a step is possible and, as a result of this hesitation, embraces fiction as a necessary part in giving meaning to the overwhelming number of facts which the human encounters constantly.

While in Platner, one of the founding fathers of anthropology as a discipline, epistemological uncertainty finds its expression in the focus on observing and expressing thoughts in an aphoristic writing style which refuses any meaningful narrative (very similar to what Kuzniar observes in Hahnemann's work), eighteenth-century anthropologists turn to autobiographical writing and to what became known as *empirical psychology*. The question of fiction, however, continued to haunt the scientific ambitions behind this project. Focusing on the narrative of life-experience, which they collect in their *Magazin der Erfahrungsseelenkunde* (Journal of Experimental Psychology) authors like Moritz and Maimon are confronted with the question of how to distinguish between fact and imaginative reconstruction. Discussing Maimon's contribution to the *Magazin*, House proposes that the production of fiction comes to be understood as a fundamental condition of human existence. Around 1800, House argues, the science of the human ultimately is a science of fiction.

Wilke takes this line of inquiry further by reconstructing the concept of "fictional feelings" that was developed in the framework of late-nineteenth-century *psychological aesthetics*. The article analyses the way in which the idea of fictional feelings, which assumes that emotions experienced as a result of aesthetic stimuli are merely "simulated states of consciousness," is the signal of a fundamental shift in the understanding of aesthetics: namely, an understanding of aesthetics which does not rely on theoretical statements (e.g., specific rules or media according to which specific art forms function), but on the study of psychological "facts" which follows an empirical methodology. Like House, Wilke observes a pronounced wish to distinguish real and "fictional" emotional responses. While there are intrinsic reasons for such a distinction, Wilke shows that the insistence on separation is also driven by strategic interests: by excluding so-called quasi-emotions from the field of psychology, psychological aesthetics hopes to establish itself as a discrete discipline. While anthropology around 1800 strives – as House demonstrates – to include a number of disciplines in order to arrive at a science of the human, psychological aesthetics insists on the limitation of the field for the sake of disciplinary clarity and survival.

The essays in the fourth part, "Relating: Biology," delve into how genealogy is negotiated in light of an increasing biologization of kinship relations. While Stefani Engelstein observes that in Gotthold Ephraim Lessing's (1729–81) *Nathan the Wise* cultural ways of establishing kinship trump biological factors, Daniel Newman explores the ways in which new and as of yet unacknowledged scientific theories inform narrative and character in E.M. Forster's (1879–1970) novel *The Longest Journey*. Literature serves here as an experimental space in which authors ask what consequences scientific theories might have for our self-understanding.

Engelstein revisits Lessing's *Nathan the Wise* in order to study its contribution to the eighteenth-century debate on human diversity. Lessing's *Nathan* played a significant role in redefining religious studies as an anthropological discipline by removing religion "from the Enlightenment quest for grounded truths."[73] However, it is important to note that eighteenth-century interpretations of anthropology – much like the one that House describes – include both biological and cultural inquiries which are considered intrinsically intertwined. If Lessing opens up a space for accepting the importance of kinship and blood relation for human self-understanding, he points out at the same time that "inherited traits must enter a history of activity and relationships to shape their expression as deeds and to acquire meaning."[74]

Newman's contribution is similarly devoted to questions of heredity and biological genealogy. However, while in Lessing's *Nathan* biological inheritance acquires meaning only through a process of culturization, Newman argues that in Forster's *The Longest Journey* new models of hereditary transmission provide the main character with a new narrative to his life. Here atomistic heredity, first described by Gregor Mendel (1822–84) and then rediscovered by the Dutch botanist and geneticist Hugo de Vries (1848–1935) and the German botanist Carel Correns (1864–1933), allows the novelist Forster to use and, at the same time, to question the narrative logic of genetic determinism. Forster's novel is informed by most recent scientific models. However, it does not only illustrate these models, but also helps to propel a scientific theory at a time when this theory is not yet fully acknowledged in the scholarly community. Like Goethe's *Elective Affinities*, Forster's novel becomes a virtual experiment in which the author anticipates and asks for the significance of specific scientific models for individual lives and human interaction.

In the fifth and last part of this volume, "Displaying: Scientific Collections," Peter McIsaac and Dana Weber examine the relationship between fact and fiction in collections of medical specimens and of ethnographic mannequins. McIsaac opens this part by studying the function of collections of medical specimens in recent literary productions by Durs Grünbein (1962–) and Thomas Hettche (1964–). In McIsaac's chapter, fictional medical museums are shown to "represent indispensable ways of probing the place of science and science knowledge in our existence as biological beings at the turn of the third millennium."[75] McIsaac's article witnesses both a new awareness for the interconnectedness of fact and fiction and an awareness that the conceptualization of their relationship is not independent of specific historical moments and particular media.

The volume is closed by Dana Weber with an chapter on ethnographic mannequins and exotic performers in early-twentieth- and twenty-first-century exhibition culture. In her article, Weber demonstrates that the boundaries between scientific display and popular spectacle, between events in which exotic performers were featured and the presentation of ethnographic mannequins in ethnological and anthropological museums which followed scientific and pedagogical goals, were not always clearly defined. She argues that the mannequin's problematic epistemological status and its uncanny effect are determined by its paradoxical position between the scientific, factual information for which it is conceptualized and the imaginative flights that it invites. Drawing on theories of the *uncanny* by Jentsch and Freud, Weber investigates "the relationship between scientific facts and the fictions emerging in their contemplation." Paradoxically, the effect that the ethnographic mannequin exerts on the viewer is uncannier when the mannequin is rendered in more realistic a manner. Weber reads the mannequin against the backdrop of the "uncanny valley," a concept introduced by Masahiro Mori in the context of robotics and later employed in studies of three-dimensional computer-generated digital animation (3D CGI) in order to articulate the insight that excessive realism leads to disturbed reactions in the viewers and users of life-like animations. Discussing the ethnographic mannequin and its relationship to contemporary adventure literature, Weber comes to the surprising and strong conclusion that "by giving some leeway to imagination, an inaccurate human representation in fact allows for a quicker and more exact ontological ascription."[76]

Dana Weber's contribution makes visible once again what renders the papers in this volume particularly fascinating, namely, the fact that they combine detailed analysis of one particular point in time with larger issues surrounding the question of the relationship between fact and fiction, thereby informing our current debate on the relationship between humanities and the sciences. The book aims to gain scholarly knowledge of disciplinary constellations in particular historical moments, but also intends to open new views and debates on questions which have far-reaching consequences for the academic landscape and society in general.

NOTES

1 Snow, *Two Cultures.*

2 In their introduction to *Victorian Science and Literature* (2011), Dawson and Lightman concede that although terminological clarity is missing, the term *literature and science* has become a useful reference. Referring to nineteenth-century Britain, they state: "While there is certainly nothing inevitable or timeless about the distinction between science *and* literature, and it is essential to resist postulating general patterns that are in fact contingent cultural formations particular only to certain historical moments or specific interest groups, it needs to be acknowledged that the disputed critical shorthand 'science *and* literature' remains no less useful than the newer 'science *as* literature' in recapturing the intricate situation of nineteenth-century Britain" ("General Introduction" x).

3 Christie and Shuttleworth, "Introduction," in *Nature Transfigured* 6.

4 Bruce and Purdy, eds, *Literature and Science*, front-matter.

5 Beer, "Translation or Transformation?" in Beer, *Open Fields* 173.

6 Beer, *Darwin's Plots.*

7 For a sketch of the debate in the history of science and bibliographic references see Turner, "Lessons from Literature" 578–89, esp. 579–80.

8 Secord, "Knowledge in Transit" 655. Another strong current has been the turn to the metaphorical language of sciences. See Bono, "Why Metaphor?" 215–34.

9 Milburn, "Modifiable Futures" 560.

10 Walls, "Of Atoms, Oaks and Cannibals" 590.

11 Bono, "Making Knowledge" 555.

12 In his contribution to the *ISIS* Focus section, Turner concentrates on how attention to form could be productive for the history of science. However, he also provides a sketch of some ways in which scientific understandings of form shaped the work of early modern playwrights, an inquiry that he has developed in greater detail in *The English Renaissance Stage* (2006). Turner, "Lessons from Literature" 581.

13 Hayles, "Deciphering the Rules of Unruly Disciplines" 25.

14 Campbell, "Ethnocentrism of Disciplines" 328–48.

15 Lenoir, "The Discipline of Nature" 94.

16 "[N]irgends wollte man zugeben, daß Wissenschaft und Poesie vereinbar seien. Man vergaß, daß Wissenschaft sich aus Poesie entwickelt habe, man bedachte nicht, daß, nach einem Umschwung von Zeiten, beide sich wieder freundlich zu beiderseitigem Vorteil, auf höherer Stelle, gar wohl wieder begegnen könnten." Goethe, "Schicksal der Druckschrift" 107. Goethe, "History of the Printed Brochure" 171–2.
17 Regarding the development of knowledge fields into scientific disciplines see Stefani Engelstein's contribution on the science of religion in this volume, chapter 9. See also Fulda and Prüfer, "Das Wissen der Moderne."
18 Knight, "Romanticism and the Sciences" 14.
19 Ann Shteir has demonstrated that women particularly contributed significantly to the study of plants around 1800. See Shteir, *Cultivating Women, Cultivating Science*. See also the recent project under the leadership of Sally Shuttleworth on citizen involvement in nineteenth-century science in Britain ("Constructing Scientific Communities: Citizen Science in the 19th and 21st Centuries," http://conscicom.org/).
20 See chapter 6, p. 155.
21 See chapter 4, p. 102.
22 Goethe, "Schicksal der Handschrift" 104. Goethe, "The History of the Manuscript" 169.
23 See the entry "fach" in the *Deutsches Wörterbuch* of the brothers Grimm, where it is defined as a spatial term and – deduced from there – as a subject area. The *Wörterbuch* connects this subject area closely with professional occupation: "fach ... das einem überwiesene, von ihm betriebene geschäft" (fach ... the profession that one has been assigned to, that one engages in). Jacob and Wilhelm Grimm, *Deutsches Wörterbuch* 1221.
24 Cf. Beer, "Translation or Transformation" 174.
25 Knight, "Romanticism" 14.
26 In another account, this prehistory is located already in alchemic thought. William R. Newman argues that "alchemy provided a uniquely powerful focus for discussing the boundary between art and nature," and thereby anticipated today's split between arts and sciences. Newman, *Promethean Ambitions* 8.
27 Osler, "Certainty, Scepticism, and Scientific Optimism" 3–28.
28 Ibid. 3.
29 Ibid. 10.
30 Ibid. 21–2.
31 Beer, "Translation and Transformation" 176.
32 See Daston and Galison, *Objectivity*.
33 Osler, "Certainty" 3.

34 Quoted in Choi, chapter 5, p. 130.
35 Quoted ibid., 144.
36 Fulford, Lee, and Kitson come to a slightly different result. While they also understand Romanticism as a counter-movement to the sciences, they see this movement less as an engagement with mechanical tendencies than with the colonial enterprise. Their "study shows how literary Romanticism arose partly in response to science's appropriation of explorers' encounters with foreign people and places" (Fulford, Lee, and J. Kitson, eds, *Literature, Science and Exploration in the Romantic Era*, front-matter).
37 Eichner, "The Rise of Modern Science and the Genesis of Romanticism" 8.
38 Ibid. 11.
39 Ibid. 12.
40 Ibid. 14.
41 Ibid. 17.
42 Ibid. 18.
43 Ibid. 24.
44 Ibid.
45 See chapter 2, 39 and 43.
46 Chapter 2, p. 61.
47 Daston and Galison, *Objectivity* 29.
48 Ibid. 30.
49 Ibid. 31.
50 Ibid. 37.
51 According to Daston, such resistance to differentiation can be observed in Germany. Cf. Daston, "Die Kultur der wissenschaftlichen Objektivität" 15–16.
52 Cf. Oexle, ed., *Naturwissenschaft.*
53 Dilthey, *Introduction to the Human Sciences.*
54 Hayles, "Deciperhing" 31.
55 Dawson and Lightman, *Victorian Science* viii.
56 Fulford, Lee, and Kitson locate the differentiation of fictional from factual writing in the middle of the nineteenth century and associate it with De Quincey. They write: "It was not customary formally to divide fictional from factual writing until De Quincey in 1848 made fiction a defining characteristic of the 'literature of power' and claimed it was distinct from the 'literature of knowledge'" (Fulford, Lee, and Kitson, *Bodies of Knowledge* 4).
57 Dawson and Lightman, *Victorian Science* ix.
58 Fulford, Lee, and Kitson, *Bodies of Knowledge* 2.
59 Christie and Shuttleworth, *Nature Transfigured* 1.
60 Ibid. 2.
61 Ibid. 2 and 9.

62 Knight, "Romanticism" 22.
63 Knight observes that "men of science in Germany were aware of their use of and need for metaphysics, while in Britain empiricism prevailed." Ibid. 19.
64 Christie and Shuttleworth, *Nature Transfigured* 2 and 9.
65 Chapter 3, p. 79.
66 Ibid.
67 Schiller and Goethe, "Über den Dilettantismus" 1121–3. More than twenty years later, when contemplating his own attempts in botanical studies, Goethe conceded that dilettanti could make decisive contributions to the sciences: "und was sind nicht überhaupt schon die Wissenschaften teilnehmenden Liebhabern, und unbefangenen Gastfreunden schuldig geworden!" ("And to how many other interested amateurs and uninhibited dilettantes is science indebted!"). Goethe, "Schicksal der Handschrift" 104 ("History of the Manuscript" 169).
68 Knight, "Romanticism" 19.
69 Cf. Luhmann, *Art as a Social System*; Luhmann, *A Systems Theory of Religion*; Luhmann, *Love as Passion*.
70 Fulda and Prüfer, "Das Wissen der Moderne" 5.
71 Chapter 3, p. 77.
72 Cf. Daston and Galison, *Objectivity*.
73 Chapter 9, p. 224.
74 Ibid., p. 232.
75 Chapter 11, p. 276.
76 Chapter 12, p. 305.

WORKS CITED

Beer, Gillian. *Darwin's Plots: Evolutionary Narrative in Darwin, George Eliot and Nineteenth-Century Fiction* [1983]. Cambridge: Cambridge UP, 2009.

– "Translation or Transformation? The Relations of Literature and Science." In G. Beer, *Open Fields: Science in Cultural Encounter*. Oxford: Clarendon Press, 1996. 173–95.

Bono, James J. "Making Knowledge: History, Literature, and the Poetics of Science." *ISIS* (Focus section: History of Science and Literature and Science, Convergences and Divergences) 101.3 (September 2010): 555–9.

– "Why Metaphor? Toward a Metaphorics of Scientific Practice." In *Science Studies: Probing the Dynamics of Scientific Knowledge*. Edited by Sabine Maasen and Mathias Winterhager. Bielefeld: Transcript, 2001. 215–34.

Bruce, Donald, and Anthony Purdy, eds. *Literature and Science*. Amsterdam: Rodopi, 1994.

Campbell, Donald T. "Ethnocentrism of Disciplines and the Fish-Scale Model of Omniscience." In *Interdisciplinary Relationships in the Social Sciences*. Edited by Muzafer Sherif and Carolyn W. Sherif. Chicago: Aldine Publishing Co., 1969. 328–48.

Christie, John, and Sally Shuttleworth. "Introduction: Between Literature and Science." In *Nature Transfigured: Science and Literature, 1700–1900*. Edited by J. Christie and S. Shuttleworth. Manchester: Manchester UP, 1989. 1–12.

Constructing Scientific Communities: Citizen Science in the 19th and 21st Centuries. http://conscicom.org/.

Cunningham, Andrew, and Nicholas Jardine, eds. *Romanticism and the Sciences*. Cambridge: Cambridge UP, 1990.

Daston, Lorraine. "Die Kultur der wissenschaftlichen Objektivität." In *Naturwissenschaft, Geisteswissenschaft, Kulturwissenschaft: Einheit – Gegensatz – Komplementarität?* Edited by Otto Gerhard Oexle. Göttingen: Wallstein, 1998. 11–39.

Daston, Lorraine, and Peter Galison. *Objectivity.* New York: Zone Books, 2007.

Dawson, Gowan, and Bernard Lightman. "General Introduction." In *Victorian Science and Literature*. Edited by G. Dawson and B. Lightman. Vol. 1. London: Pickering & Chatto, 2011. vii–xix.

Dilthey, Wilhelm. *Introduction to the Human Sciences: An Attempt to Lay a Foundation for the Study of Society and History*. Translated and introduced by Ramon J. Betanzos. Detroit: Wayne State UP, 1988.

Eichner, Hans. "The Rise of Modern Science and the Genesis of Romanticism." *PMLA* 97.1 (1982): 8–30.

Fulda, Daniel, and Thomas Prüfer. "Das Wissen der Moderne. Stichworte zum Verhältnis von wissenschaftlicher und literarischer Weltdeutung und -darstellung seit dem späten 18. Jahrhundert." *Faktenglauben und fiktionales Wissen. Zum Verhältnis von Wissenschaft und Kunst in der Moderne*. Edited by D. Fulda and T. Prüfer. Frankfurt a. M.: Peter Lang, 1996. 1–22.

Fulford, Tim, Debbie Lee, and Peter J. Kitson, eds. *Literature, Science and Exploration in the Romantic Era: Bodies of Knowledge*. Cambridge: Cambridge UP, 2004.

Goethe, Johann Wolfgang. "History of the Printed Brochure." In *Goethe's Botanical Writings*. Translated by Bertha Mueller. With an intro. by Charles J. Engard. Woodbridge, CT: Ox Bow Press, 1989. 170–6.

– "The History of the Manuscript." In *Goethe's Botanical Writings*. Translated by Bertha Mueller. With an intro. by Charles J. Engard. Woodbridge, CT: Ox Bow Press, 1989. 167–70.

– "Schicksal der Handschrift" (1817). *Werke*. Hamburger Ausgabe in vierzehn Bänden. Edited by Erich Trunz. Vol. 13. Munich: Deutscher Taschenbuch Verlag, 1988. 102–5.

– "Schicksal der Druckschrift" (1817). In *Werke*. Hamburger Ausgabe in vierzehn Bänden. Edited by Erich Trunz. Vol. 13. Munich: Deutscher Taschenbuch Verlag, 1988. 105–12.

Grimm, Jacob, and Wilhelm Grimm. *Deutsches Wörterbuch*. Vol. 3. E–Forsche. Leipzig: Hirzel, 1862.

Hayles, Katherine N. "Deciphering the Rules of Unruly Disciplines: A Modest Proposal for Literature and Science." In *Literature and Science*. Edited by Donald Bruce and Anthony Purdy. Amsterdam: Rodopi, 1994. 25–48.

Knight, David. "Romanticism and the Sciences." In *Romanticism and the Sciences*. Edited by Andrew Cunningham and Nicholas Jardine. Cambridge: Cambridge UP, 1990. 13–24.

Lenoir, Tim. "The Discipline of Nature and the Nature of Disciplines." In *Knowledges: Historical and Critical Studies in Interdisciplinarity*. Edited by Ellen Messer-Davidow, David R. Shumway, and David J. Sylvan. Charlottesville: University of Virginia Press, 1993. 70–102.

Luhmann, Niklas. *Art as a Social System*. Translated by Eva M. Knodt. Stanford, CA: Stanford UP, 2000.

– *Love as Passion. The Codification of Intimacy*. Translated by Jeremy Gaines and Doris L. Jones. Stanford, CA: Stanford UP, 1998.

– *A Systems Theory of Religion*. Edited by André Kieserling. Translated by David A. Brenner with Adrian Hermann. Stanford, CA: Stanford UP, 2013.

Milburn, Colin. "Modifiable Futures: Science Fiction at the Bench." *ISIS* (Focus section: History of Science and Literature and Science, Convergences and Divergences) 101.3 (September 2010): 560–9.

Newman, William R. *Promethean Ambitions: Alchemy and the Quest to Perfect Nature*. Chicago: U of Chicago P, 2014.

Osler, Margaret. "Certainty, Scepticism, and Scientific Optimism: The Roots of Eighteenth-Century Attitudes Toward Scientific Knowledge." In *Probability, Time, and Space in Eighteenth-Century Literature*. Edited by Paula R. Backscheider. New York: AMS Press, 1979. 3–28.

Peckham, Morse. "Toward a Theory of Romanticism." *PMLA* 66 (1951): 5–23.

Schiller, Friedrich, and Johann Wolfgang Goethe. "Über den Dilettantismus" (1799). In *Werke und Briefe in zwölf Bänden*. Edited by Otto Dann et. al. Vol. 8: Theoretische Schriften. Frankfurt a. M.: Klassiker, 1992. 1121–3.

Secord, James A. "Knowledge in Transit." *Isis* 95 (2004): 654–72.

Shteir, Ann. *Cultivating Women, Cultivating Science: Flora's Daughters and Botany in England 1760 to 1860*. Baltimore, MD: Johns Hopkins UP, 1996.

Snow, Charles Percy. *The Two Cultures and the Scientific Revolution*. New York: Cambridge UP, 1959.

Turner, Henry S. *The English Renaissance Stage: Geometry, Poetics and the Practical Spatial Arts*. Oxford: Oxford University Press, 2006.

– "Lessons from Literature for the Historian of Science (and Vice Versa): Reflections on Form." *ISIS* (Focus section: History of Science and Literature and Science, Convergences and Divergences) 101.3 (September 2010): 578–89.
Walls, Laura Dassow. "Of Atoms, Oaks and Cannibals, or, More Things That Talk." *ISIS* (Focus section: History of Science and Literature and Science, Convergences and Divergences) 101.3 (September 2010): 590–8.
Wellek, René. "The Concept of Romanticism in Literary History." *Comparative Literature* 1 (1949): 1–23, 147–72.

PART I

Reading: Electricity, Medicine

1 Facts Are What One Makes of Them: Constructing the *Faktum* in the Enlightenment and Early German Romanticism

JOCELYN HOLLAND

There is a scene in Christoph Wieland's novel *The History of the Philosopher Danischmende* (1775) where Danischmende invites the Kalender to express his views on mankind. The Kalender is a religious mendicant who has spent his life begging in the metropolises of world, and he takes the opportunity to make a few unflattering observations about human behaviour, views which Danischmende finds unacceptable. When the Kalender points out that it is not a matter of what "we wish, hope, and dream ... Facts must be the deciding factor," Danischmende retorts that "facts are what one makes of them ... from every new point of view they appear differently; and in ten cases to one the purported fact, on which one has supported his opinion with great confidence, is at heart a mere hypothesis." "This may be," replies the Kalender in turn, "But the facts of which I am speaking are of the kind which, observed from all possible perspectives, always show the same form and always give the same results" (9: 60).[1]

Danischmende and the Kalender are speaking at cross-purposes, describing two different (though not mutually exclusive) aspects of the fact: the data underlying it and its instrumentalization within a broader argument. The Kalender chooses to emphasize what he considers to be verifiable observations that constitute a fact in the first place. For him, these observations have all the neutrality of empirical data; if the evidence he has gathered in his travels yields an unflattering picture of humankind, so be it. Danischmende, without disputing what the Kalender has seen with his own eyes, nonetheless complains that facts are not stable entities and can easily succumb to subjective manipulation. His comment that facts can be crafted for individual purposes and in some cases even exposed as mere opinion underscores their instrumental value. That Wieland allowed a character like the Kalender to deliver lengthy discourses and give testimony to the innate stupidity and immaturity of the human race as irrefutable facts was also a source of irritation to some of his readers. Goethe essentially takes Danischmend's side with his complaint that, for all Wieland's eloquence, "this brilliant man liked to play with his opinions, but – as his contemporaries will testify – never with his convictions" (9: 959).[2] Such a criticism of Wieland's work, however justifiable in terms of aesthetic taste or philosophical theory, is nonetheless insufficient when it comes to a historical understanding of the fact, because what exactly it could or should be was part of an ongoing discussion which extends from the eighteenth and nineteenth centuries through to the present day. Mary Poovey has observed that there are many competing histories of the fact to be told (the one she focuses on in *A History of the Modern Fact* deals with the use of statistical tables in early-nineteenth-century Britain).[3] Nor has this situation become simpler in recent times. With regard to the fact, there is a broad spectrum between the certainty of positivism and the relativism of postmodernism. One need only consider the diverse attempts at both the definition and appropriation of facts as evinced in the fields of epistemology, critical theory, politics, and economics as well as arenas of public debate (such as the Pulitzer prize–winning website *politifact.com*). To the multiple disciplinary appropriations of the fact, one could also add the nuances of its colloquial usage, exemplified in the abundance of sometimes contradictory idiomatic expressions we have at our disposal today. Even a cursory glance at the expressions *after the fact* and *in fact* demonstrates how facts can be considered as events (and therefore situated in historical chronologies) as much as they can be used to invoke the categories of truth and reality. Any discussion of facts, including Danischmende and the Kalender's initial dispute concerning what facts are and what one can do with them, will, by necessity, confront a certain degree of terminological confusion.

Although it is no easy task to follow the manifold branches of the fact's genealogy, or to narrate even one of its many histories, this chapter participates in such a large-scale project with a focus on the fact as it was understood in the German context leading up to the Romantic era. When we speak of the fact in German thought around 1800, this problem is compounded by the situation of having more than one word that correlates to the English "fact." These include the *Factum*, a Latin import product, which had been around since the sixteenth century, as well as the *Tatsache* and, to some degree, the *Tathandlung*, both of which were understood as more or less faithful translations of the *Factum*. In order to contextualize Early German Romanticism's contribution to the discussion of the fact, this chapter begins by briefly describing the relationship between the *Factum*, *Tatsache*, and *Tathandlung* at the end of the eighteenth century before considering two aspects of the Romantic understanding of the fact. The first of these has to do with how the Romantics both draw upon pre-established usage and propose new kinds of facts with the effect of complicating the understanding of the fact at that time (this occurs above all with reference to the philosopher Johann Gottlieb Fichte and his reception by Novalis); the second concerns Romantic ideas about what one can do with facts, and even what facts can do for themselves, which I will elaborate with reference to the aphoristic work of Novalis and Friedrich Schlegel. In particular, it is Friedrich Schlegel who raises the question of to what degree facts may be considered productive or epistemological dead ends, and who taps into the operative quality of the fact to serve as both a conduit and a generator for new facts.

1. *Factum / Tatsache / Tathandlung*

When we look at the different trajectories that the words *Factum*, *Tatsache*, and *Tathandlung* follow in the German language, it is striking that they are each indebted in some way to legal discourse. The *Factum* first emerges in juridical contexts, as early as Georg Lauterbeck's *Regentenbuch* of 1559. Within a large section devoted to the governance of cities and a chapter on the importance of enforcing good hospitality, one finds the case of a poor soldier on his way home from war, who is accused of stealing money from an innkeeper. Once the trial begins, the soldier, being as honest as the innkeeper is devious, denies the *Factum* of the theft: that is, what was supposedly observed by the mendacious innkeeper, but not yet proved in the court of law. In the context of the trial, both the status of the *Factum* as event and its truth-value are disputed. The soldier, in accordance with protocol, has chosen an advocate to represent his case: it is the devil (an admittedly unusual choice for such an honest man), who has either taken on a rare case of pro bono work or, what is more likely, satisfies himself with the pleasure of escorting the evil innkeeper to Hell after the completion of the trial.[4] During the trial, the purported *Factum* is disproved and both the soldier and his lawyer are satisfied with the outcome. Other cases where the *Factum* appears in German writing during the seventeenth and eighteenth centuries preserve the legal context: it is usually defined as a deed evaluated by trial (*Streitsache*), or the circumstances described in the testimony given before a court of law. By the time Zedler publishes his universal lexicon at the beginning of the eighteenth century, however, the definition of the *Factum* has expanded: it can now be understood more generally as deeds, occurrences, and works, including the course [*Verlauff* (*sic*)] of a concluded transaction.[5] Zedler's definition of the *Factum* is therefore broad enough to encompass the double meaning of doing and making (as both the "deed" and the "work"), in keeping with its derivation from the Latin verb *facere*, but the temporal aspects of this definition merit particular emphasis. They show that the *Factum* is not only able to be assigned a place in a historical chronology, but also has its own duration. Even though one usually relegates the factum to the past around 1800 (in keeping with its grammatical status as past participle of *facere*) as opposed to the hypothetical future, a *Factum* is nonetheless able to be extended in time, as either a momentary occurrence or the course of an event. It is precisely this quality of the *Factum* that will take on new meaning in the aphorisms of Schlegel and Novalis.

Unlike the *Factum*, the *Tatsache* arrives on the scene via a translation from an English text: Joseph Butler's *Analogy of Religion, Natural and Revealed, to the Constitution and Course of Nature*, first published in 1736.[6] In the German translation of Butler's text, Johann Joachim Spalding renders the expression "matter of fact" as *Thatsache*.[7] Yet as was the case with the *Factum*, the *Thatsache* as translation of "matter of fact" owes its origins to a juridical rather than theological context and already occurs as an English legal expression in the sixteenth century.[8] Butler's text transposes the "matter of fact" from the juridical context into a theological one: it is a "Matter of Fact," for example, that "[God] governs the World by the Method of Rewards and Punishments" (*Analogy of Religion* 167). Butler also makes it quite clear that these divinely performed "matters of fact" are also "things of experience," in keeping with his overall plan to construct a parallel history between the divine and the natural.[9] Nor is he the only one. To the extent that "fact" correlates to an action, matters of fact as *Thatsachen* come to be understood as divine deeds, and it is in this sense that Johann Hamann and Johann Herder also equate the *Thatsache* with the revelation of God in natural phenomena.[10] Not everyone was pleased with this neologism, however, which was rendered both as a translation for the "matter of fact" and as a German equivalent of the *Factum* itself. Adelung's 1811 dictionary condemns both the *Thatsache* and the *Thathandlung* for being "indecorous," composed "contrary to analogy," and "subject to misunderstanding, in that an upper German [that is, someone from the Bavarian or Allemanian linguistic groups] would at first most likely think of nothing other than an act of violence, an assault" (in other words, would understand the *That* as a *Delikt*).[11] And even though one can read in the English edition of Fichte's *Wissenschaftslehre* that *Thathandlung* is "a term of Fichte's own coinage,"[12] there are examples to be found as early as the *Reichs-Fama* of 1727, which makes reference to a "murderous" *That-Handlung* (3). It would be useful to know to what degree Fichte was cognizant of the word's more violent connotations, although one should probably keep in mind that *his* family was deeply rooted in Saxony. In any event, part of the terminological proliferation of the fact was that by the mid-eighteenth century, the *Thatsache* and *Thathandlung* were just as likely to call to mind a criminal deed as they were a religious manifestation or a simple fact – with the range of possibilities, the intended meaning could only be determined by context.

2. Fichte's Fact / Romantic Facts

The proliferation of the fact and its potential confusion does not abate by the late eighteenth century, when Schlegel and Novalis become interested in the *Factum* as well as the disputed *Thatsache*. At the same time, however, the fact in its multiple forms becomes a key term in philosophy, also as the result of being imported from legal discourse:[13] yet the degree to which Kant, Fichte, and their followers ultimately subjugate the *Factum* (as well as the *Tatsache* and the *Tathandlung*) to their philosophical projects for their own purposes varies greatly. To keep things simple, the following discussion will first focus on the Romantic fact as *Factum* in the context of a reception of Fichte, in order to explore what the fact can be and do, before incorporating the other terms.

In Novalis's *Fichte Studies*, the product of a reading of Fichte's *Wissenschaftslehre* and other texts in 1795–6 (which actually extends well beyond an engagement with Fichte), one finds a compilation of excerpts which include original meditations on the fact. At one point, Novalis even characterizes Fichte's entire philosophy as a fact: "Fichte's philosophy is a process of thought production or process of organization – a *phenomenon* itself, or a *factum*" (3: 447). Structured as a chain of associations linked through repetition and accumulation, this aphorism reveals as much about Early Romantic techniques of creating definitions as it does about Fichte's philosophy, and both aspects are relevant here. Fichte's philosophy is defined as a process of thinking *or* as a process of organization, a pair immediately substituted by a phenomenon *or* a fact, suggesting a logic of accumulation rather than exclusion: all of these terms share a relationship both to Fichte's thinking and to each other. In the context of the present discussion, there are at least two things of note about the *Factum*. The first is, by connecting the *Factum* to a process, we can observe a reluctance to impose temporal constraints upon it as something made or done and then relegated to the past (which would be more in keeping with one of the definitions found in Zedler, the *Factum* as "Verlauff einer Handlung"). The second is, by linking the *Factum* with the phenomenon, as something which exists and is perceivable, Novalis allows the process-character of the *Factum* (or Fichte's philosophy) to be unified under a single sign. It also bears remembering that we are not dealing with a colloquially informed definition of "facts" in general here but rather "the fact" which, in Fichte's work (as in Kant's), has a philosophical status as a technical term.

When Novalis first refers to the *Factum* in the *Fichte Studies*, it is to assert the validity of a philosophy of the subject: "A generally valid philosophy would presuppose the *fixation* of the so-called subjectivity, thus a *free* Factum or the assumption of a hypothetical, free proposition [*Satz*]."[14] The "primal" factum is in essence the one which we are ourselves, posited in the original activity of the subject. This claim is given nuance in both the *Wissenschaftslehre* and the *Fichte Studies*, where we see the subject emerge as the synthesis of a real and ideal "fact" through the joint labour of the I and the Not-I. One of the excerpted passages from Fichte found in Novalis's notes expresses this sentiment more clearly and also explains the degree to which we are able to access the original *Factum*: "The factum should allow itself to be observed as well as, according to its *determination*, plainly posited through the I – and also, according to its being, as posited through the Not-I. It can be observed as product of the I and the Not-I, each independently of the other. It is an *intuition*."[15] Even though Novalis's reception of the *Factum* has not received much attention, this is well-travelled terrain as far as Fichte scholarship is concerned. In the process of self-reflection, according to Fichte, one has immediate access to the produced intuition or "fact" but not to the original activity of self-positing. Novalis noticed that only belatedly does the realization come that the intuition is the product of a process which originated in an undifferentiated state preceding consciousness (identified on various occasions as "Grund" or "Gefühl"); it is a state which, somewhat counter-intuitively, we can only at a later stage construct or approximate for ourselves. This aspect of Novalis's reading of Fichte has been extensively documented by Manfred Frank in his work on time and German Romanticism (*Das Problem "Zeit" in der deutschen Romantik*). For now, it suffices to remember that the *Factum* is created and, as an intuition, can be observed; this latter point aligns with the earlier connection made between the phenomenon and the process-quality of the fact.[16] In the second introduction to the *Wissenschaftslehre*,

Fichte connects the *Factum*, *Thatsache*, and *Thathandlung* in the following way: a philosopher understands that the intuition is a "fact [*Factum*] of the consciousness," with the caveat that for him it appears as *Thatsache* (i.e., *Factum* as *Datum*), whereas for the "original I" it is *Thathandlung* (an activity).[17] Robert Richards comments that "Fichte's genius was to see that a *fact* of consciousness might better be conceived as an *act* of consciousness – unification would be achieved not by a logical supposition but by an underlying action" (*Romantic Conception of Life* 75).

Just one more example from the *Fichte Studies* is necessary to lay the groundwork of facts for German Romanticism:

> Every object posits – every opposition sets up – if we attribute the particular nature of the *Factum* to the ladder [*dem Leiter*][18] – object and opposite are ladders – neither active nor passive. Activity is, however, attributed to them – because, pressured by the natural laws of reflection, this [activity] must be *posited* somewhere; and so one resorts more easily to the ladder and attributes [activity] to this – all activity belongs to the *Factum*.[19]

The translator of the *Fichte Studies* has chosen to render *Leiter* as "ladder," but the choice of words is misleading, particularly since the German text clearly indicates that *Leiter* is not a feminine noun. Whereas *die Leiter* (fem.) indicates a climbing ladder, *der Leiter* (masc.) refers to a conducting medium. The image invoked in the aphorism is therefore one of a conductor of electrical current. This allows us to align Novalis's thinking about the *Factum* with his scientific studies of electricity as well as to read the *Factum* as conduit of reflection and potential conveyer of intellectual activity. As was the case with the other aphorisms, this one is also deeply indebted to the laws of reflection. When we reflect upon an object – when we posit it in our consciousness – then, according to Fichte, it enters into a complex chain of reactions leading to our ability to compose an adequate intuition of it. And as was touched upon above, what we eventually have access to is not the object itself, but rather a mere *Schein* – an image of it.[20] Within this network of activity, the *Factum* is intimately bound to reflection, but through the reference to the *Leiter*, its processual quality comes more prominently to the foreground.

In the context of the *Fichte Studies*, Novalis focuses his attention on "the" *Factum*, but his later aphoristic work allows for modifications. The Teplitzer Fragments, for example, refer to a "specific fact" which is the source of a particular science,[21] and there is an analogous fragment in *Das allgemeine Brouillon* which makes a parallel claim for the *Thatsache*.[22]

These two cases demonstrate an attempt by Novalis to expand his reasoning about the fact beyond the immediate context of Fichtean philosophy while remaining within a theory of science. At the same time, the Romantic discussion of the fact has not yet arrived at a modern understanding of the fact in terms of what Husserl will eventually define as the "objective correlate of a true proposition."[23] What does capture the attention of Schlegel and Novalis, however, is the possibility of generalizing from "the fact" to facts by tapping into their potentially instrumental quality – the notion that one can do things with facts. To some degree, there is a precedent for this way of thinking: the idea that it is possible to experiment with facts is already a topic of the *Fichte Studies*, such as when Novalis comments that Fichte teaches us "the secret of experimentation" when he instructs us how to "transform *Thatsachen* and *Thathandlungen* ... into experiments and concepts."[24] Friedrich Schlegel's thinking about facts will, however, go much further in terms of connecting them to the experiment, without remaining indebted to the constraints imposed by Fichte's philosophy.

In Athenäum Fragment 427, Schlegel invokes the fact in the context of historical investigation when he writes that "a so-called investigation is a historical experiment. Its object and result is a fact [*Factum*]. What a fact should be has to have strict individuality, being at once a secret and an experiment, namely, an experiment of formative nature."[25] Within an analogous framework of Romantic practices of interpretation and open-ended experimentation, the essay by Alice Kuzniar in this volume on structures of signification in the homeopathy of Samuel Hahnemann offers an illuminating parallel narrative, by focusing on Hahnemann's Romantically informed "reading" of individual symptoms. As far as Athenäum Fragment 427 is concerned, although we are no longer in the realm of Fichte's fact, bound within a process of reflection, we have also still not quite arrived at the pedestrian facts of everyday life. Schlegel's understanding of the fact as the beginning and endpoint of research suggests that a fact is both something rendered to us, differentiated from the noise of sense perceptions, and something made, which preserves its individuality even in the process of transformation. If there is any new tendency to be discerned in Schlegel's comments on the fact scattered throughout his aphorisms – comments diverse enough to identify beauty and Christianity as facts in their own right[26] – then it is perhaps an inclination to let them calibrate a scale of phenomena. At one end we would have according to Schlegel a simple *Erscheinung* or phenomenon which is a "still rough and not completely historicized fact,"[27] and at the other we would have an experiment which, in the process of isolating the phenomenon as fact, eventually goes beyond it such that "the true phenomenon is representative of the infinite, thus allegory, hieroglyph – thus far more than a fact."[28] We need facts, but, as Schlegel suggests, we also need to get beyond them. As "individuals of sense," he writes, facts are constrained by being a "limited historical whole."[29] For Schlegel, the fact would seem to serve as a transit point for the work of philosophy, for history, and, one could even say, for any critical thinking. The character Marcus in Schlegel's fictional conversation "Gespräch über die Poesie" [conversation about poesy] makes precisely this point: "A true aesthetic judgment, you will agree, a fully formed, thoroughly complete view of a work is always a critical fact [*Factum*], if I may say so. But also only a fact, and that is exactly why it is empty work to want to motivate it, the motive itself would have to contain a new fact or a more precise determination of the first one."[30] The context of the quote is a discussion about the relativity of aesthetic judgments, as well as their epistemological status. An aesthetic judgment of a work of art has just as much claim to exist as any other thing that taken place, in keeping with Zedler's broad understanding of a *Faktum* as something that has occurred (*ein geschehenes Ding*). In the broader scope of Schlegel's text, however, the "critical fact" is also introduced as an argument against the limited value of aesthetic statements, claiming that despite their subjective origin they can contribute to general knowledge. Marcus's statement about the critical fact is also notable for another reason: it describes both its limit and its potential. It is certainly possible for a critical fact to be "only a fact" – to be a dead end, so to speak. But Marcus also suggests that facts and the way we work with them have the ability to generate new facts or more precise versions of the old ones. This second take on the fact recalls both Novalis's claims that facts can form the point of departure of a new science and that there is a connection between the fact and "conductor" of intellectual activity, as was discussed above with reference to Fichte. It is also important to note that we have a somewhat more cautious understanding here of the potential instrumentality of the fact. On the one hand, its mobilization could result in "empty work" – such that the instrumental value of the fact is effectively null. On the other hand, if one mobilizes it in the name of a motive which already contains a new fact (or, as Schlegel writes, a more precise formulation of the present one), then the process of critical aesthetic labour continues, albeit in a somewhat circular fashion, given that it is the motive and not the instrument which has produced something new.

The Romantic discussion of the fact can be thrown into even sharper relief with an example (one of numerous possible ones) from the scientific discussions around 1800. For the purpose of objectivity, I have chosen the scientist Paul Ludwig Simon, a professor of physics at the Bauakademie of Berlin, someone with no known ties to the Romantic circle (unless, in the interest of full disclosure, we count his financial bailout by the minister Karl August von Hardenberg, a distant relative of Novalis). Simon made contributions to one of the most hotly debated scientific ideas of his time, the composition of water. On one side of the debate were those for whom water remained a pure element in the Aristotelian sense, and on the other side were those who claimed they could experimentally prove that water was composed of hydrogen and oxygen. The latter group took advantage of the Voltaic pile, a primitive battery which generated an electric charge and allowed the process of electrolysis to take place. At the beginning of an article he published in the *Annals of Physics* (1802), Simon shows himself determined to remain impartial: "Everything which one has said so far about [the phenomena produced by water in the closed circuit of the pile] merely rests on supposition, and the theories built upon it are up until now neither evidently proven nor supported with established facts [*Thatsachen*]" (Simon 283). Of the two opinions/hypotheses – the first, that water is a composed substance, and the second, that water is "simple" – each accepts as "facts" (*Facta*) that hydrogen and oxygen result from the electrolysis of water, but neither group can adequately account for its theory. In the first case (the argument for the composition of water), there remains the question "Why do both ends of the wire of the pile only produce one component of water" (Simon 283)? According to Simon, "Everything said about this are only words, is mere hypothesis, and does not allow itself to be led back empirically [*auf sinnlich*] to justifiable facts [*Thatsachen*]" (ibid.). For its part, the other group has yet to provide a cogent explanation as to where the oxygen and hydrogen come from, if not from the water. In the context of the present discussion, it is perhaps more interesting to observe several familiar "elements" of the fact at play in a text devoted to scientific method. Not only does the passage from the *Annals of Physics* recall aspects of the Factum on trial (the fact as *Streitsache*) in the *Regentenbuch* and other juridical contexts, it can also remind us of the discussion between the Kalender and Danischmende as to whether or not facts (such as the fact that hydrogen and oxygen are the products of water electrolysis) are what we make of them. And in the question as to which version of the facts is most conducive to the generation of an adequate theory, there is also an echo of both Novalis's metaphor of the conductor (which is quite at home in the context of the Voltaic pile) and Schlegel's question of motives which result in the continued production of viable facts rather than a dead end.

A common thread in many of the examples discussed above is the duration of the fact, whether as *Factum* or *Tatsache*. The cases we have seen include Zedler's definition of the *Factum* as a process, Novalis's metaphor of a galvanic conductor and understanding of Fichte's *Tatsache* as a process; and Schlegel's notion of facts begetting other facts, if in a somewhat inverted way. These philosophical/theoretical interpretations of the fact, when considered in a broader context which accepts facts as actions and events, suggest that by the end of the eighteenth century there were multiple ways in which the temporality of the fact could be understood. Just as facts occurred in time and could be used to indicate a bygone occurrence, situated in a historical chronology, they are also events with their own mechanisms of extension and duration. The kind of facts Schlegel and Novalis have in mind may seem to be entities which bear little resemblance to the kind whose appropriation is up for grabs in contemporary political and cultural arenas. It is nevertheless worth keeping in mind that time is one of the key factors in contemporary definitions of the fact; in particular, those definitions that claim that although facts may denote temporal events, they are themselves atemporal in nature: "that every reference to facts [*Tatsachen*] is certainly a reference to temporal events … that facts themselves can however not be characterized as temporal events: they do not occur and are never past."[31] The Romantic discussion of facts challenges such constraints. Romantic facts are constructed entities with theoretical value.

Facts are what one makes of them … in the dispute over the nature of water we have heard an echo of Danischmende's words, and we can also see the connectivity of facts: each established one should lead to further precisions or altogether new facts. Otherwise it is "empty work," the dead end of a bad hypothesis. Where does that leave us? For one, with the sense that the Romantic fact is as indebted to a philosophical system as it is to linguistic context. We can also observe in the Romantic thinking about the fact an interest in exploring its temporality by connecting it to an open-ended process which, ideally, would facilitate the emergence of new facts. That means that facts, understood in this theoretical sense, have a conceptual historicity as if they were events (Schlegel's claim that Christianity is an initiated but still not concluded "Fact" would be just one additional example).

Certainly, the Romantic discussion of the fact anticipates discussions the field of science studies over a hundred years later that facts emerge through intricate processes of construction, even if science studies does not necessarily acknowledge this kinship. At the same time, it cannot be said to fit comfortably into the categories which the discussions of the past decades have circumscribed. The Romantic fact conforms neither to positivistic views nor towards the radical contingencies of postmodernism. It does not exist within a conceptual framework in which notions of "objective validity" or "reality" also play a role. Instead, the Romantic fact seems most comfortable poised on a threshold between theoretical system and event, among processes of reading and creation, and it is precisely this ambivalence which lends it its distinctive character.

NOTES

1 The entire passage reads as follows: "Die Frage, wenn ich nicht irre, war, wie die Sache sey; nicht, wie wir wünschen, hoffen, träumen, daß sie seyn sollte und möchte. Facta müssen hier den Ausschlag machen!"

"Facta sind Alles, was man daraus machen will, sagte Danischmend: aus jedem neuen Augenpunkte scheinen sie etwas Anderes; und in zehn Fällen gegen einen ist das vermeinte Factum, worauf man mit großer Zuversicht seine Meinung gestützt hatte, im Grund eine bloße Hypothese."

"Dieß mag seyn, erwiederte der Kalender. Aber die Facta, von welchen ich rede, sind von der Art derjenigen, die, aus allen möglichen Gesichtspunkten betrachtet, immer die nämliche Gestalt zeigen und immer einerlei Resultate geben" (9: 60).

2 "Der geistreiche Mann spielte gern mit seinen Meinungen, aber, ich kann alle Mitlebenden als Zeugen auffordern, niemals mit seinen Gesinnungen" (9: 959).

3 See Poovey, *History of the Modern Fact* xiii.

4 "Since the traveller denies the *Factum*, he is called upon according to custom to choose someone present" [i.e., to speak on his behalf]. "Da der Trabant das Factum leugnet, wird er dem gebrauch nach geheissen / einen aus den umbstendern zu erwehlen" (141).

5 "Eine That, das geschehene Ding, oder eine Geschichte, das Werck, die Verrichtung, der Verlauff eines ergangenen Handels" (def. "Factum," col. 65).

6 For the historical overview, see the entry "Tatsache" in Joachim Ritter and Karlfried Gründer, *Historisches Wörterbuch der Philosophie* (10: col. 910–16).

7 "For though [unbelievers] may say ... the historical Evidence of Miracles wrought in Attestation of Christianity, is not sufficient to convince them, that such Miracles were really wrought: they cannot deny, that there is such historical Evidence, it being a known matter of Fact, that there is" (Butler, *Analogy of Religion* 398). "Denn wenn sie gleich sagen mögen, der historische Beweis von den Wundern, die zur Bestätigung des Christenthums geschehen

seyn sollen, sey nicht zureichend, sie zu überzeugen, daß diese Wunder wirklich geschehen wären, so können sie doch nicht läugnen, daß es einen solchen historischen Beweis giebt, da es eine bekannte Thatsache ist, daß es dergleichen giebt" (*Bestätigung der natürlichen und geoffenbarten Religion* 378). See also the definition for "Tatsache" (10: col. 910) in the *Historisches Wörterbuch der Philosophie*.

8 See for example the *Oxford English Dictionary* definition of "matter of fact": "1583: A. Nowell & W. Day *True Rep. Disput. with E. Campion* sig. M1^v^, 'He speaketh of a matter of fact'; 1605: Bacon *Of Aduancem. Learning* i. sig. F2^v^, 'It is either a beleefe of Historie, (as the Lawyers speake, matter of fact:) or else of matter of art and opinion.'"

9 See also the definition of "Tatsache" (10: col. 910) in the *Historisches Wörterbuch der Philosophie*.

10 "These events [i.e., miracles such as the resurrection of Christ, etc.] thus belong to the course of history; their effect, partly through the impression that they make upon our minds, partly through that which follows from them as fact [*Thatsache*], lies in religion before the eyes of all the world as fact [*Factum*]." "Diese Ereignisse gehören also in den Gang der Geschichte; ihre Wirkung Theils durch den Eindruck, den sie auf die Gemüther machten, Theils durch das, was als Thatsache aus ihnen folgte, liegt in der gestifteten Religion als Factum aller Welt vor Augen" (Herder, "Von der Auferstehung als Glaube" 264).

11 See the definition for "Thatsache" in Adelung.

12 "*Thathandlung* (which is here always translated as 'Act' and capitalized) is a term of Fichte's own coinage, constructed by combining the word for 'fact' (=*Thatsache*) with the word for 'action' (=*Handlung*). It is a term employed to designate the type of originally productive act that is, at the same time, its own product and/or object) ... In other words, it designates the original, productive activity of the I itself and thus provides the starting point for a transcendental deduction of experience. Fichte first introduced this term in 1794 in his 'Review of *Aensidemus*'... and employed it extensively in GWL" (see note 12, Fichte 48–9).

13 See, for example, Pauline Kleingeld, who discusses the Factum as "a technical term that designates a particular moment in Kant's proof structure" ("Moral Consciousness" 61), drawing upon an argument by Dieter Henrich which has a direct bearing on the German tradition of legal disputes through the proof or disproof of a *factum*.

14 "Allgemeingültige Filosofie würde die *Fixirumg* der sogenannten Subjectivitaet, also ein *freyes* Factum, oder die Annahme eines hypothetischen, freyen Satzes voraussetzen." (Novalis, *Schriften* 2: 177).

15 "Das Factum soll sich betrachten lassen, als auch seiner *Bestimmung* nach schlechthin gesezt durch das Ich – und auch seinem Seyn nach, als gesezt durch das N[icht]I[ch]. Es läßt sich, als Produkt des Ich und des N[icht]I[ch] betrachten, beydes unabhängig vom andern. Es ist ein *Anschauen*" (Fichte, *Sämmtliche Werke* 1: 342; Novalis, *Schriften* 2: 345).

16 That the factum we observe is the product of two activities of positing and negation is also compatible with another eighteenth-century definition of the Factum as mathematical product. See the definition of "Product" in Adelung: "In arithmetic the product is the number that arises when one number is multiplied with another, and which is also called the *Factum*." "In der Rechenkunst ist das Product, diejenige Zahl, welche entstehet, wenn eine Zahl mit der andern multiplicirt wird, und welche auch das Factum heißt."

17 There are further specifications to be made, in that the intuition as factum is not immediately given but needs to be differentiated/discerned: "Thus the philosopher finds this intellectual intuition as fact [*Factum*] of consciousness (for him it is fact [or "matter of fact" = *Thatsache*]; for the original I action [*Thathandlung*]), not immediately, as isolated fact of his consciousness, but rather, in that he distinguishes what appears united in the common consciousness, and dissolves the whole into its constituent parts." "Sonach findet der Philosoph diese intellectuelle Anschauung als Factum des Bewusstseyns (für ihn ist es Thatsache ; für das ursprüngliche Ich Thathandlung), nicht unmittelbar, als isolirtes Factum seines Bewusstseyns, sondern, indem er unterscheidet, was in dem gemeinen Bewusstseyn vereinigt vorkommt, und das Ganze in seine Bestandtheile auflöst" (Fichte, *Sämmtliche Werke* 1: 465).

18 *die Leiter* = ladder; *der Leiter* = leader, conductor, etc.; See the "Leiter der Elektricität" in J.S.T. Gehler: "Ein vollkommner Leiter würde derjenige seyn, der der Elektricität beym Durchgange durch seine Substanz gar keinen Widerstand entgegensetzte." A complete conductor would be the one that does not offer any resistance to electricity passing through its substance. Accessed from http://echo.mpiwg-berlin.mpg.de/home.

19 "Jeder Gegenstand sezt – jeder Gegensatz stellt – wenn wir die besondre Art des Factums dem Leiter zuschreiben – Gegenstand und Gegensatz sind Leiter – weder activ noch passiv. Man schreibt ihnen aber Activität zu – weil man doch dieselbe, gedrungen vom Naturgesetze der Reflexion, wohin *setzen* muß; und da nimmt man am bequemsten mit dem Leiter vorlieb und schreibt sie diesem zu – Alle Activitaet gehört dem Factum" (Novalis, *Das philosophisch-theoretische Werk* 105).

20 Novalis proposes a creative approach to a problem already formulated by Fichte: that the product of self-reflection is a falsification that impedes access

to the original subject. Whereas Fichte negotiates this problem through a law of reflection that posits the determination of knowledge through the simultaneous recognition of its opposite, Novalis proposes a second negation of reflection. Through a double inversion that first acknowledges the falsity or *Schein* of reflection and then turns it on its head, Manfred Frank shows how Novalis believed the original, pre-reflexive state could be more closely approximated. Novalis calls for continuous philosophical activity, which, though it may never fully attain the pre-reflexive state, at least permits movement towards this goal.

21 "Jedes specifische Factum ist Quell einer bes[onderen] Wissenschaft" (Novalis, *Das philosophisch-theoretische Werk* 386, no. 330).

22 "All sciences that take their start from *facts* etc., belong to the *mixed* sciences – the *individual* sciences. Every fact is synthetic – substantial." (Novalis, *Notes for a Romantic Encyclopedia* 106). "Alle W[issenschaften] die von *Thatsachen* etc. ausgehn, gehören zu den *Gemischten* Wissenschaften – den *individuellen* W[issenschaften]. Jede Thatsache ist synthetisch – Substantiell" (Novalis, *Das philosophisch-theoretiche Werk* 609, no. 600).

23 Husserl, quoted in *Historisches Wörterbuch der Philosophie* under the definition of "Tatsache" (10: col. 912).

24 "Fichte lehrt das Geheimniß des Experimentirens, er lehrt Thatsachen und Thathandlungen, oder wirkliche Sachen und Handlungen in Experimente und Begriffe verwandeln" (Novalis, *Schriften* 3: 391, no. 657).

25 "Eine sogenannte Recherche ist ein historisches Experiment. Der Gegenstand und das Resultat desselben ist ein Faktum. Was ein Faktum seyn soll, muss strenge Individualität haben, zugleich ein Geheimniss und ein Experiment seyn, nämlich ein Experiment der bildenden Natur." Friedrich and A.W. Schlegel's *Athenaeum* (1: 135).

26 Part 2 of the second volume of the *Athenaeum* journal published by August Wilhelm and Friedrich Schlegel in 1798 contains several aphorisms on the *Faktum* written by Friedrich Schlegel (later published elsewhere in his oeuvre), including the two referred to here: "Christianity seems to me to be a fact. But a fact that has only just begun, that therefore can not be historically represented in a system, but can rather only be characterized through divinatory criticism." "Der Christianismus scheint mir ein Faktum zu seyn. Aber ein erst angefangenes Faktum, das also nicht in einem System historisch dargestellt, sondern nur durch divinatorische Kritik charakterisirt werden kann" (2: 59–60); and Schlegel's claim that beauty is "not merely a necessary fiction, but rather also a fact, namely an eternally transcendental [fact] "nicht bloss eine nothwendige Fikzion, sondern auch ein Faktum, nämlich ein ewiges transcendentales" (2: 71).

27 "*Erscheinung* ein noch rohes nicht vollständig historisirtes Factum, gehört in die Hist[orische] ϕ[Philosophie] nicht in die Tr[anszendental] ϕ[philosophie]" (*Kritische Friedrich-Schlegel-Ausgabe* 18: 55, no. 452).

28 "Das Experiment geht darauf aus, d[as] Phänomen zu isoliren d.h. es in seiner classischen Reinheit zu bekommen. Das wahre Phänomen ist Repräsentant d[es] Unendlichen, also Allegorie, Hieroglyphe – also weit mehr als ein Factum" (*Kritische Friedrich-Schlegel-Ausgabe* 18: 155, no. 380).

29 "Facta sind Individuen des Sinns ... Ein Individuum ist ein bedingtes historisches Ganzes" (*Kritische Friedrich-Schlegel-Ausgabe* 18: 88, no. 704).

30 "Ein wahres Kunsturtheil, werden Sie mir eingestehen, eine ausgebildete, durchaus fertige Ansicht eines Werks ist immer ein kritisches Factum, wenn ich so sagen darf. Aber auch nur ein Factum, und eben darum ists leere Arbeit, es motiviren zu wollen, es müsste denn das Motiv selbst ein neues Factum oder eine nähere Bestimmung des ersten enthalten" (*Athenaeum* 3: 183–84). Schlegel's "Gespräch über die Poesie" was originally published in the two parts of *Athenaeum*, vol. 3.

31 "... daß jeder Bezug auf Tatsachen zwar ein Bezug auf zeitliche Begebenheiten ist ... daß Tatsachen selbst gleichwohl nicht als zeitliche Begebenheiten charakterisiert werden können: Sie ereignen sich nicht und sind nie vergangen." See the definition for "Tatsache" (col. 912) in the *Historisches Wörterbuch*.

WORKS CITED

Adelung, Johann Christoph. *Grammatisch-kritisches Wörterbuch der hochdeutschen Mundart*. Vienna: Bauer, 1811.

– "Product." *Bestätigung der natürlichen und geoffenbarten Religion*. Trans. Johann Joachim Spalding. Leipzig: in der Weidmannischen Handlung, 1756.

– "Thatsache." *Grammatisch-kritisches Wörterbuch der hochdeutschen Mundart*. Vienna: Bauer, 1811.

Butler, Joseph. *The Analogy of Religion, Natural and Revealed*. London: John and Paul Knapton, 1740.

"Factum." In *Grosses vollständiges Universallexicon aller Wissenschaften und Künste*, vol. 9, col. 65. Ed. Johann Heinrich Zedler. Halle/Leipzig: Johann Heinrich Zedler, 1735.

Fichte, Johann Gottlieb. *Introductions to the Wissenschaftslehre and Other Writings, 1797–1800*. Ed. and trans. Daniel Breazeale. Indianapolis/Cambridge: Hackett, 1994.

– *Sämmtliche Werke*. Ed. Immanuel Hermann Fichte. Berlin: Verlag von Veit und Comp., 1845–6.

Frank, Manfred. *Das Problem "Zeit" in der deutschen Romantik*. 2nd ed. Paderborn: F. Schoningh, 1990.

Goethe, Johann Wolfang. "Zu brüderlichem Andenken Wielands." In *Sämtliche Werke*, vol. 9. Ed. Christoph Siegrist, Hans J. Becker, Dorothea Hölscher-Lohmeyer, et al. Munich/Vienna: Carl Hanser, 2006.

Herder, Johann Gottfried. "Von der Auferstehung als Glaube, Geschichte und Lehre." In *Christliche Schriften, Erste Sammlung*. Riga: Johann Friedrich Hartknoch, 1794.

Kleingeld, Pauline. "Moral Consciousness and the 'Fact of Reason.'" In *Kant's Critique of Practical Reason: A Critical Guide*. Ed. Andrews Reath and Jens Timmermann. Cambridge: Cambridge UP, 2000. 55–72.

Kritische Friedrich-Schlegel-Ausgabe. Ed. Ernst Behler, Jean Jacques Anstett, and Hans Eichner. Paderborn: F. Schöningh, 1963.

Lauterbeck, George. *Regentenbuch*. Wittemberg: Hans Kraffts Erben, 1581.

"Leiter der Elektricität." In *Physikalisches Wörterbuch*, vol. 2. Ed. J.S.T. Gehler. Leipzig: im Schwickertschen Verlag, 1798.

"Matter of Fact." *Oxford English Dictionary*. Oxford: Oxford UP, 1989.

Novalis. *Notes for a Romantic Encyclopedia: Das allgemeine Brouillon*. Trans. David W. Wood. Albany: State U of New York P, 2007.

– *Das philosophisch-theoretische Werk*. Ed. Hans Joachim Mähl and Richard H. Samuel. Munich: Hanser Verlag, 1978.

– *Schriften*. Ed. Paul Kluckhohn and Richard H. Samuel. 4 vols. Stuttgart: W. Kohlhammer, 1981.

Poovey, Mary. *A History of the Modern Fact: Problems of Knowledge in the Sciences of Wealth and Society*. Chicago: U of Chicago P, 1998.

Reichs-Fama. Frankfurt/Leipzig, January 1727.

Richards, Robert. *The Romantic Conception of Life: Science and Philosophy in the Age of Goethe*. Chicago: U of Chicago P, 2002.

Schlegel, Friedrich, and A.W. Schlegel. *Athenaeum*. 3 vols. Berlin: Friedrich Vieweg the elder, 1798–1800.

Simon, Paul Ludwig. "Beschreibung einiger Versuche über das quantitative Verhältniss, worin Volta's Säule das Oxygen- und Hydrogen-Gas aus dem Wasser darstellt." In *Annalen der Physik*, vol. 10. Ed. Ludwig Wilhelm Gilbert. Halle: Rengersche Buchhandlung, 1802. 282–300.

"Tatsache." *Historisches Wörterbuch der Philosophie*, vol. 10, col. 910–16. Ed. Joachim Ritter and Karlfried Gründer. Basel: Schwabe & Co., 1998.

Wieland, C.M. *Sämmtliche Werke*. Vol. 9. Leipzig: G.J. Göschen'sche Verlagshandlung, 1854.

2 The Competing Structures of Signification in Samuel Hahnemann's Homeopathy: Between 18th-Century Semiosis and Romantic Hermeneutics

ALICE KUZNIAR

In his essay "Lehre vom Ähnlichen" (Doctrine of the Similar) Walter Benjamin speaks of the "moment of birth" in the perception of similitude: correspondences appear to one in an instant – "im Nu" – and arise at an ingenious spark of inspiration that is "in every case bound to an instantaneous flash" (206; 66).[1] He compares this occurrence to the flash of insight that comes to the astrologist who, upon seeing the conjunction of two stars, perceives a third term or special meaning in their constellation. This magical, unanticipated instant leads Benjamin to work out a concept of a nonsensical similarity ("Begriff einer unsinnlichen Ähnlichkeit" [207; 66]). In other words, in counterpoint to the establishing of similarities stands the pivotal but paradoxical idea that what actually grounds comparison is something absurd, unexpected, arbitrary, and merely coincidental. Benjamin offers the examples of onomatopoeia and graphology as beliefs in an innate but nonsensical correspondence between a sign and that to which it refers.

This concept of a third, absurd element unexpectedly relating two separate entities is one that invites investigation in reference to one of the most renowned applications of a theory of similarity: Samuel Hahnemann's medical practice of homeopathy.[2] Hahnemann, the founder of homeopathy, came up with the idea that "like could cure like," namely, that something producing symptoms similar to an illness could in fact cure this very illness. Homeopathy indeed seems to be an absurd, nonsensical proposition; and no less a poet than Goethe made fun of it in *Faust, Part Two* when Mephisto, in response to an old woman's complaint about a sore foot, cruelly says he'll step on it, which she initially misinterprets as a sexual advance or playing footsie. But the devil's stomping on her foot is a joke, not only on her but on Hahnemann's Law of Similars: "Zu

Gleichem Gleiches, was auch einer litt; / Fuß heilet Fuß, so ist's mit allen Gliedern" (Hair of the dog, whatever ill you pick. / Foot for a foot, all parts are cured like that) (195; 181).[3] Goethe's parody aside, as a holistic medical practice, homeopathy is suspiciously seen to be effective based on the placebo effect rather than on scientific testing. But the semiotic system or tabling of symptoms that Hahnemann set up actually endeavoured to be thoroughly systematic, based on close observation and the recording of data, as well as a contribution to the compiling of facts. If we return to Walter Benjamin, though, we see undergirding Hahnemann's system of comparisons a third, nonsensical element: the moment that clinches the diagnosis for Hahnemann in determining which remedy to offer a patient is both what enables the comparison and, at the same time, threatens to disrupt the symmetrical order.

To state it differently, what I hope to pursue in this chapter are two divergent tendencies in ways of making meaning in Hahnemann's medical poesis. The one strives to list and catalogue symptoms based on their similarity; it is indebted to an eighteenth-century belief in taxonomical organization. The second tendency, running counter to the first, is a principle of the absurd, chaotic, and exceptional, in other words, Benjamin's nonsensical moment that grounds the comparison. The problem is that this pivotal moment also threatens to unhinge and unravel the system. This second tendency resembles less eighteenth-century collecting than a Romantic theorization of chaotic, fragmentary, and individualistic reading. It can be traced in Hahnemann's concepts of the unusual symptom, disease as unique to each patient, even in the piecemeal note taking of his case studies. The first requires a semiotic comparison of signs based on evident parallels, while the second depends on the ingenuity of the individual reader to single out the pertinent sign. That both "ways of knowing" – to use the phrase coined by John Pickstone – existed simultaneously is not surprising. Samuel Hahnemann straddles the eighteenth and nineteenth centuries. Extremely learned and fluent in several languages, he embodies the eighteenth-century savant. And yet he also reflects beliefs in organicism and vitalism that we have come to associate with Romanticism. In sum, he borrowed from contradictory paradigms to construct his own salient and unique philosophy of medical treatment.

The word *homeopathy* stems from the Greek *homoios* (similar) and *pathos* (sickness or feeling). Although the term gained currency only with the publication of Hahnemann's major work, the *Organon der Heilkunst* (Organon of the Art of Healing) in 1810 (a work that underwent various revisions up to 1842), as early as 1796 in his "Versuch über ein neues

Prinzip zur Auffindung der Heilkräfte der Arzneisubstanzen" (Essay on a New Principle for Ascertaining the Curative Powers of Drugs), Hahnemann laid down his Law of Similars, which was to guide all his subsequent findings: "We should imitate nature, which sometimes cures a chronic disease by superadding another, and employs in the (especially chronic) disease we wish to cure that medicine that is able to produce another very similar artificial disease, and the former will be cured; *similia similibus*" (*Lesser Writings* 265). Giving vivid examples from everyday life of *similia similibus curentur*, Hahnemann colourfully writes: "Why does the brilliant planet Jupiter disappear in the twilight from the eyes of him who gazes at it? Because a similar but more potent power, the light of breaking day, then acts upon these organs. With what are we in the habit of flattering the olfactory nerves when offended by disagreeable odours? With snuff, which affects the nose in a similar manner, but more powerfully ... In the same manner, mourning and sadness are extinguished in the soul when the news reach us (even though they were false) of a still greater misfortune occurring to another" (*Organon* 106). For Hahnemann, the homeopathic remedy exercises a "more potent power" that allows the body to regain equilibrium and overcome the initial corporeal affliction.

Hahnemann arrived at the principle of *similia similibus* via his contention that the conventional medicine of his day operated via the principle *contraria contrariis*. For example, constipation is treated by purgatives, pains by opium, or acidity in the stomach by alkalis (*Lesser Writings* 261). To comprehend the significant difference that Hahnemann offered with his concept of the minimal dose and its appeal to patients who were otherwise at the mercy of radical treatments, it is important to understand medical practice around 1800. The notion of counteracting the cause or source of an illness was prevalent because of widespread belief that one needed to "expel from the body that imaginary and supposed material cause of disease" (*Organon* 29). This expelling took the form not only of diuretics, emetics, and purgative medicines but also of bloodletting that was commonly prescribed for various manifestations of inflammation. Hahnemann writes: "They recommend diaphoretics, diuretics, venesection, setons, and cauteries, and above all, excite irritation of the alimentary canal, so as to produce evacuations from above, and more especially from below, all of which were irritatives" (*Organon* 41). He refers to "the old school of medicine ... [that] still imagined they could arrest disease by a *removal of the supposed morbid material cause*" (*Organon* 29). He even mentions the incidence of a "young girl, of Glasgow, eight years of age, having been bitten by a mad dog, the surgeon *immediately cut out the* part, which, nevertheless, did not save the child from an attack of hydrophobia" (*Organon* 36). Citing new experiments with the voltaic column in curing nervous afflictions that were the rage at the time,[4] Hahnemann rhetorically asks: "Have electric and galvanic shocks ever produced, in such cases, any other results than those of gradually increasing the paralysis of the muscular irritability and the nervous susceptibility and finally rendering the paralysis complete?" (*Organon* 53).

Hahnemann was deeply opposed to such drastic, heroic treatments. Medication that aims at producing the opposite condition, he claimed, was not only merely temporary but, in fact, injurious and destructive precisely because of its temporary nature, which could result in the aggravation of the original condition when the latter returned. After a brief period of apparent relief, the original illness would break forth again. The reason the disease returned more grievous than before, Hahnemann argued, was that "the ill-advised evacuations have lessened the energy of the vital powers" (*Organon* 45). He offered as a clear example of the rebound effect the case of opium: at first it induces a "fearless elevation of spirit, a sensation of strength and high courage, an imaginative gaiety," only to be followed by "dejection, diffidence, peevishness, loss of memory, discomfort, fear" (*Lesser Writings* 266).

It was this secondary, indirect action, following upon the antagonistic, direct action that led Hahnemann in his 1796 essay to conceive of the notion of *similia similibus*. If a drug could be administered in small doses, it could produce the counter-effect of the strong dose: for example, "valerian (*valeriana officinalis*) in *moderate* doses cures chronic diseases with excess of irritability, since in large doses ... it can exalt so remarkably the irritability of the whole system" (*Lesser Writings* 269). Another example he gives, among many, is coffee, which can produce headaches in large doses but can cure them in smaller doses (*Lesser Writings* 271–2). He adds that "other abnormal effects it occasions might be employed against similar affections of the human body, were we not in the habit of misusing it" (*Lesser Writings* 272). He was to later write in the *Organon*: "Strong coffee in the first instance stimulates the faculties (primitive effect), but it leaves behind a sensation of heaviness and drowsiness (secondary effect), which continues a long time if we do not again have recourse to the same liquid (palliative)" (*Organon* 131). Indeed, *coffea cruda* circulates today among the many homeopathic remedies that were invented by Hahnemann and is used to counteract insomnia based on this after-effect of "lassitude and sleepiness."

In his 1805 essay "Heilkunst der Erfahrung" (The Medicine of Experience), Hahnemann refines the notion of there being two incompatible responses residing simultaneously in one body, the primary effect and the after-effect. Harris Coulter explains Hahnemann's complicated line of reasoning as follows: "Discovery of the biphasic action of drugs immediately raised the question: does the 'similarity' necessary for cure lie between the primary or the secondary drug symptoms and those of the patient? For Hahnemann ... experience showed similarity to lie between the patient's symptoms and the primary symptoms of the drug; then the secondary symptoms of the drug (i.e., the symptoms of the patient's reaction) remove the disease" (*Progress and Regress* 364–5). Unlike with the effects of drugs working according to the principle of *contraria contrariis*, which can aggravate the original disease, the cure according to *similia similibus* would produce a slight aggravation only *resembling* the original disease. This slight aggravation would cause the body's own vital force to overcome the original illness, resulting in a permanent cure. Hahnemann writes in "The Medicine of Experience": "In order therefore to be able to cure, we shall only require to oppose to the existing abnormal irritation of the disease an appropriate medicine, that is to say, another morbific power whose effect is very similar to that the disease displays," and "it is only by this property of producing in the healthy body a series of specific morbid symptoms, that medicines can cure diseases, that is to say, remove and extinguish the morbid irritation by a suitable counter-irritation" (*Lesser Writings* 451). In the *Organon* Hahnemann rephrased this curative action by noting that "a remedy ... closely resembling the natural one against which it is employed ... excites ... the artificial disease ... [and], by reason of its similitude and greater intensity, now substitutes itself for the natural disease" (171). In the *Organon* the term "secondary effect" comes to also mean the reaction and reassertion of the vital life force in the living organism: "Our vital powers tend always to oppose their energy to this influence or impression [of the medicine or primary effect]. The effect that results from this, and which belongs to our conservative vital powers and their automatic force, bears the name of *secondary effect*, or *re-action*" (130).

Hahnemann then set about reading the reactions that substances produced in a healthy person, reasoning that, when this reaction mimicked a true disease, the homeopathic remedy was found. The task he undertook over the course of his life was to determine via close observation of healthy individuals, most often himself, what symptoms drugs produced. The reason he offers in the *Organon* for self-experimentation is that "a thing is never more certain than when it has been tried on ourselves" (168); moreover, the self-testing helped to "exercise our powers of observation, an indispensable talent in a physician" (168). Hahnemann then recorded and catalogued these reactions, so as to determine subsequently how they could be used to cancel and exterminate symptoms in the sick. Hahnemann's procedure was one of extremely close observing and comparing of indicators – in both the healthy and the ill as well as provoked by the primary and secondary action of drugs – and matching them so as to come up with the appropriate homeopathic remedy. His idea was that one could not truly know what occurred in the human body, but that it presented external signs to be read: "The internal essential nature of every malady, of every individual case of disease, so far as it is necessary for us to know it, for the purpose of curing it, expresses itself via the symptoms" (*Lesser Writings* 443). For him, it was not that a drug would overpower a disease, but that one symptom would overcome the other. As he writes in the *Organon*: "The particular medicine whose action upon persons in health produces the greatest number of symptoms resembling those of the disease which it is intended to cure, possesses, also, in reality (when administered in convenient doses) the power of suppressing, in a radical, prompt, and permanent manner, the totality of these morbid symptoms – that is to say – the whole of the existing disease" (105).

To restate the issue, it was not that at the root of symptoms was a disease that needed to be fought off via drugs: homeopathy operated instead according to a translation and comparison of symptoms. The underlying principle of homeopathy was thus a semiotic one, based on an association and compilation of signs. Hahnemann's process was to first distinguish indications of illness in recording what he observed and subsequently constitute them as signs by comparing them to other signs. He then formulated a law that governed how they operated. One can compare his method to what Michel Foucault categorized as typical of the scientific method in the classical age: Foucault argues that, for instance, natural history as it arises in the seventeenth and eighteenth centuries is "established within the apparent simplicity of a *description of the visible*" (*Order of Things* 137). The object is constituted or "provided by surfaces and lines, not by functions or invisible tissues. The plant and the animal are seen not so much in their organic unity as by ... visible patterning" (ibid.). To be sure, Hahnemann did regard the human body as an organic unity whose equilibrium, once disturbed, would result in malady. But it was not the *internal* circulatory, muscular-skeletal, digestive, or nervous systems that, according to homeopathy, could break down under disease so that the physician could analyse its etiology and development and then treat it; rather the *external* symptoms, or what Foucault calls "visible patterning," were the solution to the cure. Key here is that the somatic and psychic manifestations of disequilibrium do *not* reference the body – conceived as a unity of organs, tissues, and organic systems – and hence do not reference a disease that can be named. As a new science, in its self-generating productivity, homeopathy creates its own encyclopedia of symptoms and its own pharmacopeia that its practitioner consults. To be precise, Hahnemann is not involved in charting pathologies, in other words, tracking the origin, nature, and course of an illness. He does not classify diseases, as in nosology; nor for that matter does he even organize symptoms: he *compiles* symptoms.[5] Homeopathy, much like natural history, thus "traverses an area of visible, simultaneous, concomitant variables, without any internal relation of subordination or organization" (*Order of Things* 137). Hahnemann would therefore see the role of his *Materia medica pura*, inasmuch as it is a compilation, "as [a] contribution to the collective store of observations" (Pickstone, *Ways of Knowing* 68).

In order to better situate Hahnemann's discovery in terms of scientific and medical practice before the rise of hospitals and institutionalized medicine in the nineteenth century, a mode that is still dominant today, one can compare and contrast his semiotic system to that of Paracelsus (1493–1541). In referring to Paracelsian thought, Foucault notes that "the world of similarity can only be a world of signs" (*Order of Things* 26); this world view would also be true of Hahnemann. But whereas Paracelsus ascribed to the signature of things, according to which "even though he has hidden certain things, [God] has allowed nothing to remain without exterior and visible signs in the form of special marks" (cited ibid.),[6] Hahnemann does not refer to a magical analogy that reveals the workings of God. His system of analogy is without reference to the sympathy between microcosm and macrocosm. Hahnemann did not read the medicinal purpose of a plant by virtue of how it looked. In other terms, it is no longer the plant itself via its appearance that suggested an affinity with the cure it could bring about; it was solely the effect of the plant on the human body that Hahnemann examined and recorded. Thus, one does not find in Hahnemann, as in Paracelsus, a belief in a vast system of signatures that revealed the invisible workings of a divinely inspired and created universe. And certainly planetary movement was not aligned, as it was in Theophrastus von Hohenheim, with processes of healing.[7] Hahnemann believed that he was documenting observable empirical positivities; thus, he was thoroughly Kantian in his conviction that you could know phenomena but not substances. To repeat, he created a closed system, typical of eighteenth-century thought, whereby signs referred to other signs, not to the macrocosm and its divine order.

Most of the homeopathic remedies sold today stem from Hahnemann's experimentations. Harris Coulter summarizes the results of his findings as follows: "*Fragmenta de Viribus Medicamentorum Positivis* (1805) ... have the symptoms of 27 medicines ... The *Reine Arzneimittellehre* (1811–21) enlarged on the *Fragmenta*, presenting the symptomatology of 62 substances. By the end of his life Hahnemann had conducted or supervised the provings of 99 substances" (363). These substances are enumerated and discussed in great length in the compendium *Materia Medica Pura*. For each remedy Hahnemann lists a vast number of symptoms of the body, mind, and disposition which it can treat and often the time of day in which these symptoms appear. The patient portrait for each remedy is based on an accumulation of symptoms, which is to say that Hahnemann neglects either to exclude or to prioritize them. His method is synchronic in the sense that the duration, succession, frequency, and cessation of symptoms – their diachronic aspect – is not noted. For instance, more than forty pages are devoted to the remedy *nux vomica* and its various indicators such as vertigo, headache, smarting in the eyes, swelling of the gums, ringing in the ears, toothache, looseness of the teeth, heartburn, nausea, pricking pain in the hepatic region, flatulence, burning or itching while urinating, erection of the penis after the midday sleep, nocturnal cough, bloody nasal mucus, asthma, sudden powerless of the arms, frightful visions in dreams, and yawning accompanied by weepy eyes. Quite understandably if suffering from all these symptoms, the *nux vomica* patient also exhibits extraordinary anxiety, crossness, sadness, reproach of others, even mistakes in speaking and writing. This exhaustive coverage as well as listing, in which no detail is omitted of Hahnemann's investigations into *nux vomica* over several years, gives the impression of an intentional lack of hierarchy of symptoms as well as an asystematic presentation. Conceivably, there is no limit to the potential listing of symptoms, because it is not the goal of the physician to arrive at a diagnosis, pathology, or nosology. In other words, there never arrives the instant at which the doctor determines that enough symptoms have been recorded to ascertain the reason for an illness, its chronological progression, or its prognosis; these objectives or targets are not his intent.

Such a structure of asystematicity is derived in large part from the practice of "biographical" medicine current in Hahnemann's day. John Pickstone describes biographical medicine as "a continuing tradition of seeing illnesses as disturbances of individual lives" (10). Before the time of medical care conducted in hospitals,[8] the physician was devoted to hearing out the patient's maladies.[9] To be sure, Hahnemann was not so much a "bedside" physician as a practitioner who, given his renown, saw patients in his own consultation room or received long letters from them minutely detailing an illness. (In fact, he was opposed to doctors making house calls for he thought it lessened the respect that patients would have for their healers.) Nonetheless, like the bedside doctor he heard out his patients thoroughly. His philosophy, in fact, required a precise procedure for the physician to follow in sessions with his patients in order to diagnose their maladies: the physician writes down accurately all that the patient and his friends have told him in the very expressions used by them. The examination is "for the most part, to be confined to listening to his narrative" (*Organon* 167). Keeping quiet, the physician allows the patient to say all he has to say, and refrains from interrupting, even to ask questions. He should not indulge in making conjectures or suppositions (ibid.).

The result of this prescribed procedure, as amply evidenced in the vast compilation of the *Materia Medica Pura*, is a concept of the body as fragmented. In Hahnemann's patient notebooks, the *Krankenjournale*, which document the patient interviews, one clearly sees how he jots down symptoms, starting with the head and descending to the rest of the body, with notations about the disposition of the patient at the close. The only thread that joins the symptoms is this sequence, not any interpretation of the symptoms or their relation to one another. Put succinctly, this accumulation of several disjointed moments of a body in disequilibrium threatens to collapse the Law of Similars. This law attempted to create order by drawing parallels between signs in two separate human bodies, rather than between warning signs in one body. The single body thus houses chaotic, isolated, non-stratified symptoms that in fact tyrannize it as incomprehensible illness. Whether one consults the *Krankenjournale* or the *Materia Medica Pura*, each individual body presents a bewildering, cacophonous encyclopedia of symptoms. The bodily and psychic indicators of illness that are catalogued and recommended for each remedy seem infinite and unrelated, as if we were truly speaking here of a Deleuzian "body without organs," that is to say, of a body without any unifying systems, be they digestive, nervous, circulatory, etc. Such a body not only expresses its uniqueness through a plethora and mingling of affects or what Deleuze and Guattari in *A Thousand Plateaus* call "intensities," it is also exquisitely sensitive to response from the minuscule homeopathic dosage, which sets off a flow or wave of resonances. Operative in Hahnemann's system, in his note taking, and in his own patient's letters is thus less a regulatory, disciplinary monitoring of the body than a dissolving of self in the proliferation of discrete symptoms and the resonances of the remedies.[10] The coordinates are incalculable, and the results are unverifiable. Important instead are the responses of the physiological and psychological bodies, infinitely diverse from each other.

Hahnemann's schizoid practice necessarily entails revision of a belief in organic, natural wholeness that is all too quickly ascribed to homeopathy to the exclusion of this other corporeal model. In conclusion to his book *Experiencing Illness and the Sick Body in Early Modern Europe*, Michael Stolberg uses the rise in homeopathy as an example of how the body was conceived differently starting around 1800. In the early modern era, the unhindered stream of bodily fluids was considered integral to health, which meant that the body was seen as permeable and open and, when ill, required such treatments as leeching, bloodletting, drastic emetics, and laxatives in order to abet such flow. According to such a model, for instance, menopause with its cessation of menses gave rise to great concern. This medical tradition, Stolberg argues, was "superceded and replaced by a compact, internally firm body mass that was largely sealed off from the outside. The vital basis for maintaining good health was no longer the unobstructed flow of humors but the integrity and orderly performance of the solid parts and the strength of the 'life force' of the organism as a whole" (214). Bodily excretions were then seen as dangerous rather than beneficial, as the nineteenth-century anti-masturbation discourse illustrates. Stolberg continues:

> Life force became the pivotal concept in medical guidebooks, of which Hufeland's *Makrobiotik* is the most famous example. The strong response that early homeopathy earned at the beginning of the 19th century, particularly in genteel circles, is a good illustration of the positive lay response to this new view. Homeopathy's great attractiveness, according to its followers, was the fact that it "was based on the principle of temperance" ... With homeopathic treatment, human nature was not so easily deprived of the force it needed to fight the disease. (214)

Although Stolberg's insight helps explain both why homeopathy arose at the time it did and why it garnered popularity, he overlooks how Hahnemann failed to participate in the new model of science that saw "fibers and organs ... as the principal material substrate of human physiology and pathology" (214) that was instrumental in conceptualizing the body as a unified, integral whole.[11] At the very least, it is important to recognize in homeopathy two competing hypotheses about the body: Hahnemann's symptomology, that is to say, his vast compiling of symptoms, unrelated to each other within the body and to bodily organ systems, runs counter to his notion of the body as a whole, governed by a vital life force.

But if the homeopath merely jots down the symptoms that a patient relates to him and is even encouraged to refrain from interpreting them, how then is the cure to the maladjustment in the body to be found? What results in the selection of a cure is, I would like to argue, comparable to Benjamin's concept of the nonsensical similarity. What enables the decision about what remedy to select is the bizarre, unanticipated moment. The lynchpin in deciding upon a treatment was based on Hahnemann's notion that each individual patient was unique, hence, that, despite similarities with other patients, what singled out for the physician the choice of a cure is what made the patient stand out from all other cases. In short, paradoxically only the dissimilar could enable the workings of the Law of Similars.

Hahnemann criticized allopathic medicine for attempting to reduce all individual cases to one disease, whereas he saw each individual case as unique. Diseases are infinite in number, he wrote, "as diverse as the clouds in the sky" (*Lesser Writings* 504). In striking contrast to medicine as practised today, he insisted that it was always the person with the disease who was treated, not the disease itself. "Each case of the disease that presents itself must be regarded (and treated) as an individual malady that never before occurred in the same manner and under the same circumstance as in the case before us, and will never happen precisely in the same way" (*Lesser Writings* 442). On the one hand, this unique view of the patient was indebted to the "bedside" and "biographical" medical practice mentioned earlier. On the other hand, Hahnemann here parts ways with prevalent medical theories of his day, notably those of the Scottish doctor John Brown. According to the medical theory of Brown widely adopted in Germany around 1800, especially by Schelling, there were two types of illness into which a variety of maladies could fit, what he termed the asthenic and sthenic, if you will, hypo-stimulated and hyper-stimulated states.[12] The medicinal treatment also corresponds to either one of these groupings, and the physician was encouraged to test on his patient several of the drugs that belonged to either of the two categories. Hahnemann considered Brownian medicine a simplistic reduction of illness, one that also unfortunately required the use of strong medication, such as opium, in order to reverse or palliate the condition.[13] Novalis, too, criticized Brownian medicine for not attending to the individualization of illness in each patient, noting that Brown treated the body as a pure abstraction (*Werke* 2: 796). The poet wrote, for instance, that every person has their own sicknesses (2: 500), indeed, that most sicknesses seem to be very individual, like a human, or a flower or an animal (2: 797, no. 268). He goes on to observe: "Therefore interesting is their natural history, their relations (out of which complications arise), their comparison."[14] Noteworthy in this passage are two salient points. First, despite the individualization of illness, in fact paradoxically because of it, Novalis, like Hahnemann, recognizes the importance of searching out affinity and analogy between disparate entities. For both poet and physician this search was conducted intuitively and idiosyncratically – if you will, poetically. Second, it is not merely that disease and its course are uniquely manifested in each individual but that disease is specific to each individual. Moreover – and here he goes beyond Hahnemann – because of this specificity, Novalis also conjectured that illness must lead to the development of individuality; it furthered *Bildung*. Indeed, because of this potential to heighten character, he idealized illness over health: "The ideal of perfect health is only scientifically interesting. Sickness belongs to *individualization*."[15]

It now becomes clear why, as mentioned above, Hahnemann recommended the intent listening to the patient, the seemingly disorganized note taking in the *Krankenjournale*, as well as the copious accumulation of symptoms compiled in the *Materia Medica Pura*: if the manifestations of a malady are in each case different, the diseases infinite in number, and the arrival at a diagnosis of a disease impossible, the oddest symptoms need to be recorded. They, in actuality, became the key to ascertaining what made the patient unique and distinct; in Novalis's words, "sickness belongs to individualization." In determining "what kind of symptoms ought chiefly to be regarded in selecting the remedy," Hahnemann thus prescribes that

> we ought to be particularly and almost exclusively attentive to the symptoms that are *striking, singular, extraordinary,* and *peculiar* (characteristic), *for it is to these latter that similar symptoms, from among those created by the medicine, ought to correspond* ... On the other hand, the more vague and general symptoms, such as loss of appetite, headache, weakness, disturbed sleep, uncomfortableness, &c., merit little attention, because almost all diseases and medicines produce something as general. (*Organon* 173–4)

To restate, for Hahnemann the notion that illness was unique to each patient meant that the physician needed to read for what Benjamin termed the exceptional, bizarre, or dissimilar moment. Only then could the precise remedy that would exactly fit that patient be found. It was not that, as in allopathic medicine either in its Brownian variety or as practised in the nineteenth century until today, a disease would express itself in symptoms common to a host of patients, but that precisely the aberrant symptoms proper to the patient required closer attention. In terms of its new, Romantic definition that Jocelyn Holland investigates in her contribution to this volume, the "fact" (or what I have called here the symptom) gains individual, unique significance. To this effect, Holland cites Friedrich Schlegel's *Athenäum* fragment: "What a fact should be has to have strict individuality, being at once a secret and an experiment, namely, an experiment of formative nature."[16]

The reason for Hahnemann's counterintuitive procedure was, as mentioned above, that, without believing in an underlying disease, the homeopath only had symptoms to analyse. Specifically, in the search for finding the right homeopathic remedy, in other words, the *Gegenbild* (antitype) that would illicit the same overt symptoms but not be the original disease, the physician needed to read between the lines. For example, these indicators had to appear intermittently in the course of an infirmity. Harris Coulter offers this illustration: "In the treatment of malaria (intermittent fever) Hahnemann notes that the paroxysms of fever (*communia*) are of little use in the selection of the remedy, since they are experienced by everyone. Instead, the physician should look to the patient's symptoms between the seizures of fever (*propria*), since these differ greatly from one patient to the next" (381). Determining the aberrant, random symptoms meant individualizing the patient and establishing a patient profile that was attentive to such things as on which side of the body a pain came, what the general disposition of the patient was, or what other signs on other parts of the body were present that seemed to be unrelated to the malady.

To give an example of how Hahnemann desired to pay attention to the peculiarity of each symptom, one can turn to how he recommended testers record their medicinal trials. He prescribes that the experimenter

> place himself successively in various postures, and observe the changes that ensue. Thus he will be enabled to examine whether the motion communicated to the suffering parts by walking up and down the chamber, or in the open air, seated, lying down, or standing, has the effect of augmenting, diminishing, or dissipating the symptom, and if it returns or not upon resuming the original position. He will also perceive whether it changes when he eats or drinks, or by any other condition, when he speaks, coughs, or sneezes, or in any other action of the body whatsoever. He must also observe at what hour of the day or night the symptom more particularly manifests itself. All these

details are requisite, in order to discover what is *peculiar and characteristic in each symptom*. (*Organon* 164, italics mine)

That Hahnemann was attentive to the defining, bizarre symptom does not mean that all the diverse markers did not need to be recorded and taken into account. Indeed, the above passage suggests as much. He specifies that the totality of all the indicators also needed to be addressed, for they too would help select the proper remedy, for each remedy would elicit several, diverse symptoms in the healthy test case; these could not be ignored. In particular, Hahnemann recognized that the affects of "continued grief, anger, injured feelings, or great and repeated occasions of fear and alarm [i]n the course of time ... have an influence over the health of the body, and often compromise it in a high degree" (*Organon* 196). He thus exhorts the homeopathic practitioner to pay special attention to the state of mind of the patient: "The moral state of the patient is often that which is most decisive in the choice of the homeopathic remedy; for this is a symptom of the most precise character, and one that, among the mass of symptoms, by no means can escape the notice of a physician accustomed to make precise observations" (*Organon* 192).

Finally, one needs to stress the conclusion to which Hahnemann came – that is to say, the law he devised – on the basis of each patient's peculiarity. In his "Law of the Single Remedy" Hahnemann, unlike subsequent homeopaths, stipulated that only one remedy was to be tried at a time: he matched the single remedy to the singular patient. "In no instance is it requisite to employ more than *one simple* medicinal substance at a time" (*Organon* 218).[17] In short, the Benjaminian paradox is that the "Law of the Single Remedy," based as it is on the dissimilarity between patients, enables the workings of the "Law of Similars."

If the law of *similia similibus curentur* and the extensive listing evident in the *Materia Medica Pura* resembled a Foucauldian eighteenth-century semiosis, then this genial interpretation of the singular, unexpected, yet portent sign was thoroughly Romantic. Around 1800 there is a shift from a regulatory, normative poetics to the belief in individual, idiosyncratic interpretation.[18] Romantic reading is, if anything, non-predictable. "There is no universally true kind of reading, in the ordinary sense. Reading is a free operation. No one can prescribe for me how I am to read something or what,"[19] writes Novalis. The genres that come to the fore in Romanticism are non-prescriptive. Strangely enough, one could even call them non-genres – the fragment, the essay, and the mixed genre of the novel with its embedded fairy tales and digressions. Friedrich Schlegel in the most famous of the *Athenäum* fragments (nos. 116 and 238) states that modern, Romantic literary production is dynamic and reflects upon itself in ever greater exponentiation.[20] Although Hahnemann, too, used this Romantic notion of *Potenzieren* (see discussion below), what it means for Schlegel is that Romantic writing is always an after-effect, involved in the constant production of marginalia on itself or on another text. Novalis exhorted that the true reader must be an extended author (2: 282, no. 125), and Friedrich Schlegel similarly wrote that the true critic is an author to the second power (18: 106, no. 927). If the reader is an extended author, then there is no regularization of reading: *Witz*, with its attention to the unexpected, plays the more important role.[21] As we have seen, the same is the case for homeopathy. In this medical practice there is no point in running experiments, as in contemporary pharmaceutical trials, for one can't predict outcomes. The homeopath is as inventive, imaginative, and idiosyncratic as the Romantic reader: both hone in on the odd, dissimilar sign.

What is further important about the Romantic fragment is that it remains a *Bruchstück*, that is, it resists closure. It alludes (*hindeuten*) without offering up definitive interpretation (*Deutung*). It revels in surface, extraneous, or marginal observations; and it hides more than it reveals. The oracular quality of Jena Romantic writing seems to gloss the pre-Socratic fragment by Heraclitus: "The master to whom the oracle of Delphi belongs, does not speak, does not hide, he makes signs" (Fragment 93). When nature speaks, it does so via infinite signs, the key to which cannot be ascertained. In the renowned passage at the start of *Die Lehrlinge zu Sais* (The Apprentices of Sais), Novalis writes that one can see marvellous figures everywhere that seem to belong to the great script of ciphers – in the designs of bird wings, egg shells, clouds, snow, crystals, in the filings around a magnet, and in strange, chance conjunctures. This magical script would seem to resemble Paracelsus's belief in the signature of things, except that for Novalis the key to the mystery is not to be found: "Intuition alone does not allow itself to conform to particular patterns and does not seem to provide the ultimate answer."[22] The signifying abundance in nature cannot be authoritatively deciphered. This search for the perplexing signification in nature,[23] however, is just as ambivalent in Hahnemann as it is in Novalis. That is to say, the Romantic theory of fragmentary, incomplete signification subtends Hahnemann's own fragmentary, voluminous writing. Although the *Organon der Heilkunst* in its various versions is a concise treatise on the principles of homeopathy, the *Materia Medica Pura*, where Hahnemann assembles the homeopathic remedies and gives the patient profile for each, is a bewildering, cacophonous encyclopedia of symptoms.

Novalis then establishes parallels between Romantic writing and the writing in nature: when Hardenberg compares the fairy tale to nature, it is because of the chaotic ensemble they share, their unendingly accidental conjunctures, and their infinite possibilities: "A fairy tale is really a dream picture – devoid of all coherence – An *ensemble* of wondrous things and happenings – a *musical fantasy* for instance – the harmonious effects of an Aeolian harp – *Nature herself.*"[24] Again, Novalis compares nature to associative but lawless Romantic literary production: "Anecdotes, without coherence, though with association, like *dreams*. Poems – purely melodious and full of beautiful words – but also without any meaning or coherence – are at the most comprehensible as single stanzas ... At the most true poetry can ... have an indirect impact like music – nature is thus purely poetic – and so is the parlour of a magician – of a physicist – a child's room – a jangle and repository."[25] The reason why nature herself is poetic is that she is not only beautiful, but, as the passage above from *Die Lehrlinge zu Sais* similarly indicates, ultimately without coherence and meaning. This lack of apparent cohesion does not exclude the workings of association and analogy. On the contrary, the powers of association play a significant role for Novalis, but, as in Benjamin's "Lehre vom Ähnlichen," the similarities established are sheerly coincidental, free, and unforeseeable.[26]

In sum, what links Hahnemann to Romantic theories on language, nature, and interpretation and what allows one to speak of a homeopathic poesis are their shared beliefs in (1) the geniality of the gifted interpreter attentive to the marginal and surprising, (2) the chaotic, unpredictable ensemble of impressions, as well as (3) the wave of resonances or harmonies that unite life and subtend the chaos. It is this last concept of vibrational dynamism that I want, in conclusion, to touch upon briefly in respect to the second law of homeopathy about which I have said very little up to this point – the Law of Minimum. Developing his 1796 notion of the peculiar effect of the small dose, Hahnemann announced in 1799 his principle of the infinitesimal dose: then, after 1800, respecting what was to be termed homeopathy's "Law of Minimum," he gradually reduced dose sizes (Coulter 400). The impact of the catalyst was present even though the toxicity of the substance had disappeared. Hahnemann postulated that a substance would be not just still present but in fact activated after exponential dilution, as well as by trituration (grinding an insoluble ingredient with milk sugar) and succussion (vigorous shaking). This belief that the elemental, essential action of a substance could be extracted and transmitted places Hahnemann squarely in the realm of

Romantic, divinatory science, especially since Hahnemann claimed that the mysterious vital force in the remedy was somehow present in purer form once it had been so diluted that the original substance was undetectable. Homeopathy resembles the medical practice of mesmerism at the time, as well as the investigations into animal magnetism and galvanism:[27] like homeopathy, these experiments sought to provide evidence of an otherwise unseen, ubiquitous current of energy in both organic and inorganic life. Paradoxically, the more imperceptible it was, the more omnipresent, energetic, and effective the vital life force in a homeopathic remedy would be. Like the third, nonsensical term of the unique symptom, the notion that the active ingredient of a substance is not just present after several dilutions, but even more dynamically functional, demonstrates what is typical for Romanticism – an embracing of what Novalis termed "magic idealism" (2: 550, no. 399).

The law of *similia similibus curentur* operates on the eighteenth-century classification of phenomena based on a system of correspondences, whereas Hahnemann's later notion of the infinitesimal dosage capable of inversely powerful and exponential effect on the body resembles a dynamic, developmental model of life that is characteristic of the nineteenth century. As we have seen, Hahnemann thus straddles both eighteenth-century semiosis, based on the accumulation of analogies between signs, and the early-nineteenth-century Romantic hermeneutics, with its models of unpredictability, individuality, and organic dynamism. As Jocelyn Holland points out, the "fact" for the Romantics becomes involved in an open-ended process. But regardless of whether it is seen as an Enlightenment or Romantic science, the medical practice of homeopathy arises from theories of signs and how they are interpreted. In short, the therapeutic discipline cannot be separated from the fictional, poetic structures of signification that give rise to it.

NOTES

1 Here and in the rest of my article when citing a German original, the first page reference is to the German, the second, following the semi-colon, to its English translation. If no second reference is given, the translation is my own.

2 In his short study, *Der Akt der Ähnlichkeit*, art historian and homeopath Claus Just mentions Benjamin's study in the larger context of homeopathy.

3 It is amusing to see websites extolling homeopathy quoting this passage out of context so as to make it seem Goethe advocated homeopathy.

4 See Stolberg's subchapter "The Rise of the Nerves" (*Experiencing Illness* 170–3).

5 Pickstone writes: "For 18th-century philosophers, such a method [hierarchies based on maximal numbers of 'characteristics' – all treated as equally important] approximated the mental processes of 'association' which were fundamental to learning" (*Ways of Knowing* 70).

6 See also Bergengruen's subchapter "Natürliche Signaturen" where he discusses Paracelsus alongside Ficino, Croll, and other Renaissance thinkers on the signature of things. For instance, he writes that "Giovanni Pico della Mirandola [hegte] den Astrologie-unabhängigen Gedanken, dass die Philosophen die 'invisibilia [mysteria] dei' durch die 'visibilibus naturae signis' ('die unsichtbaren Geheimnisse Gottes durch die sichtbaren Zeichen der Natur') erkennen könnten" (*Nachfolge Christi* 167).

7 Gantenbein focuses on several parallels rather than fundamental differences between Hahnemann and Paracelsus in order to suggest that Paracelsus functions as a dark Jungian shadow to the founder of homeopathy, who resisted acknowledging direct influences.

8 Foucault refers to this post-1800 system as the anatomical-clinical method based on the study of cases in institutionalized settings: "a new structure in which the individual in question was not so much a sick person as the endlessly reproducible pathological fact to be found in all patients suffering in a similar way" (*Birth of the Clinic* 119). "The patient has to be enveloped in a collective, homogenous space" (242).

9 See Stolberg's subchapter "The Doctor–Patient Relationship" (64–76).

10 For an account of how the body is monitored and the self constituted by the homeopathic patient, see Brockmeyer, *Selbstverständnisse*.

11 Foucault also documents in the *Birth of the Clinic* how the early nineteenth century saw the rise of the anatomical study of tissues and organs that allowed physicians to localize and find the seat of disease.

12 On Brownian medicine, see Coulter, *Progress and Regress*; Schwanitz, *Homöopathie und Brownianismus*; and Neubauer, *Bifocal Vision*.

13 Hahnemann's observations on Brown are recorded in his essays "Fragmentarische Bemerkungen zu Browns *Elements of medicine*" (Fragmentary Observations on Brown's *Elements of Medicine* [1801]) and "Monita über die drey gangbaren Heilarten" (Observations on Three Current Methods of Treatment [1809]).

14 "Daher ist ihre Naturgeschichte, ihre Verwandtschaften (woraus die *Complicationen* entstehn) ihre Vergleichung so interessant" (2: 797, no. 268).

15 "Das Ideal einer vollkommnen Gesundheit ist blos wissenschaftlich interessant. Krankheit gehört zur *Individualisirung*" (2: 835, no. 400).

16 "Was ein Faktum seyn soll, muss strenge Individualität haben, zugleich ein Geheimniss und ein Experiment seyn, nämlich ein Experiment der bildenden Natur" (2: 249, no. 427).

17 As early as 1797 in the essay "Sind die Hindernisse der Gewißheit und Einfachheit der practischen Arzneykunde unübersteiglich?" (Are the Obstacles to Certainty and Simplicity in Practical Medicine Insurmountable?), Hahnemann recommended against mixing compounds into a single prescription.
18 I am adapting somewhat the terms that Peter Szondi used: he uses the category of the normative *Poetik*, but refers in the second instance to a "speculative poetics."
19 "Es giebt kein *allgemeingeltendes Lesen,* im gewöhnlichen Sinn. Lesen ist eine freye Operation. Wie ich und was ich lesen soll, kann mir keiner vorschreiben" (2: 399, no. 398).
20 See Neubauer, "Zwischen Natur und mathematischer Abstraktion."
21 See the section "Witz" in Lacoue-Labarthe and Nancy (*The Literary Absolute* 52–8) and its entry in their topical index to Friedrich Schlegel's fragments (164).
22 "Allein die Ahnung will sich selbst in keine feste Formen fügen, und scheint kein höherer Schlüssel werden zu wollen" (1: 201).
23 Novalis writes of "das seltsame Verhältnißspiel der Dinge" (the peculiar relational play of things) (2: 438; Schulte-Sasse, *Theory as Practice* 146).
24 "Ein Mährchen ist eigentlich wie ein Traumbild – ohne Zusammenhang – Ein Ensemble wunderbarer Dinge und Begebenheiten – z. B. eine musicalische Fantasie – die harmonischen Folgen einer Aeolsharfe – die Natur selbst" (2: 696, no. 986; translation by Wood, 171).
25 "Erzählungen, ohne Zusammenhang, jedoch mit Association, wie *Träume.* Gedichte – blos *wohlklingend* und voll schöner Worte – aber auch ohne allen Sinn und Zusammenhang – höchstens einzelne Strofen verständlich ... Höchstens kann wahre Poësie ... eine indirecte Wirckung wie Musik etc. thun – Die Natur ist daher rein poëtisch – und so die Stube eines Zauberers – eines Physikers – eine Kinderstube – eine Polter und Vorrathskammer" (2: 769, no. 113).
26 See also the fragment from *Das Allgemeine Brouillon,* in which Novalis speaks of poetic association of ideas based on intentional production of chance relations (2: 692, no. 953; translation by Wood, 168).
27 See the works by Aesch, Barkhoff, Eppenich, Holland, Steigerwald, Tatar, and Wetzels.

WORKS CITED

Aesch, Alexander Gode-von. *Natural Science in German Romanticism.* New York: AMS Press, 1966.

Barkhoff, Jürgen. *Magnetische Fiktionen: Literarisierung des Mesmerismus in der Romantik*. Stuttgart: Metzler, 1995.

Benjamin, Walter. *Aufsätze, Essays, Vorträge*. In *Gesammelte Schriften*, vol. 2.1. Frankfurt am Main: Suhrkamp, 1980.

Benjamin, Walter, and Knut Tarnowski. "Doctrine of the Similar" (1933). *New German Critique* 17. Special Walter Benjamin Issue (1979): 65–9.

Bergengruen, Maximilian. *Nachfolge Christi – Nachahmung der Natur: Himmlische und natürliche Magie bei Paracelsus, im Paracelsismus und in der Barockliteratur (Scheffler, Zesen, Grimmelshausen)*. Hamburg: Meiner, 2007.

Brockmeyer, Bettina. *Selbstverständnisse: Dialoge über Körper und Gemüt im frühen 19. Jahrhundert*. Göttingen: Wallstein, 2009.

Coulter, Harris. *Progress and Regress: J.B. Van Helmont to Claude Bernard*. Vol. 2 of *Divided Legacy: A History of the Schism in Medical Thought*. Washington: Wehawken, 1977.

Deleuze, Gilles, and Félix Guattari. *A Thousand Plateaus: Capitalism and Schizophrenia*. Trans. Brian Massumi. Minneapolis: U of Minnesota P, 1987.

Eppenich, Heinz. "Samuel Hahnemann und die Beziehung zwischen Homöopathie und Mesmerismus." *Zeitschrift für klassische Homöopathie* 38.4 (1994): 153–60.

Foucault, Michel. *The Birth of the Clinic: An Archeology of Medical Perception*. Trans. A.M. Sheridan. London and New York: Routledge, 1989.

– *The Order of Things: An Archeology of the Human Sciences*. New York: Vintage, 1973.

Gantenbein, Urs Leo. "Similia Similibus: Samuel Hahnemann und sein Schatten Paracelsus." *Nova Acta Paracelsica* 13 (1990): 293–328.

Goethe, Johann Wolfgang. "Faust: Eine Tragödie." In *Dramatische Dichtungen I*. Ed. Erich Trunz. Vol. 3 of *Goethes Werke*. Munich: C.H. Beck, 1986.

– *Faust: A Tragedy. Interpretive Notes, Contexts, Modern Criticism*. Trans. Walter Arndt. Ed. Cyrus Hamlin. 2nd ed. New York: W.W. Norton & Co., 2001.

Hahnemann, Samuel. *The Lesser Writings*. Collected and trans. R.E. Dudgeon. New York: Radde, 1852.

– *Materia Medica Pura*. Trans. R.E. Dudgeon. Vol. 2. New Delhi: Jain, n.d.

– *Organon of Homeopathic Medicine*. New York: Radde, 1849.

Holland, Jocelyn. *German Romanticism and Science: The Procreative Poetics of Goethe, Novalis, and Ritter*. New York: Routledge, 2009.

Just, Claus. *Der Akt der Ähnlichkeit. Wissenschaft. Therapie. Kunst.* Heidelberg: Haug, 1994.

Heraclitus. *The Fragments of the Work of Heraclitus of Ephesus on Nature*. Trans. G.T.W. Patrick. Baltimore: Murray, 1889.

Neubauer, John. *Bifocal Vision: Novalis' Philosophy of Nature and Disease*. Chapel Hill: UP of North Carolina, 1971.

– "Zwischen Natur und mathematischer Abstraktion: der Potenzbegriff in der Frühromantik." In *Romantik in Deutschland: Ein interdisziplinäres Symposium*. Ed. Richard Brinkmann. Stuttgart: Metzler, 1978. 175–86.

Lacoue-Labarthe, Philippe, and Jean-Luc Nancy. *The Literary Absolute: The Theory of Literature in German Romanticism*. Trans. Philip Barnard and Cheryl Lester. Albany: SUNY P, 1988.

Novalis. *Notes for a Romantic Encyclopaedia: Das Allgemeine Brouillon*. Trans. and ed. David Wood. Albany: SUNY Press, 2007.

– *Novalis: Werke, Tagebücher und Briefe Friedrich von Hardenbergs*. Ed. Hans-Joachim Mähl and Richard Samuel. 3 vols. Munich: Carl Hanser, 1978.

Pickstone, John V. *Ways of Knowing: A New History of Science, Technology and Medicine.* Chicago: U of Chicago P, 2001.

Schulte-Sasse, Jochen, et. al. *Theory as Practice: A Critical Anthology of Early German Romantic Writings.* Minneapolis: U of Minnesota P, 1997.

Schwanitz, Hans Joachim. *Homöopathie und Brownianismus 1795–1844: Zwei wissenschaftstheoretische Fallstudien aus der praktischen Medizin.* Stuttgart: Gustav Fischer, 1983.

Steigerwald, Joan. "Figuring Nature: Ritter's Galvanic Inscriptions." *European Romantic Review* 18.2 (2007): 255–63.

Stolberg, Michael. *Experiencing Illness and the Sick Body in Early Modern Europe.* Trans. Leonhard Unglaub and Logan Kennedy. New York: Palgrave Macmillan, 2011.

Szondi, Peter. *Poetik und Geschichtsphilosophie II.* Frankfurt: Suhrkamp, 1974.

Tatar, Maria. *Spellbound: Studies on Mesmerism and Literature*. Princeton: Princeton UP, 1978.

Wetzels, Walter. *Johann Wilhelm Ritter: Physik im Wirkungsfeld der deutschen Romantik*. Berlin: de Gruyter, 1973.

PART II

Imagining: Botany, Chemistry, Thermodynamics

3 "She comes! – the GODDESS!": Narrating Nature in Erasmus Darwin's *The Botanic Garden*

ANN SHTEIR

Bernard de Fontenelle's *Entretiens sur la pluralité des mondes* (*Conversations on the Plurality of Worlds*) (1686) is an exuberant popularizing French exposition of Cartesian physics in the form of a witty and imagined night-time dialogue between an intelligent noblewoman and her male counterpart and tutor on the grounds of her estate. The tutor's eyes are on seduction more than on the heavens, but the woman takes him to task for his gendered gambits – "Do you think I'm incapable of enjoying intellectual pleasures? … Tell me about your stars!" (10–11). Fontenelle's female interlocutor may lack knowledge, but, representing not only women but also others not yet introduced to the New Science, she is an avid learner, not to be trifled with. In England one century later, Erasmus Darwin joined Fontenelle's company in seeking to communicate new ideas and findings about the workings of nature to women and other audiences. Darwin's compendious poem *The Botanic Garden* (1791) brings together poetry and prose, personifications and scientific information, and mythology and reports about empirical practices. *The Botanic Garden* is studded with substantive footnotes about eighteenth-century science and technology, yet at the same time it uses mythologies old and new to promote ideas about nature that resonated with beliefs of Romantic-era writers and philosophers. A hybrid and often paradoxical piece of writing, the formal literary features and expository scientific material in *The Botanic Garden* speak in different and seemingly contradictory registers. One figure, however, links the fictive and factual aspirations of the poem. Darwin gives the role of narrator in the poem to the "Botanic Goddess," his own new-style mythological figure of inspiration and imagination. Not an abstraction, she is nature animated for botanical culture, she is the bridge in the poem between empirical botanical features of the material world and the expansive and vitalist analogies that Darwin promulgates in his verses. Like Fontenelle's seventeenth-century female aristocrat, the Botanic Goddess stands in for women whose interest in the sciences Darwin seeks to inspire. She also carries Darwin's banner for a dynamic vision of nature that expands beyond the systems and conventions of late-eighteenth-century Europe.

A two-part poem with over four thousand lines of heroic couplets, *The Botanic Garden* abounds in generic variety and fecund substance that still capture attention from literary scholars and historians of science. The first part, *The Economy of Vegetation*, is an ambitious overview of the creation of the universe that echoes Lucretius in *De rerum natura*. Darwin's verses trace the origin of stars, and the emergence of earth and moon, minerals and plants; topics include light, heat, volcanoes, tides, sensation, and stimuli. Darwin also celebrates such contemporary technological achievements associated with the Industrial Revolution as porcelain manufacture, air pumps, and electricity. The second part of the work, *The Loves of the Plants*, is filled with poetic pictures of more than eighty species of flowers. Darwin shares ideas of the Swedish botanist Carl Linnaeus about the centrality of sexuality in nature. He personifies plants and creates narratives around them that feature sexual and eroticized aspects of the vegetable kingdom.

Erasmus Darwin came of intellectual age during what David Elliston Allen has termed "the Linnaean Spring," a time in both the history of natural history and book history when the writings of Linnaeus opened new directions in plant systematics and nomenclature. Early in the eighteenth century, Linnaeus had formulated an influential system of taxonomy by dividing the plant kingdom into a hierarchy of classes and orders based in the reproductive parts of flowers. In this approach to classification, the number and placement of the "male" parts of flowers (the stamens) determine the class to which a plant is assigned, and characteristics of the "female" parts of flowers (the pistils) determine the order. Fundamental to Linnaeus's system are sharp sexual differentiation between male and female and also analogy between plant reproduction and human sexual reproduction. Metaphors abound about "virgins," "marriage," "brides" and "bridegrooms" in the vegetable kingdom, along with various other forms of sexual coupling. In part because the Linnaean system was simple enough to learn and apply, botanical writings cultivated curiosity and brought practices of collecting, identifying, naming, and classifying plants to audiences in eighteenth-century England and elsewhere. These activities were encouraged for people of all ages for their physical and mental benefits, part of fashion, and part of cultures of improvement. Erasmus Darwin's poem emerged in that climate and sought to promote it. But while the playful underpinnings of Linnaean ideas made the schema attractive for some, the erotic codings were suspect for others.

The Loves of the Plants, the better known part of Darwin's composite poem, illustrates Linnaean ideas about plant reproduction through verse narratives that personify individual flowers. In the preface, Darwin explains Linnaeus's division of the plant kingdom into 24 classes and then into about 120 orders, with further subdivisions into "families" (genera) and species. Linnaean Class I, for example, is named *Monandria*, and all plants within that grouping have one stamen on each flower. Class XXIII, *Polygamia*, consists of plants in which the male and female flowers are together; Linnaeus described Class *Polygamia* as "Twenty males or more in the same bed with the female" (Stearn, "Linnaean Classification" 244). Consider Darwin's entry for the Mimosa, or Sensitive Plant, from Linnaean Class *Polygamia* as an example of Darwin's poetic and expository practice in *The Loves of the Plants*. The verse account reads as follows:

> Weak with nice sense, the chaste MIMOSA stands,
> From each rude touch withdraws her timid hands;
> Oft as light clouds o'erpass the Summer-glade,
> Alarm'd she trembles at the moving shade;
> And feels, alive through all her tender form,
> The whisper'd murmurs of the gathering storm;
> Shuts her sweet eye-lids to approaching night;
> And hails with freshen'd charms the rising light.
> Veil'd, with gay decency and modest pride,
> Slow to the mosque she moves, an eastern bride;
> There her soft vows unceasing love record,
> Queen of the bright seraglio of her Lord. (1: 247–58)[1]

The Mimosa, still nicknamed the Sensitive Plant, does indeed close up when its leaflets are touched, whether by a hand, a breath, or a breeze. Going back to seventeenth-century writings by herbalists, the Mimosa has been treated as an object of curiosity and wonder, portrayed often as a sensitive and bashful female, but also figured as male in eighteenth-century pornographic writing (Shteir, "Sensitive, Bashful, and Chaste?"). Here, in 1791, Erasmus Darwin creates through his personification an anticipatory and sexualized *Mimosa* as one kind of gendered female for the male gaze.

Figured as in an oriental tale, she is timid, tender, and chaste, yet "alive through all her form" as an "eastern bride" on the brink of marriage and her first sexual encounter.

Darwin's verse account does not stand alone on the page in the *Botanic Garden*. A footnote to the poetic picture of the *Mimosa* contains lines of botanical discussion in prose, and in smaller font, that easily take up more than half the page. Darwin begins with the Latin name of the plant and then cites its common English name, followed by reference to its Linnaean class. Thereafter he steps away from classification and the sexual system and addresses plant physiology. He hypothesizes possible explanations for the "sleep" and "collapse" in the "sensitive" and "irritable" parts of the plant, and reports on his own observations and experiments with the *Mimosa*. Darwin writes: "I kept a sensitive plant in a dark room till some hours after day break, its leaves and leaf-stalks were collapsed as in its most profound sleep, and on exposing it to the light, above twenty minutes passed before the plant was thoroughly awake and had quite expanded itself. During the night the upper or smoother surfaces of the leaves are appressed together, this would seem to shew that the office of this surface of the leaf was to expose the fluids of the plant to the light as well as to the air" (*LP* 25). Within this one long annotation in *Loves of the Plants*, Darwin makes cross-reference to botanical notes in other parts of his poem as well. A reader who follows each such cross-reference will realize quickly that the length of *The Botanic Garden* as a poetic text is more than matched by what Darwin terms "Philosophical Notes," along with other paratextual parts of the work. Following upon the four cantos of *The Economy of Vegetation*, for example, are more than one hundred pages of notes on scientific topics in geology, chemistry, and atmospheric science that include comets, heat, phosphorus, "modern production of iron," coal, and circulation and respiration in plants. Further filling out the composite shape of *The Botanic Garden* are mythological frontispieces, intratextual prose "Interludes," illustrations of plants and of Linnaean reproductive parts of flowers, and a "Catalogue of the Poetic Exhibition" followed by an index to the "Contents of the Notes."

How are we to read such an assemblage? How are we to understand and interpret the different registers of knowledge visualized on each page of Darwin's popular and influential late-eighteenth-century poem? Numerous analyses suggest themselves. We could read the verse and the footnotes in *The Botanic Garden* as parallel forms of knowledge, separate and distinct, with the literary and scientific approaches to nature equal in value and purpose. Or, we could understand the verse and the informational notes as contradictory modes of knowledge that call upon the reader to choose one or the other. Another way of reading the generic divergence between verse and footnotes is to construe them in Darwin's text as two modes that are in tension, and perhaps in fruitful tension. A still further reading could consider the two modes as interacting in some kind of composite that embodies an approach to nature larger than each part on its own. An additional approach could explain the formats of verse and footnotes in relation to different audiences for the work, with degrees of knowledge that call for different forms of explanation. In such a case, one register of knowledge could serve pedagogically to guide readers to another.

Numerous recent scholars of Romanticism have animated discussion of Darwin's work with fresh attention to literary, scientific, and cultural aspects of *The Botanic Garden*. Alan Bewell, for one, reads *The Botanic Garden* within a nexus of British commerce and imperialism. His Darwin is the Lunar Society of Birmingham member with eyes on consumerism and expanding British national interests at home and abroad. He relates *The Botanic Garden* to eighteenth-century enthusiasms for plants and gardening, and highlights actual botanical gardens, notably the Royal Botanic Gardens at Kew. Kew carried symbolic meanings as an ecological metropole of Britain's global reach, yet also, he suggests, is a material site filled with specific plants and flowers that were collected as commodities for use, beauty, and accumulation of wealth. Seen from this vantage, he writes, Darwin's *Botanic Garden* can be considered "a very expensive gardening book, perfectly suited to appeal to a well-heeled middle-class audience interested in developing a knowledge and taste for plants" ("Erasmus Darwin" 28). Dahlia Porter, bringing a more formal literary orientation to Darwin's poem, examines how and why Darwin structures *The Loves of the Plants* around analogy in the verse and Linnaean taxonomy in the footnotes. Whereas the taxonomic aspect differentiates empirical features of nature, Darwin's analogies represent his view of connections and the vastness of relations within nature. Porter's argument is that the structural boundary between verse and footnotes in *Loves of the Plants* was a deliberate strategy by Darwin to separate out science and imagination. It is taxonomy, she concludes, that "stems the tide of unbounded analogy" in *The Loves of the Plants* ("Scientific Analogy" 219). Theresa Kelley, in a richly detailed study of botany and Romantic-era culture, looks beyond a bifurcation of verse and prose notes in *Loves of the Plants* and in *The Botanic Garden* as a whole. Although Darwin explicates and illustrates Linnaeus's sexual system as a system of order, Kelley identifies an orientation in the poem critical of Linnaeus's sexual system and of systematics as a whole. Darwin's poem is an example for her of resistances and challenges to categories and clear distinctions as "plants challenge the authority of the Linnaean system with repeated and dramatic imperiousness" (*Clandestine Marriage* 79). Furthermore, "The unruliness of … Darwin's figures gives him the space he needs to write simultaneously about and away from the Linnaean system in the same work" (81). His trajectory is towards counter-narratives of fluidity in theories of nature and practices of normative relationships.

In the proem to *The Loves of the Plants*, Darwin writes about the poet Ovid's vision of metamorphoses in nature, in which human beings are transformed into flowers and trees. Darwin declares that his own mission is to do the reverse: to restore flowers and trees to "their original animality, after having remained prisoners so long in their respective vegetable mansions" (*LP* vi). Analogy between plants and animals was a building block of the European cultural imaginary for centuries, and Darwin humanizes plants for both aesthetic and philosophical reasons in his own grand narrative of growth. Personification was his technical tool for illustrating not only reproduction in the plant kingdom but also agency and self-generating relations among plants. Darwin reflects upon his working methods in three prose interludes in *Loves of the Plants* about relations between literature and other modes of knowledge for understanding nature. Discussing the "sister-arts" of poetry and painting, he asserts an "essential similitude in the language of the poetic pen and pencil" (*LP* 119), and traces the process: "When by the Part of the Painter or Poet a train of ideas is suggested to our imaginations, which interests us so much by the pain or the pleasure it affords, that we cease to attend to the irritations of common external objects, and cease also to use any voluntary efforts to compare these interesting trains of ideas with our previous knowledge of things, a compleat reverie is produced: during which time however short, if it be but for a moment, the objects themselves appear to exist before us" (*LP* 47–8). In her analysis of Darwin's poetics, Catherine Packham argues that he gave human-style passions and behaviours to parts of nature that are already living beings, and that the personifications in *Loves of the Plants* are far from the empty mechanisms that critics attacked. She locates Darwin's botanical figures of animation within a wide spectrum of vitalist theories of nature found in eighteenth-century philosophy, natural philosophy, and literature. Darwin's transformation of plants into animals in *Loves of the Plants* can be seen, therefore, "to fulfil a scientific as much as a poetic agenda" (*Eighteenth-Century Vitalism* 156). In this regard, Darwin's way of representing plants in *The Botanic Garden* anticipates vitalistic ideas that he went on to develop further in his *Zoonomia; or, the Laws of Organic Life* (1794) and subsequent publications.

Darwin was writing at a time when "serious" science and science writing were being taken along separate paths from poetry, art, mythology, and popularizing accounts of new developments in natural history and natural philosophy. *The Botanic Garden* was issued in London in 1791 under the imprint of Joseph Johnson, who published milestone works of children's literature as well as writings by Mary Wollstonecraft and others associated with radical ferment in European politics and ideas. Erasmus Darwin, grandfather to Charles Darwin, was a busy physician in the British Midlands, an enthusiast of progressive Enlightenment thinking, a celebrated poet, author of scientific treatises and papers, and an avid communicator of ideas. He was, along with other like-minded and prosperous members, part of the Lunar Society of Birmingham that, as Jenny Uglow has documented, met from the mid-1770s into the 1790s to discuss new developments in science and technology. Absorbed by new developments in botany, Darwin translated two Linnaean botanical treatises from Latin into English at the same time that he was writing *The Loves of the Plants*.[2] *The Loves of the Plants* was a bestseller when it appeared first in 1789 as a free-standing publication that won many admirers (and garnered Darwin considerable profit), so much so that Darwin corresponded with Parliament about the possibility of a poet laureateship. Critics, however, were vocal. Poet Henry Crabb Robinson, for one, wrote of Darwin's "tinsel gawdy lines" (cited in Bewell, 34). Poet Anna Seward, who was Darwin's friend and botanical colleague, wrote in her *Memoirs* that "Dr. Darwin's excellence consists in delighting the eye, the taste, and the fancy, ... but the passions are generally asleep, and seldom are the nerves thrilled by his imagery ... or by its landscapes" (Seward 177). Goethe acknowledged that a German translation of *Loves of the Plants* had inspired his own poem "Die Metamorphose der Pflanzen," but in a letter to Schiller in 1798 he had little positive to say about Darwin's "fashionable" piece of writing ["diese englische Modeschrift"] with its pile-up of textual features and allegorical figurations, and no trace of poetic feeling to hold it all together. Odder still, Goethe adds, is that he finds no actual plants in this botanical work.[3]

Darwin had a large agenda for his poem. The prefatory advertisement to each part distinguishes between the "general design" and the "particular design" of the work. Whereas the "general design" is "to inlist Imagination under the banner of Science," the "particular design" is "to induce the ingenious to cultivate the knowledge of Botany, by introducing them to the vestibule of that delightful science, and recommending to their attention the immortal works of the celebrated Swedish Naturalist, LINNEUS" (*EV* v). Darwin intervenes through his poem in disputes about the validity of Linnaean ideas about sexual reproduction in plants; his descriptions often included botanical details that added to Linnaeus's system, and historian of science Janet Browne has made the point that Darwin likely intended his poem, above all, "to be a reaffirmation of Linnaeus's insistence on plant sexuality in the face of increasingly numerous anti-Linnaean publications" ("Botany for Gentlemen" 602). Seen from this perspective, there are ample grounds for arguing that the notes in *The Botanic Garden* were more important to Darwin than the verse.

Form and Footnotes in *The Botanic Garden* and "Die Alpen"

Darwin's *Botanic Garden* is not the first eighteenth-century poem to blend verbal modes. A notable German-language example is Albrecht von Haller's poem "Die Alpen" (1732), which brings together descriptive verse and scientific observations in an idealized vision of nature in the mountain world of the Swiss Alps. Haller (1708–77) was a Swiss polymath known throughout Europe as a poet and scholarly editor, and as author of many learned publications about anatomy, botany, and medicine. "Die Alpen" appeared first in Haller's collection of poetry *Versuch schweizerischer Gedichte*, and was reprinted and widely translated during the eighteenth century. Haller wrote with deep admiration about the lives and values of Alpine dwellers, and describes Alpine folk festivals, routines of cheesemaking, and other instances of hard work. The moral trajectory of the poem is pastoral, for Haller reflects on the simplicity and happiness that result from being in congruence with nature, by contrast to the corrupt and vapid lives of city dwellers. "Die Alpen" consists of forty-nine stanzas of tightly organized alexandrines, and Caroline Schaumann makes the point in a new study of this poem that Haller's poetic form itself manifests his overall didacticism insofar as "Haller relies on the meter in order to emphasize tradition, convention, and conscientious labor" (61). The pastoral quality in Haller's account of the bucolic world of mountain people leads him also to paint verbal pictures of Alpine topography and features of waterfalls, rock formations, minerals, and plants. Two stanzas pertinent to discussion of Erasmus Darwin's *The Botanic Garden* detail Alpine meadows, and wildflowers observed there. In the first of these stanzas Haller describes features of two species of gentian, one yellow and the other blue, and characterizes their stature among other native plants. This stanza reads as follows in a prose translation of Haller's poem into English, dating from 1794: "The noble *Gentian* lifts his proud head above the crowd of vulgar plants; a whole blossomed cohort ranges under his banner; and even his brother, distinguished by his clothing of celestial blue, bows down to yield him homage: his golden flowers encircle the grey stalk, and form a splendid crown: upon the satined leaves streaked with dark green, liquid diamonds shoot their keen sparkles."[4] While Haller's adjectives of nobility, hierarchy, and authority speak to moral dimensions of the poem, details about the colour, size, and shape of the two gentians are meant to convey the poet's careful observation of features distinguishing one plant from another. Haller strengthens the empirical linkage to the Alpine plants by inserting footnotes with Latin notations that identify them botanically. Thus, the footnote to lines 381–4 of the verse names the two gentians in the following manner: "*Gentiana floribus rotates verticillatus. Enum. Helv.* p. 478, one of the largest Alpine plants, and whose healing powers are widely known, and the blue *foliis amplexicaulibus floris fauce barbata. Enum. Helv.* p. 473, which is smaller and less attractive."[5] He goes on similarly in the next stanza to describe the size, leaf shape and configuration, colour, and habitat of other Alpine plants. The prose translation of Haller's text reads:

> Here the narrow leaves of a modest vegetable spread their net-work of ash-colour: the flower resembles a bird of amethyst, with its beak of shining gold: there a lovely plant bends its indented and glittering foliage over the surface of the river: the stream reflects its beauties; the calyx tinted with delicate purple, the velvet petals sprinkled with snow. The rose and the emerald spread all their beauties upon the meadows; and the very rocks shine in a vestment of purple.[6]

Footnotes to these lines continue to identify the plants botanically. For example, the opening four lines of the stanza refer to alpine toadflax, a low spreading plant with grey-green foliage and purple flowers that now is called *Linaria alpina*. By contrast, Haller designates the alpine toadflax botanically as "*Antirrhinum caule procumbente, foliis verticillatis, floribus congestis*." Haller did not agree with the nomenclatural system devised by Linnaeus that used a two-word shortcut practice of genus and species as the way to name plants. Instead, he used long Latin descriptive phrases to identify plants. His practice, continuing throughout his career as a writer on medical and botanical topics, placed him outside the eighteenth-century nomenclatural mainstream. The page references that follow upon the descriptive phrases in the footnotes to the stanzas shown above all refer to

Haller's own scholarly botanical compilation of Swiss plants, *Enumeratio methodica stirpium Helvetiae indigenarum* (1742). This influential work appeared after several editions of his poem "Die Alpen" had been published, and Haller integrated citations from it into the fourth edition of the poem (Shteir, "Albrecht von Haller's Botany").

In 1794, readers in England had access for the first time to a translation of Haller's poem into English, and the story around this builds a cultural bridge that connects Haller's early and mid-eighteenth-century botanical work to the content and context of Erasmus Darwin's writing in later decades. Alison Martin has studied the prose rendering of "Die Alpen" undertaken by "Mrs J. Howorth" that brought Haller's ideas to a British audience familiar by then with Rousseauistic ideas about nature and also interested in the scientific aims of Haller's poem. Mrs Howorth herself (about whom little is known) had clear botanical interests and pursued the study of plants during the decades of the 1780s and 1790s when botanical culture was burgeoning. She corresponded with Sir James E. Smith, the first president of the Linnaean Society and himself a translator of key Linnaean publications, and dedicated her *Poems of Baron Haller* to him as a fervent botanist and institution builder ("Natural Effusions" 23–4). Her translation dates from a period in the cultural history of science in Britain, America, and elsewhere when women participated in studying, collecting, drawing, translating, writing about plants, and teaching others (Shteir, *Cultivating Women*; George, *Botany, Sexuality*; Teute, "The Loves of the Plants").

Readers of Mrs Howorth's translation of Haller's mix of nature description and botanical detail, in all likelihood familiar with Erasmus Darwin's *Botanic Garden* from just a few years earlier, may well have noted similarities between the two works. Writing more than fifty years after publication of "Die Alpen," Darwin shares Haller's interest in using verse to extol nature and its workings, and both poets write out of deep involvement in technical botany and other sciences of their day. But Darwin's account goes way beyond the empirical rendering of the ideal world that Haller portrays in his praise of Alpine orderliness. Where Haller aimed for clarity and simplicity in language, Darwin's poetry and prose are exuberant and on the move, piling up images and information. The imaginative writing in Darwin's verse leads to extensive footnotes that in turn guide the reader into Linnaean systematics, as well as towards practices in plant physiology, and other new directions in scientific study of the vegetable kingdom that Darwin himself will contribute to through subsequent works.[7]

Yet those same footnotes are for Darwin part of an elaborate apparatus that surrounds his poem with explanations that are both scientific and aesthetic. His vision of nature is vitalistic as he brings forces of nature alive. Darwin also brings mythologies into the mix as part of his vision of nature, and thereby moves, in my view, past literary figuration into something else.

Mythology and the Goddess

In Darwin's day, botany was a component of fashionable activity having to do with sociability and pleasure across the broad middle range of British society. Writing in this regard in the proem to *The Loves of the Plants*, Darwin positions the verse botanical material for his intended "Gentle Reader" as "diverse little pictures suspended over the chimney of a Lady's dressing-room" (*LP* v–vi). Darwin clearly nods to gendered ideas about a feminized reader who will be attracted by ornament and aesthetics. However, Darwin had other audiences in mind, including women who looked to botany as a sphere for their own intellectual activity.

Across both parts of the poem, Darwin constructs an elaborate mythological apparatus to embody and express a vision of nature as elemental and dynamic. Classical mythology appears in references to Venus and Vulcan, Hercules, Jupiter and Juno, and to terrestrial goddesses such as Flora, Pomona, and Ceres. The overarching cast of mythological characters extends, however, outside traditional Greek and Roman gods and goddesses and the stories they have embodied across European cultures. In this regard, the dominant figure in *The Botanic Garden* is the "Botanic Goddess." Darwin's own creation, she is invoked at the start of the poem by the Genius of the Place, and her trajectory through domains of nature gives textual shape to the poem as a whole. It is her voice that guides the reader across the text. She arrives in the opening canto of *The Economy of Vegetation* and departs at the end of the fourth and closing canto of *The Loves of the Plants*:

> She comes! – the GODDESS! – through the whispering air,
> Bright as the morn, descends her blushing car;
> Each circling wheel a wreath of flowers intwines,
> And gem'd with flowers the silken harness shines;
> ... Light from her airy seat the Goddess bounds,
> And steps celestial press the pansied grounds. (*EV* 1: 59–68)

Also termed "Fair Spring," the Goddess of Botany then calls upon elemental creatures that have command of specific areas in nature and that will accompany her on a journey through her domain. Her retinue will depend upon nymphs of fire and of water, gnomes of the earth, and sylphs of the air who will keep the economy of nature on track. The myth system being called upon here is Rosicrucian, that is, European esoteric beliefs, symbols, and practices going back many centuries, and going back farther still to ancient Egyptian emblems, hieroglyphs, and allegories. Earlier in the eighteenth century, Alexander Pope had marshalled Rosicrucian sylphs and others for his witty heroicomical poem "The Rape of the Lock" (1712–14). There the coquette Belinda is assisted in her daily toilette by legions of spirits charged with preparing her for daily routines of beauty, akin to readiness for the battle that then ensues: "The busy Sylphs surround their darling care, / These set the head, and those divide the hair, / Some fold the sleeve, whilst others plait the gown" (1: 145–7). The gap in Pope's telling between the weighty machinery of multiple gnomes, mythological figures, and extravagant references, on the one hand, and the slightness of the action, on the other, is the satiric heart of Pope's wonderful poem.

By contrast, the sylphs, gnomes, and nymphs of *The Botanic Garden* personify Darwin's vision of elemental and active nature, and are not meant to be only clever machinery. Darwin's use of such figures in fact offers a productive way to think about cultural dimensions of nature and science at a time when artists, writers, scholars, sceptics and critics, translators and teachers told and retold, adapted and reshaped, stories from Greek and Roman mythology. Mythologists across the earlier and later eighteenth century used their retellings to connect to old stories in widely disparate ways. Some linked the present to the past so as to justify contemporary social codes and practices, shore up hierarchies, or confirm gender systems. Others sought to undercut earlier versions of stories, as when Enlightenment sceptics read myths from Greece and Rome as historical record rather than as divinely ordained truths; their accounts put gods and goddesses into mortal forms as historical individuals who were deified to suit politics or nation building (Feldman and Richardson). Some repudiated mythology altogether. Others, however, sought alternatives. Darwin, for one, was interested in new or less-known older accounts of origin stories. He was fascinated by a treatise on mythology by Jacob Bryant that had appeared in the 1770s, entitled *A New System, or an Analysis of Ancient Mythology*, and refers to it in footnote references in *The Botanic Garden*. Bryant was an antiquarian and Christian who believed in the scriptural Mosaic account of the Flood. Wanting to correct ancient history, he asserted that the Greeks had claimed for their own origin stories that trace way back before their time. "The Greeks," he wrote, "were so prepossessed with a notion of their own excellence and antiquity, that they supposed every ancient tradition to have proceeded from themselves" (1: 130). Instead, Bryant uses etymology and other tools as "historical evidence" that may help to win over "infidels" (3: vii). He writes about cognate rites and idols that are found in mythologies cross-culturally, and argues that these developed out of earlier Egyptian hieroglyphs and allegories and in "universal" stories that circulated among Babylonians and other early peoples. Like Bryant, Darwin seems to have found Greek and Roman mythologies limiting as well. Instead, Darwin evokes in *The Botanic Garden* typologies that are older, but that in his day were both a new style and a critical alternative style. He integrated Bryant's thinking about hieroglyphs and elemental themes and figures into his own writing as a way to get at continuities between past and present and to be both philosophical and visionary in his approaches to nature.

In the opening lines of *The Economy of Vegetation* the Goddess of Botany descends from the heavens as an embodiment of Nature but specifically in relation to plants. She gives instructions to her minions, the four elements. Nymphs of fire are instructed in canto 1 to use their heat, for example, for plant germination and growth. Gnomes of the earth are to enrich the soil:

> Go, gentle Gnomes! resume your vernal toil.
> Seek my chill tribes, which sleep beneath the soil;
> On grey-moss banks, green meads, or furrow'd lands,
> Spread the dark mould, white lime, and crumbling sands;
> Each bursting bud with healthier juices feed. (*EV* 2: 542–6)

Water nymphs, addressed in canto 3, sustain plants and breathe "sweet enchantment o'er BRITTANIA's isle" (*EV* 3: 262). The power of the Botanic Goddess and her elements is reinforced across both *The Economy of Vegetation* and *Loves of the Plants*. Darwin's Botanic Goddess might be read principally as a rhetorical creation for his intended audience, a strategic choice to help entice female readers into kinship with "her" kingdom, but she is larger than that. That she is figured in relation to the plant kingdom illustrates well later eighteenth-century orientations towards organic domains. The Botanic Goddess is apt for Darwin himself and for his time. The significance of his choice becomes clear when Darwin's creation of the Botanic Goddess is juxtaposed with the figure of Flora, the Roman goddess of flowers. Writers and pedagogues contemporary to Darwin had named Flora as their literary guide in narratives that, similarly to Darwin's, concern new directions in natural history. Darwin has a Flora too, but only as one of the handmaids that attends on the Botanic Goddess in the company of other nature divinities:

> Hither, emerging from yon orient skies,
> BOTANIC GODDESS! Bend thy radiant eyes;
> O'er these soft scenes assume thy gentle reign,
> Pomona, Ceres, Flora in thy train. (*EV* 1: 43–6)

Flora assigns dominance in the vegetable kingdom not to Flora and other terrestrial goddesses, but to the Botanic Goddess instead. She is an overarching figure that is at once explicitly scientific and, I suggest, even more powerfully mythological. The figure of the Botanic Goddess takes *The Botanic Garden* into a different kind of reading, beyond personification, and into a larger vision of nature, in which empirical features are components in a still larger whole.

With his reference to Flora, Erasmus Darwin joined himself to a rich cultural legacy. Mythologies throughout the world have some version of a Flora figure, a personified aspect of nature associated with springtime that represents fertility and the coming into flower of plants. Flora made her way into Roman popular culture and religious ritual and out into mythology textbooks, literature, science, and the visual arts. Within western European culture, into the Renaissance and Early Modern era and beyond, she was depicted in many guises. One is as the Mother of Flowers who generates growth through her body's milk. Another is as the Queen of Flowers, a figure of power who presides over seasonal and agricultural cycles of rebirth and fruition. She can be young and part of a narrative of blooming into marriage and motherhood – as in Botticelli's *Primavera*. Often Flora was depicted as sexually alluring. She has been gendered and embodied in ways that sometimes represent power, pleasure, agency, and knowledge, but often convey negative versions of womankind. Always anchored in the body, sexed female and gendered feminine, she carries traffic across the centuries, an all-too-ready vocabulary for naturalizations of difference (Shteir, "*Flora primavera* or *Flora meretrix*?"). In the eighteenth century, in particular, Flora is figured in song, on stage, in portraiture and historical painting, in garden statuary and architecture, in verse and fiction. Ubiquitous in many cultural forms, a mythological Flora certainly serves Erasmus Darwin's purposes well.

However, Darwin's figurehead in *The Botanic Garden* is the Botanic Goddess and not Flora. Because of Darwin's interest in both botany and expansive mythologies, the narrator of his poem carries a name that is less about flowers and more about systematic study of plants, that is, the science of botany. For Darwin, and for his time, the term "botany" registered as more strictly scientific than would references to "Flora." An apostrophe to the Botanic Goddess early in *Loves of the Plants* addresses her as the "Botanic Muse" who inspired Linnaeus in his work: "who in this latter age / Led by your airy hand the Swedish sage, / Bad his keen eye your secret haunts explore" (*LP* 1: 31–3). By linking Linnaeus to the Botanic Goddess and her "secrets of nature," Darwin gives tremendous power to mythology as a guide in formulating scientific ideas. In this poem, as indeed in his writings more generally, Darwin elucidates his own mythologies so as to move back and forth among types of knowledge.

Darwin's view of nature is not a binary between literary and scientific approaches to knowledge. Instead, *The Botanic Garden* is an amalgam in which literary and scientific features join to express a vision of nature that is larger than the components. The crossover point for Darwin is imagination as a resource and a tool, a force integral to both literary and scientific modes of knowing. Darwin addresses the importance of imagination in the "Advertisement" that opens his publication. He writes: "The general design of the following sheets is to inlist [*sic*] Imagination under the banner of Science; and to lead her votaries from the looser analogies, which dress out the imagery of poetry, to the stricter, ones which form the ratiocination of philosophy" (v). Imagination is Darwin's path from poetry to philosophy. It underlies science as much as poetry, and is as important for him as information. Darwin's poem abounds in references to empirical practices, yet the overarching vision is holistic and seeks to understand a unity of nature in the forces and patterns that underlie all life. For these reasons, Darwin's analogies between plants and animals and his personifications and creative mythologies make botany more philosophical than taxonomic. For these reasons, his writing includes both the fable and the footnote.

Mythology proves to be a good resource for analysing traffic across the domains of literature and science at the time when Erasmus Darwin was contributing to it as an expanding area of natural knowledge and encouraging others to join him. While the Botanic Goddess suits Darwin's late-eighteenth-century orientation as a specialized goddess that speaks to emerging disciplinary-specific directions of that time, she also embodies the larger philosophy of Darwin's poem when read as a whole. Her placement as the lead figure from the beginning of *The Economy of Vegetation* through to the conclusion of *The Loves of the Plants* gives a cosmic frame to Darwin's ideas about growth and change. The Botanic Goddess is the source of plants in their materiality and an energizing force that propels plant processes. She animates the place and ground that are the Botanic Garden, whose space is the poem. She also is the force that shapes relations among the plants and within nature. She does not impose adherence of the plants to system. Indeed, the plants in her vegetable kingdom are not reverent Linnaeans. Instead of fitting tidily within Linnaean taxonomies, they transgress boundaries and are far from walled in. Furthermore, as a female narrator, the Botanic Goddess mediates Darwin's poem to audiences, particularly to the female readers whose botanical study Darwin seeks to promote. She can serve as a narrative hook and literary way to reach them, and thus can be construed as a strategic feature in the composition and publication of the poem in that time of burgeoning popularizations of knowledge.

As much as *The Botanic Garden* can be read for literary and structural features discussed in this chapter, Darwin's embodied female Botanic Goddess also has specificity and materiality in relation to his own time and place. During the 1790s, women in England wrote about botany with the same pedagogical and popularizing purposes found in *The Botanic Gardens*, especially in *Loves of the Plants*. Didactic and expository texts such as Priscilla Wakefield's *Introduction to Botany, in a Series of Familiar Letters* (1796), and *Botanical Dialogues, between Hortensia and Her Four Children* (1797), written by Maria Elizabeth Jacson from within Darwin's own circle in the Midlands, were part of a literary marketplace of expository books about botany and other areas of natural history for women, children, and general readers that began around 1760 and extended into the mid-nineteenth century (Shteir, *Cultivating Women*; George; Kelley 103–10). Darwin was widely familiar with the interests of contemporary women in plants as objects of botanical, horticultural, and aesthetic attention, and his writing was a springboard for other women botanical writers, who themselves continued bringing botanical knowledge to female audiences. His own *Plan for the Conduct of Female Education in Boarding Schools* (1797) sets out a curriculum that includes botany as well as natural history, mythology, technology, and a range of other Arts and Sciences. There, after listing several introductory and illustrated texts that supplied instruction about botany, Darwin put in a plug for his own work: "And lastly I shall not forbear to mention, that the philosophical part of botany may be agreeably learnt from the notes to the second volume of the Botanic garden, whether the poetry be read or not" (41).

The Botanic Goddess links Darwin's creation of a new-style mythology in *The Botanic Garden* to actual "modern" Botanic goddesses, and would-be goddesses, of his time. Mythological frontispieces to the two parts of the poem illustrate this well, while also raising questions about ideas of femininity and womanhood that *The Botanic Garden* may be promoting. Indeed, despite the powerful agency of the Botanic Goddess, *The Botanic Garden* positions women within normative gendered ideas of womanhood that historically shaped women's relationship to knowledge of nature and science.

The visual aspect of Darwin's work is beyond the immediate purview of this essay, but a few remarks are relevant to the Botanic Goddess in the poem as imaginative vision, normative practices, and possible experiential realities. *The Loves of the Plants*, the chronologically earlier part of *The Botanic Garden*, carries a frontispiece captioned "FLORA at Play with CUPID" that was drawn by Emma Crewe, a socially well-placed artist. It portrays Flora languidly posed, with flowers massed in her hair and Cupid's arrow in her lap. Her face is conventionally appealing, though with a demure and flirty edge that mirrors Darwin's Linnaean verses. This image would easily find a place among other decorative representations in visual culture that would appeal to female audiences interested in the "looser" analogies of botanical poetry. The frontispiece for the overarching composite publication *The Botanic Garden* is another story. Painter and illustrator Henry Fuseli was commissioned to do this piece in line with Darwin's request for an image that would be "an allegory of the whole work" (cited in Bewell, 24), and "Flora attir'd by the Elements" captures Darwin's Romantic energy well. Fuseli's Flora (*figure 3.1*) is a force of nature being dressed by Earth, Air, Fire and Water for her work as a goddess in the plant kingdom. The image is a visual counterpart to a passage from *The Economy of Vegetation*:

> Pleased GNOMES, ascending from their earthy beds,
> Play round her graceful footsteps, as she treads;
> Gay SYLPHS attendant beat the fragrant air
> On winnowing wings, and waft her golden hair;
> Blue NYMPHS emerging leave their sparkling streams,
> And FIERY FORMS alight from orient beams. (1: 73–8)

Figure 3.1 "FLORA attired by the ELEMENTS" by Henry Fuseli is the frontispiece to Erasmus Darwin's *The Botanic Garden: A Poem in Two Parts* (London, 1791). Courtesy of the Thomas Fisher Rare Book Library, University of Toronto.

Henry Fuseli gives this passage a contemporary twist. Fuseli's gnome ascends from its "earthy bed" with budding floral growths in hand, his sylph of the air wears a butterfly hat, a figure of fire in a flaming helmet holds a mirror, and a graceful nymph points to water as an elemental source. Darwin's text does not characterize the appearance of Flora/the Botanic Goddess herself. It is Fuseli who represents her as an attractive and rather haughty and self-possessed young woman, dressed in a manner that would have looked distinctly elegant and fashionable in 1791. The position of her lower body seems modest, but the full pose is sinuous and alluring, aligned well with Linnaean ideas about sexuality and Darwin's own ideas about fecundity.

Fuseli's frontispiece to *The Botanic Garden* depicts Flora as a modern and sexualized young woman, a possible icon for her time. But how and in what ways might "Flora attir'd by the Elements" bring women over the threshold into study of botany, especially in its "stricter" analogies of philosophic and scientific thought? Several readings suggest themselves. In one kind of reading, the Fuseli/Darwin image of Flora naturalizes Woman as elementally female and the object of a sexualized gaze, preoccupied with her body rather than with intellectual directions in the study of nature. In another, Flora is the Botanic Goddess who controls the elements, and thus orchestrates both the economy of vegetation and the loves of the plants. As an exemplar for a modern botanizing goddess, she may be read as self-possessed and self-aware, modelling clever resourcefulness, inhabiting the part as a route to power. Further readings build upon or challenge traditional associations between women and flowers. Ideas about emancipatory sexualities were associated with radical politics at that time, and perhaps Fuseli and Darwin were showing in this regard a new template for women beyond the binaries of feminine/masculine and body/mind. Theresa Kelley remarks that *Loves of the Plants* is "more evidently about the role of females than males in classificatory argument," and further that "Darwin's goddess of botany supervises a system of figuration that pushes at and away from the epistemological grip of a systematic founded on figurative males as taxonomic as well as social governors" (89). Attention to the Botanic Goddess in Darwin's *Botanic Garden*, in other words, takes us out past literary features of narrative and metaphor and into considering this iconic figure as both representation and potential reality. For, as she goes, so late-eighteenth-century female and male readers, writers, and teachers may follow in her train.

Attention to the Botanic Goddess may also orient readers of the poem beyond empirical details of plants and their landscapes into spheres of elemental forces and micro and macro cosmic processes. Some older interpreters of Darwin's thought and writing, instead of analysing his poetic diction or foregrounding his progressive and evolutionary views, accentuated his "Orphic" ideas, including his preoccupation with Eleusinian mysteries and "secrets" of nature. Irwin Primer, for one, read Darwin's late poem *The Temple of Nature* as "a marriage of poetry and science" at the very time that "the humanistic and the scientific cultures … were moving steadily away from one another" ("Erasmus Darwin's Temple" 76). More recently, historian of ancient philosophy Pierre Hadot has provided an impetus of an ecological and philosophical kind to this interpretive direction in his erudite study *The Veil of Isis: An Essay in the History of the Idea of Nature.* Hadot is fervently interested in mythology and mythological figures that have been used to write about nature and science in the Western cultural imagination. Prometheus the fire-bringer and Orpheus the singer serve his purposes well. Hadot explains that mythology was "poetic physics" for medieval and Renaissance thinkers and writers (79), and he himself is drawn to metaphors, iconographies, and aesthetics as ways to understand "secrets" of nature and to admire and venerate the enigmas of life and the world. These form the Orphic attitude towards nature. The Promethean attitude shares in admiration of nature, but seeks to understand nature's secrets so as to use nature through observation and technique. While the contrast is familiar enough in analyses about organic and mechanical ideas about nature, Hadot's broad-brush study stretches across nearly twenty-five centuries from ancient thought into beliefs of more recent philosophers and scientists. Hadot wisely points out that the Promethean and Orphic orientations towards nature "do not necessarily exclude each other, and are often found united in the same person … The two attitudes … correspond to our ambiguous relation to nature, and they cannot be separated in too definitive a way" (97). Hadot has heroes in his study, Goethe notably among them as poet and scholar. Although Erasmus Darwin's *Botanic Garden* does not figure in his account, Darwin's work nicely embodies, in content and form, Hadot's thinking about contrasting but coexisting ideas in our relation to nature. *The Botanic Garden* also is congruent with Hadot's overall orientation towards the poetically Orphic rather than the scientifically Promethean.

Erasmus Darwin's expository *The Botanic Garden* blends science, poetry, and mythologies into an amalgam of information and visionary ideas. Like Haller's poem "Die Alpen," Darwin's poem showcases burgeoning eighteenth-century interest in scientific approaches to nature. Empirical features of observation, classification, and nomenclature are important to both writers, each of whom contributed directly and substantially to the elaboration and dissemination of botany. However, Darwin's integration of scientific focus and an extended literary apparatus came from a different time and place as well as from a different person and mindset within the history of European culture. Darwin embodies the intellectual, cultural, and political turmoil of the 1780s and 1790s, when analogical and organicist approaches to nature and writing were challenging earlier modes. In a recent study of German Romanticism and science, Jocelyn Holland examines procreation as both an explicit theme and a process of thought in literary writings about science at that time. She tracks Romantic discourse that includes matters of reproduction as well as metaphors and analogies of organic change on a broad scale across the arts and sciences. Holland makes a powerful case for "a productive coupling" of literature and science by studying Goethe's poem "Die Metamorphose der Pflanzen" (1798), for example, in which Goethe "embeds the scientific activities of observation and experimentation within a procreative context" (14). The same notion of a "productive coupling" applies to *The Botanic Garden*. Published in the same decade as Goethe's writings about botany, *The Botanic Garden* is an intriguing generic hybrid that takes account of new philosophies of nature and new audiences for developments in science. Although its formal features, piling up metaphor, verse, and prose, are not to most current literary tastes, Darwin's multidimensional text from 1791 still has much to teach. His poem carries ecological and cosmological provocations across the centuries to writers and readers who seek new types of relationships with animate worlds, and who are in search of effective and imaginative forms for communicating their ideas about nature and science.

NOTES

1 The original 1791 edition of *The Botanic Garden* carried separate pagination for each of the two parts of the poem. Page references, and line references within individual cantos of the poems will be shown in this way, preceded by *EV* for *The Economy of Vegetation* and *LP* for *The Loves of the Plants.*

2 Darwin's translation of Linnaeus's *Species plantarum* (1753) was published as *A System of Vegetables* (1783) and *Genera Plantarum* (1737) as *Families of Plants* (1787).

3 Goethe, *Die Schriften zur Naturwissenschaft*, ed. Dorothea Kuhn (Weimar: Hermann Böhlaus Nachfolger, 1986), 2: 9B, 130–1. I thank Christian Weber for bringing this letter to my attention.

4 Mrs J. Howorth, trans., *The Poems of Baron Haller* 31. Haller's text is:

"Dort ragt das hohe Haupt am edlen Enziane
Weit übern niedern Chor der Pöbel-Kräuter hin;
Ein ganzes Blumen-Volk dient unter seiner Fahne,
Sein blauer Bruder selbst bückt sich und ehret ihn.
Der Blumen helles Gold, in Strahlen umgebogen,
Türmt sich am Stengel auf und krönt sein grau Gewand;
Der Blätter glattes Weiss, mit tiefem Grün durchzogen,
Bestrahlt der bunte Blitz von feuchtem Diamant[.]"

(In *Die Alpen*, ll. 381–8)

5 Trans. Shteir. Haller's footnote is this: "*Gentiana floribus rotates verticillatus. Enum. Helv.* p. 478, eines der grössten Alpen-Kräuter, und dessen Heil-Kräfte überall bekannt sind, und der blaue *foliis amplexicaulibus floris fauce barbata. Enum. Helv.* p. 473, der viel kleiner und unansehnlicher ist." In Mrs Howorth's translation, the footnote is reduced to read only *Gentiana lutea* and *Gentiana bavarica*, with no further nomenclatural or botanical details.

6 *The Poems of Baron Haller* 31–2. Haller's text is:

Hier kriecht ein niedrig Kraut, gleich einem grauen Nebel,
Dem die Natur sein Blatt in Kreutze hingelegt;
Die holde Blume zeigt die zwey vergüldten Schnäbel,
Die ein von Amethyst gebildter Vogel trägt.
Dort wirft ein glänzend Blatt, in Finger ausgekerbet,
Auf eine helle Bach den grünen Wiederschein;
Der Blumen zarten Schnee, den matter Purpur färbet,
Schliesst ein gestreifter Stern in weisse Strahlen ein:
Smaragt und Rosen blühn, auch auf zertretner Heiden
Und Felsen decken sich mit einem Purpur-Kleide. (391–400)

7 The titles *Zoonomia; or, the Laws of Organic Life* (1794), *Phytologia; or the Philosophy of Agriculture and Gardening* (1800), and *Temple of Nature; or, the Origin of Society* (published posthumously in 1803) illustrate Erasmus Darwin's philosophic reach and orientation towards the life sciences and their applications.

WORKS CITED

Bewell, Alan. "Erasmus Darwin's Cosmopolitan Nature." *ELH* 76.1 (2009): 19–48.

Browne, Janet. "Botany for Gentlemen: Erasmus Darwin and *The Loves of the Plants*." *Isis* 80 (1989): 593–621.

Bryant, Jacob. *A New System, or an Analysis of Ancient Mythology*. 3 vols. London: T. Payne, 1774–6.

Darwin, Erasmus. *The Botanic Garden; A Poem, in Two Parts. Part I. Containing The Economy of Vegetation. Part II. The Loves of the Plants. With Philosophical Notes*. (1791). Menston, Yorkshire: Scolar Press, 1973.

– *A Plan for the Conduct of Female Education in Boarding Schools* (1797). New York: Johnson Reprint Corp., 1968.

– *The Temple of Nature* (1803). Menston, Yorkshire: Scolar Press, 1973.

– *Zoonomia; or, the Laws of Organic Life*. 2nd ed. London: J. Johnson, 1796.

Feldman, Burton, and Robert D. Richardson, Jr, eds. *The Rise of Modern Mythology 1680–1860*. Bloomington: Indiana UP, 1972.

Fontenelle, Bernard le Bovier de. *Conversations on the Plurality of Worlds*. Trans. H.A. Hargreaves. Berkeley: U of California P, 1990.

George, Sam. *Botany, Sexuality and Women's Writing 1760–1830: From Modest Shoot to Forward Plant*. Manchester: Manchester UP, 2007.

Goethe, Johann von. *Die Schriften zur Naturwissenschaft*. Ed. Dorothea Kuhn. Weimar: Hermann Böhlaus Nachfolger, 1986. 2: 9B.

Hadot, Pierre. *The Veil of Isis: An Essay on the History of the Idea of Nature*. Trans. Michael Chase. Cambridge, MA: Belknap Press, 2006.

Haller, Albrecht von. *Die Alpen und andere Gedichte*. Stuttgart: Reclam, 1965.

– *The Poems of Baron Haller*, trans. Mrs Howorth. London: J. Bell, 1794.

Holland, Jocelyn. *German Romanticism and Science: The Procreative Poetics of Goethe, Novalis, and Ritter*. New York: Routledge, 2009.

Kelley, Theresa M. *Clandestine Marriage: Botany and Romantic Culture*. Baltimore: Johns Hopkins UP, 2012.

Martin, Alison E. "Natural Effusions: Mrs. J. Howorth's English translation of Albrecht von Haller's *Die Alpen*." *Translation Studies* 5.1 (2012): 17–32.

Packham, Catherine. *Eighteenth-Century Vitalism: Bodies, Culture, Politics*. Houndmills, Basingstoke: Palgrave Macmillan, 2012.

Pope, Alexander. "The Rape of the Lock." In *Selected Poetry and Prose*. 2nd ed. New York: Holt, Rinehart & Winston, 1972.

Porter, Dahlia. "Scientific Analogy and Literary Taxonomy in Darwin's *Loves of the Plants*." *European Romantic Review* 18.2 (2007): 213–21.

Primer, Irwin. "Erasmus Darwin's Temple of Nature: Progress, Evolution, and the Eleusinian Mysteries." *Journal of the History of Ideas* 25.1 (1964): 58–76.

Schaumann, Caroline. "From Meadows to Mountaintops: Albrecht von Haller's 'Die Alpen.'" In *Heights of Reflection: Mountains in the German Imagination from the Middle Ages to the Twenty-First Century*. Ed. Sean Ireton and Caroline Schaumann. Rochester: Camden House, 2012. 57–76.

Seward, Anna. *Memoirs of the Life of Dr. Darwin*. London: J. Johnson, 1804.

Shteir, Ann B. "Albrecht von Haller's Botany and 'Die Alpen.'" *Eighteenth-Century Studies* 10.2 (1976/7): 169–84.

– *Cultivating Women, Cultivating Science: Flora's Daughters and Botany in England 1760 to 1860*. Baltimore: Johns Hopkins UP, 1996.

– "*Flora primavera* or *Flora meretrix*? Iconography, Gender, and Science." In *Studies in Eighteenth-Century Science*, vol. 36. Baltimore: Johns Hopkins UP, 2007. 147–68.

– "Sensitive, Bashful, and Chaste? Articulating the *Mimosa* in Science." In *Science in the Marketplace: Nineteenth-Century Sites and Experiences*. Ed. Aileen Fyfe and Bernard Lightman. Chicago: U of Chicago P, 2007. 169–95.

Stearn, William T. "Linnaean Classification, Nomenclature, and Method." In *The Compleat Naturalist: A Life of Linnaeus*. Ed. Wilfrid Blunt. London: Collins, 1971. 242–9.

Teute, Frederika J. "The Loves of the Plants: or, the Cross-Fertilization of Science and Desire at the End of the Eighteenth Century." *Huntington Library Quarterly* 63.3 (2000): 319–45.

Uglow, Jenny. *The Lunar Men: Five Friends Whose Curiosity Changed the World*. New York: Farrar, Straus and Giroux, 2002.

4 Elective Affinities / *Wahlverwandtschaften*: The Career of a Metaphor

CHRISTIAN P. WEBER

The relationship between poetry and science seems intuitively clear. They appear to be distinct from each other through mutual exclusion. Whereas poetic fiction expresses subjective ideas by imaginatively combining images and words and realizing them through the creation of mythical or literary worlds, scientific investigation – at least according to its common modern understanding – aims for the objective representation of knowledge by rigorously excluding anything that can be associated with fiction.[1] Whereas poets virtually transcend in imaginary flights the "real" world and thus the material basis of science, scientists arrive at facts as the result of strictly controlling their imagination, reducing nature to a specifically defined subject matter, and comparing the data of measurements. Yet, the presumption of this mutual exclusion is challenged by problems of distinction within each domain: How can scientists set aside subjective impulses? What determines the subject matter of a scientific investigation? What counts essentially as "matter" and what should be labelled just as evidence or inference? On what "objective" basis can these decisions and distinctions be made? And vice versa: poetic fiction requires and relies on commonly shared factual knowledge about the world in order to be able to articulate meaning and facilitate understanding. How else could a poetical, genuinely imaginary world come into existence if not by drawing its material from the "real," which is, to a certain degree, a scientifically structured world? Eventually, poetry needs to manifest its alternative ideas by leaving a material trace and having a "real" impact on peoples' lives. These probing questions defy the clear-cut distinction between "facts" and "fiction" so that, ultimately, the heuristic status of these concepts themselves oscillates between fact and fiction. Once this distinction has been blurred, fiction turns into fact and fact (re)turns into(as) fiction.

In light of this problem of definition, the following essay argues that the transmutability or translatability between scientific fact and poetic fiction is actually not only possible or unavoidable, but even desired for the progress of both (seemingly mutually exclusive) human activities. On the one hand, poetry can find inspiration in new scientific discoveries for the invention of innovative metaphors and visions of alternative (utopian) worlds. On the other hand, the strict focus of science on factual analysis encounters at some point limits of insight and overview over all facts and relations. At this point, science often reverts to poetic ideas and figurative language in order to breach new avenues of research and eventually to reach a more comprehensive, higher theoretical level of understanding. In fact, as Evelyn Fox Keller has recently argued, language, and more specifically figurative language, is the common denominator and mediator through which the opposite trajectories of science and poetry are interconnected and interact:

> Scientific research is typically directed at the elucidation of entities and processes about which no clear understanding exists, and to proceed, scientists must find ways of talking about what they do not know – about that which they as yet have only glimpses, guesses, speculations. To make sense of their day-to-day efforts, they need to invent words, expressions, forms of speech that can indicate or point to phenomena for which they have no literal descriptors … Making sense of what is not yet known is thus necessarily an ongoing and provisional activity, a groping in the dark; and for this, the imprecision and flexibility of figurative language is indispensable. (Fox Keller, *Making Sense of Life* 118)

Fox Keller's statement responds to the mysterious processes of genetic evolution as well as the phenomenal and thus conceptual instability of the term "gene." Yet her astute observation is hardly new, and neither are the described methodic problems that challenge modern biogenetic research. In fact, the situation is very reminiscent of the beginnings of modern chemistry, when Lavoisier redefined the term "element" to bring order into the otherwise confusing mixes and matches of chemical substances. Yet even this great French chemist, the embodiment of a rational and rationalist modern scientist, continued to operate with the anthropomorphic and alchemistic metaphor "elective affinities" to characterize – rather than just describe – the mysterious "motivation" of chemical reactions.

As this chapter will show, "elective affinity" has been an attractive metaphor for many other scientific discourses as well, especially at the turn from the eighteenth to the nineteenth century, and it continues to be so even today. The following case study traces the career of this metaphor as it transgresses the divide between matter and idea (spirit), fact and fiction, science and poetry. For each discourse that resorts to this metaphor, it aims to describe the gains (in insight) or losses (of sight) by using it. Or, to approach this matter from the opposite direction in recognition of the intrinsic power that Hans Blumenberg ascribed to metaphors, the chapter aims to figure out what sort of lifestyle – understood as the will and desire to (trans)form life in a certain fundamental manner – this particular metaphor has empowered and how it has changed the world.[2] The metaphor of "elective affinities" is particularly interesting for the study of these questions because it circulated in almost every discourse around the time of the French Revolution and because there is a pre-eminent literary work that emerged as a critical response to the pressing task of reflecting the aforementioned issues in light of the great transformations that this world-historic event has brought about. As I argue in the following, Goethe created his novel *Die Wahlverwandtschaften*,[3] published in 1809, (literally) as a poetical experiment to systematically explore the fundamental relations that its title metaphor has entertained by shaping various scientific discourses and even inspiring new socio-political programs and cultural life forms. However, I pursue here a different strategy than delivering a plain interpretation of the (supposedly) scientific content of this literary work, bearing in mind Helmut Müller-Sievers's warning:

> Literary texts do not contain scientific theorems as their subject matter, and science is not in need of the support of literary ornamentation ... Unless the analysis can show how science informs the literary text, unless it raises science from the unfathomable depth of the content to the surface of writing, unless the writing of science crosses over into the science of writing, the relationship between literature and science will always remain anecdotal at best. (*Self-Generation* 9–10)

This statement serves as a methodological guideline of my undertaking. My first and primary concern of analysis regards scientific, supposedly non-fictional texts that employ the metaphor of "elective affinities." Only after the specific meaning or significance of "elective affinities" has been established for each particular discourse, such as geology, chemistry, biology, and the social sciences, will I turn to Goethe's novel in order to see how – if at all – these uses or abuses of the metaphor to produce scientific "facts" influence the world view and belief of the fictive characters that then transform the poetic, pseudo-real world they inhabit. By separating as much as possible the utilization of the metaphor in the scientific discourses – or more specifically the associations and relations that were established as a result of that – from the poetic renegotiation of them by the novel, the essentially critical (and in that sense also "scientific") capacity of literature comes to light. *Die Wahlverwandtschaften* appears then as a meta-discourse that translates the "scientific" workings of its title metaphor into literary action. In the virtual reality of the novel, the characters embody and literarily "act out" the effects and consequences that the utilization of "elective affinities" has shown in various discourses. Ultimately, I argue, the poetic imagination not only invigorates scientific investigation by creating metaphors when the senses or instruments of observation have reached their limits, but also provides the means by constructing a literary simulacrum to test and critically assess the transformative power the same metaphors potentially can or actually do exercise in the real lifeworld.[4]

"Just *one* nature": Goethe's Poetics of the Simile

Before inquiring into the poetics of the various scientific discourses that employ the metaphor of "elective affinities," a short excursion into what may be called the metaphysics of Goethe's poetics helps one to understand the issue in a wider context. The author addressed the complex of metaphoric transference and substitution when he announced the publication of his new novel *Die Wahlverwandtschaften*, apparently as part of a strategy to not only explain but also reinforce the overall strategy of this literary project:

> It seems that the author has been inspired to choose this strange title by his continued scientific studies. He may have realized that in natural sciences one very often employs ethical analogies/similes [*ethische Gleichnisse*] to bring closer phenomena that are quite remote from the circle of human knowledge; and so, presumably, he also wanted, in a moral case, to trace back a chemical figure of speech [*chemische Gleichnisrede*] to its spiritual origin, all the more so since there is just *one* nature, and also since the realm of serene reason and freedom is unavoidably marked by the traces of opaque, passionate necessity. These may only be completely erased by a higher hand, and then probably not in this life. (Goethe, "Notiz" in Cotta's *Morgenblatt für gebildete Stände*, FA 1.8: 974)[5]

Goethe plays here a self-ironic game with the author role, and further plays a trick on the reader. If this piece had ever been intended as advertisement, it must have strangely missed its purpose. Its pretentious speculation creates the illusion of a meta-author who reads the author's mind, which is rather off-putting to a reader who is left clueless about the plot of this much-anticipated novel. The position assumed here mimics the ironic position of the narrator in the novel, so that the announcement can be understood as an ironically read statement of an altogether ironic novel, thus highlighting the irony and virtual reality of the whole project. Interestingly, Goethe associates this narrative strategy with the novel's "strange title," which he is most concerned to justify and clarify. Yet, he does not simply explain the origin, meaning, or significance of the crucial metaphor; he rather enacts its effects. In most condensed and stylized form, the text is composed as an intricate play of subtle figurative correlations and attractions that virtually connect concepts that are semantically far apart so that opposite meanings almost seem to belong to one and the same phenomenal complex – although their relation remains, of course, only a virtual one due to the effect of rhetorical "elective affinities." The whole text is held together by a dialectics of expanding versus retracting and displacing versus longing ("fortgesetzt," "weit Entferntes näher heranzubringen," "zu ihrem geistigen Ursprung zurückführen mögen"); the distance between 'the close" and "the far" is bridged by analogical structures such as parallelism (e.g., "nur eine Natur" – "nur durch eine höhere Hand"), opposition (e.g., "heiter[e] Vernunft-Freiheit" versus "trübe, leidenschaftliche Notwendigkeit"), and chiasm ("Naturlehre" – "ethische Gleichnisse" vis-à-vis "sittliche[r] Fall" – "chemische Gleichnisrede"). The rhetorical relations among the textual components thus simulate the immanent workings of elective affinities and yet their exposed artistry also reveals and hints at their making by a hidden, transcendent author. (To that effect, Goethe did not identify himself as the drafter of this announcement.)

Ultimately, however, all of this play serves just the purpose of illustrating the main idea of this text as well as of the novel and Goethe's holistic *Weltanschauung*, namely, that there is "just *one* nature" which springs from a "spiritual origin." For Goethe, the origins of nature and ingenious culture are essentially identical.[6] Since the "spiritual origin" of the physical world – of which the light of the sun is seen as the purest emanation – remains scientifically inaccessible, humans resort to their own minds and explore the origin of their spirituality and creativity. In two consecutive letters to his friend Knebel, who was working on a translation of Lucretius's *De rerum natura* at the time, Goethe characterizes the imagination as a faculty that even trumps natural light in its capability to illuminate the physical world:

> Lucretius's high rank as one of the most distinguished poets of all times is the result of his highly productive skill of sensory perception, which makes him capable of vigorous representations, and further of his lively imagination, which allows him to track the perceived objects even beyond the reach of the senses down to the imperceptible depths of nature and most secretive recesses. (14 February 1821, HA *Briefe* 3: 499)

In the following letter, Goethe distinguishes three types of imagination: the first he names "reproductive" (*nachbildend*), which coordinates the various sensory faculties in the effort of mimetic representation. Provided that this happens without the involvement of the mind, one may also call it the intuitive imagination. It produces pure images that are "true" in the sense of verisimilitude. This ideal of "objective" representation of natural things also serves as a fundamental criterion to determine scientific truth. The other essential quality that Goethe assigns to the great poet of nature is associated with the second type of imagination that he calls "productive" (*productiv*). Reaching beyond the senses, the productive imagination also engages the mind and creates concepts. (A concept is whole yet abstract, whereas an image is concrete yet only represents an aspect of the thing.) Only in the sphere of symbolic signification and conceptual understanding does the imagination surpass the level of purely "objective" perception and reach an "idea" of truth beyond verisimilitude that is either informed by the categorical logic of the mind as well as the fundamental maxims of reason (philosophical truth) or by the analogical procedure of the imagination (poetical truth).[7] However, when the productive imagination seeks analogies just within the symbolic sphere of language or with relation to cultural phenomena, it acts outside of its genuine field of competence where it is at the risk of establishing artificial relations and forging metaphors without "real" substance. (Such kind of "truth" is not poetic, but merely rhetorical, especially when it fulfils an ideological purpose.) Hence, to "really" create poetic truth and true poetry, a mediating third type of imagination must come into play that reconnects and constantly renegotiates the abstract symbolic meaning of words with the more concrete images of natural things:

> Moreover we can assume the existence of a circumspective [*umsichtige*] imagination, which surveys and takes hold of the same and the like during speech in order to test the validity of what has been said.

> Here now appears the desirability of analogy [*Analogie*], which places [*versetzt*] the spirit [*Geist*] onto many related points of interest so that it can reunite everything that belongs and harmonizes together [*alles das Zusammengehörige, das Zusammenstimmende wieder vereinige*].
>
> This immediately generates similes/allegories [*Gleichnisse*], which are more valuable the closer they come to match the object that they were supposed to illuminate. The most valuable, however, are those that cover the object completely and seem to become identical with it. (21 February 1821, HA *Briefe* 3: 501)

In the simile a long series of substitutions and displacements culminates that, to a certain degree, are unavoidable in the human effort to form knowledge and cultivate the world: images substitute things,[8] concepts substitute and displace images, and tropes substitute and displace concepts by a figurative recombination of the relationships between images and concepts. The simile must be considered – as it has been since ancient time[9] – a special type of metaphor. For Goethe, it retains special cultural importance as the product of the circumspective imagination, which he regards highest, since it combines both reproductive (the observance of images) and productive (the making of concepts) faculties in the act of forming a valid speech or *rapport* ("Vortrag"). Different from the rather spontaneous fusion of image and concept in the metaphor, the simile is more reflective. In creating it, the poetic "spirit" reverts to sense perception (and the making of images) in an effort to review linguistic concepts and metaphoric tropes. By determining their relationship to natural things, the analogical poetics of the simile reassesses the imagination's substitutions and displacements and performs a critique of the human language. As such, the simile also fulfils a scientific (empirical, analytic) and philosophical (critical, yet synthetic) purpose.[10] At the same time, the imagination has accomplished its genuine poetic task by establishing a symbolic harmony between concepts and images that mirrors the "original" intuitive harmony between images and things. With the creation of a truly "objective" simile, the imagination has returned to the exploratory spirit of its reproductive origin. By accomplishing an analogical identity of all its cognitive modes of representation (image, concept, and trope) in the simile, it collapses the differences and distinctions among them into *one* poetic totality and thereby completes one cycle of its formation.[11] The simile thus brings a (temporary) end and relief to the "daemonic" process of fragmenting and dividing the world in images, concepts, and metaphors. By creating one "apocalyptic" poetic vision, it reveals in a momentous epiphany that "there is just *one* nature."

In the sense described above, the famous "Gleichnisrede" (figurative speech) of the Wahlverwandten (elective relatives) certainly is no *Gleichnis*, or simile, whereas the novel as a whole is. Exemplary for their fundamental misunderstanding of the true character of the simile is Eduard's conclusion of the playful conversation, which revolved around various possibilities of how the metaphor of "elective affinities" may be applied to their situation: "Eduard interjected [*fiel ein*]: Now then! Until we will see all this before our eyes, we shall regard this formula as a parable [*Gleichnisrede*], which shall serve us as a teaching to our immediate benefit" (1.4; 118).[12] Everything that matters in the creation process of a true poetic simile is here turned inside out: the reflexivity of speech is perverted by the suddenness of Eduard's idea to declare a simile; sensory perception is replaced by speculative anticipation; the natural object of analogical comparison is here merely an abstract formula; finally, Eduard remains blind for the intrinsic poetic "value" of the simile, its esoteric vision of oneness; instead, he simply wants to utilize this "teaching" as a sort of legitimation to promote his immediate interests and practical human affairs, which bring about only further substitutions, displacements, and divisions.

Eduard's confused character disqualifies him from ever gaining an understanding of the simile, not to mention an appreciation for its poetic vision. His "daemonic" imagination is only productive, constantly creating hollow metaphors without a foundation in the "real." (To the contrary, his wife Charlotte's imagination is primarily reproductive and driven by the compulsion to make up for lost opportunities in the past.) The only character in the novel that appears to be capable of creating true similes is the old gardener, who is introduced already in the first chapter as the positive antagonist to Eduard. Whereas we first encounter the "rich baron" preoccupied with the "business" of inoculating grafts onto "young rootstocks" (1.1; 93), which serves as a symbol for his appropriating and greedy character, the gardener contains himself as a sympathetic observer of this scene.[13] Other than his selfish master, who perceives things only with pleasure as long as he has invested an interest in them, he appears to be capable of just enjoying the uninterested panning of his view "in a serene distance" (ibid.).[14] Such an attitude is the precondition for the creation of a poetic simile (an extraordinary example of which is represented in the next section). The gardener also serves as a mirroring figure of the narrator, whose omnipresence is immediately felt. He introduces himself as a tertiary meta-observer, as one who observes how the gardener observes Eduard observing. The overall task of his circumspective imagination is to fully comprehend and observe the consequences of some dubious actions and transactions by the novel's protagonists. Ultimately, the narrator describes the eventually tragic logic of displacements that has been set in motion by the misunderstanding and dubious application of the metaphor of "elective affinities," as was demonstrated by the "figurative speech" in paragraph 1.4. Later on in the novel (in paragraph 2.9), it is revealed that the conservative gardener judges Eduard's excessive grafting and the production of entirely ornamental plants as highly dubious.

Grafting means in this context not simply a horticultural practice, but represents a specific biological type of "elective affinities." The next sections discuss how this metaphor is used by various, predominantly scientific, discourses. At the same time, it symbolizes the very structure (or "nature") of the metaphor as such. If the narrator of *Die Wahlverwandtschaften* – respectively the author, whose insightful comments constitute another level of (self-)critical observation that I consider an essential part of this whole poetic enterprise – intended, as I argue, the creation of a modern meta-simile about this metaphor, his vision must comprehend and contain its wide range of uses, consequences, meanings, and overall cultural significance. The task of interpretation is then to trace back the analogical (metaphoric) relations between scientific discourses and poetry that bridge nature and human culture and to reconstruct how Goethe reconciles the tensions of this uneasy relationship in the simile, that is, the novel.

First Discourse: Geology

Goethe renders a superb poetic example of his theory of the simile in his equally scientific fragments on granite.[15] Although this group of texts does not employ the metaphor "elective affinity" directly, it provides a speculative, geological explanation for the origin of affinities in the material world, or rather, to be more precise, for the attraction of geological and especially chemical discourses to the genealogical concept of "affinity" (translated as *Verwandtschaft*).

The first fragment (subtitled *Granit I*) describes granite as a rock that exhibits the widest range of both spatial/vertical and temporal dimensions. Goethe imagines that, in primordial times, it was the "deepest" layer hidden in the earth, whereas it appears to be now the highest and most exposed layer of all geological formations. Goethe's curiosity is further sparked by the observation that granite is a composite of at least two different particles. Intriguingly, they seem to be "not joined together by something third, but to coexist side by side and to adhere just to themselves" (FA 1.25; 311). Although this natural phenomenon certainly invites speculation, Goethe adheres in the closing remark of this piece to his rock-solid and steadfast scientific principle of objective reasoning:[16] "My spirit has no wings to uplift itself to those primordial beginnings. I stand firmly on the granite and inquire the rock whether it would give us any reason to reflect about the consistency of the mass that made it" (FA 1.25: 312). The subsequent fragment (*Granit II*), however, contradicts this judgment by rendering one of the most ecstatic moments of poetic-scientific inspirations. Goethe first recalls that granite was considered even in the "most ancient times" to be a very "mysterious [*merkwürdige*] type of rock" and that its "monstrous [*ungeheuren*] masses were an inspiration for the Egyptians with their ideas of monstrous [*ungeheuren*] buildings" (FA 1.25: 312). After this historical reflection, he recollects the scientific knowledge of his time, which amounts to the "fact" that granite is both "the highest and lowest" layer of rock and therefore the "foundation of our earth" (FA 1.25: 313).[17] Feeling the insufficiency of this knowledge and the "passion" to explore the deeply hidden secrets of the earth, he introduces a metaphysical premise that opens a new avenue to poetic-scientific exploration. Similarly to his announcement of the *Wahlverwandtschaften* above, Goethe states that "all natural things entertain an exact relationship with each other," which implies that even the "human heart" as the most recent, fickle, and sensitive product and granite as "the oldest, hardest, deepest, and firmest son of nature" are interconnected and that one may be accessed by means of the other (FA 1.25: 313–14). Next, Goethe performs (and renders) a poetic soliloquy of his heart that turns into an act of "telepathic" communication, a pseudo-scientific, investigative dialogue with the earth. While sitting on a rock of granite on top of a mountain, he simultaneously summons the feelings in the depth of his soul as well as the whole world below and the sky above him. (He thus inhabits and displays a daemonic position.) Goethe takes great care in his description to emphasize the constant interplay of the introspective voice ("I say to myself") with the circumspective vision ("I survey the world"). At the climax of this experience, the inner and outer spheres coalesce and generate a complex simile at the moment of greatest enthusiasm:

> In this moment, when the inner powers of the Earth seem to affect me directly with all their forces of attraction and movement, and when the influences of heaven hover closer around me, I am uplifted in spirit to a more exalted view of nature. The human spirit brings life to everything and here, too, there springs to life within me an image irresistible in its sublimity. "This mood of solitude," I say to myself as I gaze down from the barren peak and glimpse a faint patch of low-growing moss far below, "this mood of solitude will

> overcome all who desire to bring before their souls only the deepest, oldest, most elemental feeling for the truth … I feel the first and most abiding origin of our existence; I survey the world with its undulating valleys and its distant fruitful meadows, my soul is exalted beyond itself and above all of the world, and it yearns for the heavens which are so near." (FA 1.25: 314–15)[18]

Goethe feels to have almost (*gleichsam*) an intimate relation with the rock, which inspires him to elaborate a complex "simile" (*Gleichnis*): First, he comes to see the likeness between the vivifying "human spirit" with the earth's "forces of attraction and movement." Second, he associates his daemonic mood – oscillating between a "highly tuned" (*hochgestimmte*) ecstasy and a most sober determination to explore "the deepest feelings of truth" – with the sublime moment of the "being of all beings" immediately after the act of Creation. The resulting sublime simile is simultaneously a product of all his senses, of his emotion and imagination. It thereby defies the surface of the rock and the presence of time; it accesses, conveys, and symbolically embodies the deepest and oldest secret of nature, which is the act of creating as such (see again the letter to Jacobi quoted above), especially the creating of similes. The final verses of *Faust* sum up Goethe's sublime experience in the act of creating the simile, which represent perhaps his deepest insight: "Alles Vergängliche / Ist nur ein Gleichnis" (All that is transient / Is but a simile/parable.)

This highly *subjective* and yet, at the same time, most *objective* vision informed Goethe's ideas about geological formation as well as about chemical composition. In the subsequent fragment (*Form und Bildung des Granits*), Goethe proposes the hypothesis that all matter was originally "united" in the "intimate solution" of "first chaos" (FA 1.25: 317–18). Natural history means to him a still ongoing decomposition and crystallization process that was set in motion once the primordial union of matter had been disturbed. Ever since, everything has been in flux, and Goethe seems to suggest that the constant decomposition and (re-)composition of bodies entertain "elective affinities" because all matter and all material life forms on earth are intrinsically driven by the quest to restore this previous harmony.[19] Granite is a remnant of earth's prehistory, and its indestructible composition strikes Goethe as a visible reminder of this original and intimate belonging that has been lost for all the rest. "Elective affinity" means for him essentially the expression of an essential (or even existential) longing and yearning in all material "elements" (FA 1.25: 318) that were once violently disassociated and forced to recombine in less harmonious compounds during the natural history of the earth.

I would suggest that this reasoning constitutes the foundation of the "radical idea" which Goethe reported to have followed in the composition of his *Wahlverwandtschaften*.[20] Goethe mentioned in another letter that he conceived the novel in the "Bohemian mountains" during the poetically chaotic period of the Napoleonic Wars, in which he devoted a lot of time to geological studies (Goethe to Zelter, 1 June 1809, FA 1.8: 979). This coincidence is certainly no accident. One central theme of the novel is marriage, and the primordial association of two different "elements" in granite could be considered the perfect symbol for this most intimate union between two human beings. The same analogy is actually alluded to by the most militant defender of marriage in the novel, the ominous Mittler, when he says: "Marriage is both the base [*Anfang*] and the pinnacle [*Gipfel*] of culture" (1.9: 137). Marriage thus occupies in human culture the same place as granite in nature. However, Eduard's and Charlotte's marriage proves to be anything but granite-solid. They are, as also the novella within this novel insinuates, not quite a natural match for each other; the intrinsic forces of "elective affinities" have a pull on them and continue to impact their association as well as their relationships to others. Mittler's desperate attempts to keep the couple together must remain futile since he acts, in fact, counter to the marriage symbol of granite, according to which the two elements would stick together no matter what without the need of a third, mediating person. What the couple needs are not the orthodox moral principles of a retired priest like Mittler, who does not even understand the basics of geology, but the recognition that the fundamental natural laws of creation, the interplay of attraction and repulsion, continue to have an effect even in human affairs. For that, some knowledge of chemistry may be a good start.

Second Discourse: Chemistry

The revolutionary age of chemistry, coinciding with the political revolution of France, can be easily integrated as a particularly radical episode in Goethe's idea of natural history as an ongoing process of de- and recomposition and de- and regeneration. In the historical part of the *Farbenlehre*, Goethe characterizes the emerging new discipline of chemistry accordingly:

> More recently, chemistry brought about a major transformation; it dissected natural bodies in order to artificially reassemble them in manifold ways; it destroyed a real world to construct in its stead a so far unknown,

> unimaginable new world. As a consequence, we were forced to reflect harder and harder about the likely origin of all things and everything that followed from it so that we have found ourselves confronted again and again with new and increasingly higher types of ideas [*Vorstellungsarten*]. This is even more the case since the chemist and the natural scientist have made an inseparable pact to establish among things, which previously appeared to be units, at least manifold relations – if not to decompose them completely otherwise – and thus to gain from them an admirable versatility [*bewundernswürdige Vielseitigkeit*]. (FA 1.23/1: 660–1)

The new age of chemistry does not only immensely increase the decomposition process, but, more crucially, radically alters the constitution of nature by forcefully breaking apart the natural substances of the "real world" and by recombining the fragments into artificial and fantastic composites. As Goethe points out, the unheard of possibilities of chemical syntheses are followed up by the invention of equally creative ideas and theories which also destroy the integrity of the spirit and intellect. Though he personally does not favour this modern development, Goethe accepts it as a historical fact and embraces its "admirable versatility." But he remains aware that this new scientific discipline also increases the potential of further displacements and forced associations, which consequently produce new sufferings in an ever more complicated world.

Under these circumstances, "elective affinities" – originally an alchemist term – becomes an attractive metaphor for the chemical discourse as a regulative idea. As Goethe points out, it provides the idea (and ideal) of primordial unity and thus constrains the imagination of chemists who may otherwise have fancied hypothetically unlimited new combinations. Accordingly, Torbern Bergman, whom Goethe[21] praises for the introduction of this metaphor into the chemical discourse, stresses in his *Dissertation on Elective Attractions* "the tendency to union which is observed in all neighboring bodies on the surface of the earth" (2).[22] Arguably, Bergman's great use of this metaphor assigns to chemistry its specific scientific domain by distinguishing between the chemical forces of "affinity" and the astrophysical forces of "attraction." Affinity, he writes, "only affects small particles, and scarce[ly] reaches beyond contact, whereas remote attraction extends to the great masses of matter in the immensity of space, [which] seems to be regulated by *very different laws*" (2). Even though Bergman is aware that the laws of affinity "may perhaps depend on circumstances," he maintains that a "fixed order" must exist and that the knowledge of the laws of "elective affinity" would provide the "key to unlock the innermost sanctuaries of nature" upon which "the whole of chemistry rests" (9). Hence, the metaphor of "elective affinity" encapsulates a metaphysical program of unity.

Bergman's scientific optimism regarding the possibility of taming and containing the versatile and transitory nature of chemical reactions, transformations, and circumstances is displayed in his famous affinity tables, which compile the results of his repeated observations and experiments in a very orderly manner. However, the ever-increasing dimensions of affinity tables and their failure to account for every condition and countless exceptions reintroduce the problem of how to deal with this sheer complexity. In response to these concerns, Claude Louis Berthollet has arguably reached the highest level of scientific accuracy and methodological reflection in his *Recherches sur les lois de l'affinité*,[23] published in 1801, by introducing many refinements to the guiding metaphorical principle. Among the many innovations proposed, the most relevant one is a redefinition of the term "elective affinity," which Berthollet strictly limits to displacement reactions with three agents. For him, displacement reactions of the "elective" type are not about a choice of alternatives, but rather a matter of affinity in proportion to quantity: "The very term, *elective affinity* must lead into error, as it supposes the union of the whole of one substance with another, in preference to a third; whereas there is only a partition of action, which is itself subordinate to other chemical circumstances" (146). In other words, many examples of elective affinity cannot be considered as completed and uniform displacements of absolute bodies. Instead, they often showcase partitions of bodies and actions that are not only determined by the quality of substances but also by the quantity of their "respective [chemical] masses" (6).[24] If, qua analogy, this scientific disintegration of bodies and actions is carried over to humans and their behaviour – which transfer the *Wahlverwandtschaften* seem to perform by respective actions of the "wahlverwandten" protagonists, as I will discuss later – then it is an assault on modern anthropological concepts such as free will and individuality.

Overall, Berthollet's contributions to chemistry and to epistemology are significant because they highlight the complexity and intricacy of nature. In agreement with Goethe, Berthollet recognizes the invalidity of Newton's ideal of an *experimentum crucis* as well as the insufficiency of conducting research within the confines of scientific disciplines. Only the totality of sciences constitutes for him "la physique," which brings back to mind Goethe's statement about the *Wahlverwandtschaften*, according to which there is only one nature ("nur eine Natur").

Third Discourse: Biology and Physiology

The red thread that interconnects the manifestations of both inorganic and organic nature is the metaphor of "elective affinity." By the 1790s, after it had been employed by Lavoisier in his groundbreaking *Traité élémentaire de chimie*, this metaphor was commonly accepted as a scientific concept and so well established that it spread to other discourses, including the simultaneously emerging discipline of biology. Alexander von Humboldt, for example, uses elective affinity to distinguish the principle of organic formation from the laws of inorganic association: "We call those bodies animated and organic that, though they tend constantly to change into new forms, are contained by some internal force, so that they do not relinquish that form originally introduced ... That internal force (*vim internam*) which dissolves the bonds of chemical affinity and prevents the elements of bodies from freely uniting, we call vital" (Humboldt, *Florae Fribergensis specimen* 133–5; qtd. in Richards, *Romantic Conception of Life* 257). By contrast, the physician and physiologist Johann Christian Reil[25] considers Humboldt's idea of an internal force, which he prefers to call "life force" (*Lebenskraft*), not an objective quality but a subjective concept, a hypothetical metaphor that helps conceive and represent otherwise inconceivable relations and reactions. Inspired by French modern chemistry, he aims to substitute this rather mystically sounding concept with a full-fledged theory of elective affinity.[26] Reil traces back the origin of organic life to elementary matter, which he defines in accordance with Lavoisier's famous conceptualization of "elements" as substances "which we are not able to reduce further by decomposition" (Reil, *Von der Lebenskraft* 6).[27] However, he emphasizes more than Lavoisier that all "elements have one unique and essential quality in common, which is elective affinity [*Wahlanziehung*]" (6). And he believes that elective affinities also determine organic matter, since it consists to the greatest extent of inorganic matter. Living matter then only differs from dead matter in an additional, distinctly organic "basic material" (*Grundstoff*) that has certain features of "composition [*Mischung*] and form [*Form*]," which themselves are the resulting manifestations of particular laws of elective affinity between inorganic substances and the specific basic material:

> Per se, organic matter is peculiar to the organic realm and not to be found anywhere in dead nature. And yet, the origin of organic material is securely stored in the womb of dead nature. One must only find the core or stock of

> an organic being [*Wesen*] to which raw materials can attach themselves and they will be organized in a purposeful order. Plants are begotten out of the materials of dead nature and constitute, so to speak, the first level of ennobling matter [*Veredelung der Materie*] into organic beings. (11)

This passage serves as a great example for the desire of natural philosophers and scientists of the eighteenth century to imagine and construct a metaphoric bridge to cross the divisions between species and different forms of organized matter, perhaps even to find an access to the primordial union of all nature that also Goethe envisioned. For Reil, everything that consists of matter is basically identical, except that organic matter displays an organizing skill. He assumes that the organic core material or "stock" consists of very "fine, perhaps entirely unknown matter" which transforms and refines the crude matter by intermingling with it (13–14).[28] Curiously, he characterizes the general form of this relationship metaphorically in terms of grafting, which he applies to growth – the inoculation of "foreign matter" (nutrients) onto the organic life-stock – and to plant cultivation: "We are able to engraft a tree with scions of different kind; each scion is its own stock that attracts the common matter, which it draws from the tree according to the laws of its own affinity [*Verwandtschaft*] and by which it increases in mass from its own kind" (42–3). Hence, grafting is the basic modus operandi, the elective affinities of organic life forms, which is also why it is so prominently featured in the opening sentence of the *Wahlverwandtschaften*. (The symbolic meaning of "grafting" is discussed in the next section.)

According to Reil, variants of elective affinity also occur on the level of the human organism, which he subsumes under the heading of "sympathy (consensus)." He mentions that "similarities of the constitution and composition of organs can cause the generation of sympathetic phenomena" that even affect remote organs: "Similar organs like nerves or blood vessels have similar affections and similar affinities [*Verwandtschaften*] to the fine matter" (62–3). Moreover, sympathetic effects can result "from the habit and association of our motions [*Bewegungen*] and representations [*Vorstellungen*]" (63). More refined human organs like the eyes and the brain are especially palpable; they develop their faculties (e.g., vision, understanding) by adapting to the widest range of "matter," which they process as information: "Almost every new idea, every new concept changes the system of their faculties [*Kräfte*], intermingles with [*mischt sich*] their operations and increases the potential [*Kraft*] of new products in the future" (69). Thus, Reil even conceives the formation of cognition and cultural forms essentially as manifestations of elective affinities.

At the same time, this metaphor loses its original elementary pull the more it is associated with intellectual and spiritual (moral) faculties. Eventually, these higher faculties transgress and challenge the predetermined order of the physical world by creating a symbolic order of signs that produces desires beyond immediate necessity and stimulates ideas of free will and autonomy. Human behaviour very often runs counter to the (hypothetical) pre-established harmony of elective affinities. In Goethe's novel, the actions of the Wahlverwandten Eduard and Charlotte, the Hauptmann and Ottilie represent this basic conflict between the laws of nature and the (more or less) rational decisions and actions of human beings. Especially the egotistic decisions and actions of the first two institute a series of displacements which range from grafting exotic plants onto the native trees and soil of their grounds to the transplanting of the "delicate plant" Ottilie, who was in Charlotte's custodial care but is sent away to an institution of education against her own inclination. Altogether, the enforced actions of displacement[29] result in modern biographies of suffering (*Werther*'s theme) and in a romantic longing for love, friendship, and community that mirrors nature's yearning for a return to its primal state of unity. Human history is thus a part of the general decomposition process of natural history.

Fourth Discourse: National Ideology

To return once more to the discourse of physiology, Reil further suggests that organs, which once cooperated in a "community" (*Gemeinschaft*), have the inclination to form lasting associations (81). He explicitly likens the organic body to the body politic of a republican state, since both "consist of many parts that stand in a determinate relationship with one another and contribute to the maintenance of the whole; but each part does so through its own faculties and its own perfections, deficiencies, and afflictions independently from the other parts of the body" (59). The body metaphor has been often employed to illustrate the abstract idea or ideal of the republican state, for example, to name prominent examples of the eighteenth century, in Rousseau's *Social Contract* and Schiller's *Aesthetic Letters.* As part of a rhetorical strategy, it makes "visible that which could not be seen otherwise" (Koschorke et al., *Der fiktive Staat* 58), namely, the apparatus of the state as a whole. Still invisible, however, remain the principles and fundamental program that unite and coordinate all the people of one state by providing them with a distinct cultural and thus national identity.

I suggest that, complementary to the effect of the body metaphor of the state, biopolitical metaphors, such as "grafting" and "elective affinities," promote within diverse discourses an implicit programmatic idea of how life is organized in nature *and* how, in turn, society should be organized as a nation. They thereby define the national ideology that assigns only specific cultural content to fill the abstract political form of state government.[30] Concerning "grafting," I can present here only one example for how this metaphor has informed other discourses of national relevance, especially in England. In his *Reflections on the Revolution of France*, Edmund Burke reminds his British readers of the unique constitutional principle of their nation and warns them against the potential attraction they may feel towards the newly "fabricated" one across the Channel in France: "The very idea of the fabrication of a new government is enough to fill us with disgust and horror. We wished at the period of the Revolution [in 1688], and do now wish, to derive all we possess as *an inheritance from our forefathers*. Upon that body and stock of inheritance we have taken care not to inoculate any scion alien to the nature of the original plant" (27). For Burke, the natural "law of inheritance" must remain the sacrosanct basis of the state, and "grafting" its national principle. He believes that the British nation will not fall prey to the ills of modernity and another revolution as long as it sticks to its foundational principle of inheritance and the cultivation of blood-conscious grafting. At the same time, his insistence on grafting indicates that he acknowledges some need for continued national reform, but only within this clearly defined limit. What Burke so vehemently opposes is not so much the "new government" of France, but rather the new national idea that justifies its "fabrication," which is derived from another, at this time most popular, scientific metaphor: "elective affinities."[31]

It is hardly just a curious coincidence of history that the most prominent scientific work that made use of "elective affinities" was published right in the centre and at the climax of the Revolution: Antoine Lavoisier's *Traité élémentaire de chimie* appeared in Paris in 1789. This major accomplishment did not only revolutionize sciences by introducing a system of elements and thereby articulating the clearest and most radical version of the chemical life form. It also proposes a new scientific ethos that strives to exclude imagination, tradition, and prejudice from the laboratory and that accepts nothing but facts. As a consequence, Lavoisier breaks down the appearances of organic bodies and reduces their essences until they cannot possibly be decomposed further, which results in his famous definition of chemical elements (as mentioned earlier). That this scientific revolution is related to the political revolution has been noted by Friedrich Schlegel, who called the French in one of his famous *Athenaeum* fragments a "chemical nation," since in them "the chemical sense is excited more universally than in others. Even in moral chemistry they conduct their experiments always at a grand scale. Likewise, the age is a chemical age. Revolutions are universal movements, not organic but chemical" (87, no. 426).

But the analogy between chemistry and the French nation alludes not only to the melting and composition of masses during the revolutionary events, it also and perhaps even more convincingly informs about the more critical stage of instituting and constituting a new political order. After the most radical break from past traditions, values, and institutions, which destroyed the "organic" self-understanding and communities of many French people, the revolutionaries were pressured to restore order quickly. To justify the destruction of the old aristocratic "nation," the Revolution demanded in its stead the implementation of a radical, anti-organic conception of nature as an alternative ideal life form that unites the renewed French nation. Lavoisier's chemical model of life and his experimental, yet strictly rational, method provided much inspiration for the revolutionaries' desire to redefine humanity in terms of their slogan "Liberty, Equality, and Fraternity." The new chemistry's pursuit of decomposing organic units down to elements, which are from the standpoint of objective scientific observation equal, correlates with the attacks of the political revolution on venerable organicist traditions and socio-political hierarchies that were grounded in the notion of natural law. As a result of events of collective uprooting during the ancient regime, theoretically everybody is equal and free to form new associations. This coincides with another important claim of Lavoisier's theory. He acknowledges agency in chemical elements and recognizes their innate capability of forming associations freely, that is, without the interference of the experimenter: "They act with regard to us as simple substances, and we ought never to suppose them compounded until experiment and observation has proved them to be so" (4). In other words, the analytically truthful chemist must strictly observe the principal rights of chemical elements, namely, to regard them as equals that can associate freely and, as such, form "elective affinities." Since these are elementary rights, they should be considered universally. From here it is only a relatively small step – although it remains an enormous jump from elements to human beings, of course – to the declaration of universal human rights and to Rousseau's republican ideas that inspired the Revolution.

The advantages of the chemical model for the (re-)formation of the French nation are obvious: it promotes the principle of equality, which theoretically grants every human being the right to become a citizen and to have equal opportunities, and allows for very progressive and flexible political structures that can justify even radical transformations. However, there are certainly also risks and dangers attached to it: First, the transfer of materialist scientific principles to the socio-political sphere contradicts the genuinely intersubjective and often idealist nature of human interactions. Social and political decisions cannot be based exclusively on mere facts and rational factors, but are also driven by compassion and directed by distinctly humanistic ideals. A nation that considers its citizens merely as human "elements," without respect for individual biographies, familial ties, or cultural traditions, tends to approve the confiscation of private property and the displacement of people more readily than a nation that is governed by more organicist ideas. Second, chemical as well as social and political experiments have often unpredictable outcomes that may result in catastrophic explosions. To counterbalance these dangers, a "chemical" nation is susceptible to individuals who may usurp – as the embodiment of reason – the supervising position of the master chemist and thus incapacitate other people. The history of the French Revolution shows how easily Robespierre and Napoleon Bonaparte could turn the new Republic of France into a "laboratory" and determine the parameters for their social and political experiments.

Goethe wrote the *Wahlverwandtschaften* during the chaotic period of the Napoleonic Wars, which affected his own life and caused unease to his family and community.[32] The political and social ideas that the revolutionaries and Napoleon, their culminating master chemist, experimented with in the laboratory of the French nation are repeated and mirrored en miniature by Eduard's and Charlotte's efforts to live together in the seclusion of their estate. In their conversation about the arrival of the Hauptmann in the first chapter, they explicitly emphasize the experimental character of their chosen lifestyle. Charlotte remarks that "inviting the Captain does not quite fit in with our original intentions, plans, and arrangements" (1.1; 95), and she insists that they "try [*versuchen*] for a time at least to see how we can get along in this way with each other's company" (1.1; 96). This whole setting, which includes Eduard's efforts of grafting and Charlotte's endeavour to transform the natural landscape into a "new creation" (1.1; 93), displays a willingness to experiment with nature, with their own lives as well as with the lives of others, especially of the misplaced Hauptmann and displaced Ottilie. Their experimental lifestyles indicate the shifts and rifts that the Revolution has caused in the attitudes of common people. Essentially, the *Wahlverwandtschaften* simulate the chemical, social, and political experiments of this time in one literary meta-experiment to envision what good or bad results from these tendencies. Hence, the novel aims not only to represent but actually to (re)enact the conditions that brought about the Revolution and the consequences that it brought about.[33]

Elective Affinities, "Elective Affinities," and *Elective Affinities*

The novel is, of course, not just about the Revolution; more fundamentally it is about the consequences and effects – positive and negative, imaginary and real – of the title metaphor's inherent potential. Goethe was generally very sensitive about the application of metaphors in scientific discourses[34] and warned scientists to not confuse its artificial and to a certain degree arbitrary status with the real natural phenomenon. Yet the phenomenal scientific career of "elective affinities" must have awoken in Goethe a sense of urgency to excavate the intrinsic structure and psychological logic that make this particular metaphor so attractive and to reveal this dangerous mechanism to a wider audience in the more popular form of the novel.

For Goethe, the crux of all culture and the sciences in particular rests in the problematic, that is, metaphoric origin of the human language in general, as he expressed with great clarity and verve in a letter to Wilhelm von Humboldt from 22 August 1806. This letter arguably can be considered the founding document of the *Wahlverwandtschaften.*[35] The following crucial passage stands in the context of Goethe's review of Steffen's idealistic and speculative natural philosophy, which he mainly criticizes for its "strange language" (*seltsame Sprache*):

> It was certainly due to the nature of the problem that one had to penetrate the depth of nature with words which were based on signs from in-depth inquiries of other scientific and human endeavors. That way a symbolism came about, which I don't want to criticize, but which entails, however, something highly miraculous [*höchst Wunderliches*] and dangerous at the same time. The formulas of pure and applied mathematics, astronomy, cosmology, geology, physics, chemistry, natural history, ethics, religion and mysticism are all confused and mixed into the mass of a metaphysical [or metaphoric?][36] language which, though often used with good and great sense, will always appear barbaric ... In this very complex and highly artificial language [as in any language in general], very dire consequences result from the fact that one substitutes the symbolic proxy for the thing itself and that one internalizes the implied external relation, which loses by this replacement with figures of speech [*Gleichnisreden*] its representative quality [*Darstellung*]. For

> example, North and South, East and West, oxygen and hydrogen are already such phantoms of strange figures of speech [*wunderliche Topik*] that they exorcize the best of our intentions. (HA *Briefe* 4: 484–5)

In contrast to the constructive scientific-poetic simile that the circumspective imagination has created in the *Granit* fragment, Goethe warns in this passage against the potential catachrestic and eclectic use of metaphors and allegories in the sciences, since the confusion of any symbolic representation for the "real" thing may create "whimsical figures of speech" and consequently produce whimsical scientific results.[37] (As mentioned before, Goethe's poetics of the simile is meant to counteract this common phenomenon that we observed in the discussed scientific discourses.) An illustrative example for such misunderstanding and misappropriation is presented by the famous "figure of speech" (*Gleichnisrede*) in the *Wahlverwandtschaften*. Eduard, Charlotte, and the Hauptmann literally enact the negative dialectic of metaphorization and further promote it by naively transferring the metaphor of "elective affinities" to their human affairs in the hope of making sense of them that way.[38] Their conversation ends in the fatal decision to add Ottilie to the mix simply because she fits in the equation. It reinforces the dubious motivation of their decisions and actions, of which the protagonists themselves seem to be subconsciously aware: "What strange [*wunderliche*] people we are" (1.2; 100), Eduard exclaims at the beginning. And Charlotte wraps up the whole story in an equally curious statement close to the end: "If true things are said in strange [*wunderlich*] ways ..., in the end strange things [*das Wunderliche*] appear as true" (2.7; 208). These remarks show the protagonists' quest for orientation and certainty due to the crumbling of the aristocratic culture that experiences the decline of its political and economic status and the depreciation of its values and norms. How the nobility responds to this transformation is nicely reflected by one particular change of Eduard's habits. As the narrator reports, the baron had an inclination to entertain his evening societies with "his lively and expressive recitation of poetry and rhetorical pieces," but now "he read from other texts, and for some time had chosen by preference works on physics, chemistry and technology" (1.4; 111). In other words, Eduard searches and yearns for a new stable foundation on which he can rebuild his life. He seems to have found a new life form in the metaphor of "elective affinities," yet he does not realize that this is just a pseudo-scientific metaphor which itself rests on instable ground. To build a new life upon this idea just perpetuates and increases the contingency and insecurity of his existence, as the Wahlverwandten painfully experience. Their decision to complete the formula by sending for Ottilie releases the "natural" forces of elective affinities in the human imagination, which result in an erosion of common-sense reason and a general detachment from reality. This has fatal consequences especially for Eduard and Charlotte's "fantastically" conceived "Wunderkind" Otto, whose facial appearance shows a striking resemblance to both Ottilie and the Hauptmann and who dies due to the collective neglect of all four "elective relatives." Through his death he becomes the "living allegory"[39] of the negative dialectic of "elective affinities," both of the "real" imaginary play of the protagonists' fantasies and the just imagined power that has been attributed to it in terms of pseudo-scientific metaphor.

With regard to the latter, the uses of it in scientific and socio-political discourses reduce the physical complexity of the respective phenomena by providing a supposedly simple and quick explanation where actually there may be none. At the same time, its use also unnecessarily complicates research by inventing associations between in fact unrelated phenomena. Hence, metaphors may not just open up innovative avenues for future scientific inquiry, as was argued here in the opening paragraph, but also have the opposite effect of obscuring and mystifying issues that would require further empirical investigation. Berthollet's contributions to chemistry were so important – not least to Goethe – because his *Recherches* highlighted this concern. He argued, as we have seen, that chemical reactions are caused or altered by many contingent factors, which reveal the limit of elective affinity as a formal measure, based on the general assumption that certain elements have specific qualities and thus entertain certain relations with other elements accordingly. But that even Berthollet was not yet ready to disregard this basic assumption and completely dismiss this metaphor, which instead continued to enjoy popularity in almost every newly emerging scientific discipline, is a symptomatic reaction to the enormous increase of complexity and contingency around 1800. Biopolitical metaphors are attractive because they provide or rather pretend pseudo-scientific guidance; as such, they introduce a kind of new mythology with increasingly national and nationalistic implications.

But how shall one deal with the emergence of ever more complex subject matters when even the sciences fail and when one remains sceptical against national ideologies? How is a representation of dynamic processes and transformative developments – both in society at large and in the psyche of individuals – at all possible? I argue that Goethe's poetics of the simile, as it manifests in the novel *Die Wahlverwandtschaften*, responds to this very issue by employing poetic strategies that reflect the three modes of the imagination discussed earlier. First, like the reproductive imagination, it is the author's ambition to render a realistic representation of the situation, attitudes, and actions of the aristocratic society around 1800, which is essentially characterized by its desperate attempt to integrate itself into the emerging civil society. This notion has been noted by many contemporary readers.[40] Second, the action of the novel equals the actions of the main protagonists Eduard and Charlotte, whose productive imagination is informed by the title metaphor – though at first negatively. To salvage their marriage – basically to escape from the pull of the "real" elective affinities as they manifest themselves, for example, in sexual attraction – they decide to live secluded from society and to unite their otherwise drifting apart personalities by creating for themselves a perfect environment. For the realization of this common project, they radically alter their lifestyle and the landscape of their property by compulsively displacing rocks, plants, and people (most notably Charlotte's daughter Luciane and her foster child Ottilie). Their efforts to gain control over the uncontrollable only increase in intensity once the Hauptmann and Ottilie come into play. Ironically, they now try to regain composure and restrain the (real, natural) elective affinities of their imaginative powers by implementing the pseudo-scientific metaphor of "elective affinities" as a general principle of orientation. (The "Gleichnisrede" of chapter 1.4 marks this turning point.) Fighting elective affinities with "elective affinities," they are fighting the blindness caused by their consuming passions with the blindness of (false) reasoning that is (mis-)informed by an unfounded, pseudo-scientific metaphor. (Even though, it should be mentioned in parentheses, it is often the narrator who alludes to this metaphor when reporting or rather commenting on their behaviour, for example, in chapter 1.7. He probably does so to remind his audience about the importance that this metaphor plays for their idea of shaping their lives, but also for the poetic sake of instituting the simile.) This negative dialectic triggers a series of tragic events and basically seals their doomed fate.

At the same time, equally detrimental to their state of affairs is the fact that the Wahlverwandten are not only losing sight of their core values and touch with the conditions and consequences of their behaviour for their immediate environment, but that they also take every slightest issue of their petit community far too seriously. What Eduard and Ottilie, but also Charlotte and the Hauptmann, are lacking most is circumspective vision. To accomplish that, certain qualities are required like dispassionateness, calmness, and serenity, which they do certainly not possess. The notable exceptions in the novels are the old gardener and, of course, the above all (between plot and author) hovering narrator. His display of circumspective vision satisfies the third requirement for the accomplishment of a poetic simile, which Goethe himself associated with the *Wahlverwandtschaften* in another of his many insightful statements about his novel:

> Man encounters problems everywhere, yet he is incapable of ignoring a single one, which is fair enough, since otherwise research would stop. However, we should not take the *positive* too seriously, but transcend it with irony in order to recognize the *characteristics of the problem*. After exhausting years of dealing with Berthollet in the *Wahlverwandtschaften*, the public is now as unwilling to accept his science as my novel.[41]

Irony functions for Goethe as a poetic strategy to represent serious and complex problems without direct engagement and entanglement. The ability to transcend the pressing problems, to hover above them and to comprehend them in one big picture is a quality that distinguishes the true poet[42] as much as the true scientist[43] from the mere actors and spectators of the world. Peter Schwartz aptly noticed the affinity of Goethe's "ideal of morally neutral contemplation (*Schauen*)" with Spinoza's ultimate philosophical goal to strive for an "adequate knowledge of the formal essence of things" (*After Jena* 214). This perspective is reflected also in the narrator of the novel, who presents us, without compromising the complexity of the issue, only traits of characters that are essential for the demonstration of the unfolding effects and consequences of "elective affinities" in human relations.

To facilitate such a critical perspective is a very important function and accomplishment of modern poetry. The novel is a favourable genre to contain and represent the complexities of modern life, because it possesses the poetic capacity to associate a wide range of discourses and to condense them in graphic manner. Goethe also associated his novel with a container or barrel ("faßlich")[44] through which he expresses his desire to counteract the fragmenting tendencies of modernity and the emerging dissociation of nature into scientific disciplines by resynthesizing nature in one text. *Die Wahlverwandtschaften* thus exercises a critical meta-discourse about the uses of its title metaphor in scientific discourses and human life as much as it executes a poetic simile, a super-realistic *Gleichnis* that does not represent reality, but rather recreates a virtual model of reality based on some essential parameters.

Astonishingly, Goethe's poetic ambition is matched or even trumped today by some vanguard scientists, who write computer programs to simulate and study complex environments and evolutionary processes in virtual realities. According to Christopher Langston, "the ultimate goal of the study of artificial life would be to create 'life' in some other medium, ideally a *virtual* medium where the essence of life has been abstracted from the details of its implementation in any particular model. We would like to build models that are so life-like that they cease to become *models* of life and become *examples* of life themselves."[45] At this vanishing point of (future) science, the boundary to poetry in its highest form – the visionary yet reflected use of the reproductive, productive, and circumspective imagination in the creation of a living simile – collapses. The sciences' as much as poetry's ultimate goal is to withdraw the distinction between fact and fiction, that is, as Langton states, to create another "example" of life in a different medium, which eventually asserts its right to live just as any life that unfolds in the material and historical world. The latter part of this sentence actually paraphrases a letter from Goethe to his friend K.F. von Reinhard that accompanied the sending of a copy of his newest brainchild, which presents a wonderful opportunity to close also this investigation of the *wunderliche* similarities among elective affinities (as elementary/imaginary forces), "elective affinities" (as metaphor) and *The Elective Affinities* (as a poetic simile in the form of the novel):

> When despite all criticism the content of this small book stands before the imagination as an immutable factum [*unveränderliches Factum*], when the readers realize that all their willpower and aversion will not alter it; then they will eventually accept an apprehensive *Wunderkind* in fiction [*in der Fabel*] just as they have come to accept in history, after a few years, the execution of an old king and the crowning of a new emperor. Poetic events assert their rights just as historical events do. [*Das Gedichtete behauptet sein Recht, wie das Geschehene*.] (31 December 1809, FA 1.8: 982)

NOTES

1 About the vicissitudes of the ethos of "objectivity" in the sciences, see Daston and Galison, *Objectivity*.
2 Cf. Blumenberg, *Paradigms* 15.
3 Another literary text that reflects the potential consequences of the metaphor of "elective affinities" by enacting an equally rigorous discourse analysis is E.T.A. Hoffmann's novella *Die Bergwerke zu Falun*.
4 I should emphasize that my ambition in this essay is not to deliver a full-fledged interpretation of Goethe's perhaps most interpreted work. (For

a lucid review of the novel's scholarly reception until 2001 see Tantillo, *Goethe's "Elective Affinities."*) I only relate to the *Wahlverwandtschaften* as the most important literary document to reflect on the metaphoric relation between the scientific and the poetic imagination, which, I argue, the novel itself does in poetic terms.

5 Since the original wording of this short "note" matters, I add the German text: "Es scheint, daß den Verfasser seine fortgesetzten physikalischen Arbeiten zu diesem seltsamen Titel veranlaßten. Er mochte bemerkt haben, daß man in der Naturlehre sich sehr oft ethischer Gleichnisse bedient, um etwas von dem Kreise menschlichen Wissens weit Entferntes näher heranzubringen; und so hat er auch wohl in einem sittlichen Falle, eine chemische Gleichnisrede zu ihrem geistigen Ursprunge zurückführen mögen, um so mehr, als doch überall nur *eine* Natur ist und auch durch das Reich der heitern Vernunft-Freiheit die Spuren trüber, leidenschaftlicher Notwendigkeit sich unaufhaltsam hindurchziehen, die nur durch eine höhere Hand, und vielleicht auch nicht in diesem Leben, völlig auszulöschen sind." Unless indicated otherwise, all translations of German sources are my own.

6 Goethe expressed this belief most prominently in the famous verses which he adapted from Plotinus and which form, appropriately, a simile: "Wär' nicht das Auge sonnenhaft, / Wie könnten wir das Licht erblicken? / Lebt' nicht in uns des Gottes eigne Kraft, / Wie könnt' uns Göttliches entzücken?" (FA 1.23/1:24) – "Something like the sun the eye must be, / Else it no glint of sun could ever see; / Surely God's own powers with us unite, / Else godly things would not compel delight" (trans. Christopher Middleton, GCW 1: 179).

7 I am elaborating on Goethe's typology with reference to Kantian terminology given that Goethe himself employed it here and at other occasions. Cf. esp. the essays "Glückliches Ereignis," "Einwirkung der neueren Philosophie," and "Anschauende Urteilskraft" in the first volume of his *Hefte zur Morphologie* (FA 1.24: 434–8, 442–8).

8 Fritz Breithaupt (*Jenseits der Bilder*, 131–88) describes the substitutive structure of the image/picture and its working in the *Wahlverwandtschaften* in his interpretation of the novel. Relevant for the poetics of the simile is his observation that "no comparison" exists that could make visible the destructions caused by the image, "since according to the program of substitution reality does only appear as a substitute" (134–5), that is, reality can be only conceived in the mode of representation. The simile, however, juxtaposes and compares two different modes and layers of representations so that one may serve as the critique of the other.

9 Cf. Robert Stockhammer's entry "Gleichnis" in the *Goethe-Handbuch* 4.1: 388.

10 In a letter to Jacobi (23 November 1801, HA *Briefe* 2: 423), Goethe expresses this expectation from philosophy, which he only considers beneficent "when she unifies, that is to say, when she increases, secures and transforms our genuine sense *as if we were one with nature* into a deep and quiet contemplation [*Anschauen*] of the eternal unifying [συγχρισις] and separating [δίαχρισις], in which we feel divine life."

11 Goethe appreciates oriental poets especially for their similes, which he regards as felicitous expressions of their cultural identity. He describes the ideal, i.e., quasi "natural," creation process of some exemplary similes in his notes to the "West-östlichen Divan," cf. FA 1.3/1: 196–200.

12 All direct quotes from the *Wahlverwandtschaften* are cited by providing first the chapter number of the novel (here: 1.4) followed by the page number of the English edition of *Elective Affinities* in Judith Ryan's translation (GCW 11, 89–262, here: 118). I have also used the German edition edited by Waltraud Wiethölter (FA 1.8: 269–529).

13 Actually, the narrator reverses the relationship between master Eduard and his serving gardener in this very first paragraph, since it is indeed the gardener who feels "enjoyed" (the German *ergetzte* is reminiscent of God's satisfied contemplation of His Creation) about the "participating diligence of the lord."

14 My analysis has been informed by Breithaupt's precise close reading of the first chapter, cf. 131–3.

15 I refer here to five texts that the Frankfurter edition compiled under the heading "*Granit, Gebirgsbau und Epochen der Gesteinsbildung 1784–1785*" (FA 1.25: 311–21). For a thorough survey of Goethe's interest in geology, see von Engelhardt, *Goethe im Gespräch mit der Erde*.

16 Goethe translates his ethos of "obstinate realism" into a scientific method of observation and experimentation in the essay *Der Versuch als Vermittler zwischen Objekt und Subjekt* (FA 1.25: 26–36).

17 What Goethe considered fundamental and imperturbable knowledge at his time is, as matter of fact, no longer accepted in most of the present geological theories and models of earth formation.

18 My translation follows Douglas Miller's (GCW 12: 132). I add here the first part of the original German text to emphasize (by putting in italics) the character of the simile that is lost in the translation: "In diesem Augenblicke da die innern anziehenden und bewegenden Kräfte der Erde *gleichsam* unmittelbar auf mich wirken, da die Einflüsse des Himmels mich näher umschweben, werde ich zu höheren Betrachtungen der Natur hinauf gestimmt, und *wie* der Menschengeist alles belebt *so* wird auch *ein Gleichnis* in mir rege dessen Erhabenheit ich nicht widerstehen kann. *So* einsam sage ich zu mir selber indem ich diesen ganz nackten Gipfel hinab sehe und kaum in der Ferne am Fuße ein geringwachsendes Moos erblicke, *so* einsam sage ich wird es dem Menschen

zu Mute der nur den ältsten ersten tiefsten Gefühlen der Wahrheit seine Seele eröffnen will."

19 I cannot go in detail here, but Goethe's basic idea of world history was influenced by Plato's and Spinoza's philosophy and, more specifically, by Hamann's ideas about the loss of unity in God's Creation and the original poetic language through human reason, as expressed in his writings *Sokratische Denkwürdigkeiten* and *Aesthetica in nuce*.

20 See his correspondence with Eckermann, 6 May 1827 (FA 1.8: 984).

21 See Goethe to Riemer, 24 July 1809: "The ethical symbols in the natural sciences (for example, that of elective affinities which was invented and used by the great Bergman) are wittier and more readily connectable with poetry and even society [*Sozietät*] than all others, though the latter, too, are merely anthropomorphic, even the mathematical ones" (FA 1.8: 979–80).

22 First published in Latin in 1775 and quoted here after its English translation by Thomas Beddoes as rendered by Mi Gyung Kim, 264–6. Cf. also the recapitulations of Bergman's *Dissertatio* in Jeremy Adler, "*Eine fast magische Anziehungskraft*" 63–73 and Nils Reschke, "*Zeit der Umwendung*" 121–45.

23 Here quoted after the English translation *Researches into the Laws of Chemical Affinity* from 1809 with page numbers in brackets, cf. Kim 411–33.

24 On how the introduction of quantities changed the conception of "elective affinities" in the chemical discourse and on how this translates into Goethe's novel, cf. Hoffmann, "'Zeitalter der Revolutionen.'"

25 Richards (*Romantic Conception* 252–88) provides an instructive recapitulation of Reil's theories of life and mind.

26 The irony here is, of course, that he simply replaces one metaphor with another, because the other was scientifically more established. Nowadays, "elective affinity" sounds as mystical as "life force," but so will probably a metaphor like "genetic engineering" in a couple hundred years.

27 Cf. the definition in Lavoisier, *Elements of Chemistry* 3.

28 Today, we identify this "fine basic matter" as DNA.

29 The narrator reveals the psychology of displacements, which Eduard and Charlotte are entangled in, as a systematic problem of modernity by using the multivalent term "versetzen" (which means, among many other possible things, "to displace," but is here primarily used in the sense of "to counter an argument") in the novel's first chapter no less than seventeen times, thus setting the thematic leitmotif. According to Martina Schwanke, it is the most frequently used word in the whole novel.

30 The content of this section is discussed in greater detail in my article "Particular Universals – Universal Particulars: Biopolitical Metaphors and the Emergence of Nationalism in Europe (1650–1815)."

31 In his recent interpretation of Goethe's *Wahlverwandtschaften*, Nils Reschke argues that Goethe's novel reflects the events of the French Revolution by assuming the same critical position that Burke expressed in the *Reflections* (cf. esp. chap. 3, "Wahlverwandtschaften: Goethe – Burke," 85–119). This attitude is prominently articulated by the ironic opening sentence of the novel, in which Eduard is introduced while "grafting freshly cut shoots onto young rootstocks" (1.1; 93). He is thus completely inverting the practice of grafting as recommended by Burke – we learn later that Eduard, in doing so, acts against the horticultural practice of his father – and is thus characterized as a revolutionary.

32 See Schwartz for a thorough "historical contextualization" (*After Jena* 39) of the novel.

33 Cf. Reschke 124–5.

34 Cf. Pörksen, "Goethes Kritik."

35 Besides its criticism of "metaphoric symbolism," there are two more aspects of this letter that make me think that it contains the nucleus of the plan for the future novel. First, Goethe articulates his shock about the suicide of Karoline von Günderode, whose life and fate show some striking parallels with the tragic figure of Ottilie. Second, he speaks about the "fate of the German fatherland" during the Napoleonic occupation and how this political event is reflected in the writings of certain nationalist authors, namely, Müller, Gentz (Burke's translator), and Arndt.

36 This passage is also discussed by Pörksen, 297–8, who reads "metaphorischen" instead of "metaphysischen," which is probably the correct rendering.

37 "Wunderlich," like "Gleichnis," is a favourite term of Goethe during these years of the Napoleonic Wars and frequently appears in his letters between 1805 and 1810. It is difficult to translate and can mean all of the following: wondrous, strange, curious, fantastic, and whimsical. Moreover, it is related to marvellous (*sich wundern* = to marvel) and miraculous (*das Wunder* = miracle) and even evokes an association with wounded (*die Wunde* = wound); all of these meanings resonate in Goethe's use of the word in the novel.

38 Cf. the detailed analysis of the "Gleichnisrede" and how it can be translated into chemical formulas in Adler 84–139. Attempts to read the poetics of the *Wahlverwandtschaften* exclusively in terms of these chemical formulas, however, must fail in light of Goethe's criticism and warning of unsubstantiated/unmotivated transferences in the letter to Humboldt.

39 Cf. Müller-Sievers, *Self-Generation* 162.

40 For example Achim von Arnim, who saw in it "a segment of vanishing history portrayed for the future in exact and exhaustive detail." Letter to Bettina Brentano, 5 November 1809, as cited in Schwartz, 15).

41 Goethe to Kaspar von Sternberg, 19 September 1826, quoted from Reschke, 136.
42 See Goethe's *Dichtung und Wahrheit*: "True poetry announces itself [to us], as a secular Gospel, by freeing us through inner cheerfulness and external comfort from the earthly burdens that press on us. Like a balloon, it lifts us and all the ballast attached to us to higher regions and lets us see, from a bird's perspective, the confused paths of the world spread before us" (FA 1.15: 631).
43 See his essay *Der Versuch als Vermittler von Objekt und Subjekt*: "The true botanist shall be neither touched by the beauty nor by the usability of plants. He shall just study their forms and relations among each other. As they are all raised and shined on by the sun, the botanist shall look at them all and survey them in the same calm manner" (FA 1.25: 26).
44 See Goethe to Johann F. Cotta, 26 July 1808: "The novel is a generally comprehensible [*faßliches*] and, also for the writer, a comfortably entertaining genre; I feel a great urge to put more of what I have to say into this form than previously" (FA 1.8: 978). Cf. his statement to Eckermann, 5 May 1827, FA 1.8: 984.
45 Quoted in Fox Keller, 267.

WORKS CITED

Adler, Jeremy. *"Eine fast magische Anziehungskraft": Goethes* Wahlverwandtschaften *und die Chemie seiner Zeit*. Munich: C.H. Beck, 1987.

Baecque, Antoine de. *The Body Politic: Corporeal Metaphor in Revolutionary France, 1770–1800*. Trans. Charlotte Mandell. Stanford: Stanford UP, 1999.

Bell, David A. *The Cult of the Nation in France: Inventing Nationalism, 1680–1800*. Cambridge, MA: Harvard UP, 2003.

Bergman, Torbern. *Dissertation on Elective Attractions*. Trans. Thomas Beddoes. London: J. Murray, 1970.

Berthollet, Claude Louis. *Researches into the Laws of Chemical Affinity*. Trans. M. Farrell. Baltimore: P.H. Nicklin & Co., 1809.

Blumenberg, Hans. *Paradigms for a Metaphorology*. Trans. Robert L. Savage. Ithaca: Cornell UP, 2010.

Breithaupt, Fritz. *Jenseits der Bilder: Goethes Poetik der Wahrnehmung*. Freiburg im Breisgau: Rombach, 2000.

Burke, Edmund. *Reflections on the Revolution in France*. New Haven: Yale UP, 2003.

Daston, Lorraine J., and Peter Galison. *Objectivity*. Brooklyn: Zone, 2007.

Engelhardt, Wolf von. *Goethe im Gespräch mit der Erde: Landschaften, Gesteine, Mineralien und Erdgeschichte in seinem Leben und Werk*. Weimar: Böhlau, 2003.

Fox Keller, Evelyn. *Making Sense of Life: Explaining Biological Development with Models, Metaphors, and Machines*. Cambridge, MA: Harvard UP, 2002.

Goethe, Johann W. *Goethes Briefe und Briefe von Goethe*. Hamburger Ausgabe in 6 vols. Ed. Karl Robert Mandelkow. Munich: Deutscher Taschenbuch Verlag, 1988. [= HA *Briefe*]

Goethe, Johann W. *Goethe's Collected Works*. 12 vols. Ed. Victor Lange et al. New York: Suhrkamp, 1983–9. [= GCW]

Goethe, Johann W. *Sämtliche Werke: Briefe, Tagebücher und Gespräche*. Ed. Dieter Borchmeyer et al. 40 vols. Frankfurt am Main: Deutscher Klassiker Verlag, 1985–99. [= FA]

Goethe-Handbuch. Ed. Bernd Witte et al. 4 vols. in 5. Stuttgart: Metzler, 1996–9.

Hoffmann, Christoph. "'Zeitalter der Revolutionen': Goethes *Wahlverwandtschaften* im Fokus des chemischen Paradigmenwechsels." *Deutsche Vierteljahrsschrift* 67 (1993): 417–50.

Humboldt, Wilhelm von. *Florae Fribergensis specimen, plantas cryptogamicas praesertim subterraneas exhibens*, Berolini: Rottman, 1793.

Kim, Mi Gyung. *Affinity, That Elusive Dream: A Genealogy of the Chemical Revolution*. Cambridge, MA: MIT UP, 2003.

Koschorke, Albrecht, Susanne Lüdemann, Thomas Frank, and Ethel Matala de Mazza. *Der fiktive Staat: Konstruktionen des politischen Körpers in der Geschichte Europas*. Frankfurt am Main: Fischer, 2007.

Lavoisier, Antoine. *Elements of Chemistry*. Trans. Robert Kerr. Chicago: U of Chicago P, 1952.

Müller-Sievers, Helmut. *Self-Generation: Biology, Philosophy, and Literature 1800*. Stanford: Stanford UP, 1997.

Pörksen, Uwe. "Goethes Kritik naturwissenschaftlicher Metaphorik." *Jahrbuch der Deutschen Schillergesellschaft* 25 (1981): 285–313.

Reil, Johann Christian. *Von der Lebenskraft* (1795). Leipzig: Johann Ambrosius Barth, 1910.

Reschke, Nils. *"Zeit der Umwendung": Lektüren der Revolution in Goethes Roman* Die Wahlverwandtschaften. Freiburg: Rombach, 2006.

Richards, Robert J. *The Romantic Conception of Life: Science and Philosophy in the Age of Goethe*. Chicago: U of Chicago P, 2002.

Schlegel, Friedrich. *Philosophical Fragments*. Trans. Peter Firchow. Minneapolis: U of Minnesota P, 1991.

Schwanke, Martina. *Lemmatisierter Index zu Goethes "Die Wahlverwandtschaften."* Stuttgart: Metzler, 1994.

Schwartz, Peter J. *After Jena: Goethe's* Elective Affinities *and the End of the Old Regime.* Lewisburg, PA: Bucknell UP, 2010.

Tantillo, Astrida O. *Goethe's "Elective Affinities" and the Critics.* Rochester, NY: Camden House, 2001.

Weber, Christian P. "Particular Universals – Universal Particulars: Biopolitical Metaphors and the Emergence of Nationalism in Europe (1650–1815)." *History of European Ideas* 39.3 (2013): 426–48.

5 Physics Disarmed: Probabilistic Knowledge in the Works of James Clerk Maxwell and George Eliot

TINA YOUNG CHOI

In his 1873 *Nature* article, British physicist James Clerk Maxwell introduced readers to the molecule, a particle about which little had heretofore been known. "Every substance ... has its own molecule," the renowned scientist methodically explained in his opening remarks, and every molecule a characteristic mass and composition ("Molecules" 437). Yet there were significant limitations to the investigator's knowledge, he admitted, in spite of Britain's many advances in the physical and thermodynamic sciences. Even in the article's first paragraph, he conceded that "no one has ever seen or handled a single molecule," and characterized his own work as "deal[ing] with things invisible and imperceptible by our senses, and which cannot be subjected to direct experiment" (437). After devoting several pages to an explanation of the principles of molecular velocity and diffusion, he returned in his concluding paragraphs to the more fundamental methodological problem with which the article began, the problem of seeing and knowing, and noted that in spite of these obstacles to traditional scientific methods, molecular research had compensated by "develop[ing] a method of its own, and it has also opened up new views of nature" (440).

Rather than naming this revolutionary new "method" at once, however, Maxwell left readers in suspense while he embarked on an unusual digression for the space of a few paragraphs. He first turned to ancient Roman philosopher-poet Lucretius's assertion that the invisible movements of atoms might be understood through their indirect effects, the movement of dust particles rendered visible in shafts of light, and then quoted Lord Tennyson's 1868 poem "Lucretius," with its vivid description of "flaring atom-streams" (440). Only after these two examples of ways in which the invisible might imaginatively be rendered visible did Maxwell identify the new "method" he had mentioned earlier: statistics.

The juxtaposition of Lucretius's and Tennyson's accounts of the molecule with nineteenth-century statistical models feels unexpected, even strange. Maxwell may have wished to highlight the contrast between older forms of understanding and recent research methods; but rather than dismissing the attempts of his predecessors, he seems instead to draw attention to the continuities between poetic and scientific modes of representation. Like Lucretius and Tennyson, his article suggests, the nineteenth-century molecular scientist can only speculate about the subject of his inquiry. The scientist cannot know "the actual motion of any one of these molecules," Maxwell explains, and his "experiments can never give … anything more than statistical information" – averages, likelihoods, a range of chances and possibilities – impressionistic data beyond which finer examination yields imprecision and uncertainty (440). In place of empirical knowledge that would come from direct observation and measurement, statistics offers a speculative, indirect vision of its object. The molecule itself, imperceptible and unfixable, is a "mental representation" in Maxwell's words, something generated by and resident in the imagination (438). Like poetry's visions of illuminated dust, statistics – with its probabilities and indeterminacies – provides what can only be, as he puts it, a "probable conjecture" about the molecule (439).

For physical scientists of the mid- and late-nineteenth century, these seemingly abstruse questions about epistemology and imagination were concerns to be grappled with on a regular basis, both in the laboratory and in the pages of professional journals. As the thermodynamic sciences, in particular, turned their attention to the realm of unseen atoms and molecules, new epistemological questions arose about the very nature of scientific inquiry: What kind of knowledge could be considered legitimate, or even possible, about this invisible and largely imperceptible world of molecules? What constituted knowledge in the absence of direct empirical evidence about one's subject?

As historians of science have observed, the proffered answers to these questions were correlated, in large part, with the respondent's national affiliation (Smith, *Science of Energy* 233–5; Dear, *Intelligibility of Nature* 115–19). Leading German physicists, men like Carl Friedrich Gauss and Wilhelm Weber, contended that molecules and the unseen magnetic and electrical forces governing the interactions between them could best be described mathematically. In the 1850s, as British scientists like Maxwell were studying the mechanics of electromagnetism, Weber directed his efforts to the calculation of distance and potential energy between particles, to the mathematical description of forces. Yet these Continental accounts met with resistance from British scientists like chemist Michael Faraday, the director of the Royal Institution and the first to describe electromagnetic induction, as well as prominent mathematician and energy physicist William Thomson (later Lord Kelvin), among others. Like them, Maxwell argued that Weber's mathematical solution, what he called "action at a distance," reduced molecular phenomena to little more than "a system of points" and overlooked "the perseverance of matter" (qtd. in Smith, 221). For Maxwell and his colleagues, particles and the spaces between them were not mathematical abstractions, but material bodies whose actions needed to be explained in terms of mechanics and physical causalities. Understanding molecules thus meant examining not only these invisible particles themselves but also and especially the intervening spaces between particles, the fields within which one particle might collide with or affect another.

The larger epistemological question posed by the molecule, however, reached beyond the limits of the laboratory, as Maxwell's *Nature* article suggested – and touched as well upon concerns both theological and aesthetic. Indeed, Christian Weber's essay in this volume demonstrates that this interest in what could not be apprehended through the senses had its origins in eighteenth-century philosophy and science; Romantic thinkers across Europe, but especially German intellectuals like Goethe and Kant, sought a language for describing the immaterial relationship between the self and the world. As Christian Weber reveals, Goethe's chosen metaphor, drawn from the language of experimental chemistry, was "elective affinity," a word that not only reflected the relational quality of perception but also suggested the act of imagination at its core. Yet the leading German physicists of the nineteenth century, Gauss and Wilhelm Weber, ultimately turned away from the language of philosophy and literature – the language of affinity, inclination, faith, and desire – and towards mathematical precision and certainty. By contrast, as this chapter will reveal, their British counterparts embraced the spirit of imaginative speculation. Indeed, by the 1870s, both Maxwell and one of his most prominent contemporaries in the literary world, George Eliot, were engaged in their own representational experiments, using the language of probability.

The first section of this chapter focuses on efforts by British scientists, especially by Maxwell and his contemporary, physicist John Tyndall, to investigate the realm of sub-microscopic particles in the 1860s and 1870s, and to accustom readers not to expect direct empirical knowledge about the subject, but to accept the kinds of speculative activity and indeterminacy that such research entailed. The second section considers Eliot's novel *Daniel Deronda* as an exploration of forms of understanding about the unverifiable and the unknown in human motivation and feeling. Both Maxwell and Eliot formulated new models for understanding that did not avoid but rather acknowledged and even embraced uncertainty. Literary historian Christopher Herbert asserts that a wide range of intellectuals began to question forms of absolute knowledge during this period (*Victorian Relativity* xiv), and Maxwell and Eliot are, without doubt, to be counted among them. But their work also proposed that not knowing could become the basis for a different way of knowing, a knowing that was statistical rather than empirical.

According to historians of science Lorraine Daston, Ian Hacking, and Theodore Porter, the emergence of the statistical sciences in the 1830s and 1840s had a significant impact on professional and popular discourse. With the founding of a statistical section of the British Association for the Advancement of Science in 1833, the contemporaneous creation of statistical societies in London and Manchester, and the open support of political economists like Thomas Malthus and social reformers like James Phillips Kay, statistical methods gained legitimacy not only in scientific circles but in political ones as well (Porter, *Rise of Statistical Thinking* 31–3). The creation in 1837 of the General Register Office, which was tasked with collecting comprehensive population statistics for all of Britain, and the establishment of the *Journal of the Statistical Society* the following year gave these professional concerns a more public voice. By the middle of the century, proportions and percentages were referred to as matters of common parlance.

It soon became clear from this widespread application of the statistical sciences in insurance policies, social reform, public health planning, and political economy that there were two seemingly contradictory phenomena that emerged from the collection of numerical data. On the one hand, statistics illustrated the mathematical regularity with which events (e.g., death, crime, sickness, fire) occurred when measured in large populations and over long stretches of time. This law of large numbers lent such incidents the effect of determinacy and certainty. Although one might not be able to predict their time or location, the fact of their occurrence gave statisticians and laypersons the impression of a world governed, if no longer by providence, then by a secular principle at once consistent and transcendent in its application. But on the other hand, statistics spoke through the language of uncertainty. Its percentages and proportions might have calculated the chances and risks of an event's occurrence, but particulars – where, when, who – were left to the imagination and the future. Recent scholarship has tended to focus on the former, on the containment and control represented by statistical regularities (Poovey, Rosenthal), and particularly on the role of numbers and averages in reinforcing the middle class's normalizing disciplinary agendas. But the uncertainties conjured by statistics, while not exactly liberatory, nonetheless moved beyond predictability and determinism, and instead encouraged readers to think in terms of probabilities and possibilities, to contemplate what theorist Niklas Luhmann has described as the fertile space between the "necessary" and the "impossible" (*Observations on Modernity* 45). But where this realm of the possible is, for Luhmann, most characteristic of twentieth-century thought, my work traces its origins to the nineteenth century and suggests, more specifically, that it was contemplated and cultivated by science and literature alike.

By the 1850s and 1860s, as the language of statistics extended beyond the specialized report and became all but commonplace, lay writers began to contemplate the disjunction between large-scale certainties, the law of large numbers that might describe populations, and the vagaries and indeterminacies associated with the individual. One anonymous essayist, for instance, complained that public health statistics, rather than providing certainty or assurance, left the individual ever in doubt: for "the one death that must come ... the time is to him personally – in spite of libraries full of statistics – utterly unknown and uncertain" ("Registration" 228). More typical was Charles Dickens's treatment of statistics in his 1854 novel *Hard Times*, which criticized the period's proliferation of numbers and tables for their overdetermined, dehumanizing qualities, for how little they concerned themselves with the individuals they claimed to represent. The character Sissy Jupe, for example, learns that in a population of "a million of inhabitants ... only five-and-twenty are starved to death in the streets, in the course of a year" (97). Statistics, for the novel's characters, are not only unsympathetic but also wrong-headed in their narrow focus on populations and their failure to account for the experiences of the individual. For many Victorians, the incontrovertibility of such "facts" represented the limitations of statistical methods and the impersonal quality of the political or social efforts that employed them.

But later writers like Maxwell and Eliot, turning their focus away from statistical certainty, saw value in the uncertainties that statistics also allowed one to represent. Rather than dismissing statistical modes of understanding as irrelevant, they considered how the uncertainties that emerged at the level of the particular might in fact be generative of alternative forms of knowledge about what could be neither seen nor measured: the precise qualities of any one of Maxwell's molecules, the emotions of Eliot's characters. In place of the verifiable constants that described populations, both Maxwell and Eliot suggested that probabilities – imprecise and indeterminate though they might be in application – could provide a way of approaching the particular, not of knowing it directly through empirical observation or measurement, but of generating a fertile field of possibilities around it.

Molecular Realms of Speculation

British scientists discredited "action at a distance," the theory favoured by Gauss and Weber to explain magnetic and electrical phenomena between discrete particles, and sought instead causal explanations to describe the relationship between one body and another.[1] They promoted the idea of "aether" as a material – and possibly even mechanical – substrate that could mediate and transmit such effects across space. But knowledge about the ether, which was understood to be omnipresent but imperceptible, as well as about the individual molecules within it, lay outside the scope of scientific certainty. Faraday posited the existence of "lines of force," and Maxwell, citing the plausibility of Faraday's explanation for the "intervening medium" between particles, also speculated that something like intricate cogwheels could be thought of as the responsible intermediaries (Maxwell, *Treatise* x, 36; Dear 132–5; Smith 220, 225–7).[2] Scientific evidence about these or other hypotheses was, however, inconclusive. Describing the realm of the molecular – the motions and interactions of molecules, and the ether surrounding them – to other scientists and to laypersons thus presented a significant challenge.

Indeed, what these scientists emphasized was that the molecule and the ether surrounding it were indescribable by traditional modes of scientific investigation and representation. Tyndall, an experimental physicist who had succeeded Faraday to the directorship of the Royal Institution in 1867, considered this aspect of scientific research in his 1870 address to the British Association for the Advancement of Science. He focused primarily on the microscopic, but, he asserted, once scientists moved beyond the microscope's limits and towards the molecular, "the speculative faculty" necessarily compensated in "regions where the hope of certainty would seem to be entirely shut out ... Beyond the present outposts of microscopic inquiry lies an immense field for the exercise of the imagination" ("Scientific Use," 63).[3] As an example of imagination supplementing more traditional forms of scientific investigation, Tyndall referred to the work of his contemporary, Lord Kelvin, observing, "When William Thomson tries to place the ultimate particles of matter [molecules] between his compass points, and to apply to them a scale of millimeters, it is an exercise of the imagination" (36). Beyond the limits of the visible, more speculative forms of knowledge took the place of epistemological certainty and empirical knowledge. Maxwell might elsewhere have disagreed vehemently with Tyndall, but in his own address to the British Association the same year, he offered an account of molecular research that accorded with that of his fellow scientist.[4] Knowledge about the molecule, according to Maxwell, lay in "the still more hidden and dimmer region where Thought weds Fact," a region in which "molecules ... in their true relation" might be apprehended only through a combination of empirical and theoretical study ("Address" 216).[5] As he concluded, "the way to [the molecule]" passes not through the scientific laboratory or the mathematician's notebook, but rather "through the very den of the metaphysician" (ibid.).

The difficulty in obtaining information about the individual molecule was due, in part, to the technical limitations of available instruments; the resolution of microscopes did not allow scientists to visualize the particles they studied. But as Maxwell's dynamical theory of molecules asserted, the very nature of the particle and its motions also rendered imaging or measurement impossible. Never a "single hard body" whose contours and motions could be determined with mathematical accuracy, the molecule was a site of "vibration" internally as well as externally, engaged in what he evocatively described as a "dance" with other molecular bodies ("Address" 224, 228). Thus, he could state with assurance that particles in air travel at an average velocity of "1505 feet per second" and experience an average of "8,077,200,000 collisions per second" (*Scientific Letters* 2: 615). Such figures might well strike the uninitiated reader as providing access to empirical knowledge – but these data were, as Maxwell emphasized elsewhere, "of an essentially statistical nature, because no one has yet discovered any practical method of tracing the path of a molecule, or of identifying it at different times" (*Theory of Heat* 329). Moreover, this shift from empirical to statistical knowing was, he declared, of both scientific and epistemological significance: "This is a step the philosophical importance of which cannot be overestimated. It is the equivalent to the change from absolute certainty to high probability" (*Scientific Letters* 2: 930).[6]

In explicating this distinction for lay readers, Maxwell resorted to an analogy with the population statistics with which most of them would already have been familiar. What one could know about individual molecules, like what one could know about individual persons, was different from what one could know about a group, he explained. Indeed, he made this comparison between molecules and populations explicit in his 1873 *Nature* article, explaining that just as surveys by "registrars and tabulators" differed in fundamental ways from "the study of human nature by parents and schoolmasters," so by analogy "the smallest portion of matter which we can subject to experiment consists of millions of molecules, not one of which ever becomes individually sensible to us. We cannot, therefore, ascertain the actual motion of any one of these molecules, so that we are obliged ... to adopt the statistical method" ("Molecules" 440).[7] Offering a similar comparison in his letter to social scientist Herbert Spencer that same year, he declared that our knowledge of the molecule – of its rotations, which "var[y] at every encounter with another molecule," and of its differential velocity – can be "*statistical* only – there is nothing definite in any other sense than the death-rate of a city is definite" (2: 959–60).[8] Just as the law of large numbers might provide information about populations but not individuals – a distinction which most readers of the 1870s would have comprehended – scientific investigation yielded certainty and accuracy for the mass but not for the single molecule. Specific knowledge in both cases, Maxwell suggests, would necessarily be probabilistic in nature.[9]

But this epistemological uncertainty applied not just to the molecule, but also and especially to the intervening spaces between molecules, the ether of molecular influences, movement, and potential. As twentieth-century physicist and philosopher Freeman Dyson puts it, the focus of Maxwell's research was not only "things," but also the fields within which these "things" move and exert their influence on others ("Why Is Maxwell's Theory" 3–4). Moreover, while molecules might have some known properties, such as chemical composition and mass, the chemical essence and mechanism of the ether (Faraday's proposed lines and Maxwell's hypothetical cogs notwithstanding) remained undefined. Indeed, the ether's most consistent characteristic lay not in any physical feature assigned to it, but in the indeterminacy associated with scientific investigations into its nature. Just as the ether's very existence was a matter of scientific hypothesis without empirical proof, so the intervening spaces between molecules were rendered thick, not by any discernible matter, but by the multiple probabilities understood to reside there – the velocities, vibrations, influences, and impulses that were at once imaginable and yet incalculable.

Probabilistic Intersubjectivity

Maxwell was keenly aware of how this probabilistic approach might extend beyond the sciences. After all, he asserted, there was little difference between a metaphysician who contemplated human motives and behaviours and "a physicist disarmed of all his weapons" (*Scientific Letters* 2: 815), and as he admitted in his *Nature* article, the physicist who studied the molecule was himself "disarmed" of empirical methods and data. For novelist George Eliot, the world was filled with observers who, like Maxwell's scientist, were "disarmed," denied omniscience or assurances of perfect understanding. Indeed, sympathy and scientific observation function in analogous ways, she suggests in her final novel, *Daniel Deronda*, as they are ever moving towards but never achieving epistemological resolution.

Eliot's interest in the period's science, including nineteenth-century naturalism and the medical sciences, spanned the length of her career as a novelist (Beer, *Darwin's Plots*; Levine, *Darwin*; Rothfield, *Vital Signs*). Moreover, while a number of other Victorian novelists demonstrated an interest in contemporaneous scientific discoveries and theories – notably Charles Dickens, who was fascinated by the period's physical chemistry, and Charles Kingsley, who actively promoted sanitary principles in his fiction – Eliot was perhaps unique among them in the depth of her engagement with and understanding of contemporaneous scientific research. Her lifelong companion, editor George Henry Lewes, was Tyndall's personal friend and correspondent; she herself had read Tyndall's and Maxwell's published essays, and had assiduously transcribed excerpts from their two 1870 British Association lectures into her working notebooks in preparation for writing *Daniel Deronda* (*George Eliot's Notebooks* 16–23). A consideration of Eliot's literary oeuvre as a whole, however, belies any suggestion that science's epistemological grapplings served as the prerequisite and foundation for her fictional equivalents. Her earlier writings, too, had explored versions of these same questions both from a theological perspective, through translations of key Christian philosophical texts that were among her first publications in the 1840s and 1850s, and from a secular stance, through novels that asked readers to consider the difficulties inherent in the process of seeing and knowing. The narrator of *Middlemarch*, for example, famously made appeals to the novel's readers, inviting them to turn a critical eye to the limitations of vision and perspective; she shed light on the difficult process by which characters might know each other or, as in the case of her well-meaning but often fatally myopic hero, Dr Tertius Lydgate, might know themselves. These questions permeate

Daniel Deronda as well, and the notebooks she kept in preparing this 1876 novel seem to suggest the common ground she observed between recent scientific developments – as they questioned the possibility of empirical knowledge and considered the meaning of incalculability – and the direction of her own literary endeavour. For Eliot, scientific investigation and understanding, and specifically, their handling of the broader epistemological challenges of knowing something about the invisible world, provided one way of thinking through and describing the limits of knowing, a useful model – and sometimes a useful metaphor – for describing her own experiments in narrative, where omniscience gave way to speculation, certitude to productive doubt.

Scholars investigating the intersections between science and literature in Eliot's work have typically looked to *Middlemarch* as a critical case study. Her last novel, *Daniel Deronda*, which traces the intertwined histories of two young English persons confronting unsettling circumstances – Daniel Deronda, a wealthy gentleman who discovers and ultimately embraces his Jewish ancestry, and Gwendolen Harleth, a woman who attempts to resolve her social and financial difficulties through marriage to the aristocratic Charles Grandcourt – has tended to attract critical attention to its social thematics, namely, the place of Jews and of women in Victorian London. But given that the notes Eliot made in preparing to write this novel included material drawn from Maxwell's and Tyndall's writing, I suggest that we might read *Daniel Deronda*, too, as a "scientific" novel. Unlike *Middlemarch*, with its doctor protagonist and its focus on the rise of the medical profession, science plays no thematic role in *Daniel Deronda*. Yet as critics such as George Levine (*Dying to Know* 172–85; "George Eliot's Hypothesis") and Jesse Rosenthal have noted, the latter investigates epistemological questions about the relationship between scientific and sympathetic, objective and subjective ways of knowing. Indeed, like *Middlemarch*, with its recurrent turns to the language of light and microscopy as figures for perception and epistemology, *Daniel Deronda* features science – and as these pages will demonstrate, probability theory in particular – as central to its narrative strategy. It provides one way of responding to the question, How can one know something about the unknowable? For Eliot's characters, religious faith – in this case, Judaism – offers one viable response to the problem of arriving at knowledge about the unknowable. But the narrative also invites us to contemplate the power of probabilistic thinking as another mode of approaching the unknowable. While their objects of investigation necessarily differed – for Maxwell it was the molecule, while for Eliot it was human emotion – both explored ways of knowing that extended beyond the empirical, beyond what observers could see and measure. In this sense, the novel offers its own meditation on an issue that Maxwell had raised some years before, in a provocative letter to friend and classics scholar Lewis Campbell: "What is believing? When the probability ... in a man's mind of a certain proposition being true is greater than that of its being false, he believes it with a proportion of faith corresponding to the probability ... This is faith in general" (*Scientific Letters* 1: 198). In other words, rather than opposing religious and scientific explanation, Maxwell places them on a single continuum of belief. Just as probability, for the scientist, was the likelihood of a hypothesis holding true, so too was faith a matter of ever-increasing probabilities, of an asymptotic, not identical, relation to truth.

As if elaborating two decades later on Maxwell's privately expressed idea, Eliot contemplates the relationship between religious and scientific belief in chapter 41 of *Daniel Deronda*, the first chapter of the novel's sixth book, "Revelations," a title that aptly suggests the convergence of secular and religious truths that occurs within. The narrator explores the continuities between religious faith and scientific research from Daniel's perspective, as he reflects on the surprising insistence of his Jewish friend, Ezra Cohen, that the hitherto Christian Daniel is destined to serve as Ezra's own "executive self," to fulfil his spiritual desires (510). For Daniel, who has not yet discovered his Jewish parentage, his friend's zeal verges on fanaticism; at the same time, he acknowledges, many secular men, including the "social reformer ... [the] enthusiast in sewage," and even great scientists such as Copernicus, Galileo, and James Watt, might well have been described as possessing an enthusiasm more akin to prophetic fervour than to scientific detachment (510). Indeed, he speculates that Ezra's passion might be likened to "even strictly-measuring science," whose "forecasting ardour ... feels the agitations of discovery beforehand, and has a faith in its preconception that surmounts many failures of experiment" (513). The operations of science, like the inclinations of religion, are driven forward by belief. Filling the space of the unknown with guesses, premonitions, and desires, scientific speculation operates like another version of spiritual faith. Moreover, Ezra, in believing that Daniel is Jewish, is not alone in his speculative fanaticism; Daniel acknowledges that he, too, has transformed probabilistic belief (what he, borrowing the language of science, terms a "hypothesis") into faith when he assumes, as he has for many years, that he is Hugo Mallinger's biological son (512). But rather than seeking "valid evidence" that would support or refute any of these speculations, Daniel accepts these forms of irresolution at chapter's end, "regard[ing] his uncertainty as a condition to be cherished" (515).

This language of scientific speculation recurs throughout the novel, as a figure for other modes of speculative thought: religious faith in a time of secular rationalism, emotional attachment to a certain vision of one's future, sensitivity to what others feel but cannot express. What Eliot's last novel suggests is that these forms of knowing are, in large measure, necessarily probabilistic; in the absence of empirical evidence to confirm or deny, it is the observer who helps to generate around his or her object a field of possibility, actively filling the unknown spaces between the necessary and the impossible with hypothetical narratives of what might be.

The difficulty of knowing, particularly when knowing necessitates the overcoming of distance between oneself and another – whether between one character and another, or between reader and character – is central to Eliot's oeuvre as a whole, and a number of recent critics, including Thomas Albrecht, Elizabeth Ermarth, Catherine Gallagher, Rae Greiner, George Levine ("*Daniel Deronda*"), and Forest Pyle, have ably explored the attendant problematics of sympathetic feeling in Eliot's work. As with Maxwell's molecule, however, sympathy's epistemological difficulty arises not merely from limitations of perception, but also from the nature of the perceived object itself. Maxwell had referred to a "dance" to describe the unfixed condition of the molecule at the centre of his study, and so too Eliot was interested, not in securing her subject under a microscope, but in portraying its ever-shifting condition. In an essay presented to a private club, Maxwell, ruminating on the extension of physical principles into the domain of metaphysics, suggested that "our free will at the best is like that of Lucretius's atoms – which at quite uncertain times and places deviate in an uncertain manner from their course" (*Scientific Letters* 2: 820). Perception might be one part of our difficulty in knowing, that is, but another, significant part lies in the undetermined path of our object, whether molecular or human. Eliot's *Daniel Deronda* explores this indeterminacy with characteristic psychological depth and complexity, focusing attention on the "iridescence of character – the play of various, nay, contrary tendencies," the often imperceptibly shifting emotions of the individuals at the novel's centre (42).

The narrator of *Deronda* introduces us to a range of characters, and while she occasionally dwells on appearances and generalizations, she also reveals that such forms of knowledge are not to be trusted. For example, in introducing Grandcourt, the narrator lingers for a moment on the surface of this "correct Englishman," on his "faded fairness" and "long grey eyes" (111). But she cautions us about coming to any conclusions about the individual based on certitudes about "correct Englishmen" as a population – and then, pressing further still, she exclaims, "Attempts at description are stupid: who can all at once describe a human being? even when he is presented to us we only begin that knowledge of his appearance which must be completed by innumerable impressions under differing circumstances" (111). The supposedly legible surfaces of the body tell us little; they represent only the beginning of epistemological difficulty, revealing primarily the limits to our understanding. Even when "complete," our empirical knowledge consists only of an assemblage of fleeting observations, "impressions," rather than facts or certainties. The narrator's stance here constitutes a striking difference from the nineteenth century's typical literary omniscience, in which the authoritative third-person narrator of a Dickens or Flaubert novel implicitly knows – even if he does not reveal – all. Here, such knowing is a delusion, based on generalizations or assumptions; as the chapter's epigraph admonishes us, "The beginning of an acquaintance whether with persons or things is to get a definite outline for our ignorance" (111).

What kind of knowledge might we as readers hope to gain about these characters, then? To resign ourselves to the impossibility of understanding is hardly a reassuring beginning for someone embarking upon a nine-hundred-page novel. Eliot revisits this question throughout, when she invites us into those spaces of encounter between one character and another, or even between reader and character. For instance, she offers us the perspective of Mr Lush, Grandcourt's assistant, who contemplates the possibility of a union between his employer and Gwendolen:

> What was the probable effect that the news of [Gwendolen's] family misfortunes would have on Grandcourt's fitful obstinacy he felt to be quite incalculable. So far as the girl's poverty might be an argument that she would accept an offer from him now in spite of any previous coyness, it might remove that bitter objection to risk a repulse which Lush divined to be one of Grandcourt's determining motives; on the other hand, the certainty of acceptance was just "the sort of thing" to make him lapse hither and thither with no more apparent will than a moth. Lush had had his patron under close observation for many years, and knew him perhaps better than he knew any other subject; but to know Grandcourt was to doubt what he would do in any particular case ... Lush had some general certainties about Grandcourt ... Of what use, however, is a general certainty that an insect will not walk with his

> head hindmost, when what you need to know is the play of inward stimulus that sends him hither and thither in a network of possible paths? (281–2)

More than the content of Lush's thought processes, this passage reveals their limitations – the first half of the passage inhabits Lush's limited perspective through indirect discourse, then turns away to the narrator's point of view, a third-person commentary on Lush's reflections. Yet if we expected narratorial omniscience in the passage's second half (beginning with "Lush had had his patron"), the novel disappoints us. We receive no further insight, rather an exposition on the necessarily imperfect state of Lush's knowledge as well as, by extension, our own. Moreover, that imperfection is hardly particular to Lush; indeed, as the narrator suggests, it is as fundamental to observation of a creature like Grandcourt, as to any act of scientific observation of a moth or other insect. Like the scientist, Lush is familiar with generalities, average behaviours deduced from "close observation for many years," but he cannot know particulars for any one case, including the case that interests him most.

Significantly, as the narrator pauses over the divide between Lush and Grandcourt, her subject is not Grandcourt himself, but rather the difficulty that characters like Lush or Gwendolen (or even we as readers) face in ascertaining Grandcourt's feelings and motivations. Drawing our attention to the felt space between individuals – to what narratologists have termed intersubjectivity, one character's conscious appraisal of another's interiority,[10] and what we might call a version of human ether, filled with emotions, inclinations, and influences – *Daniel Deronda* reveals that it is not readily accessed by empirical knowledge and useful data, but rather by speculative and imaginative effort. Thus, the condition of uncertainty that Lush experiences applies generally, not just to the inscrutable Grandcourt. For example, Gwendolen, contemplating Grandcourt's offer of marriage, speculates on the relationship between husband and wife: "For what could not a woman do when she was married, if she knew how to assert herself? Here all was constructive imagination. Gwendolen had about as accurate a conception of marriage – that is to say, of the mutual influences, demands, duties of man and woman in the state of matrimony – as she had of magnetic currents and the law of storms" (298). What seems at first a deprecatory comment about Gwendolen's ignorance of married life (not to mention science) might also be read, in light of the narrator's description of Lush some pages earlier, as a commentary on the epistemological difficulties that such invisible influences and effects present to any observer, who can perceive little more than their outer manifestations. Just as the mundane interactions and expectations that constitute the intersubjective experience of married life are unknowable to someone like Gwendolen, so too are the physical interactions of particles or of masses of air invisible even to the physicist or the meteorologist, whose objects of study are resistant to more traditional, empirical modes of study. She might indeed be ignorant, but so too the trained observer, as Maxwell himself had admitted, needed to extrapolate from limited data by engaging the "constructive imagination." Indeed, these parallels between scientific and lay observation are the mirror image of those in Maxwell's 1873 *Nature* article; just as, for Maxwell, probability theory might be explained through analogy to Tennyson's poetic visions of the atom, so for Eliot might the layperson's imaginative interpersonal speculations be understood by comparison to the scientist's necessarily probabilistic hypotheses.

The epistemological challenge presented by intersubjective space is a central feature in many of Eliot's writings, but what distinguishes this last novel from her earlier work is the degree of certainty characterizing moments of intersubjective feeling. Much is left unarticulated by characters and narrator in *Middlemarch*, for example, but this earlier novel nonetheless leaves us with the sense that the characters have reached a deep understanding with each other, and we as readers with them; thus, in its final chapters, the novel's primary characters find themselves joined in moments of mutual insight. Describing the sympathetic touch of hands and meeting of eyes, the narrator reassures us that such secular communion of feelings between persons can exist. In *Daniel Deronda*, Eliot invites us to explore the indeterminacy of interpersonal spaces, but she denies us the certainties she offered in her earlier novel. While she resolves the lingering question of Daniel's parentage with a perhaps uncharacteristic certainty,[11] the realm of the unseen – questions of faith, emotion, attachment, motivation – remains one of uncertainty. *Deronda*'s characters approach each other, but the sympathetic resolutions that take place in *Middlemarch* are elusive in this last novel. Its final pages, in which the widowed Gwendolen sends one last letter to Daniel, and Daniel, inspired by the dying Ezra's religious fervour, sails off to Palestine, leave both her characters and us as readers in a state of emotional irresolution: What effect does Gwendolen's last letter have on Daniel? Will Gwendolen carry out Daniel's encouragement to become "one of the best of women"? Will Daniel fulfil the dying Ezra's final, prophetic wish?

For a novel characterized by such indeterminacy, the opening scene begins, appropriately, with Gwendolen being viewed through a haze, both literal and epistemological, by Daniel, who can only guess at her feelings as she plays at roulette. The roulette game, like the accidents that occur throughout – the Harleth family's financial losses, Daniel's encounters with Ezra and with Mirah Lapidow, Grandcourt's drowning – reflects the fact that these characters inhabit a secular rather than a providential world, filled with indeterminate causes and outcomes. The traditional certainties of knowledge, whether those of empiricism, religious faith, or even narratorial omniscience, have little hold here. Perhaps for this reason, when faith does emerge in the novel Eliot represents it in a form that would have been unfamiliar to most of her Victorian readers (including the devoutly Christian Maxwell); rather than a turn towards nostalgic assurances, Daniel's Judaism represents, both for him and for readers, a step towards the unknown.

But for Eliot, a modern world unguided by providence or traditional certitudes need not be an unfeeling or unsympathetic one. Deep feeling and sympathy are possible, she suggests in this last novel, but require a new mode for their generation and sustenance, guided by probabilistic thinking and approximation rather than absolute knowledge.[12] Acknowledging the limitations of one's vision, the hindrances to seeing or knowing with certainty, as the narrator herself does when she admits how little Grandcourt's "faded fairness" tells us, is the prerequisite for a new form of knowledge. By this criterion, Grandcourt himself fails miserably; compared to a "terrier" by the narrator, he understands his wife's feelings "in dog fashion ... with the narrow correctness which leaves a world of unknown feeling behind" (678). To insist on an exact account of others' emotional life, as Grandcourt does, is necessarily to fall short in human sympathy. Like Maxwell, Eliot directs us rather to an epistemological stance defined by uncertainty, where precise empirical information about the objects that interest us is unavailable. We might know the molecule's characteristics in terms of likelihoods and averages, just as Lush might know Grandcourt's general characteristics, but we cannot ascertain the behaviour of our object for any one moment in space and time. Moreover, this acceptance of ignorance, about molecules or persons, is generative of new modes of knowledge; indeed, as Eliot's narrator declares, "ignorance gives one a large range of probabilities" (137). The acknowledgment of ignorance, the novel suggests, is thus a productive starting point for probabilistic understanding.

Further, such imperfect knowledge is not only a result of the fundamental opacity of the individual, the lack of correspondence between appearance and emotion, between averages and particulars, but also, as the narrator reminds us, an effect of the many circumscribing social codes, rituals, and circumstances of Victorian London. The ether of social interaction, as it were, surrounds and fills the spaces between persons, at once invisible and congested with unexpressed, unknowable desires, impulses, temptations, and constraints. Eliot's novel explores what it means to act ethically and sympathetically in this world, where the possibilities for feeling, speech, and action that *might* exist, play a much larger role and occupy many more pages than those which can find utterance or actualization. Such intersubjective ignorance is, for characters like Daniel, Lush, and Gwendolen, as well as for us as readers, a rich landscape of possibility, and Eliot encourages us to envision those intervening spaces between observer and observed, where exactitude and empirical measurement are unattainable, as available to probabilistic modes of understanding.

When, for example, Daniel contemplates Gwendolen's marriage, the narrative tells us that "his mind had perhaps never been so active in weaving probabilities," and indeed, as the narrator reveals, his feeling for her is conveyed here not through any one insight, but through a series of possibilities: What "caused her to shrink from [marriage] – a shrinking finally overcome by the urgence of poverty? … Was [she,] under all her determined show of satisfaction, gnawed by a double, a treble-headed grief – self-reproach, disappointment, jealousy?" (433). Similarly, his attachment to Mirah begins when he sees her by the river, and "fell again and again to speculating on the probable romance that lay behind that loneliness and look of desolation" (188). This condition of not knowing, far from being futile, is instead what enables the development of a sympathetic imagination, the capacity to generate multiple hypotheses about the feelings and experiences of others. Two chapters later, the act of speculating consumes Daniel's attention again, as thinking back on his discovery of Mirah, he "saw and heard everything as clearly as before – saw not only the actual events of two hours, but possibilities of what had been and what might be which those events were enough to feed with the warm blood of passionate hope and fear" (205), followed by several paragraphs of speculation: about Mirah's past and about her future, about the true character of her lost relatives. In similar fashion, Gwendolen's connections to other characters can never achieve the resolution she longs for; her emotional isolation, a result of her marriage to the domineering Grandcourt, "caused her to live through [conversations with others] many times beforehand, imagining how they would take place and what she would say" (607). Much of the pleasure and satisfaction she takes in such social interaction comes, then, not from actualized conversations, which are too often kept in check by the presence of others, but from the time spent generating hypotheses about the many directions these conversations might take – conjuring that intersubjective space for herself in the imagination. Speculation acts as a positive, generative force here, filling the unknowable space that divides observer from observed, empirically available "actual events" from the unavailable emotions of lived experience, with a multiplicity of narratives, which reach out towards their object like so many benevolent tentacles of potential understanding. Indeed, Eliot's novel proposes, a sensitivity to qualities "which can never be written or even spoken – only divined by each of us" in "our neighbours' lives" constitutes a kind of "genius" of sympathetic feeling (179). Daniel's speculative ability thus serves as a model for intersubjective experience, not only for other characters but also for us as readers. Sympathy, even the exceptional sympathy of someone like Daniel, is only ever an approximation, an epistemological asymptote to its object.

In this sense, Eliot's last novel seems to pick up where *Middlemarch* leaves off in its final paragraph, with its contemplation of a single person's "incalculably diffusive" influence on others, of his or her "unvisited" grave as a marker of unrecognized effects (896). Where the preceding chapters of this earlier novel had assured us of the possibility of true mutual understanding – between Lydgate and Dorothea Brooke, between Dorothea and Rosamond Vincy, even between Will Ladislaw and James Chettam, characters divided by temperament and social class – its last lines dwell on the ethics of unreciprocated feeling, on the value of what cannot be calculated or identified. *Daniel Deronda* elaborates on the significance of unconfirmed influence and emotion, where Ezra's feeling for Daniel, Daniel's feeling for Gwendolen, even Daniel's feeling for God, elude definition or calculation.

The unlived, unrealized, hypothesized landscape of speculative knowledge is the primary dwelling place for the novel's characters throughout. The narrator shows us characters again and again weighing probabilities, and for this reason, these moments are more present, and possibly even more potent, than the novel's realized moments. As with Daniel, she leads us into the speculative reflections of other characters; we witness, too, the young artist Hans Meyrick thinking about the romantic inclinations of Mirah, Daniel, and Gwendolen ("Mrs Grandcourt"):

> Suppose Mirah's heart were entirely preoccupied with Deronda in another character than that of her own and her brother's benefactor: the supposition was attended in Hans's mind with anxieties which, to do him justice, were not altogether selfish. He had a strong persuasion, which only direct evidence

> to the contrary could have dissipated, that there was a serious attachment between Deronda and Mrs Grandcourt; he had pieced together many fragments of observation ... which convinced him not only that Mrs Grandcourt had a passion for Deronda, but also, notwithstanding his friend's austere self-repression, that Deronda's susceptibility about her was the sign of concealed love. Some men, having such a conviction, would have avoided allusions that could have roused that susceptibility; but Hans's talk naturally fluttered towards mischief, and he was given to a form of experiment on live animals which consisted in irritating his friends playfully. His experiments had ended in satisfying him that what he thought likely was true. (729–30)

The intersubjective, emotional spaces between characters – what Hans knows about Mirah's emotional state, what Mirah might feel for Daniel, what Daniel and Gwendolen feel for each other – occupy the centre of this long passage. As with her account of Lush's reflections, Eliot's narrator begins with indirect discourse, in which she lightly mediates Hans's thoughts, only to intercede without warning, shifting from Hans's limited perspective on his fellow characters to her own commentary on Hans's behaviour towards them. Like Lush, Hans is figured as a scientist, and yet in both cases, science represents not the power of comprehensive knowledge, but rather its limitations. Hans as the scientific observer draws the only conclusions he can about what he can neither see nor measure, and these limited data lead him, as we learn, to incorrect judgments. As the narrator's analogy reveals, in place of the empirical conclusiveness Hans seeks, he accumulates only "fragments of observation" and "sign[s]"; his answers come from a probabilistic interpretation of his observations ("what he thought likely").

What is more, the novel shows us that this probabilistic stance is not limited to its characters; indeed, even the reader is invited to generate his or her own speculations around the narrative. For instance, in describing Daniel's thought processes, the narrator makes her now characteristic move, first inhabiting Daniel's speculations about Gwendolen through free indirect discourse, then turning her third-person gaze onto Daniel himself: "Was she seeing the whole event – her own acts included – through an exaggerating medium of excitement and horror? Was she in a state of delirium into which there entered a sense of concealment and necessity for self-repression? Such thoughts glanced through Deronda as a sort of hope. But imagine the conflict of feeling that kept him silent" (689). But here the narrator departs from the pattern she follows in the examples discussed earlier; rather than offering a generalizing commentary about speculative knowledge, she moves our attention from the intersubjective space between Daniel and Gwendolen, to the intersubjective space between Daniel and ourselves as readers. Moreover, rather than filling that space with the certainties of her own omniscient knowledge, she encourages us to speculate ("imagine the conflict of feeling"), to generate our own narratives to describe Daniel's emotional state at that moment.

Daniel Deronda depicts a world in which characters are necessarily limited in what they can know about others; however, in contrast to *Middlemarch*, where the characters' epistemological constraints were offset by the narrator's own transcendent wisdom, the narrator of *Daniel Deronda* points to a more general condition, where we and she share in the experience of not knowing, of generating fields of possibility through speculative activity. This aspect of Eliot's fiction marks an important difference, then, from Maxwell's vision. Maxwell might have turned to the probabilistic to compensate for the lack of empirical evidence, but he also envisioned a being, whether idealized automaton or God, possessed of perfect perception, who could, for example, look at the movements of molecules in a box and determine the velocities and paths of individual molecules.[13] Yet Eliot seems to disavow even that possibility in *Daniel Deronda*. The goal for both characters and for us is not to aspire to that perfect insight, but to acknowledge the value of uncertainty as an ideal form of knowledge.

Eliot's narrator, then, provides a vision of this invisible world – a world of seemingly empty spaces between persons, between separate consciousnesses – and reveals that it is thick with feeling, intention, sympathy, and desire. But she also reveals that our knowledge can only ever be an approximation, a good guess about the object of our attention. The very nature of that space is, like the ether, probabilistic, a space of potential rather than of resolution, of all those things that might be rather than the one thing that has been. As Maxwell wrote to Campbell, "They say that Understanding ought to work by the rules of ... Logic; but the actual science of Logic is conversant at present only with things either certain, impossible, or *entirely* doubtful, none of which (fortunately) we have to reason on. Therefore the true Logic for this world is the Calculus of Probabilities" (*Scientific Letters* 1: 197). Maxwell's assertion is that an understanding of "this world" (and by this he seems to mean, not simply the world of molecules, but the "world" more generally) is constituted not so much by what is "certain" or what is "impossible," but by what lies between the two, by possibilities. To understand that world of the probable, of potential rather than of resolution, requires, as both Eliot and Maxwell understood, a redefinition of knowledge itself.

NOTES

An earlier version of this chapter appeared in the Proceedings of the Membranes, Surfaces, Boundaries Workshop, ed. Mathias Grote, Laura Otis, and Max Stadler, Max-Planck-Institut for the History of Science, Berlin, Germany (2011): 105–12.

1 As Maxwell summarized it, "According to a theory of electricity which is making great progress in Germany, two electrical particles act on one another directly at a distance ... Another theory of electricity, which I prefer, denies action at a distance and attributes electric action to tensions and pressures in an all-pervading medium" ("Address" 228). See also Dear 13, 116; Smith 211, 219.

2 Both Dear and Smith note that Maxwell offered this model as a hypothetical explanation for electromagnetic phenomena, rather than as an illustration of a physical reality.

3 This was originally delivered as an address to the British Association for the Advancement of Science, 16 September 1870.

4 As Smith recounts, Maxwell and Tyndall were involved in a bitter dispute over the direction of the energy sciences and their relationship to theology (Smith 170–2, 249), but little, if any, of that rivalry is evident in these addresses. Indeed, they seem in remarkably cordial agreement here in their characterization of the scientific imagination.

5 This was originally delivered as an address to the British Association for the Advancement of Science, 15 September 1870.

6 Porter's account traces Maxwell's gradual turn to probability through his interactions with other scientists, starting from the late 1850s (Porter 194–208).

7 Quoting La Rochefoucauld, Eliot offers a similar statement in one of her epigraphs for *Daniel Deronda*: "Il est plus aisé de connoître l'homme en général que de connoître un homme en particulier" (309); i.e., "It is easier to know mankind in general than to know one man in particular."

8 Spencer seems to have struggled with Maxwell's argument, a result perhaps of his own belief in a perfect epistemological clarity; in an ideal society, Spencer wrote, "emotions ... will visibly exhibit themselves" and a "simultaneous increase in the power of interpreting ... signs of feeling" will take place (*Data of Ethics* 286, 287). I am grateful to Kathy Psomiades for clarifying and helping me to locate this element in Spencer's work.

9 Indeed, according to Dyson, Maxwell's work anticipated twentieth-century quantum mechanics by describing a probabilistically rather than empirically known world of energies, movements, and collisions (5).

10 For an extensive discussion of intersubjectivity in the British literary tradition, see Butte, *I Know*.

11 Levine makes this observation as well ("George Eliot's Hypothesis" 18–19).
12 Levine likewise identifies the world of *Daniel Deronda* as characterized by epistemological uncertainty, but he is primarily interested in the relationship between knowledge and feeling in achieving sympathy ("*Daniel Deronda*" 69).
13 As Smith and Porter observe, Maxwell's thought experiment pointed to the statistical nature of the Second Law of Thermodynamics; see Smith 249–52, Porter 200–1.

WORKS CITED

Albrecht, Thomas. "Sympathy and Telepathy: The Problem of Ethics in George Eliot's *The Lifted Veil*." *ELH* 73 (2006): 437–63.

Beer, Gillian. *Darwin's Plots: Evolutionary Narrative in Darwin, George Eliot and Nineteenth-Century Fiction*. Cambridge: Cambridge UP, 2000.

Butte, George. *I Know That You Know That I Know: Narrating Subjects from* Moll Flanders *to* Marnie. Columbus: Ohio State UP, 2004.

Daston, Lorraine. *Classical Probability in the Enlightenment*. Princeton: Princeton UP, 1988.

Dear, Peter. *The Intelligibility of Nature: How Science Makes Sense of the World*. Chicago: U of Chicago P, 2006.

Dyson, Freeman. "Why Is Maxwell's Theory So Hard to Understand?" Delivered at and published in the Proceedings of the Second European Conference on Antennas and Propagation, 11–16 November 2007. London: Institution of Engineering and Technology, 2007.

Eliot, George. *Daniel Deronda*. 1876. London: Penguin Books, 2003.

– *Middlemarch*. 1871–2. London: Penguin Books, 1965.

Ermarth, Elizabeth. "George Eliot's Conception of Sympathy." *Nineteenth-Century Fiction* 40.1 (1985): 23–45.

Gallagher, Catherine. "George Eliot: Immanent Victorian." *Representations* 90 (2005): 61–74.

George Eliot's Daniel Deronda *Notebooks*. Ed. Jane Irwin. Cambridge: Cambridge UP, 1996.

Greiner, Rae. "Thinking of Me Thinking of You: Sympathy v. Empathy in the Realist Novel." *Victorian Studies* 53 (2011): 417–26.

Hacking, Ian. *The Taming of Chance*. Cambridge: Cambridge UP, 1990.

Herbert, Christopher. *Victorian Relativity: Radical Thought and Scientific Discovery*. Chicago: U of Chicago P, 2001.

Levine, George. "*Daniel Deronda*: A New Epistemology." In *Knowing the Past: Victorian Literature and Culture*. Ed. Suzy Anger. Ithaca: Cornell UP, 2001. 52–73.

– *Darwin and the Novelists: Patterns of Science in Victorian Fiction*. Chicago: U of Chicago P, 1991.
– *Dying to Know: Scientific Epistemology and Narrative in Victorian England*. Chicago: U of Chicago P, 2002.
– "George Eliot's Hypothesis of Reality." *Nineteenth-Century Literature* 35 (1980): 1–28.
Luhmann, Niklas. *Observations on Modernity*. Trans. William Whobrey. Stanford: Stanford UP, 1998.
Maxwell, James Clerk. "Address to the Mathematical and Physical Sections of the British Association." In *The Scientific Papers of James Clerk Maxwell*, vol. 2. Ed. W.D. Niven. Mineola, NY: Dover Publications, Inc., 2003. 215–29.
– "Molecules." *Nature* 8 (1873): 437–41.
– *The Scientific Letters and Papers of James Clerk Maxwell*. Ed. P.M. Harman. 3 vols. Cambridge: Cambridge UP, 1990.
– *Theory of Heat* (1871, 1888). Ed. Peter Pesic. Mineola, NY: Dover Publications, 2001.
– *A Treatise on Electricity and Magnetism*. Vol. 1. Oxford: Clarendon Press, 1873.
Poovey, Mary. *A History of the Modern Fact: Problems of Knowledge in the Sciences of Wealth and Society*. Chicago: U of Chicago P, 1998.
Porter, Theodore. *The Rise of Statistical Thinking 1820–1900*. Princeton: Princeton UP, 1986.
Pyle, Forest. "A Novel Sympathy: The Imagination of Community in George Eliot." *NOVEL: A Forum on Fiction* 27.1 (1993): 5–23.
"Registration of Sickness." *All the Year Round* 4 (1860): 227–8.
Rosenthal, Jesse. "The Large Novel and the Law of Large Numbers; Or, Why George Eliot Hates Gambling." *ELH* 77 (2010): 777–811.
Rothfield, Lawrence. *Vital Signs: Medical Realism in Nineteenth-Century Fiction*. Princeton: Princeton UP, 1992.
Smith, Crosbie. *The Science of Energy: A Cultural History of Energy Physics in Victorian Britain*. Chicago: U of Chicago P, 1998.
Spencer, Herbert. *The Data of Ethics*. 1879. New Brunswick, NJ: Transaction Publishers, 2011.
Tyndall, John. "On the Scientific Use of the Imagination." In *Scientific Addresses*. New Haven: Charles Chatfield & Co., 1870. 33–74.

PART III

Sensing: Anthropology, Psychology, Aesthetics

6 Herder's Unsettling of the Distinction between Fact and Fiction

JOHN K. NOYES

In this chapter I show how, in his earliest writings, Johann Gottfried Herder sets in place a program of research that calls into question the distinction between fact and fiction. In a number of early papers, he develops two fundamental principles that render the fact/fiction distinction problematic: the first is the unknowability of Being; the second is the discursive nature of knowledge. Taken together, these principles ensure that any attempt to formulate statements of fact has to be measured on the same scale that is applied when reading poetic language. This is not to say that the notion of factuality is clouded by its rhetorical strategies, but that there is something about the poetic that resides at the heart of factuality.

In 1764 Herder wrote a short paper, *Versuch über das Sein* (Essay on Being), on the impulse of Kant's lectures on metaphysics, and on some of Kant's pre-critical writings. Herder refers again and again, both directly and indirectly, to Kant's publications of the years 1762 and 1763, such as *Die falsche Spitzfindigkeit der vier syllogistischen Figuren* (The False Subtlety of the Four Syllogistic Figures, 1762), *Versuch, den Begriff der negativen Größen in die Weltweisheit einzuführen* (Attempt to Introduce the Concept of Negative Magnitudes into Philosophy, 1763), and, above all, *Der einzig mögliche Beweisgrund zu einer Demonstration des Daseins Gottes* (The Only Possible Argument in Support of a Demonstration of the Existence of God, 1763). Herder also references the works of Crusius, and Baumgarten's metaphysics and aesthetics, which formed the backbone of Kant's lectures on philosophy in the 1760s.[1]

The general philosophical problem Herder addresses is what Pross calls the "crisis in causality and the problem of evidence" (*MA* 1: 844), which, in the wake of Locke and Hume, had split the philosophical debates of the Enlightenment, forcing writers to think about how best to use the rules of logic and/or observation and experimentation to explain the phenomena of the natural world. Like Kant, Herder examines Being as a concept that cannot be further analysed, and he follows his teacher in denying the status of a predicate to Being: nothing is explained by stating that an object has existence. Herder also rejects any attempts to explain either Ideal Being (*Idealsein*) or Existential Being (*Existentialsein*) on the basis of the other, as Descartes had done by declaring *cogito ergo sum*, or Crusius in asserting the existence of the self on the basis of self-consciousness.[2] The point of departure, and the guiding principle of the essay, is stated clearly in the Prolegomena, where Herder declares his adherence to a philosophy that follows the "*human* paths of attention, abstraction and reflection" ("Versuch über das Sein" 576). Kant, too, in his writings of the 1760s repeatedly emphasized the need to consider the human dimension of thought.[3] The human dimension of thought is characterized by the specificity of sensory experience on the one hand and the universality of logical thought on the other. Herder links the two through innate cognitive processes. Attention is the capacity of the mind to focus on the information imparted by the senses, and the processes of abstraction and reflection are the cornerstones of the analytic method, which Herder recognized as the cognitive distinction that sets humans apart from the rest of creation.

With this declaration, Herder is announcing his philosophical lineage. But as the essay progresses, he will begin to push these ideas in a remarkable direction. It is not simply that he attempts to revise Baumgarten's views on aesthetics, following what Gaier calls a characteristic move in eighteenth-century philosophy – the shift in focus from "the aporia of philosophy to aesthetics as a metatheory" (*FA* 1: 857). He also wants to dwell on the intersection of philosophy and aesthetics by studying the conditions under which the information given to the senses is converted to thought processes. Philosophy, he felt, is not in a position to add to the store of existing knowledge. It can only provide a better understanding of knowledge through relating concepts to experience.[4] As Herder puts it, "One has to *really exist* if one is to think" (*MA* 2: 11). And to really exist is to exist in time and space. Philosophical inquiry has to confront the fact that the concepts it uses have a history, a genesis within the thought processes of the perceiving subject, in the same way that they have a geography, a location in the natural world.

When he demonstrated in the *Essay on Being* that experience becomes increasingly inaccessible to the operations of logic as it comes closer to the saturated fullness of unmediated sensory perception, Herder felt that he had also shown the error in the founding premise of Baumgarten's aesthetics. Baumgarten followed Wolff and Leibniz in regarding sensory cognition as taking place on a lower order than rational cognition, but he applied their concept of rational analogy – which they had used in order to compare the cognitive faculty of animals to that of humans[5] – in order to argue that there is a science of sensory cognition, just as there is a science of rational thought, and that this science can serve as a guiding principle in making true judgments about sensory experience, and in the production of objects of beauty. The problem with this approach to aesthetics is that it applies the same formalism that undermines the effectiveness of logic,[6] and it consequently prescribes artificial rules to artistic production, thereby inscribing them with the limitations of rational thought. Rational thought needs to confine itself to the sphere of cognition where it remains effective. Aesthetic experience, as it comes closer to the experience of Being – the "most sensory of concepts" – recedes from the grasp of logic, and no attempt to bring it back will succeed. What remains for the philosopher is to investigate the genesis of concepts and the factors influencing aesthetic experience. This is what Marion Heinz and Heinrich Clairmont call the "anthropocentric turn" in Herder's epistemology, whereby "pointless attempts to solve the problem of truth as the central task of classical epistemology are to be renounced in favor of meta-reflection on which kind of certainty is possible for which kind of subject" ("Herder's Epistemology" 46–7). In turning the philosophical pursuit of truth to an aesthetics of human life, Herder is pushing the philosophical project in the direction of an anthropology of cognition, which will ask questions about the material factors influencing the subjective processes that lead from experience to a world view.

At the same time that he was working on the *Essay on Being*, Herder was attending Kant's lectures on geography. The topics of Kant's lectures were wide-ranging and included physical geography, which he was later to declare as the cornerstone for an understanding of humanity's place in the world. Around the time Herder arrived in Königsberg, Kant's announcements of his forthcoming classes almost always included physical geography.[7] In fact, looking back on his career shortly before his death in 1800, Kant observes that over the course of thirty years he had been careful to include courses on both anthropology and physical geography in his duties as a teacher of philosophy. He is explicit in stating that these two disciplines complement one another in imparting "*Weltkenntniß*" (knowledge of the world) (*Anthropology from a Pragmatic Point of View*, note to page 6). One of the reasons why geography assumed foundational importance in Kant's thinking was that it provided him with the grounds for discussing various other aspects of human life and thought.[8] It formed the basis for what he called a general pragmatic anthropology, the study of the self-apprehension of human beings, in their relationship to the natural world and their own human nature.

The view of physical geography Kant imparted to his students placed it on the cusp between nature and human life. In the report on the plan of his lectures for the winter semester 1765–6, the year after Herder left Königsberg, Kant suggests a threefold conception of the discipline that would include "physical, moral and political geography." The basis of this threefold geography is "the natural relationship which holds between all the countries and seas of the world," as well as the basis of their interconnection. Kant calls this basis "the real foundation of all history," without which "history is scarcely distinguishable from fairy tales." The second step is to investigate "humanity according to the variety of its natural properties," with the aim of acquiring "a comprehensive map of the human species." Finally, the interaction of these two aspects allows a study of "the condition of the *states* and nations throughout the world" (Kant, "Announcement" 229).[9]

If geographical knowledge points to the diversity of the human condition, it presented Herder with a set of problems that are closely related to the problem of Being. The grounding of history in geography suggests that the story of humanity's development through the ages derives in some as yet unexplained manner from experiences of geographical diversity. The priority of geography as the "real foundation" of historical narratives indicates a collective experience of geographical Being that has, through time, been translated into various collective narratives of historical becoming. What this means is that there must be something in the stories history tells that harks back to sensory cognition and the experience of Being. Geography does not secure the truth of history in contradistinction to fairy tales by giving it a location, as Kant had hoped. Instead, history is itself grounded in and merges with a more fundamental discourse of Being – that of poetry. In Herder's opinion, Baumgarten was right in identifying poetry as a pure discourse of the experience of Being, but he was mistaken in his attempts to explain poetry in terms of Wolffian logic. Poetry, like the other art forms, is an aesthetic expression of aesthetic experience: *aisthetic* perception is subject to *aesthetic* reflection (Greif, "Herder's Aesthetics" 143).[10] Artistic products testify in different ways to what it is like to be located in time and space, and to what kind of models of nature's hidden forces can be used to link the spatial and temporal aspects of embodied being. To draw up a catalogue of the different genres that does justice to the complex poetic reflections on time, space, and force would be to draft what Herder calls a "map of the human soul" (*MA* 2: 11). This map would show how the different sense perceptions of time, space, and force give rise to different forms of artistic reflection.[11] Here, literary criticism is forced to engage with the fundamental problems of philosophy.

The challenge facing literary criticism is to write of poetry in a language that does not supplant the immediacy of originary experience with the "totally univocal language" towards which philosophy strives (Zammito, *Kant, Herder* 160). Instead, the descriptive language of criticism needs to trace the self-understanding that arises from the apprehension of the world. History works together with philosophy and poetry in providing the theoretical framework for this project. Herder called this project anthropology, and "he pronounced it philosophy's legitimate successor" (ibid.), since any philosophy which was to be for humanity will have to re-centre scientific inquiry on its real object – humanity, in all its manifestations. The focus on humanity sent Herder on a quest for a model capable of explaining the force determining the unitary development of humanity in its diverse manifestations – just as Copernicus and Kepler had sought the force at the centre of the universe that determines the motion of all heavenly bodies. As Palti notes, in the 1770s, Herder came to see history as analogous to cosmology.[12]

Herder's move from philosophy to anthropology or, as he put it in 1765, the "withdrawal of philosophy into anthropology" (*FA* 1: 103), seemed to provide an appropriate shift in perspective, since it drew on empirically verifiable data in order to reconstruct a perspective on that which could not be verified. But it also brought with it a problem that becomes apparent as Herder begins to turn his attention to the historical development of the different art forms that express diverse experiences of social life. Herder was so convinced of the fundamental correctness of his departure from Wolff, Baumgarten, and Kant that he began to think of the individual genesis of concepts out of sensory cognition not only in terms of the individual but also in terms of the social collective, and of the species as a whole. The philosophical formulation of this coincidence of the individual with the species will lead Herder to take the position that Marion Heinz calls (in the title of her 1994 book) "sensual idealism."[13] According to Heinz and Clairmont, this position is first taken in the sketch *Plato sagte* (Plato Said, 1767). Here Herder describes the soul as a finite force that enters into dialogue with the body via "a specifically organized body-soul constitution produced by itself" (Heinz and Clairmont 49).[14] What is being described here is not only the psychological genesis of concepts in a particular individual or a particular apperceptive event, but a fundamental quality and a central process of human nature. It is part of the objective constitution of human beings that cognitive faculties of the soul point to a being which they cannot grasp, while our physiology organizes sensory concepts according to the concepts of time, space, and force. Starting in 1767, with *Plato Said*, Herder begins to address the paradoxical position of the mind or soul (*Seele*) with respect to Being. Here, "representations mediated through external sensory perception are considered as consequences of inner thought occasioned by the perception of objects" (Heinz and Clairmont 49–50). This appears to invite Descartes in through the back door by assigning primacy to the mind in grasping Being, while time, space, and nature's force are concepts relating to bodily experience. What Herder is in fact trying to do – and what he will continue to attempt in his subsequent writings – is to find a way to describe the conceptual unity that resides within the infinite variety of phenomena and experiences. The assumption that there is such a conceptual unity grounding creation is central to Herder's theology and cosmology. It contains the idea, as Pross shows, that the infinite diversity of creation only makes sense if we think of it as preceded by the "purely intellectual anticipation of their unity" (*MA* 3.2: 348). Furthermore, this is built into the diversity of nature as a structural potential for unity, and natural as well as historical development is motivated by a drive to realize this potential. In the realm of thought, the progression from the physiological apprehension of time and space through to thinking about Being follows this structural potential, and it leads to the realization that thinking about Being is "purely symbolic" and that it is "the opposite of sensory representation" (*MA* 3.2: 347–8). Symbolization is what Heinz and Clairmont call a "spiritualization of nature" and a "naturalization of spirit" (Heinz and Clairmont 52).

Because Herder understands himself to be speaking not only of unique individual psychological processes but of human nature, the objectivity of knowledge can be thought of not only in epistemological or psychological terms, but also in terms that would later provide the field for social anthropology. Representations of the world are not only individual; they are shared, and they have a shared history. In approaching the concept of Being through the concepts of time, space, and natural force, the body represents its environment to the mind – and here Herder was thinking of Spinoza. But in the shared genesis of these representations – and in the shared medium of their communication (language and art) – the individual appropriates the world and the culture in which he or she lives.[15] This is why the philosopher in pursuit of the essence of human life cannot begin by tracing human expression back to an act of divine intervention (this conviction forms the backbone of Herder's later essay on the origin of language). Instead, he has to take account of the fact that, in acts of linguistic creation, human expression works in analogy with and according to the same laws as the divine force at work in nature. The essence of divine force causes it to manifest itself as a diversity of cultural expressions, which themselves retain structural traces of the idea of their unity. For Herder, language could not be traced back to a single, ideal purpose that might be named divine. Language is a social arrangement that expresses the diversity of human life. Writing in 1766, Herder asked what would remain for him the fundamental question of linguistic diversity: "Are there not a thousand indications in one language, and in the diversity of languages millions of vestiges, of how it was precisely through language that the nations gradually learned to think, and through thinking that they gradually learned to speak?" (Herder, "Über die Bildung einer Sprache" 154).

In Herder's analysis, nature's force reveals itself in the relationship between various unifying and diversifying impulses, each of which requires a corresponding conceptualization on the part of the philosopher – to the point where philosophy needs to take on board the various other discourses aimed at understanding human life: psychology, biology, physiology, cultural anthropology, and so on. These discourses cast human life into a set of disciplines that establish the terms of their own factuality, and in the process they run the risk of posing as transparent windows onto the objective world. Herder saw scientific model-formation in the disciplines within the context of his aesthetic theory – as rhetorical systems for articulating well-defined aspects of experience.

Herder began early on to think of aesthetics as an inquiry into the common foundations of this process, but at the same time he saw the endless possibilities for studying the historical development of shared representations in specific cultures. Any such study would have to remain grounded in the essential insight into human nature: that "all human beings have *aestheticam connatam*, since they are *all born* as sensory animals, and since they are more animal than spirit, the aesthetica connata is *necessarily* greater than innate logic ... Here lies the origin of the *sensory* sensibility for beauty, which all humanity has in common" ("Plan zu einer Aesthetik" 660). Because of this, there is something about the poetic that remains essential to discourses of fact. The test case would be history.

In 1764, at the same time that he was working on the *Essay on Being*, Herder drafted a study of poetry as evidence of this single human drive to expression, but a drive whose forms of expression are infinite in variety.

In his posthumously published *Versuch einer Geschichte der lyrischen Dichtkunst* (Outline of a History of Lyric Poetry), he ties this problem of formal multiplicity and unity of purpose to the question of the origin of things, and the genesis of the world. "One of the most pleasant fields in which human curiosity can stray," he tells us in the opening sentence, is the recognition of "the origin of that which exists" (*Geschichte der lyrischen Dichtkunst* 85). This study of origins is even more appealing when it is concerned with the products of human artifice.

In the opening paragraph of this essay, it becomes clear that Herder is already thinking of epistemology as parallel to history. The pursuit of the origin of knowledge in sensory concepts follows the historical pursuit of human knowledge in the depths of prehistory. He speaks of the drive to knowledge (*Wißbegierde*), which "pushes forward, unsatisfied," following a path "into the darkest times, in order to experience historically the beginning of things, or else to explain them philosophically, or to speculate on their possibility" (*Geschichte der lyrischen Dichtkunst* 85). The framework here is anthropological in the sense Zammito claims, in that it brings philosophy, poetry, and history into dialogue with one another in the name of holistic human knowledge. In speaking of the darkest times in which knowledge seeks its own origins, he is evoking the Leibnizian obscurity of the sensory (Norton 40). In the *Essay on Being* he declared that "all my representations are sensory – they are obscure; sensory and obscure have been synonymous expressions for a long time" ("Versuch über das Sein" 11). But he is also evoking the problem of historical origins, where historical knowledge merges with oral tradition, myth, and the unknown, and where truth slips from the field of philosophical discourse, or at least from the discourses of rationalism, and enters the domain of poetic language, the form of expression that is both epistemologically and historically prior to the language of philosophy.[16] "Philosophers came forth quite late in time; they themselves hailed from poets; they spoke in the language of poets; they derived their wisdom from poets and from common life" (*EW* 81); and so the natural drive to seek origins leads directly to a history of humanity. This, he continues, is the reason why "we take such pleasure in reading the poetic or philosophical hypotheses on the origins of familiar objects"; and here he cites the opening chapters of the Bible as presenting "the oldest reports on the childhood of the world" (*Geschichte der lyrischen Dichtkunst* 85).

In formulating the challenge facing the study of origins in poetry or philosophy, Herder emphasizes how all nations have responded to this historicizing explanatory drive in a similar manner, with the development of "cosmogonies that contain the grounds of their wisdom." The diverse forms of these cosmogonies cannot themselves be traced back to a single origin, although their form of expression may point in that direction. Herder rejects from the outset the possibility that "all nations appropriated these treasures from a single people; that everything has to be traced back to the lands of the East, that all streams arise from a single spring." Instead, he insists that it is more helpful "to seek within each people itself the seeds that were capable of giving rise to the arts and sciences" (*Geschichte der lyrischen Dichtkunst* 94–5). This is not to deny the common ground of poetic expression, but to shift it away from facile models of geographical origins in favour of the common anthropological condition. Monogenesis is a biological fact, but culture is polygenetic.

The project of a history of the forms of expression of humanity in all its diverse manifestations is itself like the cosmogonies of the nations. In taking cognizance of the single drive to expression that unites all peoples, such a history must at the same time recognize that the more we study the origin of this drive, the more it fades away into the far distant past, becoming ever more fictional as its recedes. In its place, we are left with the certainty that all people share an intense desire for knowledge, an epistemological drive, as well as a form-giving drive, an aesthetic drive, and that the forms of expression of these drives are infinite in variety. The historian of humanity is like the poet – he responds to a desire for knowledge by creating aesthetic products that mark the limits of this knowledge. And if there is such a thing as a single origin of human expression, its traces lie in the multiplicity of poetic form throughout the world. The diversity of expression is like a mosaic, a composite picture of that which each nation can only dream in its cosmogonies.

By outlining the historiographical challenges of poetic expression in this way, Herder is setting the markers for his future aesthetic project. Wolfgang Pross speaks of a "program of research" that sets itself the goal of grasping the universal nature of the human being in its anthropological constitution while "taking account of the legitimacy of the divergent historical forms of this constitution" (*MA* 1: 694). One of the earliest attempts to do justice to this program of research was the essay *Über den Fleiß in mehreren gelehrten Sprachen* (On Diligence in the Study of Several Learned Languages, 1764), and it marks the point where Herder's epistemology first leads him to confront some of the contemporary effects of European imperialism.

On Diligence was one of the last essays Herder wrote before leaving Königsberg for Riga. It was published in the *Gelehrte Beiträge zu den*

Rigaischen Anzeigen in October 1764, but was composed in the form of a speech earlier in the year.[17] On the surface, it addresses the question of priority in the teaching of the mother tongue and foreign languages in schools, a matter that was much debated in Herder's day, and that continued to occupy him in the years he spent in Riga (Gaier, *FA* 1: 870).[18] As Michael Morton has shown, there has been a recurrent tendency in Herder criticism to read the essay on this surface level, and to derive the interesting but not particularly surprising position Herder takes: that the mother tongue will always have priority over acquired languages, since "nature imposes upon us an obligation only to our mother tongue," but that, in the developmental history of humanity, the learning of foreign languages plays a key role (*On Diligence* 30). However, reading this essay within the epistemological framework Herder developed in *On Being*, it becomes clear that much more is at stake.[19]

The opening paragraphs of the essay are built upon a number of assumptions that relate directly to *On Being*. The first of these concerns the central task of Herder's anthropology: bringing philosophy into dialogue with history and poetry in order to gain insight into the genesis of humanity. In order to clarify what exactly the terms of this dialogue should be, he begins the essay by setting himself apart from the commonly held view that poetry can serve to revitalize the originary language of nature. The most important proponent of this view for Herder was Johann Georg Hamann, whom Herder had met in church in Königsberg earlier that year. Like Herder, Hamann was intent upon demonstrating the importance of sensory experience and, above all, of feelings and emotions in the life of the mind, since "nature works by way of the senses and passions" (Hamann, *Aesthetica in nuce* 131). Language for him was the key to unity in human life. This grants poetry and the poetic arts a special place, since they provide a form of expression that allows experience to move beyond the shackles of the rational mind. Furthermore, they allow specific cultural experiences to be expressed in accordance with the unique qualities of a specific language. In his *Aesthetica in nuce* of 1760, he wrote that poetry is "the mother-tongue of the human race; even as the garden is older than the ploughed field, painting than script; as song is more ancient than declamation; parables older than reasoning; barter than trade" (*Aesthetica in nuce* 121). This historical priority of poetic language has an epistemological correlate, since poetic language focuses on and reproduces the imagery of the senses and the passions. Nature is to be read as a compendium of signs, and the key to human happiness lies in the correct deciphering of nature's signs. "The senses and passions speak and comprehend nothing but images. In images lie the entire treasure of human knowledge and happiness" (ibid. 121–2). The imagery of poetic language is thus one step closer to originary experience than the concepts of logic.

Hamann's ideas on the history of expression connected well with Herder's conviction that the poetic expression of individual cultures cannot be evaluated in absolute terms, nor measured on a scale given by European culture. In fact, there is something about the lives of more innocent cultures (Hamann speaks of "the heathens") that allows them, in their "blindness" to "recognize the invisibility which humans have in common with GOD" (*Aesthetica in nuce* 122). The underlying assumption of this recognition of linguistic diversity, together with the belief in a common human communion with God and Nature, is that there is a single unidirectional movement of human development, which issues from some primary divine or natural force, or some primal creative event. "Speak, so that I may see you! – This wish was granted in the act of Creation, which is speech through created beings to created beings. For one day speaks to the next, and one night heralds the next. Their watchword runs through all climates up to the end of the world, and their voice can be heard in every language" (ibid. 123). Not only did Hamann believe that poetic language could transport humanity back to its childhood, where the communion with divine creativity had not been tarnished by the rational mind, but he felt there must be other cultures that were closer to this process than his own. When he wrote *Aesthetica in nuce*, he was beginning to tentatively explore the idea that other cultures held the potential for reinvigorating what had ossified or decayed in the European context. He asked himself how it would be possible to "raise the defunct language of Nature from the dead," suggesting immediately that the answer was by "making pilgrimages to the fortunate lands of Arabia, and by going on crusades to the East, and by restoring their magic art. To steal it, we must employ old women's cunning, for that is the best sort" (ibid. 16). The terms in which he imagines this process are still rudimentary, to say the least, still rife with imagery borrowed from popular tales of crusade, conquest, and plunder, but his ideas on poetic language and on cultural cross-fertilization pose a pressing question to Herder: if poetry is the mother tongue of humanity, how well do we speak it?

The answer to this question can be sought on a number of levels. It is true, the golden age has past, but this did not stop Hamann from attempting to revitalize the language, if not the age, and to harness it against the "murderously deceitful philosophy" of his day (*Aesthetica in nuce* 131). Hamann's writing was intended to evoke the muse that would "dare to purify the natural use of the senses and cleanse it from the unnatural uses of abstraction, through which our concept of things is deformed to the same extent that the Creator is suppressed and blasphemed" (ibid. 13). Herder was to take a plain stance on this in his essay on Hamann, *Dithyrambische Rhapsodie über die Rhapsodie kabbalistischer Prose* (Dithyrambic Rhapsody on the Rhapsody of Cabalistic Prose), written in early 1765, where he stated: "If poetry is the mother tongue, then ours is prose" (31).

Similarly, the earlier, unpublished version of *On Diligence* begins with the words "It has vanished, that flourishing age ..." (*FA* 1: 22). In stating the passing of the golden age, Herder draws a line between himself and the age of humanity's earliest communion with nature, which Hamann had characterized in *Aesthetica in nuce*. And Herder casts this age irrevocably into the past even while retaining Hamann's understanding of what the poetic age looked like: it was a "golden age," when "our earliest ancestors dwelt round the patriarchs like children round their parents," and when "all the world was of one tongue and language" (*On Diligence* 29). Like Hamann's "mother tongue of the human race" (*Aesthetica in nuce* 2), the language of Herder's golden age is poetic in the sense that it presents the imagery in which "the senses and the passions speak and comprehend" (ibid. 12). And it is the language of nature, since "nature acts (*würkt*) via the senses and the passions" (ibid., translation modified). And like Hamann, Herder registers the chasm that separates this language from our own, which is marked with "the burden of our learning and the masks of our virtues" (*On Diligence* 29). But unlike his friend, Herder sees no point in sustaining the rhapsodic evocation of the lost language of a lost age: "But why do I sketch a lost portrait of irreplaceable charms? It is no more, this golden age" (*On Diligence* 29). In a prosodic age, critical discourse can attain the goals Hamann sets himself only by drawing the full methodological and topical consequences of the impossibility of analysing Being.[20] But the problem with the prosodic age is that it speaks in a rhetoric of factuality, while intending to mediate the insights of poetry.

In beginning *On Diligence* with a concealed criticism of Hamann, Herder is once again raising the problem of philosophical method. Herder's rejection of the rationalist school's attempt to apply mathematical method in philosophy and transfer this to aesthetics was in agreement with Hamann.[21] But the methodological consequences he drew were quite different. In *On Being*, Herder stated that idealism cannot be refuted on the basis of that which is logically possible.[22] Logical possibility is embedded in philosophical language, where it serves to link concepts to one another through the use of grammar. Since logical possibility and grammar mutually guarantee the validity of propositions of being, the Being of which they speak cannot be proved or disproved using logical possibility. Similarly, common sense shows that no experiential concept can be proven a priori ("Versuch über das Sein" 584).[23] What this means from a methodological point of view is that the idealist position must be unmasked by demonstrating, using the method of analysis, that idealist claims to make meaningful statements about Being are all based on the unspoken assumption of Being's unanalysability. Once analysis has pointed to the moments where idealism is built upon the knowledge of Being as its own unanalysable foundation, it can be shown how grammar hides its founding premises. This is the point at which Herder solicits poetic language. As a formalization of Being's unanalysability, it speaks within, not outside of, philosophical language.[24]

This is how Herder is asking to be read when he begins *On Diligence* with an imaginary foray into mythological time. The opening images of a golden age, followed by the whirlwind tour from the Tower of Babel through the Greeks and Romans to present-day Germans, Spaniards, and Africans is intended to present the process whereby knowledge of history becomes possible. When it confronts the origin of things, historical discourse devises stories about the Being that has enabled it, and that will forever escape its grasp. Only after Herder has uncovered this process does he begin to speak of the mother tongue as the material perpetuation of one particular way of moving from prehistory to history, and from Being and sensation to consciousness. Once we see it in these terms, another methodological question presents itself, and this one will prove to be much more problematic for Herder. This is the principle of the analogous development of individual language speakers, of individual linguistic communities, and of humanity as a collective language-speaking organism. This is, as Morton observes, "a key element of Herder's thought" (*Herder and Poetics* 30). With his image of "our earliest ancestors" placed in juxtaposition with the image of children in the presence of their parents, Herder is establishing the link between species and individual as one of the most important assumptions of his essay. He uses it not only to describe the initial poetic communion with nature, but also the growth out of this condition and into maturity. In doing this, he sets himself the task of explaining how the processes that shape individual life are different from, and how they are similar to, the processes at work in the development of the species. In *On Diligence* Herder begins to sketch one of the most important aspects in the coincidence of individual development and the development of the species: the role of language. Language mediates the individual's experience of the world and the collective thought processes that make sense of the world. And it also provides the building blocks for repeating this mediation on a collective level – the level of a linguistic community, or a culture, but perhaps even a species level.

Herder embeds the question of language learning in the context of the historical development of humanity out of mythical origins into its current state. Herder's age is characterized by a multiplicity of languages and cultures scattered across the earth, each with its own set of traditions, each with a distinct relationship to its specific environment. Each of these has its own national characteristics, interpretations of the world, and characteristic sets of skills. After the failed Tower of Babel, humanity began to split into "families and dialects" that were "transplanted to various points of the compass; and a thousand languages were created in tune with the climes and mores of a thousand nations" (*On Diligence* 29). It is only natural that languages and cultures drift apart in the course of history, since they are acted upon from without by the different environments in which they take root (*Clima*, climes), and from within by the perpetuation of tradition and shared memory (*Sitten*, mores). This becomes increasingly pronounced throughout history. But it raises another problem that will occupy Herder for years to come. As the languages and cultures drift apart, where is the cultural location from which its unity can be imagined? In what language can its unity be described? And how do we imagine the many cultures of the world developing into an organic whole, without imposing our world view and value system on them?

Within the life of an individual, there are various forces at work to ensure a tight bond among psychological development, the development of the mind, and the cultural context in which development takes place. This tight bond ensures that the individual experiences culture as possessing a natural dimension, since culture mediates the effects of climes; and a historical one, since culture appears as a collection of historically transmitted mores. Within this cultural context, the most important force at work in the psychological and cognitive development of the individual is the mother tongue, since "it is perhaps better attuned to our character and coextensive with our way of thinking" (*EW* 30). In describing the primacy of the mother tongue in human development, Herder is careful to emphasize the blurry line between historical and environmental factors. The language of the fatherland forms a cultural bond that ties its members together, while at the same time creating an inner drive that presents one's own language as the most attractive one of all. In using the word *Reiz* (attraction, allure, stimulus, charm) to describe this attraction, Herder is also blurring the line between emotional forces and physiological ones. It is the experience of attraction that bonds the individual to his language and gives preference to the mother tongue as part of the developmental psychology of the human being. The early experiences of pleasure in the mother tongue "impressed themselves upon us first and somehow shaped themselves together with the finest fissures of our sensibility" (*On Diligence* 32). But they are also part of the individual's physiological constitution, since, as he argues in *On Being*, the mental life of the individual is grounded in the senses. It follows that not only the organs of sense themselves, but also the regime of concepts built upon them have a particular affinity with the language into which an individual is born. In Herder's words, "Our mother tongue really harmonizes most perfectly with our most sensitive organs and our most delicate turns of mind" (*On Diligence* 30). What this means is that the mother tongue is "the instrument with which the child collects a world of images and concepts into his or her soul by means of words; the specific ways and methods of thinking characteristic of a people are as it were planted in its language, and the learning child forms soul, ear, and organs of speech synchronically" (Gaier, "Core Cognition" 303).

In acquiring a mother tongue, a person is shaped, developmentally and physiologically, into an individual who is also a member of a group, who exists in time and space, and is subject to the forces, both environmental and social, that make up that person's culture. The experience of becoming human means confronting one's own Being as it is moulded by the forces associated with the Crusian *ubi* and *quando*, which amounts to confronting the forces of history and geography. But it also means striving to live in the consciousness of one's historical and geographical determination, and to understand how the organism one has become is a result of these forces. This is why the limits of cognition Herder described in *On Being* also mark the limits at which one is able to confront one's own cultural, historical, and geographical determination as something factual, objective. It is in the nature of cognition that the ability to make statements about the world external to oneself is always compromised by the speaker's own organic condition, its organic life as a material extension of the "external" world. Confronting factuality means confronting the limits of cognition, and the medium of this confrontation resides at the very core of the discourses of truth and factuality. Wherever poetic language can be shown to inhere in statements of factuality, the mind comes a little closer to understanding its strange relationship with a truth it can never quite grasp.

NOTES

1 Rudolf Haym's appraisal that Herder is steering a course remarkably close to Kant's pre-critical writing has been the subject of much critical revision, and more recent readings are much more conscious of the independent moves in the essay. Herder is using his teacher's ideas to position himself critically within the labyrinth of mid-century metaphysics, and while his points of reference focus on Kant and the philosophers Kant lectured on, they extend beyond this in complicated ways. In *Kant, Herder and the Birth of Anthropology* (410n78), John Zammito repeats the opinion of Marion Heinz that Herder is attempting to establish his own philosophical status by engaging critically with the core ideas of his teacher. More recent readings suggest a more striking originality in the essay. For example, Heinz herself, writing with Heinrich Clairmont, speaks of Herder's stance against Kant's claim that philosophy could be a demonstrative science (Heinz and Clairmont, "Herder's Epistemology" 46). Ulrich Gaier (*Herders Sprachphilosophie* 35) describes the project in the essay as a "transcendental philosophy of sensory, existential experience," and places this in direct opposition to Kant; and in his notes to the critical edition, Gaier claims that Herder is anticipating Kant's own position on the proof of the existence of God which he later takes in the critical writings (*FA* 1: 845). Pross emphasizes the importance of Moses Mendelssohn and Johann Heinrich Lambert for this essay (*MA* 1: 844–5).

2 "For this reason, Descartes also reached the wrong conclusion with 'I think, therefore I am.' Crusius too with: 'I am conscious of myself, therefore I am.' Both deduce existential being on the basis of ideal being" ("Versuch über das Sein" 587).

3 *In Träume eines Geistersehers* (Dreams of a Spirit-Seer, 1766), he puts it like this: "The other advantage is more adapted to human reason, and consists in recognizing whether the task be within the limits of our knowledge and in stating its relation to the conceptions derived from experience, for these must always be the foundation of all our judgments. In so far metaphysics is the science of the boundaries of human reason. And as a small country always has many boundaries, and is generally more careful to intimately know and defend its possessions than blindly to set out upon conquests, it is this use of metaphysics, as setting boundaries, which is at the same time the least known and the most important, and which further is obtained only late and by long experience" (113).

4 See Norton, *Herder's Aesthetics* 33.

5 Leibniz and Wolff ascribed to animals lower orders of cognition, which they share with humans, such as memory, anticipation, association, etc. These

orders function as *analogon rationis*, in that they are able to link separate facts of cognition without understanding the causes. See Leibniz, *Monadology*, para. 26, 28; *Theodicy*, Preliminary Dissertation, para. 65; Wolff, *Psychologia empirica*, para. 506, *Philosophia rationalis*, para. 766, and *Vernünfige Gedanken*, I, para. 872.

6 See Heinz and Clairmont 49–50.

7 Some of Herder's handwritten notes on Kant's geography lectures are to be found in the Berlin Akademie Archiv under AA-Kant: 29 0069–0071 NL.-Kant Nr. 15 and NL.-Adickes U 4; also in Berlin, Staatsbibliothek Preußischer Kulturbesitz, Haus II: NL.-Herder: XXV, 44 and XXV, 44a.

8 This is explained by May (*Kant's Concept of Geography* 113).

9 By the mid-1770s he is referring to geography as "the preliminary exercise in the *knowledge of the world*," lending a pragmatic aspect to all other forms of knowledge and skills ("Of the different races of human beings" 97).

10 See also Menges, "Particular Universals" 193.

11 See the tabular representation of this in Norton, 201.

12 Here too, Herder was reading Kant. In 1755 Kant had published his *Allgemeine Naturgeschichte und Theorie des Himmels* (Universal Natural History and Theory of the Heavens), in which he argues the unity of diverse phenomena on a cosmic scale. In his reading of this idea, Herder emphasized the notion of a *Kette der Wesen* (chain of beings) (*SW* 4: 381), which would later form the basis for his inquiries into the geographical distribution of diversity across a planet characterized by human unity.

13 Heinz, *Sensualistischer Idealismus*.

14 Heinz and Clairmont 49.

15 See Heinz and Clairmont 52. Gaier speaks of Herder's "brand-new systems theory of cognition" ("Core Cognition in Herder" 295). See also Gaier, "Herders Systemtheorie."

16 In 1765, Herder will draw on Blackwell's studies of Homer as evidence of the fact that "in everyday life, poetry is older than prose. This is also the reason why the first writers were poets, the first *νόμοι* were songs, and the oldest religions were mythologies, all of which spoke the sensory language of the people" (*FA* 1: 133).

17 See Morton, *Herder and Poetics* 8. I follow Morton in using the Suphan edition of Herder's essay, which is the version he published in the *Gelehrte Beiträge* (*SW* 1: 1–7), and I cite Menze's translation in *EW*, which also follows the Suphan edition.

18 See also Herder's comments in *Journal meiner Reise* (*SW* 4: 388ff.).

19 In his book on *On Diligence*, Morton doesn't mention *On Being*, but he uncovers a wealth of themes that relate directly to that study, themes which

Herder will continue to develop in the following decades. Morton is evasive on the question of the centrality of *On Diligence* for Herder's corpus (6), though the tenor of his book is to argue for the germinal nature of this essay. But in failing to link *On Diligence* to *On Being*, he misses its position in the development of Herder's studies in history out of his epistemology. Pross makes a similar move when, in volume 1 of *MA*, he decides to place *On Being* directly before *This Too a Philosophy*. The latter work is, he claims, the most immediate realization of the principle of evidence postulated in *On Being* (*MA* 1: 845). This is probably correct, but *On Diligence* needs to be read as an important intermediate statement between these two essays.

20 See Norton 67.

21 "We contemporaries of the templates for letters concerning recent literature are all the happy ones privileged to be schooled by taste, which becomes a mathematical teacher of the aesthetic average, building in the playful caprice of its declamations and of the most recent literature on foundations which no eye has seen and no ear heard" (Hamann, *Hamburgische Nachricht* 492–3). My translation.

22 Gaier notes that Diderot made the same observation in *Lettre sur les aveugles, à l'usage de ceux qui voient* (Letter on the Blind, for the Use of Those Who Can See, 1749). *FA* 1: 854–5.

23 This is the famous problem of synthetic judgment a priori which Kant will tackle in *Critique of Pure Reason*, and which Herder will address in his Metacritique. See Kaupert, "Verstand und Erfahrung."

24 This is the "actual relationship between poetic and discursive language" of which Morton (12) speaks.

WORKS CITED

Adler, Hans, and Wolf Koepke, eds. *A Companion to the Works of Johann Gottfried Herder*. Rochester: Camden House, 2009.

Blackwell, Thomas. *An Enquiry into the Life and Writings of Homer*. London, 1735.

Fox, Russell Arben. "J. G. Herder on Language and the Metaphysics of National Community." *Review of Politics* 65.2 (2003): 237–62.

Gaier, Ulrich. *Herders Sprachphilosophie und Erkenntniskritik*. Stuttgart-Cannstatt: frommann-holzboog, 1988.

– "Herders Systemtheorie." *Allgemeine Zeitschrift für Philosophie* 23.1 (1998): 3–17.

– "The Problem of Core Cognition in Herder." *Monatshefte* 95.2 (2003): 294–309.

Greif, Stefan. "Herder's Aesthetics and Poetics." In Adler and Koepke, *Companion* 141–64.

Hamann, Johann Georg. *Aesthetica in nuce*. In *Classic and Romantic German Aesthetics*. Ed. J.M. Bernstein. Cambridge: Cambridge UP, 2003.

– *Hamburgische Nachricht aus dem Reiche der Gelehrsamkeit. Nach dem ein und sechzigsten Stücke des Jahres 1762. Hamanns Schriften*, vol. 2. Ed. Friedrich von Roth. Berlin: Reimer, 1820.

Haym, Rudolf. *Herder nach seinem Leben und seinen Werken*. Berlin: Rudolph Gaertner, 1870.

Heinz, Marion. *Sensualistischer Idealismus: Untersuchungen zur Erkenntnistheorie des jungen Herder*. Hamburg: Meiner, 1994.

Heinz, Marion, and Heinrich Clairmont. "Herder's Epistemology." In Adler and Koepke, *Companion* 43–64.

Herder, Johann Gottfried von. *Dithyrambische Rhapsodie über die Rhapsodie kabbalistischer Prose. FA* 1: 30–9.

– "Plan zu einer Aesthetik." *FA* 1: 659–69.

– *Sämtliche Werke*. Edited by Bernhard Suphan. Hildesheim: G. Olms, 1967–8. Cited as *SW* (Suphan Werke).

– *Selected Early Works 1764–1767. Addresses, Essays, and Drafts; Fragments on Recent German Literature*. Ed. Ernest A. Menze and Karl Menges. Trans. Ernest A. Menze with Michael Palma. University Park: Pennsylvania State UP, 1992. Cited as *EW*.

– *Selected Writings on Aesthetics*. Trans. and ed. Gregory Moore. Princeton: Princeton UP, 2006.

– "Über die Bildung einer Sprache." *MA* 1: 143–210.

– "Versuch einer Geschichte der lyrischen Dichtkunst." *SW* 32: 85–140.

– "Versuch über das Sein." *MA* 1: 571–87. Citations of this essay are my translation.

– *Werke*. Ed. Wolfgang Pross. Munich: Carl Hanser, 1984–. Cited as *MA* (Münchener Ausgabe).

– *Werke in zehn Bänden*. Ed. Martin Bollacher et al. Frankfurt: Deutscher Klassiker Verlag, 1985–. Cited as *FA* (Frankfurter Ausgabe).

Kant, Immanuel. *Anthropology from a Pragmatic Point of View*. Trans. and ed. Robert B. Louden. Cambridge: Cambridge UP, 2006.

– *Dreams of a Spirit-Seer Illustrated by Dreams of Metaphysics*. Trans. Url F. Goerwitz. Ed. Frank Sewall. London: Swan Sonnenschein, 1900.

– "M. Immanuel Kant's Announcement of the Programme of His Lectures for the Winter Semester 1765–1766." In *Immanuel Kant, Theoretical Philosophy 1755–1770*. Trans. and ed. David Walford and Ralf Meerbote. Cambridge: Cambridge UP, 1992.

– "Of the Different Races of Human Beings." In *Anthropology, History, and Education.* Ed. Günter Zöller and Robert M. Louden. Cambridge UP, 2007. 82–97.

– *Universal Natural History and Theory of the Heavens, or An Essay on the Constitution and Mechanical Origins of the Entire World Edifice treated according to Newtonian Principles.* Trans. Stanley L. Jaki. Edinburgh: Scottish Academic Press, 1981.

Kaupert, Christa. "Verstand und Erfahrung in Kants Vernunftkritik und Herders Metakritik". Diss. Rheinische Friedrich-Wilhelms-Universität, Bonn, 2006. http://www.johann-gottfried-herder.net/Christa_Kaupert_Metakritik.pdf.

Leibniz, G.W. *Discourse on Metaphysics, and The Monadology.* Trans. George R. Montgomery. Mineola, NY: Dover Publications, 2005.

– *Theodicy: Essays on the Goodness of God, the Freedom of Man and the Origin of Evil.* Trans. E.M. Huggard. London: Routledge & Kegan Paul, 1951.

May, J.A. *Kant's Concept of Geography and Its Relation to Recent Geographical Thought.* Toronto: U of Toronto P, 1970.

Menges, Karl. "Particular Universals: Herder on National Literature, Popular Literature, and World Literature." In Adler and Koepke, *Companion* 189–213.

Morton, Michael. *Herder and the Poetics of Thought.* University Park and London: Pennsylvania State UP, 1989.

Norton, Robert. *Herder's Aesthetics and the European Enlightenment.* Ithaca: Cornell UP, 1991.

Palti, Elias. "The 'Metaphor of Life': Herder's Philosophy of History and Uneven Developments." *Eighteenth-Century Natural Sciences* 38.3 (1999): 322–47.

Pénisson, Pierre. "Kant et Herder." *Revue germanique internationale* 6 (1996): 63–74.

Rudolph, Enno. "Kultur als höhere Natur: Herder als Kritiker der Geschichtsphilosophie Kants." In *Nationen und Kulturen: zum 250. Geburtstag Johann Gottfried Herders.* Ed. Regine Otto. Würzburg: Königshausen & Neumann, 1996.

Terzakis, Katie. *The Immanent Word: The Turn to Language in German Philosophy.* New York and London: Routledge, 2007.

Wolff, Christian. *Philosophia rationalis.* Francofurti and Lipsiae: Prostat in officina libraria Rengeriana, 1732.

– *Psychologia empirica.* Hildesheim: Olms, 1968.

– *Vernünfftige Gedancken von dem gesellschafftlichen Leben der Menschen: Und insonderheit dem gemeinen Wesen.* Hildesheim, New York: Olms, 1975.

Zammito, John H. *Kant, Herder, and the Birth of Anthropology.* Chicago: U of Chicago P, 2002.

7 Fictional Feedback: Empirical Souls and Self-Deception in the *Magazine for Empirical Psychology* and Beyond

MICHAEL HOUSE

The Problem of Psychology: Science of the Human as Science of Fiction

In his famous unpublished essay "On Truth and Lie in an Extra-Moral Sense" (1873), Nietzsche confronts the hubris of the philosophic tradition with the cold realization that the intellect may serve a biological and not spiritual function:

> The intellect as a means of preserving the individual unfolds its main powers (*Hauptkräfte*) in dissimulation (*Verstellung*); for this is the means by which the weaker, less robust individuals preserve themselves, having been denied the ability to fight for their existence with horns or the sharp teeth of a predator. In the human this art of dissimulation reaches its peak: here deception (*Täuschung*), flattery, lying and deceit, speaking behind someone's back, posing, living in borrowed splendor, masking oneself, hiding behind convention, acting in front of others and one's self (*das Bühnenspiel vor anderen und vor sich selbst*), in short, the continuous fluttering around the one flame of vanity has become so much the rule and law, that nothing is more inconceivable than how the human could have come to a noble and pure drive to truth. ("Über Wahrheit und Lüge" 1: 876; "On Truth and Lie" 254, translation modified)

Nietzsche presents our claim to a "drive to truth" as incomprehensible in the face of what more accurately defines the "rule and law" of human activity, namely, "the art of dissimulation." The logic, in its most distilled form, reveals that if there is anything true about us, it is that we have a strong natural proclivity to falsify, lie, deceive, and generate fiction. As a result of this observation, our sanctimonious account of our perpetual desire to come closer to the truth can only be understood as a subordinate manifestation of a biological imperative. With this passage and the text as a whole Nietzsche initiates a second project that undermines the dualism between mind and body that quarantines and purifies the intellectual realm from its bodily contamination. Now this art of deception is our survival mechanism; it maintains our existence where our pathetic physical constitution – our lack of predatory attributes – would fail. Remarkably, Nietzsche's conflation of the traditional dualism and reduction of all intellectual activity to its materialist basis in no way eliminates the spontaneous, aesthetic component of human activity in favour of causal laws. Instead, it amplifies the constitutive role of fiction in human experience. We cannot eliminate the acts of cloaking, masking, and playing a role in order to reveal what is truly human; rather, the human is found in these very acts. To know the human is to know the human deceiving.

It is possible to view Nietzsche's essay as the culmination of a project that has its start in the previous century. In particular, it is in the interdisciplinary drive to create a hybrid science of the "whole man" – a science that combines disciplines traditionally limited to knowledge of the "body" or the "mind" – that we find not only a similar melding of the traditional dualism, but also a sustained reflection on the same question of the human's "deceptive" nature.[1] *Empirical psychology* and *anthropology* stand at the forefront of this pursuit and their anticipation of Nietzsche's proclamation emerges from a reflection on both methodological problems as well as the very characteristics of human nature that makes it resistant to scientific pursuit. They both attempt to provide an account of human subjectivity from the basis of its concrete embodiment, while still understanding their pursuit as a synthesis of two distinct realms of human activity. The result, however, is that the enterprise – and this is especially the case with empirical psychology – becomes obsessed with fiction not only as a potential threat to the scientific status of the emerging discipline, but also as a potential condition for human experience.

Overcoming the dualist account of the human in order to form a total science of the whole man faced two main problems: the first pertained to the potential for disciplinary interference and the breakdown of disciplinary unity; and the second pertained to the impossibility of studying a human subject. With respect to the first problem, Ernst Platner's influential *Anthropology for Physicians and Philosophers* (1772) serves as an illustrative example. For Platner the aim of anthropology is nothing more than an adequate representation of what a human being truly *is*: "The human is neither body nor soul alone; he is rather the harmony of both and the physician (*Arzt*) should not be permitted to reduce his focus to the former as much as the moralist on the latter" (iv). From this recognition, anthropology as the science of "the whole man" upholds the dualism while at the same time attempting to demonstrate pathways between souls and bodies. Platner's division of the knowledge of man (*Erkenntnis des Menschen*) into three separate fields of inquiry demonstrates the drive to both maintain physiology and psychology as independent sciences and, at the same time, reconcile them under the umbrella of anthropology:

> The first considers the parts and operations (*Geschäffte*) of the *machine alone* without thereby taking into consideration which of these movements (*Bewegungen*) are received from the soul and which are experienced by the soul; these are known as anatomy and physiology. Secondly one can in the very same way examine the powers and qualities of the *soul* without at the same time considering the concurrence (*Mitwirkung*) of the body and the consequent changes in the soul on account of the machine. And this I call psychology ... Finally, one can consider *body and soul together in their reciprocal relationships, restrictions and affiliations, and that is what I call anthropology*. (xvi–xvii; emphasis added)

What anthropology, as an examination of the exchange relations in the psychosomatic complex, gains in its claim to a total account of the human, it loses in disciplinary specificity and unity.[2] Each domain represents a closed system adequate to itself, but (at least previously understood as) incommensurate with the other: one treated the body as a mechanistic entity; the other, in complete opposition, treated the spontaneous freedom of the soul. Anthropology unites the two only insofar as it applies the operative assumption of "the immanent interrelation of two intrinsically connected substances" (Hess, *Reconstituting the Body Politic* 134). Still, insofar as it does not present a monist account, it remains in the interstices between mind and body, where "reciprocal relationships, restrictions and affiliations occur," a site which for Nietzsche remains connected only through the non-logical structure of metaphorical exchange.[3]

For Platner, however, the speculative quality of all metaphoric assertion seems to have no place in a science that concerns itself with that which is "more historical than speculative" (xxvi). Platner's corrective occurs in the mode of presentation that he deems most adequate to avoiding the fictional narratives produced by philosophical systems and adopts what he calls an "aphoristic writing style" (xvii). As Adler notes, he conceives of his anthropology more as "observing and collecting than systematizing" ("Aisthesis"

100), and thus the aphoristic style allows for the presentation of raw, unmediated facts. However, in reducing all action to its historical-empirical ground without eliminating the existence of the soul, his project becomes a mechanistic fiction in which each action is metaphorically translated into a discrete physiological function. Even more damaging, the physiological register can only account for the mechanistic dimensions of human action, reducing it all to the "unfree" movement of nature's machine.[4] Thus, what is observed empirically is at best a paradoxical expression of an unobservable state (i.e., the mechanistic expression of spontaneity) and as such can do nothing to explain, except in an inadequate register.

The second problem concerns the very tight definition of what constitutes a science at the time. In the *Metaphysical Foundation of Natural Science* (1786), Kant determines that we have to have the ability to construct laws about objects on the basis of a priori knowledge (i.e., on the basis of their mere possibility) for the study to attain this status. Chemistry, for instance, as it exists before Kant's eyes, fails this test, as it is impossible to construct laws of chemical interaction strictly within our minds, and as a result, it can, at best, attain the status of a "systematic art of analysis (*systematische Zergliederungskunst*)" or "experimental doctrine (*Experimentallehre*)" (AA 4: 471).[5] For a science of our mind, things are far worse. Imagine if the chemicals were non-quantifiable, endowed with free will, and demonstrated a strong proclivity towards dissimulation. For Kant, the "empirical study of the soul" has (slightly less than) no chance whatsoever of attaining the status of a science. If the ambitions were, however, downgraded, what then? Could we still talk about empirical psychology as a "systematic art of analysis" or "experimental doctrine"? Not simply, and Kant identifies three problems: (1) while I can think of the manifold of internal observation separately, I cannot separate them and reconnect them at will; (2) I cannot possibly see the contents or internal observations of the mind of another subject; and finally, and most importantly for the problem at hand, (3) if the other is aware of observation, the observed subject alters itself and dissembles (*alterirt und verstellt*). However, while Kant excludes empirical psychology from the status of science, this does not preclude some sort of study of the human mind. It would, no doubt, neither be a "science of the soul" (*Seelenwissenschaft*) nor a "psychological experimental doctrine" (*psychologische Experimentallehre*), but would have to go by another name: "a natural description of the soul" (*Naturbeschreibung der Seele*) (AA 4: 471).

While Kant's reclassification of empirical psychology as less-than-scientific does not decommission it, the set of problems he raises are certainly pressing for its self-definition and realization. For Kant, the shift from a transcendental to an empirical account of man must reconcile the deceptively simple problem that the observed subject is capable of distortion. "Dissembling" and "alteration" produce fictional surrogates, potential red herrings in the search for "true selves." As a subject narrates its past, conveys its "state of mind" to itself or others, it is impossible to overlook the imaginative reconstruction that occurs. For this reason, the methodological question of how to treat "fiction" not only haunts this program as a tangential problem, but also at times becomes its central focus. Nowhere else does this occur with greater consistency and frequency than in the journal *Gnothi Seauton oder Magazin zur Erfahrungsseelenkunde* (*Know Thyself or the Magazine for Empirical Psychology*). In its ten-year run (1783–93), its editors – most notably Karl Philipp Moritz and the Kantian Salomon Maimon[6] – offer a continual reflection on the methodological problems faced by an empirical psychology, while its other contributors provide narrative accounts of their own lives, and reflect on various psychological dispositions and disorders they encounter in themselves and others.[7] Kant's concerns with the possibility of such a pursuit certainly do not go unaddressed in the context of this journal, and at numerous junctures we find a sustained engagement with the question of "fiction" and "deception." Recent scholarship has pointed to some of the key articles on deception in the *Magazine* – most notably Moritz's contribution "On Self-Deception"; what is left unaddressed is how the theory of fiction in fact defines the science of the human.[8] The human's production of fiction is no longer addressed as a problem that needs to be overcome, but as constitutive element of human experience, and thus as a self-understanding of the human, the production of fiction is fundamental. For the history of the *Magazine*, this emerges as a trajectory in which the reformulations of empirical psychology continually move.

Performing Subjectivity: The Subjects of Real Fictions

For all its concrete, historical, and empirical presence, the "subject" of empirical psychology seems to have always lacked all stability, consistency, and permanence. It is not "given," but is instead created, and as much as this subject creates itself, it is likewise capable of self-annihilation. Moritz's concurrent project, the novel *Anton Reiser*, which he first publishes in fragments in the *Magazine*, attests to the problematic subject position in a number of ways. First, Moritz's psychological novel – which is in fact an autobiography – foregrounds the construction and alteration of identity through the construction of a surrogate identity, the titular character "Anton Reiser."[9] Second, Moritz further emphasizes the alterability of the subject position by beginning the novel with his father's engagement with the "Quietist or Separatist" sect led by Mad. Guion. Here, the teachings lead subjects to "exterminate," "deny," and "depart" from themselves: "The entire household, down to the lowliest servant consisted only of such people whose efforts were directed at or appeared to be directed at returning to their *Nothingness* (as Mad. Guion calls it), the *annihilation* of all passion, and the *extermination* of all individuality (*Eigenheit*)" (1: 37; author's emphasis). He further emphasizes this possibility moments later: "One believed to read *annihilation* and *disavowal* in every expression, and *departure from oneself* and *entry into nothingness* in every act" (1: 37; author's emphasis). While these acts serve a religious function – namely, preparation for a truly "disinterested love of God" unmarred by even a minute "flicker of self-love" (1: 38) – in a text that carries the subtitle *A Psychological Novel*, beginning with a cult that promotes the negation of the self certainly points not to the historical permanence and empirical immutability of the subject, but to a void that can be filled or emptied at will. The subject is anchored only by its mobility, its potential for creation, recreation, and annihilation. What lies beneath these acts is, for an empirical account of the human subject, irrelevant.

Moritz further entrenches human experience in an inescapable fictionality in his preparatory work for the *Magazine*, in particular in the article "Prospects for an Experimental-Psychology" (1782).[10] Amid his account of the modes of observation available to the practitioner of this science, he cannot depart from an obsession with the mediality of the human subject as a condition of familial and social existence. And at this time Moritz is still concerned with the potential to escape from a totally illusory existence. However, as much progress as he makes, dissemblance becomes more and more an inescapable condition of human existence. In fact, for Moritz, acts of dissemblance predate their own understanding: "The child learns to dissemble (*sich verstellen*), before it knows that there is dissemblance and that dissemblance is a vice" (3: 87). Later in the text, he addresses another more contemporary and culturally specific issue that impedes access to some "authentic" self lurking behind its medial counterpart: namely, reading-addiction. Reading becomes pathological the moment a subject's actions are dominated by imitation: "The addiction to imitation (*Nachahmungssucht*) extends so far, that one carries over ideals from books into one's life. Indeed nothing makes the human more *untrue* (*unwahr*), than too many books. How difficult it has become for the observer, with everything that has come to the character through the reading of novels and plays, to retrieve the authentic and original (*das Eigne und Originelle*). Instead of humans, o wonder! one now hears books speaking, and sees books acting" (3: 96).[11] Moritz's lamentation of the mimetic inauthenticity that plagues Europe appears as a reflection on its potential inescapability.[12] While he holds this possibility out there, these questions become a running concern that threatens to disrupt the very model of inquiry that would define the *Magazine*. The impositions of customs (courtesy, politeness, etc.) and culture (literature and theatre) on the subject erect such veneers of mere appearance that the deeper reality of empirical subjectivity appears at this juncture unattainable. Still, Moritz holds out hope that there is something beyond the veneer, and that it can be attained.

The Theory of Fiction: Imagining Kantians in the *Erfahrungsseelenkunde*

Theatricality, deception, self-deception, and fiction all have their place in the scholarship that deals with the *Magazine* and historically affiliated projects. However, the subtle theoretical framework that Moritz and Maimon develop to address the fictionality of empirical existence still requires attention. In particular, Salomon Maimon's contribution to the question of fiction gives the project a form, in which Moritz's perpetual insistence on "antitheatricality," and statements against "idealism" (see Wild, "Theorizing Theater Antitheatrically") make sense in relationship to the real subject's inevitable slide into the "unreal." That is, although the ideality of experience is inescapable, this does not preclude the possibility of a rigorous science of fiction, one that distinguishes, for instance, between kinds of ideality (e.g., good and bad). For Maimon, the claim goes so far as to suggest that the foundation of empirical experience can only be worked out in terms of a solid theory of fiction. The heightened rhetoric of fictionality occupies a central place in Maimon's thought, as we find in the shift in emphasis from the Kantian language of "*representation* (*Vorstellung*)" to that of "*fiction* (*Fiktion*)" and "*fabrication* (*Erdichtung*)."[13] Thus, Maimon, the self-proclaimed "empirical skeptic,"[14] occupies a unique position to orchestrate a project on empirical psychology: through a reflection on the mechanisms through which we generate fictions, he can differentiate between the production of fiction and deception. Bracketed by the terms "superstition (*Aberglaube*)" and "doubt (*Zweifel*)," even his 1791 *Philosophical Dictionary* (*Philosophisches Wörterbuch*) is disproportionately dedicated to an exploration of the unreal.[15]

So what is fiction for Maimon, and why does it seem to describe an unavoidable condition of empirical existence? In the *Philosophical Dictionary*, under the entry "Fiction," he provides the following definition: "Fiction (Fabrication) is in its most general meaning an operation of the imagination in which a not objectively necessary unity in the manifold of an object is brought forth."[16] For Maimon, this means that the meaningful experience of a world of discrete objects occurs at the hand of imagination (*Einbildungskraft*). He begins with the manifold itself (*das Mannigfaltige an sich*), which alone does not yet constitute an object of experience. Only when the subject modifies the manifold through the reflexive concepts (*Reflexionsbegriffe*) of "unity (*Einerleiheit*), difference (*Verschiedenheit*) and the like" does it become an object of thought (*Gegenstand des Denkens*) (3: 61). Maimon then draws the following conclusion: "The mere sensible gathering together (*Zusammennehmung*) of the manifold to a unity in the object, is on the other hand, much like the object that emerges from this activity, an object of the faculty of fabrication or productive imagination (*Erdichtungsvermögen*)" (3: 61). The external world is a subjective and fictitious rendering produced by the faculty of fabrication. For Maimon, the study of empirical subjects, in part, must begin with an understanding of how the "productive imagination" produces a world for the subject; and how this co-constitutes the production of the empirical subject. As a key founder of German Idealism, Maimon maintains that there is no escape from the "circle of consciousness"; we have no access to an object outside of consciousness.

As Maimon's extreme subjective idealism serves as the theoretical backdrop for his own contributions to the *Magazine*, it is clear that Kant's potential issues for an empirical science of the soul have not disappeared, but have rather doubled. The fictional status of the experience of the external world – a point arrived at through the definition of the a priori conditions of knowledge – emerges as an issue for both the observing and observed subject. And the self-proclaimed quest of the project, "knowledge of the human (*Menschenkenntnis*)," now experiences the full brunt of its grammatical ambiguity. Knowledge of the human is all-too-human.

To speak now of a theoretical framework in advance of the empirical collection of data, however, betrays the method the *Magazine* itself employs. It desires only to be a repository that collects the various "appearances or episodes" (*Erscheinungen*) from its "learned and unlearned"[17] contributors and readers. This is outlined by Moritz in his proposal for the *Magazine* that he published a year before its first issue, in 1782: "All these observations will first be collected in a magazine under certain rubrics, *without engaging any reflection*, until a sufficient number of facts are there, and *then, at the end all of this, it will be ordered into a purposeful whole*. And what an important work for mankind this could become!" (Moritz 3: 90; emphasis added). Thus, on one level, we encounter the project as a truly enlightened "public scientific project," to use Gailus's phrase, in which "cultural and scientific progress are intertwined" (75). On another, however, activities of accumulation and ordering remain distinct; and there is no myth of an organic order that crystallizes at the culmination of the project. Instead, the project parallels Maimon's distinction between the sensation and the production of an objective reality: as the data streams in, it accumulates as an unruly manifold until it attains the critical mass that would allow its editors to transform the repository into a "systematic understanding" of the human: a mirror image that forever remains just that, an image.[18] Episodic, contingent, arbitrary events will later be retold as a meaningful narrative. On an individual level this occurs as a restructuring of one's life as a temporally continuous and meaningful narrative, and on a disciplinary level, that is, for empirical psychology, this occurs as the unification of the data into a systematic whole.

The generic qualities of accumulated parts themselves are also revealing in terms of the question of fiction. The genre-blurring and -blending contributions from philosophers, lawyers, clergymen, and anonymous self-observers produce a truly unsystematic manifold ready for ordering.[19] The *Magazine* contains a mixture of contributions that range from clinical accounts of "sicknesses of the soul," disturbances in language and consciousness (aphasia, deafness), evaluations of spiritual power such as divination and clairvoyance, anonymous autobiographical accounts (for instance, a multipart sequence entitled "From the Journal of a Self-Observer"), reflections on proclivities towards various forms of criminality, as well as selections that would later be republished as their own literary texts (Maimon's *Autobiography* and Moritz's *Anton Reiser*). Thus, from a perusal of the table of contents, it seems that the editors maintain the diverse manifold of a public repository for accounts of empirical subjectivity. At the same time, the journal erodes the division between "fabricated" and "true" accounts of human behaviour. A great example occurs as Maimon seems to slip in and out of the fabricated world of one suffering from "reading addiction" and freely cites a long passage (the Heinrich encounter) from Goethe's *Sorrows of Young Werther*, in a recurring article, "Plan for the Magazine of Empirical Psychology," and then remarks: "And although this is also not a true anecdote, but a mere fabrication (*Erdichtung*) from the author, this remark is no less true, which can be verified through thousands of examples" (9: 1.13). Certainly, the need to provide non-literary evidence for a fabricated claim demonstrates a continued commitment to the empirical dimension, but the line between the two grows ever more thin.

Maimon, whose work primarily engages with transcendental philosophy, provides an epistemological account of why an account of empirical existence and the work of the *Magazine* must have as its focus the human capacity for fabrication. In the first instalment of his 1791 "Plan" article, Maimon intervenes to begin the work of systematizing the "science of the soul." He first acknowledges the division between "pure and applied psychology"; the former constitutes a "doctrine of the main powers (*Hauptkräften*) of the soul" (8: 3.1). As an empirical science, Maimon argues that "the only correct method is the following: to connect all appearances so much as possible through the reduction to common principles; not to fabricate unknown principles" (2). Immediately following this statement, however, he turns to a more abstract metaphysical enumeration of the powers of the soul and their division into higher powers (understanding and reason) and lower powers (sensation, imagination, memory, etc.) (4). For Maimon, the higher powers have no place in empirical psychology, as they are the same in all "rational entities" (5). Individuality is not a question for the "higher powers" of reason and understanding; instead, it works itself out in terms of the "lower powers" used to process the empirical world. Individuals would be indistinguishable if you were to control the variable element (empirical experience): "If you were to give Duns Scotus the same sensible representations and series of associations that Newton had, he would discover the exact same world system" (5).[20] What remains for Maimon as the variable element that gives each individual its own discrete world and allows for discrepancies between their worlds relates to the "Imagination (*Einbildungskraft*)" (6). The imagination processes the same objects in "different successions of association," and according to different degrees of "strength and speed (*Stärke und Geschwindigkeit*)," and in different relations of "freedom and necessity" (6). For Maimon this not only accounts for the differences in human perception but also for a systematic understanding of the "diseases of the soul" to which the division of applied psychology can turn; they could only ever be "diseases of the productive imagination," as reason and understanding are universal and do not vary among individuals. The whole project turns on understanding the "different modes of activity of the imagination" (6), a science that he boasts is a priori and not a posteriori. More importantly, the general conclusion that Maimon draws from this is that whether or not we speak of the differentiation as a matter of health and sickness of the soul, the possibility of individuality (distinctions between humans) relies on the discrepancy in the worlds they produce with their imagination. The only fact about distinct individuals is that they live according to different fictions.

Are They Deceiving Themselves? Self-Deception and Self-Observation

The use of fabrications to establish facts about conditions of human existence proceeds also in the reverse direction, in which the contributing subjects express their inability to escape the fictionality of their existence. Perhaps the most sustained discussion of this issue occurs at a moment in the third volume, which appeared in 1791, and in which Moritz and Maimon feel compelled to interject, in the middle of the aforementioned anonymous self-observer's journal entry, two independent pieces, each titled "On Self-Deception (*Über Selbsttäuchung*)." Occurring first as a harsh insertion of the *Magazine*'s editorial voice, Moritz contradicts his promise to remain "hands-off" and feels compelled to respond to a statement made by the self-observer,[21] who complains of the impossibility of presenting to himself or anyone else who *he truly is*: "In these morning hours, in this garden under the open sky, I only want to make the following resolution: in the future only to *be true*, and not to *appear*, neither to myself nor to others; that is precisely what has until now robbed me of so much happiness" (7: 3.44; emphasis added). The psychological predicament is one in which there is a rift between the moments of action and observation. In the loud interruption, before allowing the reported journal to continue, Moritz not only chastises the author for his desire to transcend his "mere appearance" and "be real" as a fundamental self-deception, but also argues that we can no longer conceive of authentic individuality as anterior to the production of a fiction. For Moritz, at the moment one expresses "the desire to be true" an inversion occurs and "the desire of truth, becomes a lie, the hate of dissemblance itself dissemblance, and the fear of self-deception itself deception" (7: 3.47). Wild identifies in this the "will to truthful self-observation and its programmatic enactment" as representing "the highest degree of self-deception" (537). This is true, and the problem pertains not only to the act of self-observation and the feedback generated from the self observing itself observing itself, but also to the mediated condition of experience in general. Moritz does not propose to overcome this problem, but presents the drive to overcome it as misplaced; what is, however, uncovered in this self-deception is the hidden outline of what the subject truly "is." The very moment of deception becomes the moment that warrants our attention, "because there, where our being deceives itself, certainly resides the undiscovered traces of its hidden limits and delineations" (7: 3.47). Here, in the act of self-deception we find the anonymous self-observer, who has made himself present in writing; he does not reveal him*self*, but is the act of presentation. The self is nothing more than the ever-changing self-generation of its own image. Thus, the object of the science of man seems to move far from a static empirical object to the ever-evolving mechanisms of deception, dissimulation, or, to put it less negatively, representation.

In fact, within philosophical discourse at the same time and the scepticism debate in which Maimon is a central voice, we find the emergence of a similar line of argument. Gottlob Ernst Schulze's sceptical attack on the edifice of Kantian philosophy (or at least the form it takes with Reinhold) leads Maimon and Fichte to some of the most original statements on the self in which it would be absurd to draw the conclusion that there is a static "subject" (self-in-itself) that exists behind the stream of representation, or independently of its activity. Fichte's famous conclusion that emerges from this debate reduces the subject to its own activity, thereby ending the metaphysical search for a "soul" or "self-in-itself" that underwrites existence.[22] The subject is reduced to a pure production. However, this does not mollify the paranoia that persists and drives the question of self-deception forward: the paranoia grounded in the conviction that there exists an internal split in the self. For Moritz in the 1791 article "On Self-Deception," the phenomenon of self-deception must be greeted first as enigmatic: "In human nature, there is certainly no more unexplainable phenomenon than the possibility of deceiving oneself, as if one is at the same time a being that is distinct from itself that has two separate interests" (8: 3.32). Moritz's response to this possibility is less than satisfactory, as he merely subjects "deception" to a cost-benefit analysis, and argues that no man would deceive another without there being some sort of advantage, and the same must hold for self-deception. In the case of self-deception the benefit, for Moritz, is lost.

Maimon's response to this paradox promises a solution – and gives rise to his own article "On Self-Deception" – one that first must give specificity to the terms of the debate, and argues that what is required is a distinction between "Deception (*Täuschung*)" and "Deceit (*Betrug*)." Maimon begins by setting the former in an aesthetic context: here it can obtain a positive valance, even though it contains the possibility of deception. In fact, Maimon, who follows Sulzer's aesthetics and a mimetic understanding of the work of art, perceives its effectiveness in its capacity to deceive, arguing in the end that "the good effect of the fine arts (in so far as they are an imitation of nature) depend on deception" (8: 2.38). Maimon's account of *deception* takes its cues from his belief that Kant does not overcome Hume's scepticism, in which he argues that what "deception" holds in common with historical and empirical truths is the fact that they both rest on the "Association of Imagination (*Association der Einbildungskraft*)" (8: 3.39). What is associated or connected are different appearances, such as the colour, weight, and density of gold, that are constantly connected in space and time, and through this habitual connection we come up with "gold" as that in which we combine all these appearances as its "qualities." It is on this basis as well that historic or empirical truths attain their contingent structure; they depend on a unity that is manifested by the imagination. Thus, Maimon, through a Kantian logic, has negated the question: "Should it mean, for example, that sugar, which tastes sweet, can also, independent of my own capacity for sensation (*Empfindungsvermögen*), be sweet in itself (*an sich*)? This contains a contradiction, that something independent of my faculty of sensibility indeed still can be called a sensation" (8: 3.40). Maimon's point is that the deception and the question of deception lie not in the relationship to the external thing, but rather in its association with other appearances. Nonetheless, Maimon can maintain a distinction between deception (*Täuschung*) and deceit (*Betrug*). He writes: "They are different from one another, insofar as a deceit is destroyed through its discovery; on the other hand, deception, even in the conviction that it is a deception, is not destroyed" (41). Deceit only differs insofar as the conditions for the production of the "image" reveal that the assumptions drawn by the subject in its encounter with the illusion were wrong.[23] For Maimon, thus, that we deceive ourselves is certainly the case, a fact of empirical existence, in which we constantly construct out of a manifold another reality; that we would will to deceive ourselves and know that we carry out an act of deceit with respect to ourselves, on the other hand, is an impossibility.

The Truth of Fiction: The Narrated Unity of Subjectivity

Empirical truth, no longer beholden to the narrow definition of the correspondence between a subjective image and an external object, can now be sought in the internal unity and consistency of the associated episodes drawn together by the imagination. This proposal is, even for Moritz, tenuous, leaving a great deal of discomfort; but it marks the transition from a soul understood as fixed and hidden, needing to be recovered from the veil of language, to the temporalized entity that is its expression in language. I say tenuous, because it remains a tension that permeates even his own *Anton Reiser*: he sees his being, his self and soul, as "a *mere deception*, an *abstract idea* – a consolidation of similarities, which in every following moment in life disappears" (227).[24] This revelation, however, marks the moment that the pursuit of empirical psychology changes from one of uncovering truth to one of reconstructing meaning.

For this reason, Moritz, in his "radically empirical" psychological novel *Anton Reiser* focuses on the possibility of bringing the life of a single, ordinary, everyday human subject to writing; it is at once a scientific and literary pursuit that entails a recalibration of the observer's (or author's) representational faculties in such a way that it becomes coldly attuned to all events. Moritz describes this process as follows: "It is intended not to disperse the representational power, but to concentrate it, and to give the soul a sharper insight into itself" (136). This concentrated focus of the representational faculty produces a kind of microscopic vision that does not allow the initial perception of events to determine whether they will be included in the narrative of the character, leading to the obvious problem that much of what he writes appears, in his own words, too "small and meaningless" (136). However, as we read on, we discover that the process is far from complete, and that he is only asking for the readers' patience. The temporal structure of the plot simply displaces the question of meaning, and it is only through the totality of a life, only "in the process of life" (136) that the hermeneutic context for reading life is revealed.

In the *Magazine* a similar determinative structure emerges, but here it is clear that the displacement defines the limitation of possibility, and childhood impressions gain their importance insofar as they make "indeed the foundation for all that follows" (Moritz 3: 104). Both *Anton Reiser* and the *Magazine* carry the problematic structure, however, that the material – the original impressions, or the small and unimportant events of childhood – attain their determinative force not through empirical observation, but rather through a secondary act. This is necessarily the case, as these events and impressions are generally available only as "memories of memories" (ibid.). Thus, the significance and meaning do not emerge solely out of themselves; instead, the power of reconstruction takes on the form of an imaginative return to a natural origin. Methodologically, this underlines the very tension between a literary enterprise that attempts to eradicate the literary imagination and a scientific one that seems to depend on the imaginative reconstruction of the individual.

In this way, we can read Moritz's generic obsession – which primarily takes the form of the self-reflexive, extradiegetic question: am I writing a psychological novel that is still a novel or a biography that is a faithful reproduction of life?[25] – as exemplary of a larger concern as to whether or not life writing (*biography*) can ever achieve the status of a "life science." Moritz is nonetheless committed to the possibility of his human science as a "Seelennaturkunde" produced through "dispassionate self-observation" (Krupp, "Observing Children" 34). What emerges, however, is the suggestion that the literary reconstruction of the *small* and *meaningless* as significant and meaningful is not merely a phenomenon restricted to observation, but is also a process integral to the human condition. The status of these determinations (of meaning and significance) becomes the tension that permeates the entire early history of anthropological disciplines (the so-called sciences of man). Are they fictions generated only in the moment of (self-) observation? If so, do they nonetheless have an ontological status, expressing a condition of existence by which empirical subjects live?[26]

Postscript: The Playful Art of Anthropology

Kant's *Anthropology in a Pragmatic Sense* responds to this question from another point of view. Kant starts with a critique of the deterministic implications of a reductive physiological account of man present in the materialist vein of the sciences of man. The model of strictly spatial causality allows all capacities of the soul to find their origin in the constitution of the body. Moritz's model for human science already establishes its complexity through the introduction of a temporality, and it becomes clear that his subject attains an arbitrary freedom in the open-ended possible interpretations of particular events. For Kant, any determinist account of man as a fixed mechanical or material subject is abhorrent to his fundamental understanding of man as a "free acting being (*freihandelndes Wesen*)," who is likewise a free citizen of the world (the human as *Weltbürger*). Kant's rejection of a physiological basis for anthropology immediately sets up the poles between internal freedom and external determination. Under this model, we are merely passive observers of the necessary, but indecipherable, processes that occur in our body, but are inaccessible to our mind. That is, we become enslaved to the play of representations of unknown origins:

> He who ponders natural phenomena, for example, what the causes of the faculty of memory may rest on, can speculate back and forth (like Descartes)

> over the traces of impressions remaining in the brain, but in doing so he must admit that in this play of his representations (*Spiel seiner Vorstellungen*) he is a mere observer and must let nature run its course, for he does not know the cranial nerves and fibers, nor does he understand how to put them to use for his purposes. Therefore all theoretical speculation about this is a waste of time. (Kant, *Anthropology* 3; AA 7: 119)

Regaining access to these representations, and more specifically to the play of representations, becomes both the basis for his anthropology and the chief impediment to its execution. It would be far easier to study sedate, passive objects that present themselves in the tangible clarity of a physical structure. However, for Kant this would do injustice to the fundamental self-determining freedom man experiences with respect to the "play of representations." And because it is a free self-directed *play* – we play with our representations – a ludic element creeps in the backdoor.

For Kant, in his *Anthropology*, the problems expressed at the beginning are reformulated as they pertain to pragmatic anthropology. In addition to the problem of dissembling, Kant adds the fact that cultural entrenchment makes certain habits second nature (Kant, *Anthropology* 5; AA 7: 121). These concerns all point to the question of *access* to what is authentically human. Expressed as a problem for the very possibility of an anthropology or empirical psychology, Kant directs us to what might be called a productive negation, a failure that reveals that the self-generated or socially generated construction does not merely obfuscate man, but might define what man, in fact, is. No doubt, the concluding paragraphs of this preface take this wager seriously when he argues: "While not exactly sources for anthropology, these are nevertheless aids: world history, biographies, even plays and novels" (ibid.). As we move closer to understanding what Kant in this context means by man, as an I-object constituting a *Weltbürger*, it becomes increasingly clear that we are dealing with a hybrid entity, one that not only is known through its literary aids, but also constitutes itself through these aids.

Foucault – in his *Introduction to Kant's* Anthropology – makes the point that "we see a field proper to anthropology being sketched out, where the concrete unity of the syntheses and of passivity, of the affected and the constituting, are given as phenomena in the form of time" (39). In this sense, Kant comes closer to what in Moritz appears as the play between the determinative contingency of external conditions (*Umstände*) and the continuous reattribution of meaning that the subject gives these former conditions. On this basis, Foucault aligns this back and forth with the notion of play at the heart of Kant's reclaiming of the *Spiel der Vorstellungen* (i.e., man as the constant, free-acting moderator of the play):

> This notion of *Spielen* is singularly important: man is nature's play; it is the game that he plays, and [he] is played by it; if he is sometimes played with – as when his senses are deceived – it is because he is playing the victim of the game, despite it being within his power to be in control, to take back control by feigning his intention. In this way, the game becomes a "*künstlicher Spiel*" [*sic*] and the show he puts on receives its moral justification. *Anthropology* thus develops on the basis of this dimension of human exercise that goes from the ambiguity of the *Spiel* (game-toy) to the indecision of the *Kunst* (art-artifice). (53)

Even for Kant, what originally constitutes the chief impediment for the possibility of anthropology becomes its very subject matter.

The means of the playing, and what it means to be a *human* for anthropology, for Foucault, for his Kant, and even for Moritz, has its answer in the question of language: "Anthropology's man is indeed a *Weltbürger*, but not in the sense that he belongs to a given social group or such and such institution. He is *Weltbürger* purely and simply because he speaks. It is in the exchange of language that he manages on his own account both to attain and to realize the concrete universal. His living in the world is, originarily, residence in language" (Foucault 102). Language thus emerges immediately for Moritz and Kant as the science's problem preventing anthropology from penetrating the dissimulations and façades erected by an I-object's literary nature. The truth of man is no longer something "anterior to language" (ibid.) – a physiological structure or originary, small, meaningless moments – but rather is to be found in the negotia tion between observer and observed, and their linguistic exchange. Thus, Moritz, when returning to the same methodological concern at the beginning of the second book, focuses on the synthetic process, the linguistic re-rendering of the minuscule: "For anyone who gives value to a faithful representation (*Darstellung*) will not be irked by what appears initially to be trivial and unimportant; but will take into consideration that the artistically interwoven web of a human life consists of an infinite number of details (*Kleinigkeiten*), all of which assume the greatest importance upon being interwoven" (Moritz 3: 120). It is only with this notion of the *web* that is "artistically interwoven" that the human subject as an object of literary science emerges. In this way – so long as we are reading an autobiography – the temporally determined interconnections and causal networks do not have their origin in an externally determinative source, but rather in the subject's own artistic and linguistic capacity. It is in this free act of self-production and in this act alone that the empirical soul exists.

NOTES

1 For the most comprehensive anthology on this period in German history, which accounts for the diversity of sciences that propose to provide an account of the "whole man," see Schings, ed., *Der ganze Mensch*. The anthology is based on the 1992 DFG-Symposium, and the authors take into account the complete spectrum of scientific perspectives, methods, and theories that contribute to the attempted account of "the whole man." Everything from physiognomy, crainioscopy, neuroanatomy, to (animal) magnetism, as well as those sciences that define the focus of this chapter: empirical psychology (*Erfahrungsseelenkunde*) and anthropology.

2 Jonathan Hess provides a good overview of the impact of Platner's project in his book *Reconstituting the Body Politic.* There he argues that there is an ideal of the interdisciplinary, which he characterizes as follows: "Platner's *Anthropologie* addresses and hopes to bring together both physicians and philosophers, the anatomists and physiologists who specialize in the body, and the philosophers who traditionally limit themselves to studying the mind and soul" (134). At the same time, the discourse privileges the "empirical observations of the medical doctor over the philosopher's quest for systematic knowledge" (135).

3 Nietzsche famously refers to the series of metaphors that separate "things in themselves" from our experience of them: "The 'thing in itself' (for that is what pure truth, without consequences, would be) is also completely incomprehensible to the creator of language and not at all worth striving after. He designates only the relationship between things and men, and to express them one employs the boldest metaphors. A nerve stimulus, first transposed into an image – first metaphor. The image, in turn, imitated by a sound – second metaphor. And each time there is a complete overleaping of one sphere, right into the middle of an entirely new and different one" ("On Truth and Lie" 256; "Über Wahrheit und Lüge" 1: 879; translation modified).

4 In the preface to Kant's *Anthropology in a Pragmatic Sense*, it is precisely this dimension of "physiological anthropology" that he views as deficient. I will return to this in the concluding section.

5 All references to Kant's work are to the *Akademische Ausgabe* (AA).

6 Friedrich Pockels was the second editor of the *Magazine*. The focus of this chapter is on Moritz and Maimon's stewardship.

7 For those interested in the specifics of the publication, its popularity, and the history of its editorial changes, see Bennholdt-Thomsen and Guzzoni, "Nachwort" and Gailus, "A Case of Individuality" 70–1.

8 Schreiber, following the path of Wild, points to the theatrical metaphor that Moritz employs in his article: "In his theatrical Vorstellung, then, the risk of Verstellung is not overcome, but rather remains immanent. In attempting to peer through the curtain of courteous convention by distancing oneself from oneself, yet another curtain falls" ("Pressing Matters" 145). Thus, the moment the subject observes itself, or becomes observed, he suffers the problem foretold by Kant: a projected identity created for the observer (even if the observed and observer are one and the same). Schreiber points to the inevitable doubling of the self into observing subject and observed object as well, and demonstrates the common psychological configuration in both "self-deception and self-observation": "The role-playing of self-deception would then only be a logical extension of the theatrical model of (self-)observation" (537). Schreiber, building upon Bezold's comprehensive work on the subject, demonstrates that the "self-observer" doubles himself and becomes performer and audience at once (161). Gailus comes closest to the understanding that the problem of self-deception does not need to be solved for there to be a "true" representation of the self. "Language is not a transparent window onto the soul but a narcissistic mirror that enables the self to imagine its own wholeness" (97). What I would contend is that, in all cases, what Moritz (and Maimon) encounter is that the science of the self can only reveal the self as non-stop representational activity, and not as some thing or entity that resides beyond or outside of the activity. And this represents a complete transformation of the nature of empirical psychology itself. It should also be noted that what remains especially underappreciated in the scholarship on Moritz's article "On Self-Deception" is Maimon's contribution. This paper attempts to demonstrate that through Maimon the fictionality of the subject attains a scientific understanding that allows for a far more subtle account of what "self-deception" could possibly mean.

9 In a much more "real" way, this is the case for Salomon "Maimon," whose own name is a construction that stands in for his given name, Salomon Ben Joshua. For an account of the question of name and identity see Weissberg ("Erfahrungsseelenkunde" 303–39). Maimon likewise published his autobiography in fragments in the *Magazine*.

10 A good overview of the road to the *Magazine* can be found in Davies's article "Karl Philipp Moritz's Erfahrungsseelenkunde" (15–21) and Bell's *The German Tradition of Psychology* (esp. 85–103).

11 This concern with an oversaturated book market is repeated in the inaugural remarks, in which he speaks of the journal itself contributing to "the

Flood of books." His retort is that he is offering neither "moral prattle, nor a novel, nor a comedy" but "facts" (3: 103).

12 Wild makes a similar point, while retaining the fundamental aim of the *Magazine* to undermine the "idealism" and "theatricality" of a mediated life: "While Moritz never tires of warning against 'sich in eine idealische Welt hinüber zu träumen' and promotes Erfahrungsseenlenkunde as a method 'in seine eigne wirkliche Welt immer tiefer einzudringen,' this bookish variant of 'Nachahmungssucht' poses the danger that there is no real world left to which one can return from one's foray into the ideal" (535).

13 Maimon is perhaps more famous for his role in the skeptical reception of Kant's *Critique of Pure Reason*. His skepticism serves to widen the Kantian rift between subjective knowledge and a mind independent external reality, leaving the subject to reside solely within the ideality of his own mind.

14 He makes this statement, which is the point of departure for most interpretations, in his most famous work, *Essay on Transcendental Philosophy* (232), which is an extended exegesis on Kant's *Critique of Pure Reason*.

15 To get a sense of this tendency, consider the following entry titles dedicated to the exploration of issues surrounding fictional dimensions of human existence: "Superstition" (*Aberglauben*)," "Idolatry (*Abgötterei*)," "Imagination (*Einbildungskraft*)," "Fiction (*Fiktion*)," "Belief (*Glauben*)," "Imitation (*Nachahmung*)," "Play (*Spiel*)," "Deception and Appearance (*Täuschung und Schein*)," "Probability (*Wahrscheinlichkeit*)," "Reality [in us] (*Wirklichkeit* [*in uns*])," and "Doubt (*Zweifel*)."

16 "Fiktion (Erdichtung) ist in der allgemeinsten Bedeutung eine Operation der Einbildungskraft, wodurch eine nicht objektiv notwendige Einheit im Manigfaltigen eines Objekts hervorgebracht wird" (3: 60).

17 The subtitle for the journal reads: "As a Primer for Scholars and Nonscholars (als ein Lesebuch für Gelehrte und Ungelehrte)."

18 From his preparatory texts, Moritz claims that the empirical psychology would constitute "a universal mirror, in which the human species could see itself" (3: 90). Gailus cleverly and accurately acknowledges that it is not a mirror, but "a multi-perspectival montage of a population in its psychosocial diversity" (81).

19 This overstates the case a tad, as there is a slight tension in Moritz's empirical method. Moritz does include in the introduction to the *Magazine* rubrics that would define the basic subdivisions of the discipline (as proposed by his friend Moses Mendelssohn) and they are, "without any structural mechanisms: natural psychology (Seelennaturkunde), psychopathology (Seelenkrankheitskunde), psychosemiotics (Seelenzeichenkunde), psychodietetics (Seelenediätetik) and psychotherapy (Seelenheilkunde), etc." (see Moritz

3: 104; and *Magazine* 1: part 1. 3). All future references will be made to the original *Gnothi Seauton oder Magazin zur Erfahrungsseelenkunde* (volume number followed by part number and page number), and the author's name will be mentioned if known.

20 His point is that these higher powers give the "thinking being" the capacity to think an object this way or that way at all: "Understanding thinks concepts of objects and makes judgments about the relationships of these objects a priori"(4). These relationships are necessary and universally valid, as in the case of a triangle: "The concept of a triangle is only possible, because the three sides (as the determinations) without space (as that which is through this determined) cannot be thought" (4). The elements of a triangle must be thought together for there to be a triangle at all. Thus, the differences and discrepancies between individuals must reside in another capacity.

21 For a sense of the hard-handedness of this intervention, here is the sequence as it appears in the table of contents:

"Anonymous. From the Journal of a Self-Observer
Moritz. On Self-Deception. A Parentheses to the Journal of the Self-Observer
Anonymous. Continuation of the Journal"

22 As Fichte writes: "The I posits itself, and it is, by virtue of this mere positing by itself and conversely: The self is, and it posits its being, in virtue of its mere being. It is at once the agent and the product of action; the active, and that which is brought about by the activity; action and deed are one and the same; and hence: 'I am' expresses a Tathandlung" (97).

23 He gives the example of a stick partially submerged in water (41–2). From the angle of the stick you could believe it to be broken, but with knowledge of optics and an understanding of why the angle of the stick changes in the medium of water, the deceit (that the stick is broken) is destroyed. However, it is always the case that the stick, as it appears, is just that, an appearance.

24 Minter presents this as the radical empiricism and an expression of a "Humean sentiment" ("Psychology of Association" 70). Historically, there is no doubt that this is the case, and it is in part due to the rise of Hume in German intellectual circles at this very time. Maimon himself, certainly in his engagement with Kant, does not believe the problems raised by Hume to be solved by the first *Kritik*. And his *Essay on Transcendental Philosophy* explores the way in which Kant fails to answer the questions quid juris and quid facti. The radical Humean scepticism that would lead Anton to doubt the existence of the soul comes with the liberating realization that the self has a form-giving function, and cannot be estranged from the world it produces.

In a different venue, linking this to the role of association psychology in *Anton Reiser*, Minter makes a similar point: "Against the backdrop of *Anton Reiser*'s radical empiricism and its implications for the nature of the central character's experience of self, the principle of association offers itself as a potential psychological form-giving element: Anton's fragmentary perceptions are capable of becoming connected according to the laws of association" (70).

25 The famous introductory lines in the preface (certainly not promising as a page turner) read: "This psychological novel could also be called a biography, because the observations are for the most part taken from real life" (Moritz 3: 36).

26 The fact that fiction can constitute a real ontological category in psychology becomes a perennial topic for the discipline, especially as it attains disciplinary specificity around 1900, as is evident in Wilke's contribution to this very anthology. And in this context, in particular in the formation of psychological aesthetics as a field of knowledge, the epistemological and ontological relationships between fact and fiction are not merely a problem that the nascent discipline must overcome; instead, it is again a constitutive, formative negotiation.

WORKS CITED

Adler, Hans. "Aisthesis, steinernes Herz und geschmeidige Sinne. Zur Bedeutung der Ästhetik-Diskussion in der zweiten Hälfte des 18. Jahrhunderts." In *Der ganze Mensch: Anthropologie und Literatur im 18. Jahrhundert*. Ed. Hans-Jürgen Schings. Stuttgart: J.B. Metzler, 1992.

Bell, Mathew. *The German Tradition of Psychology in Literature and Thought, 1770–1840*. Cambridge: Cambridge UP, 2005. Print.

Bennholdt-Thomsen, Anke, and Alfredo Guzzoni. "Nachwort." In *Gnothi Sauton oder Magazin zur Erfahrungsseelenkunde*. Vol. 10. Lindau: Antiqua-Verlag, 1978.

Bezold, Raimund. *Popularphilosophie und Erfahrungsseelenkunde im Werk von Karl Philipp Moritz*. Würzburg: Königshausen and Neumann, 1984.

Boulby, Mark. *Karl Philipp Moritz: At the Fringe of Genius*. Toronto: U of Toronto P, 1979.

Brantigan, Martha Jane. *Magazin zur Erfahrungsseelenkunde: Editors, Text and Context*. Diss., Johns Hopkins University, 1981.

Davies, Martin L. "Karl Philipp Moritz's *Erfahrungsseelenkunde*: Its Social and Intellectual Origins." *Oxford German Studies* 26 (1985): 13–35.

Fichte, Johann Gottlieb. *The Science of Knowledge*. Ed. and trans. Peter Heath and John Lachs. Cambridge: Cambridge UP, 1982.

Foucault, Michel. *Introduction to Kant's* Anthropology. Ed. Roberto Nigro. Trans. Roberto Nigro and Kate Briggs. Los Angeles: Semiotext(e), 2008.

Gailus, Anreas. "A Case of Individuality: Karl Philipp Moritz and the Magazine for Empirical Psychology." *New German Critique* 79. Special issue on Eighteenth-Century Literature and Thought (Winter 2000): 67–105.

Gnothi Seauton oder Magazin zur Erfahrungsseelenkunde. Ed. K.P. Moritz, K.F. Pockels, and S. Maimon. 10 vols. Berlin, 1783–93. http://www.ub.uni-bielefeld.de/diglib/aufkl/magerfahrgsseelenkd/index.htm.

Hess, Jonathan. *Reconstituting the Body Politic: Enlightenment, Public Culture and the Invention of Aesthetic Autonomy.* Detroit: Wayne State UP, 1999.

Kant, Immanuel. *Anthropology from a Pragmatic Point of View.* Trans. and ed. Robert B. Louden. Cambridge: Cambridge UP, 2006.

– *Kants gesammelte Schriften. Edition Königlich Preussische Akademie.* 29 vols. Berlin: Georg Reimer Verlag, 1910–. (= AA)

Krupp, Anthony. "Observing Children in an Early Journal of Psychology." In *Fashioning Childhood in the Eighteenth Century*. Ed. Anja Müller. Burlington, VT: Ashgate, 2006.

Maimon, Salomon. *Gesammelte Werke.* Ed. Valerio Verra. 6 vols. Hildesheim: Georg Olms Verlagsbuchhandlung, 1965–71.

– *Versuch über die Transzendentalphilosophie.* Ed. Florian Ehrensperger. Hamburg: Felix Meiner Verlag, 2004.

Minter, Catherin. "The Psychology of Association in Karl Philipp Mortiz's *Anton Reiser.*" *Forum Modern Language Studies* 44.1 (2008): 67–75.

Moritz, Karl Philipp. "Vorschlag zu einem Magazin einer Erfahrungs-Seelenkunde." *Deutsches Museum, 1776–88*, vol. 1 (1782): 485–503.

– *Werke.* Ed. Horst Günther. Frankfurt am Main: Insel Verlag, 1981.

Nietzsche, Friedrich. "On Truth and Lie in an Extra-Moral Sense." In *Writings from the Early Notebooks.* Ed. Raymond Guess and Alexander Nehamas. Trans. Ladislaus Löb. Cambridge: Cambridge UP, 2009.

– "Über Wahrheit und Lüge im außermoralischen Sinne." In *Kritische Studienausgabe.* Ed. G. Colli and M. Montinari. 2nd ed. Munich, Berlin, New York: dtv and de Gruyter, 1988.

Platner, Ernst. *Anthropologie für Aerzte und Weltweise.* Leipzig: Dyckische Buchhandlung, 1772.

Schings, Hans-Jürgen, ed. *Der ganze Mensch: Anthropologie und Literatur im 18. Jahrhundert*. Stuttgart: J.B. Metzler, 1992.

Schreiber, Elliott. "Pressing Matters: Karl Philipp Mortz's Models of the Self in the Magazin zur Erfahrungsseelenkunde." *Goethe Yearbook* 11 (2002): 133–58.

Weissberg, Liliane. "Erfahrungsseelenkunde als Akkulturation: Philosophie, Wissenschaft und Lebensgeschichte bei Salomon Maimon." In *Der ganze Mensch: Anthropologie und Literatur im 18. Jahrhundert*. Ed. Hans-Jürgen Schings. Stuttgart: J.B. Metzler, 1992.

Wild, Christopher J. "Theorizing Theater Antitheatrically: Karl Philipp Moritz's Theatromania." *MLN* 120.3 (April 2005): 507–38.

8 Fictional Feelings: Psychological Aesthetics and the Paradox of Tragic Pleasure

TOBIAS WILKE

"Do aesthetic quasi-emotions [*Scheingefühle*] exist?" (191),[1] the German philosopher Moritz Geiger asks in the opening part of a lecture delivered at the first Kongreß für Ästhetik und allgemeine Kunstwissenschaft, a large-scale gathering of aestheticians, psychologists, and art historians held in Berlin in 1913.[2] The question he poses in this manner is, to be sure, a rhetorical one, for Geiger himself has no doubt that the object of his inquiry – conceived as a particular class of psychological responses to aesthetic stimuli – is, in fact, empirically "real." And he proceeds to dispel any potential uncertainty on the part of his audience by citing various examples of experiential evidence, all of which attest, according to him, that "there are" emotions of the kind he is going to talk about. In particular, he invokes the familiar experience of feelings aroused by dramatic representations – those feelings, that is, with which the viewer in the theatre either personally reacts *to* the characters on stage or re-*en*acts *their* condition through a mechanism of empathetic identification. As Geiger points out, the two kinds of response are categorically different: In the first case, the spectator's own emotion is directed at the fictional characters and their actions – Geiger writes in this context: "I *detest* Franz Moor, I *pity* Maria Stuart" (192)[3] – while in the second case it is directed at the object of the feelings experienced (fictionally) by the characters themselves: "One fears *with* Wallenstein, or *with* Agnes Bernauer and so forth" (192). Yet both kinds of emotional response fall equally – so Geiger goes on to claim – into the larger category of "aesthetic quasi-emotions." For they both display the characteristics that he takes to be symptomatic of quasi-emotions in general. He writes:

> So-called quasi-emotions are shorter in duration and alternate more rapidly than real emotions ... Moreover, quasi-emotions are significantly less effective

> in psycho-motoric respects than real emotions. In the theatre, fear does not prompt us to jump up and run away, pity does not compel us to help the hero of a play. And finally, there exists the strange fact that the most intensely unpleasant feelings, such as fear and fright, do not interfere with the experience of aesthetic enjoyment but even increase it. (Problem of Dubos.) (192)[4]

The central aspect named here to distinguish "quasi-emotions" – phenomenologically – from "actual" ones is the different behavioural pattern they involve. Experienced in a fictional context like the dramatic representation on stage, neither pity nor fear trigger the psycho-physical repertoire of standardized actions that would (likely) be activated under "normal" or "real" circumstances; and they do not trigger those actions because they are not defined by the same emotional "valence"[5] as their non-aesthetic counterparts – because they are, in fact, not the same emotions at all.

Within the course of but a few paragraphs, Geiger has arrived in his deliberations at the issue of tragedy's peculiar emotional economy, and the fact that he has done so is no coincidence, for the so-called paradox of tragic pleasure – "the strange fact," as he puts it, "that the most intensely unpleasant feelings, such as fear and fright, do not interfere with the experience of aesthetic enjoyment but even increase it" – forms the primary context within which the late-nineteenth-century concept of "quasi-emotions" initially emerged.[6] The issue of the tragic paradox in itself, to be sure, long pre-existed this conceptual development. Perhaps most canonically stated in the opening sentence of David Hume's treatise "Of Tragedy" (1757) – "It seems an unaccountable pleasure, which the spectators of a well-written tragedy receive from sorrow, terror, anxiety, and other passions, that are in themselves disagreeable and uneasy" (258) – it had been addressed repeatedly from the early eighteenth century onwards. (Geiger briefly gestures towards this history in his parenthetical remark "Dubossches Problem.")[7] And indeed, Aristotle's even earlier, if more implicit, treatment of the paradox in his theory of tragic *pathos* famously marks the very beginning of (Western) poetics in general. What uniquely characterizes the late-nineteenth-century debates, however, to which Geiger's 1913 lecture offers a kind of belated postscript, is a significant transformation within – and *of* – this theoretical genealogy. For starting in the 1870s, the tragic paradox becomes the object of, and testing ground for, new explanatory strategies that are inextricably tied to a fundamental methodological shift in the field of aesthetics: namely, the shift towards the rigorous study of psychological "facts" and a discipline governed by the laws, on a par with the standards, of (modern) empirical science.[8]

The beginning of this transformational process is typically identified with Friedrich Theodor Vischer's anti-formalist declaration in 1866 that "the beautiful" be conceived and investigated as (the result of) a dynamic psychological "act" ("Kritik meiner Ästhetik" 224).[9] Throughout the following decades, this pronounced reorientation unfolds, with ever increasing discursive intensity, in various descriptive models designed to explicate the essentially *e*motional "nature" of aesthetic experience. In the works of authors like Robert Vischer, Johannes Volkelt, Theodor Lipps, and Karl Groos (figures who are relatively little known today but were of decisive influence at the time), "psychological aesthetics" takes shape as a field of knowledge constituted by newly developed conceptual instruments and argumentative patterns; and it involves, though often only in nominal form, the incipient deployment of "experimental" research methods.[10] What unifies the evolving discipline (which enters into a phase of methodological and institutional consolidation in the 1890s)[11] is the avowed conviction that aesthetics, "like any other science [*Wissenschaft*], must proceed anti-metaphysically [*unmetaphysisch*] by deriving its point of departure and its objectives from the world of experience" (Volkelt, *System* 31). Rejecting any kind of speculative reasoning – which they take to be characteristic of traditional, "merely" philosophical aesthetics (Volkelt, *Ästhetik des Tragischen*, 1st ed., 2; Groos, *Einleitung* 310) – the proponents of this paradigmatic "turn" claim that aesthetic experience can be adequately studied only by means of systematic empirical observation. Aesthetics is to be transformed from a body of theoretical "principles" into a body of demonstrable "facts" – from a *Prinzipienwissenschaft* into a *Tatsachenwissenschaft* – in which the notion of "functional law" takes the place of central concept (Nachtsheim, *Kunstphilosophie* 35). And while the various ways in which this shift is actually implemented may not always live up to the standards of a strictly empiricist endeavour, the underlying aspiration nevertheless remains, discursively speaking, effective. For it is precisely this aspiration – the objective of re-conceiving aesthetics as a science of observable facts – that produces the need to maintain, or rather re-establish, a specific area of competence from within the methodological framework of empirical psychology.[12] And it is, in turn, due to this very need that the categorical notion of "aesthetic emotions,"[13] and the notion of "aesthetic *quasi*-emotions" more specifically, begins to acquire its central conceptual status. The notion of inherently fictional feelings, in other words, first arises within, and consequently testifies to, a discursive process in which the new formation of psychological aesthetics begins to stake out a territory of its own. And in the context of this process, the concept of *quasi*-emotions serves to articulate a qualitative difference between certain specifically aesthetic processes of consciousness and other, more general psychological functions – a difference, that is, from which a corresponding (partial) difference at the level of disciplinary formations can then be derived by means of analogy.

The question to be pursued here is not whether this kind of discursive strategy actually succeeded from a systematic point of view, but rather *how* the emerging notion of quasi-emotions relates – epistemologically and rhetorically – to the self-demarcation and self-legitimization of a nascent disciplinary field situated at the crossroads between an aesthetic tradition and contemporary scientific paradigms. The particular significance of this dynamic interaction between methodological claims and conceptual developments, when viewed from a genealogical perspective, lies in the way in which the reorientation towards a decidedly scientific standard of factuality – a factuality anchored at the methodological level of empirical analysis and description – ultimately leads the newly conceived branch of psychological aesthetics to *fictionalize* emotional processes by claiming that "fictional" emotions like "quasi-fear" and "quasi-pity" *are* psychological facts. Viewed in this light, Geiger's initial question "Do aesthetic quasi-emotions exist?" turns out to revolve around the central issue of how, and in what sense exactly, those fictional feelings can be said to be actually "the case." And any solution to this problem requires, as he asserts right after the passage quoted above, "a psychological theory as to whether mere illusion [*Schein*] is at all possible within the psychological realm" (192). The way in which this very possibility gets addressed and maintained throughout the late nineteenth century is therefore to be understood as the negotiation of a two-levelled relationship – the epistemic-ontological relationship between fact and fiction on the one hand, and the methodological-discursive relationship between "scientific" analysis and (the experience of) aesthetic objects on the other hand – at a crucial juncture in the history of aesthetics as a field of knowledge. To reconstruct this negotiation, conversely, is to trace the process through which the theoreticians of "aesthetic quasi-emotions" *arrived* at this peculiar notion of real yet fictional feelings in the first place.

Not coincidentally, it is in the very text usually credited with initiating the psychological turn in late-nineteenth-century aesthetics – Friedrich Theodor Vischer's treatise "Kritik meiner Ästhetik" (1866) – where the first traces of the conceptual development towards quasi-emotions can be discerned. Contending at one point that it would be virtually impossible to follow the stage presentation of a play like Schiller's *Wallenstein* without experiencing any emotional involvement whatsoever – and that, consequently, the peculiar nature of this emotional involvement must be analysed – Vischer provides the following preliminary characterization:

> None of this, to be sure, happens in reality; it is not "earnest" in the usual sense of the word. Just as the object is mere illusion, so also is the impression. In both cases, however, it is no empty, frivolous kind of un-earnestness; after all, it is with earnest intentions that the illusion is presented to us, and as viewers we likewise take our feelings very earnestly – without any earnestness in the everyday sense of the word. Interest has been divested of the sting of interest, stimulus is stimulus without stimulus, fright is fright without fright, hatred is hatred without hatred and so on for every emotion. (327–8)[14]

The passage is significant for the way in which it relocates the kernel of aesthetic experience – while transforming the classic Kantian notion of "disinterested interest" – to a generalized economy of feeling (Müller-Tamm). In doing so, it extends the notion of illusion from the level of aesthetic object – the stimulus – to the level of emotional response ("just as the object is mere illusion, so also is the impression"). More specifically it transfers, by means of analogy, the fictional logic inherent to the poetic object of aesthetic experience ("None of this, to be sure, happens in reality") on to the psychological object of (future) scientific observation. According to this model, then, the spectator of *Wallenstein* reproduces the fictional representation that occurs on stage in the form of an emotional experience in which every feeling corresponds to – but is not identical to – a "real" counterpart. This, however, does not mean that these aesthetically induced emotions are merely *un*real ("no empty … un-earnestness"). As Vischer goes on to emphasize, they rather possess their very own and distinctly empirical factuality – after all, something happens on stage that can be seen and heard – and they are thus to be conceived, paradoxically, in rhetorical forms like "fright is fright without fright, hatred is hatred without hatred," and the like.

This focus on the paradox of tragic pleasure – already inscribed into Vischer's *Wallenstein*-inspired reflection – begins to unfold more fully at the point where psychological aesthetics, over the course of the 1890s, develops comprehensive typologies designed to capture the entire spectrum of dramatically aroused feelings. As a central means of laying claim to the practice of rigorous empirical analysis – to an exhaustive categorization of what can be "observed" – these typologies serve to differentiate more precisely among the various kinds of aesthetically relevant emotions;

and they do so, in particular, by establishing under the umbrella category of quasi-emotions the two different subclasses of fictional feelings as distinguished in Geiger's lecture. The first subcategory, and most basic form, of tragic "quasi-emotions" identified in this context comprises the "empathetic feelings [*Einfühlungsgefühle*],"[15] that is, those feelings that the spectators, while following the dramatic representation, "project into" the figures on stage – as is the case, for example, when they experience the wrath of King Lear or Gretchen's despair as the emotional states lived through by the fictional characters themselves. As Johannes Volkelt puts it in the third edition of his *Ästhetik des Tragischen*: "In reality, this pain is being projected out of our own soul and into the tragic character, with whom it then 'fuses,' so that it appears to us – in a manner completely detached from its origin in our own consciousness – as though it pervaded the tragic characters themselves" (297).[16] The second subcategory of tragic "quasi-emotions," by contrast, is not subject to any such psychological mechanism of projection ("feeling into"). Instead of being ascribed to the fictional characters, the "sympathetic feelings" (Witasek, *Grundzüge* 148)[17] or "reactive feelings" (Volkelt, *Ästhetik des Tragischen*, 1st ed., 358) are experienced by the spectator as a kind of meta-response to the dramatic action on stage (Witasek, "Zur psychologischen Analyse" 2); and they therefore imply, as Theodor Meyer concludes, an awareness of lasting emotional difference: "We are well aware that these sympathetic feelings differ from empathetic feelings; we know very well that the fear we begin to feel for Gretchen when she – full of love and confidence – makes the fatal pledge to her loved one is entirely our own feeling, a feeling that we must not project into her" (534).[18] Likewise, the pain experienced by the spectator at the moment of the tragic catastrophe must precisely not be identified with the suffering of the tragic characters themselves; rather, it is to be described – as Volkelt underscores once again with his own kind of pathos – in the structurally different mode of compassion: "When we see how the mighty Lear, every inch of whom had once been king, has been broken, overwhelmed by his pain, and has fallen prey to the misery of madness, we are softened and shaken by compassion. Another example for this almost passionate excitation of pity is Goethe's Gretchen in the dungeon scene" (*Ästhetik des Tragischen*, 2nd ed., 282).[19] Despite this crucial difference, however, both "empathetic" and "sympathetic/reactive" feelings are considered to be "merely imagined and not truly real feelings" (Witasek, "Zur psychologischen Analyse" 7), manifestations of an "emotional illusion" (Lange, *Das Wesen der Kunst* 97) in which the fictional plot of tragedy translates, as it were, into the psychological form of a similarly fictional "affect script."[20] Neither kind of emotion – so the consensus among the most important proponents of psychological aesthetics[21] – is "real" in the sense that it would originate from an *actual* affection or activation of the spectator's personal *self*hood – his "ego-state [*Ichzustand*],"[22] as Moritz Geiger puts it in his lecture (193). Since their dramatic generation occurs within an established aesthetic frame, both "empathetic" and "reactive" feelings lack any notable connection to pragmatically relevant contexts, and this fundamental disconnect has, in the words of Stephan Witasek, the effect that "the aesthetically relevant sympathetic feelings, just like the empathetic ones, are usually not real feelings but merely quasi-emotions. After all, the events on stage that we observe from the auditorium are not real but merely illusory; consequently, there is no actual reason for fear and pity, since nobody is being truly harmed" (*Grundzüge* 150).[23] This passage unmistakably recalls – and reiterates – the causal nexus drawn by Vischer in his originary characterization of "quasi-emotions." Yet it also indicates – by placing its focus explicitly on the two most classic tragic affects – that the notion of fictional feelings now figures plainly as a *counter* model to the oldest and most prominent explanation of tragic pleasure, namely: to the idea of "catharsis" which had traditionally revolved around the dramatic arousal of *real* pity and *real* fear.

Specifically in its dominant nineteenth-century conception, tragic catharsis had been construed as a mechanism in which harmful emotional conditions on the part of the spectator are stimulated, intensified, and ultimately released from the psycho-physical apparatus. As the philologist Jacob Bernays in his seminal treatise *Grundzüge der verlorenen Abhandlung des Aristoteles über Wirkung der Tragödie* (1857) claims, catharsis in its original, Aristotelian definition derives from an analogy between the fields of medicine and poetics; it is to be understood as a "medical metaphor" (21) that serves to semantically transfer the principle of therapeutic purgation from the context of metabolic processes to the sphere of psychological phenomena. In a move directed against Lessing and his "moralizing" take on the Aristotelian notion of tragedy,[24] Bernays states that "catharsis is: a designation transferred from the somatic to the mental for the type of treatment given to an oppressed person, which does not seek to transform or suppress the element oppressing him, but rather to arouse and drive it into the open, and thereby to bring about the relief of the oppressed person" ("On Catharsis" 329).[25] What Aristotle describes as the effect (and objective) of tragedy must therefore be seen – so Bernays argues – from a "*pathological* point of view" (325); and the famous passage from the *Poetics*, also known as the *Tragödiensatz*, is to be translated, according to Bernays, like this: "Tragedy brings about through (excitation of) pity and fear, the alleviating discharge of such (pitiful and fearful) affections of the mind" (325).[26] According to this model, then, the final purpose of tragic fiction is to address emotional tensions in the spectator in order to temporarily *liquidate* these affective energies; and the pleasure associated with this aesthetically induced process lies in the experience of retroactive relief. Not least owing to its suggestive imagery, Bernays's interpretation of catharsis as energetic "discharge" ("Entladung") became tremendously influential throughout the late nineteenth century and was widely accepted in both philological and literary circles.[27] For the proponents of a psychological aesthetics, however, it serves as a decidedly negative foil against which they begin to situate, in the 1890s, their very own explanation of tragic pleasure. The basic thrust of their critique turns on the argument that Bernays – though he pursues, as a matter of fact, an essentially psychological line of reasoning – does not adequately account for the specifically aesthetic nature of the emotional response to tragic fiction. What the psychological aestheticists seek to contest, in other words, is the idea that the pleasure of tragic pity and tragic fear can be derived from a merely quantitative intensification of pre-existing feeling states.

In his treatise, Bernays does indeed ascribe to the tragic affects of pity and fear the status of general emotional "dispositions." According to him, the state of arousal induced in the spectator by the fictional plot of tragedy serves to release potentials of affective energies that do not themselves belong specifically to the realm of aesthetic experience. What is "discharged" from the viewer's psycho-physical apparatus, in other words, does not qualitatively originate from (or with) the dramatic representation. Rather, it precedes the latter in the form of habitual and chronic conditions – conditions that have been acquired biographically by the spectator and that are merely acted *upon* by the tragic plot.[28] This understanding of pity and fear as affects whose actual sources lie in pragmatic contexts of life – in "real" events, that is, that have led to the formation of lasting character traits – effectively renders tragedy a means of psycho-hygienic therapy, designed in particular for the treatment of pathologically fearful or compassionate "patients."[29] And it is precisely this functional linkage between general emotional "affections" and their tragically elicited discharge against which the proponents of late-nineteenth-century psychological aesthetics raise their objections.[30] In an essay entitled "Die tragische Entladung der Affekte" (1898), Johannes Volkelt, for example, declares that any "legitimate" explanation of tragic joy must rigorously distinguish between "pathological" and "aesthetic" effects (2–3). While he concedes that cathartic processes as envisioned by Aristotle/Bernays may occur as part of the tragic impression, he seeks to systematically play down their prominence and scope, with the aim of constraining the explanatory value attached to them. In this regard, his position is typical of the way in which Bernays's theory is negotiated throughout the field of late-nineteenth-century psychological aesthetics more generally: Whereas the semantic equation between catharsis and energetic "discharge" remains uncontested from a conceptual point of view – indeed, is regularly taken for "fact"[31] – the mechanism of emotional purgation is simultaneously recast as an "extra-aesthetic" (Volkelt, *Ästhetik des Tragischen*, 1st ed., 391) factor of tragic pleasure – as a factor, moreover, that informs "some cases" (Volkelt, *Ästhetik des Tragischen*, 2nd ed., 318) of subjective experience at best. Two arguments, accordingly, come into play here: On the one hand, the effect of cathartic discharge is conceived as exception rather than rule precisely because it presupposes, on the part of the spectator, a *particular* disposition to pity and fear. On the other hand, this limited scope is rendered not only an empirical given but also a theoretical necessity. Where the conceptual focus lies primarily or exclusively on the mechanism of cathartic discharge – so the critical argument goes – it becomes impossible to draw a categorical line between aesthetic and (other) therapeutic forms of psychological stimulation.

Whereas Bernays ties the Aristotelian purpose of tragedy to the metaphorical function of catharsis – understood as "a making visible [of] the processes in the mind by alluding to analogous bodily manifestations" ("On Catharsis" 328)[32] – the proponents of psychological aesthetics counter this notion with the claim that "aesthetic feelings, inasmuch as they remain *aesthetic*, do not reach the stage of sensory discharge" (Groos, *Einleitung* 344).[33] In line with the metaphorical field at stake here, this counter-strategy can be characterized as a way of *defusing* the explosive power of the cathartic model on two interrelated levels: By neutralizing the suggestive force of the physiological-medical metaphor, psychological aesthetics – at its object-level – seeks to shift the focus from a psycho-hygienic "side-effect" to the central characteristic of genuinely aesthetic pleasure.[34] And this very shift serves, in turn – at the level of description – to combat a form of psychologization that threatens to "contaminate" (Volkelt, *Ästhetik des Tragischen*, 2nd ed., 310) and even undermine the specific area of competence to which psychological aesthetics lays disciplinary claim. Seen from this point of view, the critical references to Bernays primarily bear witness to a process of systematic *self*-articulation in which a newly defined field of "scientific" investigation attempts to secure its particular authority, by sealing itself off from the potentially volatile consequences of its own psychological (re)constitution. In this context, the typologies of emotions sketched out above become discernible as a strategic means of implementing this self-definitional process with particular regard to the two (most) classic tragic affects. The conception of tragic pity and tragic fear as aesthetic "quasi-emotions" serves to withdraw them from the subject area of a general psychology of affect, and in doing so, ultimately serves to negotiate the discursive identity of psychological aesthetics as a discrete field of knowledge.

Against the negative backdrop of this anti-Bernaysian critique, the positive model of tragic pleasure prevalent in late-nineteenth-century psychological aesthetics begins to take shape: Whereas both "empathetic" and "sympathetic" emotions figure, in the words of Karl Groos, as "feelings *within* aesthetic contemplation [*Anschauung*]" (*Einleitung* 150) – that is, as discrete affects that change and alternate over the course of the tragic plot – the "pleasure *of* [*an*] aesthetic contemplation" (150) gains the status of a separate "dimension" of emotional experience which in itself remains independent of the specific "valences" of those changing and alternating affects.[35] According to this two-tiered model, the effect of what Groos terms "*pleasure in the image of pain* [*Lust am Bilde des Schmerzes*]" (168) becomes possible insofar as the decidedly negative quality of affects like pity and fear remains confined to a first plane of psychological processes within which it is then neutralized so that the positive valence of pleasure can unfold on a second functional level for which the first level serves as a kind of contrastive "foil" (Utitz, *Funktionsfreuden* 64; Döring, "Die ästhetischen Gefühle" 165). The phrase "pleasure in the image of pain" is thus to be read in a dual sense: It locates the source of tragedy's pleasurable effects not only in the dramatic representation of painful affects in the "images" created on stage, but also, and primarily, in the fact that the spectator experiences his own emotional affection in the theatre *as* a mere "image" of pain. This is, then, where the decisive contrast to the model of cathartic discharge ultimately turns out to lie: The pleasure-inducing mechanism of tragedy does not depend here on a solicitation of certain real "affections of the mind" but – on the contrary – on a *de*-realization of these (displeasurable) emotions by means of their psychological *simulation*.

It would be a task in its own right to pursue in detail the various ways in which the very *act* of psychological simulation – an act labelled "conscious self-deception [*bewußte Selbsttäuschung*]" (Lange, *Die bewußte Selbsttäuschung* 28) or "playful inner imitation [*spielende innere Nachahmung*]"

(Groos, *Einleitung* 347) – is rendered the actual source of a truly aesthetic pleasure derived from tragedy.[36] Instead, it must suffice here to sketch out the crucial dynamic in a few lines: When the proponents of psychological aesthetics ascribe to the two classic tragic affects of pity and fear the status of merely simulated forms of emotional excitation – the status of feelings, that is, that are "strictly speaking *neither pleasant nor painful*" (Witasek, *Grundzüge* 115)[37] – they do so to ensure that at a "higher" functional level the dimensional phenomenon of aesthetic pleasure can emerge as a *real* emotional effect. Aesthetic pleasure is conceived in this context as the positive experience of a state of affective arousal *as such* – as an experience that can only be realized where the psychological process of the tragic impression is not fully imbued with, and absorbed by, the specific qualities of certain "empathetic" or "sympathetic" feelings like pity and fear. According to this logic, then, the purpose of the particular stimulation as accomplished through tragedy would be to neutralize the negative valence of these otherwise "disagreeable and uneasy" (Hume 258) affects, thereby facilitating their conversion into the feeling of dynamic emotional *activity* for its own sake. Contrary to the teleological notion of cathartic discharge, this model seeks the source of tragic pleasure in the very fact of being aroused – in a kind of autotelic "self-feeling" ["Selbstgefühl"] that originates not from the qualitative "what" and "how" but from the "that" of an inner movement and its successive unfolding (Volkelt, *Ästhetik des Tragischen*, 3rd ed., 299). The aesthetic enjoyment derived from tragedy, in short, emerges in this perspective as a form of second-order "functional pleasure" (Döring 164) in which the dynamic of affective processes is experienced in its own energetic structure constituted by rhythmic "vibrations" (Utitz 11). And the prerequisite for the empirical facticity of this experience – its condition of possibility – comes to be identified with the very fictionality of the tragic plot which serves to separate between simulated emotional qualities (quasi-pity, quasi-fear) and the actuality of their simulation.

It is precisely this argumentative pattern that can be seen to recur, about a century later, where the notion of quasi-emotions re-enters academic discourse in its most recent (and English-language) form. In his study *Mimesis as Make-Believe* (1990), the analytic philosopher Kendell Walton writes: "Must we declare Aristotle wrong in decreeing that tragedies should evoke fear and pity? Not unless we naively insist on a literal-minded reading of his words" (249). And he goes on to provide the necessarily figurative understanding of what tragic affect in a fictional context really *is*: "Realizing it to be fictional that Anna Karenina suffers misfortune, it is fictional that we are aware of her suffering, and we experience quasi pity as a result" (251).[38] When confronted with the fictional representation of a fear- or pity-inducing object – so Walton argues to support his claim – the spectator/reader engages in a process of mental simulation which is qualitatively set apart from his "actual" mental life (255) and in which he "actually experiences his 'fictional fear'" (247).[39] This discursive recurrence of a distinction first developed in the late nineteenth century may indicate that the question addressed in and by the term of aesthetic quasi-emotions did not disappear entirely with the historical formation of fin-de-siècle psychological aesthetics – a formation whose prominence began to dissipate rapidly in the years leading up to the First World War. The term did, however, first come into being with that formation, emerging from a constellation in which poetic fiction not only figures as the object *of*, but also functions as the model *for* the emotional processes it generates – emotional processes which, in turn, not only form the object of, but also serve as foundational "facts" for a nascent field of psychological investigation.

NOTES

1 A note on terminology: The term "quasi-emotions," which was coined by the analytic philosopher Kendell Walton in his study *Mimesis as Make-Believe* (1990), will be used here to translate the German word *Scheingefühle*, as it has come to be – in the context of recent debates on the subject matter – the most commonly used corresponding expression in English. It is important to keep in mind, however, that the term does not capture the double meaning inherent to its German counterpart. As the compound structure of the word *Scheingefühle* implies, the noun *Schein* (which means fiction or illusion) can be taken to designate both the (fictional) object/cause and the (fictional) status of the attached *Gefühl* – a linguistic effect to which the concept of quasi-emotions does not offer a full semantic equivalent. For Walton's discussion of emotional phenomena like "quasi-fear" and "quasi-pity," see *Mimesis* 244–9.

2 For a discussion of this conference and its historical background, see Bernhardt, "Dialog und Konkurrenz."

3 Unless otherwise noted, all translations from German sources are my own. In the case of longer quotations, the German original will be given in the footnotes.

4 "Die sogenannten Scheingefühle sind von kürzerer Dauer und wechseln miteinander schneller ab als die wirklichen Gefühle ... Fernerhin haben die Scheingefühle eine weit geringere psychomotorische Wirksamkeit als die

wirklichen Gefühle: die Furcht im Theater veranlaßt uns keineswegs, aufzuspringen und davonzulaufen, das Mitleid treibt uns nicht, dem Helden eines Dramas zu helfen. Und endlich existiert die merkwürdige Tatsache, daß die heftigsten Unlustgefühle, wie Furcht und Angst, den ästhetischen Genuß nicht stören – ja sogar ihn noch erhöhen. (Dubossches Problem)." See note 7 regarding Dubos.

5 The notion of emotional "valence" – which refers to the basic qualitative distinction between pleasure (*Lust*) and displeasure (*Unlust*) – was introduced into empirical psychology by Wilhelm Wundt in the 1870s and quickly adopted by many scholars throughout the late nineteenth and early twentieth centuries. See, for instance, Wundt, *Grundriss* 99.

6 The aim of the following deliberations, therefore, is not to examine the late-nineteenth-century category of aesthetic quasi-emotions as such, but to explore the particular way in which it relates to the psychological discussion of the paradox of tragic pleasure, and more specifically even to the notion of cathartic "discharge" that had dominated earlier nineteenth-century conceptions of tragic affect. A more general and more comprehensive investigation into the historical debates on quasi-emotions has been conducted in the context of the research project "Aesthetic Thresholds: Emotion and Fiction," directed by Jutta Müller-Tamm at the Freie Universität Berlin, to which this paper offers a complementary focus and perspective. I thank Jutta Müller-Tamm for her suggestions and for comments on an earlier version of this text.

7 This refers to French writer Jean-Baptiste Dubos, whose *Réflexions critiques sur la poésie et sur la peinture* (1719) had already been credited by David Hume with having initiated serious philosophical discussion of the subject matter ("Of Tragedy" 259).

8 As Michael House's paper in this volume demonstrates, these late-nineteenth-century developments by no means constitute the first historical occurrence of "empirical" approaches in the study of psychological phenomena and their fictional character. What distinguishes these developments from the understanding of *Erfahrungsseelenkunde* prevalent in the eighteenth century, however, is the way in which they respond both to the rise of new experimental paradigms since the 1860s and to the challenges that result from the (methodological and institutional) rise of psychology as a scientific discipline in its own right – a process set in motion primarily by the pioneering works of Gustav Fechner and Wilhelm Wundt.

9 See also, paradigmatically, the appropriation of this definition in Lipps, "Ästhetik" 349, and the corresponding characterization in Groos, *Der aesthetische Genuss* 2. For a more detailed discussion of Vischer's claim and its methodological implications, see Perpeet.

10 In this particular context, "experiments" are not conceived in the form of psycho-physiological testing methods – methods that would involve the measuring of changes in respiration, heartbeat, or pulse – but as systematically executed processes of introspective self-observation. In his *Einleitung in die Aesthetik* (1892), for instance, Karl Groos paradigmatically states that the origin of the beautiful must be sought "in purely psychological processes that can only be approached by means of introspection and not by means of levers and screws" (283). Johannes Volkelt, in his *System der Ästhetik*, remarks accordingly that the apparatus-based gathering of physiological data could serve to address "only preliminary aesthetic questions of the most basic kind" (38–9). Nonetheless, it is precisely in response to the scientific boom of psycho-physiological testing practices à la Wilhelm Wundt – and to the competitive pressure exerted by these practices – that the "method" of introspection is now frequently recast as "a kind of experiment" (Groos, "Ästhetik" 508). See also, in this context, the critical distance to Wundt's psycho-physiological research as staked out in Lipps, "Zur Lehre von den Gefühlen" 329–30 and 361, and the following passage in Lipps, "Ästhetik": "In the realm of aesthetics, the facts of history and everyday life will always prevail, due to the nature of things, over the experiment conducted in the laboratory. No such experiment, at any rate, can replace the experiment to which the aesthetician subjects himself, that is: an introspective self-analysis under varying conditions" (386).

11 For a discussion of this development within the institutional context of nineteenth-century Germany's university system and its disciplinary organization, see Drüe.

12 When Johannes Volkelt, in the foreword to the first edition of his *Ästhetik des Tragischen* (1897) declares, "Aesthetics can only be pursued on psychological grounds" (2), his statement paradigmatically embodies the twofold aim of relating and differentiating the two fields. For a more general discussion of this interdisciplinary dynamic, see Allesch.

13 The earliest text in which the category of "aesthetic emotions" appears is Alexander Bain, *The Emotions and the Will*, published in 1859. In German, the corresponding term "ästhetische Gefühle" is first employed in August Döring's essay "Die ästhetischen Gefühle," which appeared in 1890.

14 "Nun aber geschieht ja dies Alles nicht wirklich, es ist im gewöhnlichen Sinne des Wortes nicht ernst. Wie der Gegenstand bloßer Schein, so der Eindruck. Auf beiden Seiten ist es jedoch kein leerer, leichtfertiger Nicht-Ernst; es ist ja doch sehr ernst gemeint, daß man uns den Schein vormacht, ebenso ist es uns mit unserem Fühlen beim Anblick sehr ernst – ohne allen Ernst im alltäglichen Sinne des Worts. Dem Interesse ist der Stachel des Interesses genommen,

Reiz ist Reiz ohne Reiz, Angst ist Angst ohne Angst, Haß ist Haß ohne Haß und so jedes Gefühl."

15 See Witasek, *Grundzüge* 148; Volkelt, *Ästhetik des Tragischen*, 2nd ed., 273; Meyer 530.

16 "Dieses Leid wird in Wahrheit aus unserer eigenen Seele in die tragische Person hinaus- und hineinverlegt, mit ihr 'verschmolzen', so daß es uns, unter völligem Zurücktreten seines Ursprungs aus unserem eigenen Bewußtsein, als die tragischen Personen selbst erfüllend erscheint."

17 For a concise discussion of the semantic difference between empathy and sympathy, see Keen, "Theory of Narrative Empathy" 208–9.

18 "Diese Anteilsgefühle sind uns in ihrer Verschiedenheit von den Einfühlungsgefühlen wohl bewußt, wir wissen ganz genau, daß die Furcht, die uns für Gretchen befällt, da sie liebe- und vertrauensselig dem Geliebten die verhängnisvolle Zusage gibt, nicht ein Gefühl Gretchens ist, sondern ganz nur unser eigenes Gefühl, das wir in diesem Augenblick nicht in sie einfühlen dürfen."

19 "Sehen wir den gewaltigen Lear, an dem jeder Zoll ein König war, zerbrochen, von Qualen überwältigt, dem Jammer des Wahnsinns verfallen, so werden wir von Mitleid durchweicht und durchschüttelt. Ein anderes Beispiel für diese, fast leidenschaftliche Mitleidserregung bietet Goethes Gretchen in der Kerkerszene."

20 In the first edition of his *Ästhetik des Tragischen*, for example, Johannes Volkelt characterizes empathetic feelings as "images [*Abbilder*] of emotions" (357). In the same vein, Witasek states that "in the process of empathy … quasi-emotions [*Phantasiegefühle*] are generated in the appreciating subject and projected by the latter into the expressive object" (*Grundzüge* 148).

21 There are merely two exceptions to this rule: Volkelt stresses at one point that "reactive feelings" experienced in response to the tragic characters on stage do not fall under the umbrella category of "quasi-emotions," as they are part of the spectator's actual personal condition (*Ästhetik des Tragischen* 1st ed. 358), and Theodor Lipps goes so far as to reject the notion of quasi-emotions altogether ("Weiteres zur Einfühlung" 479–80).

22 "In the theatre," Geiger adds to underscore this point, "horror, fear *for*, and fear *with* Wallenstein are present as experiences [*Erlebnisse*], without, however, turning into states of the I" (193).

23 "Daß die ästhetisch in Betracht kommenden Anteilsgefühle, geradeso wie die Einfühlungsgefühle in der Regel nicht Ernst-, sondern bloß Phantasiegefühle sind. Die Vorgänge auf der Bühne, die wir vom Zuschauerraum aus verfolgen, sind ja nicht Wirklichkeit, sondern nur Schein, es liegt also ein tatsächlicher Grund zu Furcht und Mitleid gar nicht vor, weil ernstlich niemandem etwas zuleide geschieht." Cf. also, in this context, the characterization in Hermann

Siebeck's *Grundfragen zur Psychologie und Aesthetik der Tonkunst*, where tragedy's emotional economy is conceived as follows: "The dramatic poet, for instance, creates images of conditions in ourselves that we would have brought forth for real, had their causes – as represented in the play – truly occurred" (15).

24 Bernays critically remarks that Lessing, in his (mis)translation and (mis)interpretation of Aristotle's notion of catharsis, conceives of tragedy as a "moral house of correction" ("moralisches Correctionshaus") that serves to purify rather than purge the tragic affects of pity and fear (3).

25 "dass Katharsis sei: eine von Körperlichem auf Gemüthliches übertragene Bezeichnung für solche Behandlung eines Beklommenen, welche das beklemmende Element nicht zu verwandlen oder zurückzudrängen sucht, sondern es aufregen, hervortreiben und dadurch Erleichterung des Beklommenen bewirken will" ("Grundzüge der verlorenen Abhandlung" 16). Translation modified.

26 "Die Tragödie bewirkt durch (Erregung von) Mitleid und Furcht die erleichternde Entladung solcher (mitleidigen und furchtsamen) Gemüthsaffectionen." (Bernays, "Grundzüge der verlorenen Abhandlung" 21).

27 The degree to which Bernays's interpretation of Aristotle's notion of catharsis – initially the cause of a controversial and heated debate among contemporary philologists (see Gründer) – eventually acquired canonical status can be inferred from various late-nineteenth- and early-twentieth-century sources. See, for example, the obituary of Bernays published by Viennese classicist Theodor Gomperz in 1881, a text in which the semantic equation between catharsis and discharge is authorized in no uncertain terms: Bernays's "pathological" viewpoint – so Gomperz claims – has "solved the riddle of the sphinx and put an end to the catharsis controversy" ("Jacob Bernays" 122). In his own translation of the Aristotelian *Poetics*, published in 1897, Gomperz accordingly chooses to render catharsis as "discharge," thereby endorsing – and further disseminating – Bernays's account. Another protagonist of Vienna's literary circles, Hermann Bahr, likewise remarks in his "Dialog vom Tragischen" (1903) that Aristotle's notion of catharsis permits "no other interpretation than the one provided by Bernays," and that, therefore, the identification of the term's "pathological" meaning is to be considered the final word on the subject matter (719). On the catharsis-related debates in turn-of the-century Vienna, see also Worbs.

28 Bernays states that it is the viewer's "permanent affection [*dauernde Affection*] ... that Aristotle must be concerned with if the process he calls catharsis is to take place" ("Grundzüge der verlorenen Abhandlung" 30).

29 At the end of the nineteenth century, the Viennese philosopher Alfred von Berger generalizes – and radicalizes – this therapeutic model even further. Whereas for Bernays/Aristotle, tragic catharsis remains confined to the (temporary) liquidation of pity and fear, Berger claims that these two affects can serve as (metaphorical) vehicles to discharge any kind of unhealthy "affective tensions" ["Affect-Spannungen"] from the viewer's psyche. Berger's reflections on this mechanism – inspired by Breuer and Freud's *Studien über Hysterie* (1895) – were published in 1897 as an appendix to Gomperz's translation of the *Poetics.* For a detailed discussion of this therapeutic model in relation to Breuer/Freud's "cathartic" method of the "talking cure," see Gödde.

30 See Volkelt, *Ästhetik des Tragischen*, 2nd ed., 304; Groos, *Einleitung* 345–6; Utitz, *Funktionsfreuden* 29.

31 See Stumpf, "Die Lust am Trauerspiel" 54–5; Siebeck, *Grundfragen* 90; Groos, "Das Spiel als Katharsis" 356.

32 "Eine Versinnlichung des Vorgangs im Gemüth durch Hindeutung auf analoge körperliche Erscheinungen" ("Grundzüge der verlorenen Abhandlung" 14).

33 Emphasis mine.

34 See Volkelt, *Ästhetik des Tragischen*, 3rd ed., 347; Witasek, *Grundzüge* 151; Groos, *Einleitung* 344–8.

35 The conceptual distinction between "discrete" affects like anger, fear, pity, etc. and general affective "dimensions" like pleasure and displeasure is Wilhelm Wundt's. See Wundt, *Grundriss* 99.

36 In his discussion of tragic affects, Groos introduces the notion of "inner imitation" – the core element of his own aesthetic theory – explicitly as a counter-concept to the concept of cathartic "discharge." As he claims, tragic pleasure "originates exclusively from the play of inner imitation, and discharge is but a special side-effect of very limited significance" (*Einleitung* 357).

37 For Witasek, the distinction between "real" emotions and "quasi-emotions" explicitly results from the different non-emotional premises under which they arise: The former are based on judgments about reality, whereas "quasi-emotions" are based on assumptions about fictitious objects (*Grundzüge* 116). For a detailed discussion of this particular aspect, see Vendrell Ferran, "Ästhetische Erfahrung."

38 The reference point for Walton in this context is Colin Radford's seminal paper "How Can We Be Moved By the Fate of Anna Karenina?" (1975), which had initiated in the field of analytic philosophy an extensive debate devoted to the so-called paradox of fiction (Yanal, *Paradoxes* 1–18).

39 For a more detailed examination of Walton's theory and its premises, see Yanal 49–66.

WORKS CITED

Allesch, Christian G. *Geschichte der psychologischen Ästhetik: Untersuchungen zur historischen Entwicklung eines psychologischen Verständnisses ästhetischer Phänomene*. Göttingen: Hogrefe, 1987.

Bahr, Hermann. "Dialog vom Tragischen." *Neue Deutsche Rundschau* 14 (1903): 716–36.

Bain, Alexander. *The Emotions and the Will*. London: Parker & Son, 1859.

Berger, Alfred von. "Wahrheit und Irrtum in der Katharsistheorie des Aristoteles." In *Poetik* by Aristotle. Trans. and ed. Theodor Gomperz. Leipzig: Veit, 1897. 69–98.

Bernays, Jacob. "Grundzüge der verlorenen Abhandlung des Aristoteles über Wirkung der Tragödie." In *Zwei Abhandlungen über die aristotelische Theorie des Drama*. Berlin: Hertz, 1880. 1–118.

– "On Catharsis: From Fundamentals of Aristotle's Lost Essay on the 'Effect of Tragedy.'" Trans. Peter L. Rudnytsky. *American Imago* 61.3 (2004): 319–41.

Bernhardt, Toni. "Dialog und Konkurrenz: Die Berliner 'Vereinigung für ästhetische Forschung' (1908–1914)." In *Konzert und Konkurrenz: Die Künste und ihre Wissenschaften im 19. Jahrhundert*. Ed. Christian Scholl, Sandra Richter, and Oliver Huck. Göttingen: Universitätsverlag, 2010. 253–67.

Döring, August. "Die ästhetischen Gefühle." *Zeitschrift für Psychologie und Physiologie der Sinnesorgane* 1 (1890): 161–86.

Drüe, Hermann. "Die psychologische Ästhetik im Deutschen Kaiserreich." In *Ideengeschichte und Kunstwissenschaft: Philosophie und bildende Kunst im Kaiserreich*. Ed. Ekkehard Mai, Stephan Waetzoldt, and Gerd Wolandt. Berlin: Mann, 1983. 71–98.

Geiger, Moritz. "Das Problem der ästhetischen Scheingefühle." In *Kongreß für Ästhetik und allgemeine Kunstwissenschaft, Berlin 7.–9. Oktober 1913; Bericht*. Stuttgart: Enke, 1914. 191–4.

Gödde, Günter. "Therapeutik und Ästhetik: Verbindungen zwischen Breuers und Freuds kathartischer Therapie und der Katharsis-Konzeption von Jacob Bernays." In *Grenzen der Katharsis in den modernen Künsten: Transformationen des aristotelischen Modells seit Bernays, Nietzsche und Freud*. Ed. Martin Vöhler and Dirck Linck. Berlin and New York: de Gruyter, 2009. 63–91.

Gomperz, Theodor. "Jacob Bernays [1824–1881]." *Essays und Erinnerungen*. Stuttgart and Leipzig: Deutsche Verlags-Anstalt, 1905. 106–25.

Groos, Karl. "Ästhetik." In "Das Spiel als Katharsis." *Zeitschrift für pädagogische Psychologie und experimentelle Pädagogik* 12.7/8 (1911): 353–67.

– *Der aesthetische Genuss*. Gießen: Rieker'sche Verlagsbuchhandlung, 1902.

– *Die Philosophie im Beginn des 20. Jahrhunderts. Festschrift für Kuno Fischer.* Ed. Wilhelm Windelband. 2 vols. Heidelberg: Winter, 1907. 2: 487– 528.
– *Einleitung in die Aesthetik*. Gießen: Rieker'sche Verlagsbuchhandlung, 1892.
Gründer, Karlfried. "Jacob Bernays und der Streit um die Katharsis." In *Die Aristotelische Katharsis: Dokumente ihrer Deutung im 19. und 20. Jahrhundert*. Ed. Matthias Luserke. Hildesheim: Olms, 1991. 352–85.
Hume, David. "Of Tragedy." In *Essays: Moral, Political, and Literary*. Ed. Thomas Hill Green and Thomas Hodge Grose. Vol. 3 of *The Philosophical Works*. Aalen: Scienta, 1964. 258–65.
Keen, Suzanne. "A Theory of Narrative Empathy." *Narrative* 14.3 (2006): 207–36.
Lange, Konrad. *Das Wesen der Kunst*. Berlin: Grote, 1901.
– *Die bewußte Selbsttäuschung als Kern des künstlerischen Genusses*. Leipzig: Veit & Co., 1895.
Lipps, Theodor. "Ästhetik." In *Systematische Philosophie*. Ed. Wilhelm Dilthey. Berlin and Leipzig: Teubner, 1907. 349–87.
– "Weiteres zur Einfühlung." *Archiv für die gesamte Psychologie* 4 (1905): 465–519.
– "Zur Lehre von den Gefühlen, insbesondere den ästhetischen Elementargefühlen." *Zeitschrift für Psychologie und Physiologie der Sinnesorgane* 8 (1895): 321–61.
Meyer, Theodor A. "Kritik der Einfühlungstheorie." *Zeitschrift für Ästhetik und allgemeine Kunstwissenschaft* 7 (1912): 529–67.
Müller-Tamm, Jutta. "Nähe und Distanz: Über den Raum und die Räumlichkeit der ästhetischen Erfahrung um 1900." In *Bewegte Erfahrungen: Zwischen Emotionalität und Ästhetik*. Ed. Anke Hennig et al. Zurich/Berlin: diaphanes, 2008. 97–110.
Nachtsheim, Stephan. *Kunstphilosophie und empirische Kunstforschung, 1870–1920*. Berlin: Mann, 1984.
Perpeet, Wilhelm. "Historisches und Systematisches zur Einfühlungsästhetik." *Zeitschrift für Ästhetik und allgemeine Kunstwissenschaft* 11 (1966): 85–111.
Radford, Colin. "How Can We Be Moved by the Fate of Anna Karenina?" *Proceedings of the Aristotelian Society* 49 (1975): 67–80.
Siebeck, Hermann. *Grundfragen zur Psychologie und Aesthetik der Tonkunst*. Tübingen: Mohr, 1909.
Stumpf, Carl. "Die Lust am Trauerspiel." In *Philosophische Reden und Vorträge*. Leipzig: Barth, 1910. 1–64.
Utitz, Emil. *Die Funktionsfreuden im aesthetischen Verhalten*. Halle/Saale: Niemeyer, 1911.

Vendrell Ferran, Íngrid. "Ästhetische Erfahrung und Quasi-Gefühle." In *The Aesthetics of the Graz School*. Ed. Venanzio Raspa. Heusenstamm: Ontos, 2010. 129–68.

Vischer, Friedrich Theodor. "Kritik meiner Ästhetik." In *Kritische Gänge*. Ed. Robert Vischer. 6 vols. Munich: Meyer & Jessen, 1914–22. 4: 222–419.

Volkelt, Johannes. *Ästhetik des Tragischen*. 1st ed. Munich: Beck, 1897.

– *Ästhetik des Tragischen*. 2nd ed. Munich: Beck, 1906.

– *Ästhetik des Tragischen*. 3rd ed. Munich: Beck, 1917.

– "Die tragische Entladung der Affekte." *Zeitschrift für Philosophie und philosophische Kritik* 112 (1898): 1–16.

– *System der Ästhetik*. 2 vols. Munich: Beck, 1905–10. Vol. 1.

Walton, Kendall L. *Mimesis as Make-Believe: On the Foundations of the Representational Arts*. Cambridge, MA, and London: Harvard UP, 1990.

Witasek, Stefan. *Grundzüge der allgemeinen Ästhetik*. Leipzig: Barth, 1904.

Witasek, Stefan. "Zur psychologischen Analyse der ästhetischen Einfühlung." *Zeitschrift für Psychologie und Physiologie der Sinnesorgane* 25 (1901): 1–49.

Worbs, Michael. "Katharsis in Wien um 1900." In *Grenzen der Katharsis in den modernen Künsten: Transformationen des aristotelischen Modells seit Bernays, Nietzsche und Freud*. Ed. Martin Vöhler and Dirck Linck. Berlin and New York: de Gruyter, 2009. 93–113.

Wundt, Wilhelm. *Grundriss der Psychologie*. Leipzig: Engelmann, 1907.

Yanal, Robert J. *Paradoxes of Emotion and Fiction*. University Park: Pennsylvania State UP, 1999.

PART IV

Relating: Biology

9 Coining a Discipline: Lessing, Reimarus, and a Science of Religion

STEFANI ENGELSTEIN

In 1782, Johann Christoph Adelung coined the name *cultural history* for a phenomenon recently put into practice by Johann Gottfried Herder. In the *Treatise on the Origin of Language* (1772) and again two years later in *This Too a Philosophy of History for the Formation of Humanity*, Herder embeds "culture" in a list of characteristics that define a particular people in a particular age and that vary over time: "*arts, science, culture and language*" (italics in the original).[1] Culture as a concept, in other words, was largely concomitant with its historicization. It would be anachronistic, however, either to think of cultural history as a discrete discipline or to categorize it within a two-cultures divide of sciences and humanities that still lay in the future. Instead, cultural history was one of a panoply of allied new approaches to understanding both Europe as a whole and particular European cultures in the context of other cultures around the world. Indeed, by the beginning of the nineteenth century, a growing obsession with human diversity in all of its cultural and physical forms had led to a variety of attempts to trace and classify relationships between groups genealogically, that is, through inheritance either biological or cultural. This pattern held true from biology and its subfield of race theory to comparative linguistics and comparative religion, and to the related fields of ethnology, anthropology, and cultural history. These proto-disciplines followed a pattern of repeated anastomoses and generally failed to remain distinct. As each of these fields traced genealogical developments over time, they created complex patterns of relatedness among peoples, languages, and cultures. Sigrid Weigel has recently noted the rise of family trees at this time, and the way that the logic of genealogy applies to histories of both natural and cultural transmission, which were segregated into the natural sciences and the humanities over the course of the nineteenth century (9).[2]

Among the fields investigating human diversity, the one we are today least likely to refer to as a science is religious studies, and yet comparative religion shared a methodology with other investigations of human diversity and claimed for itself a scientific basis through the nineteenth century. Eric Sharpe's classic history of comparative religion locates Darwin's 1859 publication of *On the Origin of Species* as the decisive moment in the formation of the discipline, when "an attempt was beginning to be made to view religion on the criteria provided by science, to judge its history and growth and evolution as one would judge the history, growth, and evolution of any organism – and to dissect it as one would dissect any organism" (*Comparative Religion* 32).[3] Darwinian evolution provided, in other words, "the principle of comparison" (ibid.). The directionality and chronology of methodological influence is far more complicated, however. Darwin was heavily indebted to linguists from Friedrich Schlegel to August Schleicher in his establishment of the theory of descent with modification as the principle for determining the relationship between population groups over time.[4] Schlegel, in turn, had acknowledged comparative anatomy as the foundation of his methodology (*Über die Sprache* 137). By the time Schlegel wrote "On the Language and Wisdom of the Indians," moreover, comparative anatomy had already branched out into anthropology in the 1770s and 1780s, at precisely the same time that Herder and Adelung ventured into the arena of cultural history. Adelung, who explicitly included the study of the history of religion within cultural history (Preface, *Versuch einer Geschichte* ii), positioned culture in an inverse relationship to the physical needs of the human animal. Far from excluding physical anthropology from the study of culture, this paradigm correlated cultural advances with increased physical delicacy and decreased sensuality. Bodies mattered in culture. The religious studies that emerged at this time participated in the same concerns as other anthropological pursuits; in fact, comparative religion modelled in exemplary fashion basic tensions in physical and cultural anthropology: between value-laden and value-neutral analysis, and between progressive models of history and contingent models. Indeed, the nascent paradigm for each of these approaches can be found within the work of a single early practitioner, namely, Gotthold Ephraim Lessing.

In Germany, the emergence of comparative religion out of theology crystallized in a very public manner in 1777, when Lessing anonymously and posthumously published several fragments from a manuscript written by the deist Hermann Samuel Reimarus, a professor of oriental languages at an academic preparatory school (*Gymnasium*).[5] The infamous *Fragmentenstreit*, or fragment-controversy, that ensued engulfed Lessing in a series of polemical disputes with theologians, in particular Johann Melchior Goeze, the senior pastor of Hamburg. At the centre of the controversy was not only the acceptability of the idea of a rational or natural religion, but also implicitly the application of ethnographic methodologies to religion, including historical investigations of the events in the Gospels. As a result of the exchange, Lessing was officially censored from any further publications on religion by the duke of Braunschweig. Lessing's most famous literary work, *Nathan the Wise*, has regularly been read as a barely covert continuation of this dispute in a literary form likely to circumvent the censors. Most Lessing critics interested in the fragments have focused on the advocacy of a religion of reason in the play, but *Nathan the Wise* also picks up Reimarus's comparative approach to understanding the relationship between the monotheistic religions and his cultural-geographical approach to belief systems around the world. Moreover, the famous ring parable at the literal centre of the drama, which recasts the relationship between the monotheistic religions as a sibling relationship, was also part of the new investigation of the historical connections between religions that the Reimarus fragments heralded. The ring parable and the play as a whole can together be read as a particular variant of the eighteenth-century transition from patriarchy to fratriarchy, a shifting of focus from vertical lineage to genealogically informed horizontal relations, here framed within the global-cultural field. The narrative structure of *Nathan the Wise* did more than help the piece elude censorship, however – it also facilitated a new kind of object and a new methodology for comparative religion and even for anthropology itself.

Lessing's *Nathan the Wise* thus becomes a paradigmatic moment for reading classifications of human population groups through the structure of the family, and interrogating the role of innate and cultural traits in both cases. Willi Goetschel has noted Lessing's departure from norms represented by Johann David Michaelis, among others, who erected essentialist ethnic categories ("Lessing's 'Jewish' Questions," esp. 63). Helmut Schneider similarly depicts Lessing's valorization of the autogenesis of reason above the material morass of body, sex, race, and national identity (*Genealogie*, esp. 176).[6] I would argue, however, that Lessing gives both more credence and more respect to inherited physical difference than Goetschel and Schneider allow for. This material component of identity serves as a structural enabler of human worth. Within a milieu that serves as a perfect setting for a study of human population diversity, *Nathan the Wise* reframes the combined effects of physical and cultural determinants of group identity.

The play is not Lessing's only reflection on these issues. In his theoretical responses to the fragment controversy, including the piece "The Education of the Human Race," Lessing's historiography takes a far different shape. This treatise can be read as a bridge from the older genre of History of Humanity [*Menschheitsgeschichte*] to the equally progressive Philosophy of History [*Geschichtsphilosophie*] of the nineteenth century. While "The Education of the Human Race" complicates the notion of universal human progress by connecting the nature of belief to historical circumstance, it does ultimately represent the Christian religion as a cultural advance. In *Nathan the Wise*, however, Lessing shifts the object of inquiry away from the content of belief and onto the contingencies of custom themselves. He thereby removes *religion* from the Enlightenment quest for grounded truths, on the one hand, while on the other, making *religions* available to anthropology. In this shift, Lessing provided a foundation for a "science of religion" equally removed both from deist debunking of positive religion and from theological attempts to find proof for Christianity in the assembled mythologies of the world.

1. Letter and Spirit

The text by Reimarus participates in the deist project of discrediting positive religion. The passages Lessing chose to publish from Reimarus's manuscript, against the advice of friends and fellow enlightenment thinkers Moses Mendelssohn and Friedrich Nicolai,[7] not only employ a comparative and cultural-geographical approach to religions, but also question the plausibility of a single revealed religion as a divine strategy for salvation, problematize the relationship of belief to justification, and cast doubt upon both the authorship of the gospels and the veracity of what is reported in them – most controversially, the resurrection. Lessing accepted the concerns raised about the Bible as the word of God, but, unlike Reimarus, did not see these doubts as fatal for the idea of a revealed Christian religion. Lessing simply increased the distance between letter and spirit, asserting in the first section of his response to Reimarus, "In short, the letter is not the spirit, and the bible is not religion."[8] He explicitly claims that salvation does not depend on "this *particular revelation*" (78; emphasis in original, trans. modified), but rather that God "might very well wish to save the good people of all religions out of this *particular consideration* and for these *particular reasons*" (78, trans. mod.). What is particular here is not the content of revelation, but rather the reasons for salvation, namely, ethical goodness, so that the core of religion is not an essence but a function, that of providing "motives for virtue" (69). Not only does this shift allow Lessing to open the doors of heaven to the myriad peoples with no exposure to Christianity, but it also enables him to avoid making of religion a business in which one counts converted souls as profit, a perspective he finds distasteful and whose origin he locates as Jewish.[9] If the content of revelation is not the salient feature of its salvific power, then conversion is merely a superficial change sanctioned by a dubious authority, very much like the stamping of new coins Lessing will later have Nathan complain of, and to which I will return below.

For Reimarus, this notion of religion as an arbitrary stamp reaches beyond the issue of conversion. Reimarus claims that 'each person has his religion and sect impressed upon [*eingeprägt*] him as a child, merely as a prejudice, through memorized formulas that are not understood and a drilled-in fear of damnation" (8:176).[10] Each individual's "inherited religion" ("angeerbte Religion," 8:175) is a consequence of indoctrination during a time when children are not yet able to exercise reason. This practice leaves them permanently stunted, unable ever to attain the impartial power of judgment. The teaching of religion to children comes across as a kind of child abuse, an impression strengthened by the emphasis on fear of damnation presumed to structure the religious upbringing. In Reimarus's schema then, *Erziehung*[11] itself becomes suspicious, a view we find echoed unexpectedly in the self-serving rhetoric of Lessing's blood-thirsty church patriarch in *Nathan the Wise*: "For isn't everything that one does to children violence?" he declares, with the crucial caveat, however, "except what the Church does to children" (85, trans. modified).[12] If we leave aside the hypocritical addendum, however, what remains is Reimarus's vision of the parent–child relationship as irredeemably tainted. Childhood becomes a dangerous waiting period. It is only from one's equals and as an equal, after the age of majority, that one can properly judge truth. The only acceptable transmission of religion implied by Reimarus would thus be a horizontal one. And yet, any thorough and mature investigation of the specific claims of a religion are bound to reveal inconsistencies and inaccuracies. In a historical investigation of the truth value of religious beliefs, all religions fail equally. As Robert Leventhal points out, deists such as Remairus actually shared with their rival orthodox adherents a need to find a fixed foundation for religious beliefs. The deists chose reason as their foundation, and hence jettisoned all narratives of divine involvement with history, and all positive religions along with them. The orthodox, by contrast, insisted on the Bible as a source of revealed truth about history, as well as about God ("Parable as Performance" 509). Lessing introduces a third option: a valorization of the transmission of belief and hence of the cultural practice of religion.

While, like Reimarus, Lessing also envisioned horizontal community as crucial to proper religious activity, he departed from Reimarus's view of childhood. For Lessing, childhood education in religion was the necessary foundation of an ethical habit that was its salient feature. "Education is revelation imparted to the individual," he declares in "The Education of the Human Race." *Nathan the Wise* spells out still more explicitly what Reimarus has overlooked in the parent–child relationship that Lessing finds redemptive, namely, love. It is love that keeps the *inherited religion* from representing violence. Love provides a counter-model to the objectionable business of trading in souls. Nonetheless, Lessing's ring story illustrates how love can recreate the effect of fear as long as truth in religion is viewed as attached to a single doctrine. The three siblings in Nathan's story are equally loved by their father, but are unable to accept this equality. Their love leaves them equally blind to the truth and unable to judge the equal legitimacy of their siblings' claims to it. Nathan's ring parable can thus be read as a rebuke to the author's own philosophical treatise, because the treatise retains the notion of a progressive approach to religious truth.

The universalizing tendency that seems in Lessing's treatise an argument for respectful coexistence has another side, therefore. Lessing's own metaphor of soul-usury implies that Christianity has a moral imperative to leave behind a materialism envisioned as imparted by its Jewish roots. Indeed, even the notion of shared roots is too disturbing for Lessing, for whom "The Christian peoples ... were grafted onto the trunk/tribe of Judaism"[13] rather than growing organically out of it. If tolerance and progress require a divorce of spirit from letter, and a move away from particularism, then it becomes merely an acclamation of an understanding of Protestant Christianity that was coming to stand for the universal. "The Education of the Human Race" restricted the usefulness of Judaism to a certain stage of human development later superseded by the purportedly more spiritual and abstract Christianity. Islam, meanwhile, because it is subsequent to Christianity, but deemed less advanced, fails to appear at all. Willi Goetschel is not wrong, however, when in his exploration of *Nathan the Wise* he emphasizes Lessing's recognition of the debt owed by Christianity to the Judaism from which it sprang, a debt that amounts to an obligation for respect and acknowledgment and, more, an acceptance of national and civic equality without reference to religious identity ("Lessing's 'Jewish' Questions" 62–4). Lessing's depiction of religion and coexistence in the drama is predicated on characters with individual rather than universal histories and therefore constructs a more nuanced vision of community than does his philosophical treatise. Indeed, it is this narrative form that gestures towards an ethnographic alternative to universal histories.

The debate over the degree of tolerance and respect for religious difference in *Nathan the Wise* has raged for decades, focusing on the question of how Jewish Nathan is. Is Nathan a proponent of a denuded rational religion that bears little resemblance to the practice of Judaism? And why is he alone excluded from the "universal" family relations revealed to exist between all the other main characters at the end of the play?[14] Like the grafting of Christianity onto Judaism quoted above, the relationship of Recha to Nathan remains one of adoption, not blood. The question of whether the conclusion truly allows for Jewish particularity, or whether the universal family merely points to the imposition of a universal religion, thus hinges on the relationship between blood and upbringing in establishing identity, character, and human value. If upbringing supersedes blood, then Judaism gains a status of respect, love, and belonging in the play; if blood remains a tainting essence that undermines the practice of reason, then, as Helmut Schneider puts it, Judaism "is in the end the blemish, the stain of irreducible bodiliness per se, that cannot dissolve into any universality" (*Genealogie*, 179, my trans.). The reason the controversy continues unabated is because the text undermines this dichotomy, proposing a far more complex interaction of the terms of the debate. As in his aesthetics and his ethics, Lessing here shifts from essence to process, from substance to history, from being to acting. In order to integrate a view of human identity as material with a view of identity as cultural, Lessing must similarly transform the terms of this dilemma. Thus, any heritable trait in the play, material or immaterial, requires experience to mould, to interpret, and to weave it into a history without which it is meaningless.

2. Matter and Meaning

While *Nathan the Wise* is often read as a coda for universal brotherhood, Lessing's focus on the three monotheistic religions had long since become anachronistic as an indicator of universality. The European medieval and early modern division of the world into four religions, namely, Judaism, Christianity, Islam, and polytheism or heathenism had given way over the course of the seventeenth and eighteenth centuries to an increasingly vast panoply of known religions, ancient and modern.[15] Guy Stroumsa has recently argued that this proliferation of acknowledged belief systems along with secularization in Europe increasingly reframed religion as an element of culture parallel to habits, customs, and language. The notion of civil religion advocated by Rousseau meanwhile reinforced the status of religion as a national characteristic (*A New Science* 171–3). Alain Schnapp has outlined the result for the British and French context: "What emerges unmistakably ... is the appeal to a new form of knowledge, uniting natural science with human history, theological inquiry with the study of antiquity" ("Antiquarian Studies" 162). This new approach soon expanded in scope, adopting the same methods in the study of more recent and indeed contemporary religious practice and belief. Religion thus came to represent private devotion while serving simultaneously as a sign of group identity within a historical, cultural framework. Comparative religion correspondingly reflected ethnographic practices. It is not a coincidence that Saladin, when countering Nathan's figuration of the three monotheistic religions as three identical rings, insists on their variety in "clothing, ... food and drink" (72), while Nathan himself refers to differences between religious groups "in color [that is, skin color] and clothing, in form" (56). If these external features generally characterize the religious groups, they nonetheless prove throughout the course of the play to be inadequate to their signifying task. Not only does Nathan mistake his Parsi friend al-Hafi for a Muslim once he has changed into the uniform of Saladin's court,[16] but the terms "Jud'" and "Christ" used as forms of address based on visual judgments of exteriors, are shown to be indicative of a category mistake which equates individuals with their "Volk" (9: 533; 56–7).[17] Skin colour and build can be similarly misleading. The adopted Recha, for example, passes as Jewish without problem although her inherited physical traits come from a European Christian mother and a Muslim-born, Middle Eastern father. Meanwhile, Daja sees nothing odd about Curd's claim to be a simple Swabian (43) in spite of the resemblance to his Muslim-born, Middle Eastern father noticed by both Saladin and Nathan.

One way in which Lessing approaches this relationship between culture and body is through the metaphor of the coin. Economic transactions, monetary gifts, and depicted financial prejudice against Jews recur pervasively and play multiple roles in this text.[18] My interest in coins and rings in this essay moves in another direction, however. In its configuration as a material symbol for an immaterial value, coin, I argue, is used by Lessing to comment on signification and on the connection between letter and spirit in religion, and also to interrogate the valence of human bodies.

When Lessing's wise Nathan appears before the sultan Saladin he is prepared for trouble – money trouble to be precise. And he is not wrong.

The sultan has called him in to borrow money. Saladin's request for truth, for an accounting of the true religion, is a trick, meant to loosen Nathan's purse strings by backing him into a corner. And yet, there is something in the request itself that reminds Nathan of money. He muses: "He wants ... truth. Truth! And he wants it like that, so bare, so shiny, as though the truth were a coin!" (70). But what then is truth, to speak with Nietzsche? Struggling with this question, Nathan resorts again to coin: "Now if it were an age-old coin that was weighed, that might work. But such a new coin, that only a stamp can make, that you can just count on a counter, that's not what the truth is" (70, trans. modified). By insisting on weighed money as a figure more appropriate for truth than new coin dependent on an arbitrary stamp, Nathan simultaneously fits into and modifies the role known as *Münzjude*, the Jewish mint-master and financier to the nobility. Münzjuden, employed by Prussian kings for generations by the time Lessing wrote, were regularly publically abused for devaluing currency by changing the stamps, and thus causing inflation.[19] Nathan's preference for weighed metal coin counters this image of the false-dealing Jew, but does not uphold the possibility of uniting sign and referent in any simple way. The metal coin serves after all as a complicated figure of speech. The phrase "that might work" ("Das ginge noch!" 9: 554) cannot be read as a simple declaration of inherent truth value; it suggests instead an activity in the context of a social interaction, a kind of *weighing* on Nathan's part of the ability of human-crafted metaphors to affix value. The coin figure serves several purposes here, then. First, it reveals Nathan in the process of considering metaphor as a strategy for responding to the sultan; second, it tests the coin as a rough draft of the valuable ring he will eventually choose for his story; and finally, in the reflection on age-old and new coin, Nathan develops an approach that establishes the value of transmission as dependent on material, while side-stepping an evaluation of the material itself, an approach in other words that allows him to assign worth to all three religions and escape the "tyranny" of a singular truth. The shifting of value from matter to transmission is a shrewd political move that illuminates Nathan's strategic intelligence, but we need not therefore dismiss his claims. The peaceful coexistence of different faiths that Nathan's reading facilitates would have made this formula quite as compelling for Lessing as for Nathan, and just as desirable for each to deliver to his respective audience.

In order to fulfil these functions, the coin passage engages with the conventional value of even weighed money, which was recognized and debated throughout the eighteenth century, as well as with the referential status of stories and metaphors such as Lessing's own.[20] As Richard Gray has discussed, mining operations in the New World at this time had demonstrated the volatility of the value of gold and silver, and greater acquaintance with other cultures had revealed their status as valuable objects to be a relative cultural phenomenon (26–7). Unlike paper bank notes that wear their conventional status on their sleeves, however, metal money participates in an illusion of security.[21] Nathan's *age-old coin* could be idealized as an example of transparent unity between stamp and intrinsic worth, and yet the value of a weighed coin as Nathan describes it lies more in its age than its weight, that is, it accrues significance through transmission over time.[22] Indeed, the passage, particularly read in conjunction with the ring story and the play as a whole, reveals that, in spite of its own age-old association with the word, coin is never *bar* or *bare*, never nakedly self-valuing. Not only its arbitrary, authorized stamp, but also its function as substance is unsuited to serve as a symbol of truth. To resemble truth, the coin must be entered into circulation within a society that accepts and upholds its value. It is worth comparing this genealogical view of truth to Nietzsche's extraordinarily similar and oft-quoted one a century later:

> What then is truth? A mobile army of metaphors, metonymies, anthropomorphisms, in short, a sum of human relations which ... after lengthy use, seem firm, canonical and binding to a people: truths are illusions that are no longer remembered to be illusions, metaphors that have become worn and stripped of their sensuous force, coins that have lost their design and are now considered only as metal and no longer as coins. ("On Truth and Lie" 357)

For Nietzsche, as for Reimarus before him, the genealogical reading discredits truth. For Lessing, however, the same procedure reveals and *validates* the source of truth as transmission rather than substance.[23] While in "The Education of the Human Race," Lessing was content to separate letter from spirit, in *Nathan the Wise* he finds a new way to combine them.[24]

In his coin musings, Nathan presents us with a view of worth he will consistently espouse throughout the play. The sultan, however, only treats truth like new coin as part of a temporary strategy for borrowing money of the less metaphorical variety. Saladin has already expressed his philosophical preference for a naive view in which true value both inheres in a thing and can be reliably discerned through its outer form. In accordance with Muslim prohibitions on figurative art, Saladin and his sister Sittah play chess with "smooth stones, which are reminiscent of nothing, don't depict anything" (45, trans. modified). Saladin's exasperation with them expresses his yearning for a revelatory correspondence between matter and meaning in things both human and divine. Saladin's wish would seem to be upheld by at least one incident in the course of the play: the Templar Curd, whom Saladin anomalously pardons because the Christian crusader resembles Saladin's brother, will turn out to be the son of that brother.[25] Not only Nathan's ring story, however, but also the play itself, ultimately includes human bodies in its challenge to the idea of natural signs.

Nathan's ring story is thus particularly well chosen because it directly addresses Saladin's qualms about arbitrary signs. In Nathan's famous story, the original ring was passed down from father to best-loved son for generations until it was eventually replicated by a father who loved his three sons equally and who gave a ring to each of them. As the judge in Nathan's story notes, not only the knowledge of which ring is the original, but the true ring itself, may very well have been lost in transmission. All three rings are likely copies and, like the once-weighed coin, now depend upon faith in transmission for their value. Significantly, the value of even the original ring lay in its role as a marker of a loving relationship between two people, rather than in its material. After the proliferation of rings, one could still imagine authenticating the true ring or the true religion through its ostensible power to make its wearer beloved, if it is worn with that intention. While vertical transmission motivates the adoption of a particular religious truth claim, therefore, it is horizontal affirmation of regard from siblings or contemporaries that distinguishes the bearer of the true ring. This qualification suggests the replacement of a competition over truth, which is singular, by a competition in goodness, which can be shared without diminishing. As truth content devolves into process, and substance dissolves into a history of relationships, the replication of a single father in each generation proliferates into a complex set of affective kinship relations. This pattern complicates Friedrich Kittler's now commonly accepted claims about the rise of a new bourgeois nuclear family at this time, centring in Lessing on paternal *Bildung* rather than biological inheritance, and in the later Romantic period on maternal love, but in both cases positioning the child in a linear relationship to parents while overlooking siblings.

3. Family Matters

Between "The Education of the Human Race" and *Nathan the Wise*, Lessing subtly but significantly altered his portrayal of the common elements of religions. In both cases Lessing refers to common *Gründe*, but in the drama he no longer means the intellectual justification for religion, namely, the "motives [*Bewegungsgründen* (8: 321)] for virtue" (69) from his response to Reimarus.[26] Instead, he now focuses on the historical and narrative foundations of religions. With this move, he replaces an emphasis on individual rational analysis with an emphasis on the affective quality of familial relationships embedded in transmission. In both cases, however, the foundations are a set of behaviours and motivations rather than solid substances. "After all, aren't they [religions] all grounded in history? Written or passed down [*überliefert* (9: 557)]! And history can only be accepted on faith and belief, right? Well, whose faith and belief is one least likely to call into question? Isn't it that of his own people? Of those of our own blood? Of the people who from childhood on have given us proof of their love?" (73, trans. modified). Belief, in other words, is not a rational judgment about truth, but a question of identity. The passage raises the same question inherent in the coin, the rings, and Saladin's chess pieces, but now levied more directly at human population groups. This question needs to be addressed to the entire late eighteenth century and the sciences that emerged from this period: religious studies, linguistics, race theory, ethnography, and anthropology. What does it mean to belong? Who are "his own people" ("die Seinen") – those of whose blood *we* are (to follow Nathan's sudden shift from third to first person here), *or* those who raise us with love? How do the material and the cultural inform each other? The parable, like the play as a whole, dismisses neither birth nor emotional ties as legitimate foundations for the transmission of belief and culture, but intertwines them. The eventual discovery that the Templar and Recha are brother and sister, and are Saladin's nephew and niece, is not disregarded as irrelevant to their behaviour, their emotions towards one another, or what one could call their cultural identity. Blood, however, is not a defining substance here, any more than metal defines the coin. Saladin unexpectedly gets this right when he reassures Recha, "Truly blood, blood alone does not make the father! It hardly makes the father of an animal! At the most it confers the right to earn that name!" (113). True to this notion of *earning* value, the play dramatizes the way that inherited traits must enter a history of activity and relationships to shape their expression as deeds and to acquire meaning. Moreover, blood alone does not communicate itself without a history of shared experience. Not only does Saladin recognize Curd because of his memory of his brother, but the drama also suggests that Curd recognizes Recha, although less distinctly, because of his vaguer memories of his parents. Significantly, Recha, orphaned as an infant, cannot reciprocally recognize him, and therefore does not react to him with the same passion that he immediately feels for her.

While on a first acquaintance Saladin and Curd are each attracted to these new objects of affection, more interaction is required to solidify the bond. Lessing's commitment to moving beyond physical traits and first impressions is programmatic rather than accidental. The relationships must both develop a history and be recognized as historical by the participants. This process entails establishing a complex interaction of inherited and learned traits, through an integration of temporal and spatial experiences. While Curd's appearance, for example, highlights the persistence of inherited characteristics, these inherited characteristics are not limited to the physical, and cannot be isolated from their lived contexts. While Recha's behaviour, on the other hand, emphasizes the significance of learned characteristics, the effect of these learned characteristics is influenced by her innate traits.

The plot of *Nathan the Wise* turns on Curd's resemblance to Nathan's friend and to Saladin's brother, who are, of course, revealed to be both one and the same and Curd's father. The traits Curd shares with his father range from the most concretely material to the intangible. While Saladin pardons the Templar at first glance because of a visual resemblance, he later notes that the tone of their voices also coincides (9: 582). Saladin also regularly compares the Templar's behaviour, rash as well as brave, to that of his long-lost brother, while Nathan reasons without hesitation from appearance to character. After just one look at the Templar and before their first conversation, Nathan concludes, "The shell might be bitter; the core certainly isn't" (54).[27]

Recha, unlike her brother, seems to be first and foremost the product of her education, and to resemble Nathan more than her biological parents. Her features are never described and it would seem that her physical traits exist in no relationship, in no history. Mild and soft, as both her Jewish and Christian names suggest, she would seem the ideal imprintable blank slate.[28] And yet, as with Curd and Saladin, Recha awakens memories in the Templar through both her appearance and her voice. In an early draft of the play, Curd asks himself: "I have seen just such a heavenly form somewhere before – heard just such a heavenly voice. – But where? In a dream? Images from dreams do not impress themselves so deep" (9: 649; my trans.). The two most prominent rescues in the play are thus analogous in motivation: Saladin acts on a visual cue of recognition when he pardons Curd from execution, Curd on an aural one when he hears Recha cry out for help from the burning building.[29] Curd's own bemusement over this action, which makes him a "mystery" to himself (43), can only be unravelled once he has discovered his own identity in relationship to Recha.

Lessing removed such explicit allusions to Recha's resemblances from the final version, however, creating an initial tension between appearance and voice in Curd's perception of Recha that he must overcome.

Curd's initial attachment to Recha therefore seems to play out in the field of the visual. His defensive insistence after the rescue that "the girl's image disappeared long ago from my mind, if it was ever there in the first place" (43), argues against its own import. A second meeting reinforces a bond created specifically through appearance: "Seeing her, and the decision never to let her out of my sight ... Seeing her, and the feeling of being bound up with her, of being interwoven with her, were one and the same ... If that's love, then the Templar truly loves, the Christian truly loves the Jewish girl" (75–6).[30] After conversing with Recha, he feels a sense of disjunction, crying out, "How my soul is divided between eye and ear" (65). Educated exclusively orally by her foster father, who discouraged her from reading, her speech echoes his empirical bent. We must therefore surmise a glimmer of awareness on Curd's part of the contrasting pull of her appearance towards her birth family, towards his own parents.[31]

We soon realize, however, that the perceived division between eye and ear in Curd's reaction to Recha is another of his groping misinterpretations. Recha's voice combines Nathan's instruction with the timbre of her ancestry, while visual traits such as her smile are integrated into a history of action and behaviour. Curd himself determines that Recha's smile alone would not appeal to him, were it not for the thoughts that motivate its appearance, thoughts attributable to her upbringing. Helmut Schneider reads the emphasis on paternal instruction in the evaluation of Recha's smile as a male appropriation of female generative abilities (196). While Schneider is right to critique the absence or inadequacies of maternal education here and throughout Lessing's work, it is noteworthy here that the paternal inhabits both body and mind. The already mercurial image of the smile or the material timbre of voice,[32] which might be inherited, are thus replaced by the actions of smiling and speaking which represent the unique combinatorics of nature and nurture, and complicate the discrepancy between time and space.[33]

The split between eye and ear was at the centre of Lessing's great aesthetic treatise *Laocoön: An Essay on the Limits of Painting and Poetry*. Lessing's preference there for the thoughts and empathy awakened by the arbitrary signs of language above the beauty achieved by the natural signs of visual art reappears here, when Curd turns his head aside to hear Recha without distraction from his eyes. And yet, Curd is unable to keep his eyes averted. While drama always combines visual and verbal material, Curd's and Saladin's reflections are more than cues for how the audience should interpret the play. Rather, they model how the audience should read bodies in action as signs in general. Lessing here expands his semiotics, merging aesthetics, ethics, and epistemology. David Wellbery has argued that visual and audible signs ultimately fail to remain distinct in Lessing's *Laocoön* because language, however arbitrary, performs a mimesis of thought, which occurs through the same arbitrary medium (*Lessing's* Laocoon 198–200). Wellbery is too quick to collapse Lessing's nuanced semiotics, however. Verbal discourse, precisely because it is non-mimetic, creates a space necessary for the material to achieve meaning. Claudia Brodsky Lacour notes this chiasmus "by which signs attain natural status and the things they signify are denaturalized" ("'Is that Helen?'" 245). This "revers[al of] the order of semiosis" (246) allows a material thing – whether tone or smile – to be freed from the pure mimesis of inheritance and refer to the historical experience of a person in time.

It is no accident that Lessing's text, like many others of the period, depends prominently on investigations of the relations between siblings to explore this interaction between bodies and identity. One could speculate that it was the disturbingly proximate relationship of the monotheistic religions that accounts for the prevalence of Muslims in European tales of sibling incest, particularly in British literature, but also in German.[34] At the same time, as in so much later social and genetic science, siblings foreground questions of how shared or divergent upbringing interacts with shared biological origins. If with a coin, it is not only the stamp, but also the metal itself whose value depends on convention, the matter/meaning constellation is still more complicated in humans. It is significant in this vein that the story's familial denouement departs from traditions in which an orphan discovers a father who provides a name, a title, and often a fortune, enabling a happy ending based on marriage. Here, the reunited family conspicuously excludes vertical lineage, extending the dismantling of reproductive relationships that has structured the story throughout. Even in the symbolic terms of church titles, the sympathetic and open minded lay *brother* is clearly to be preferred to the fanatical *patriarch*.[35] Discovering that the beloved Recha is his sister creates a moment of dismay for Curd, but only a moment, after which he declares to Nathan that in providing him with a sister rather than a wife, "You've given me more than you've taken from me! Infinitely more!" (117).[36]

What are we to make of this preference for siblinghood over spousal and parent–child relations? The answer lies in the disparity between two versions of history, exemplified also in the discrepancy between Lessing's treatise "The Education of the Human Race" and his drama *Nathan the Wise*. Any universal, progressive history requires abstracting ideas and cultural affiliations from individuals and positing a story of linear descent as supersession. Such descent, in order to be progressive and teleological, necessarily implies the preference of new over old, necessarily distorts by ignoring developments that do not fit the desired vision of advance. Hence Lessing's denigration of Judaism in comparison to Christianity, and his avoidance of Islam altogether, in his philosophical treatise. A narrative fiction works differently, however. In the play, history is always personal, and the abstract becomes concrete and particular. Religious succession becomes religious coexistence; the genealogy of the monotheistic religions metamorphisizes from one of generational descent to one of common ancestry; and parental relationships melt away in favour of complex lateral and step-relationships. While the universal histories of idealism construct a vision of advance viewed from a distance that renders them indifferent to individual lives, focusing on cultural history in the moment reveals stark ethical choices that do not end with the close of the Crusades: respectful coexistence and recognition of the bonds of individual histories, or fanaticism in the service of a vision of progress. In the play, Lessing constructed a defence of both the ethics and the anthropological value of weighing particular histories and relationships above universal progress. Meanwhile, both forms of history left lasting and conflicting legacies.[37]

4. Revelation

Writing nearly a century after Lessing, Friedrich Max Müller announced the birth of a "Science of Religion," and attributed it to the accumulation of new material from around the world over the preceding fifty years, and to the new ability to read this material as a result of advances in linguistic knowledge in Europe. At least as important in the establishment of this field, however, was the wider shift in the methodologies of knowledge work in which Reimarus and Lessing participated. While it is true that more Europeans were travelling more widely and reporting their experiences for large and rapt audiences, comparative religious studies would not have developed without the internal application of ethnological tools to the roots of European culture: in particular, biblical philology and the historical study of early Christianity.

The stakes of early comparative religion were very high. As Jonathan Z. Smith indicated in the 1980s, "Religion is solely the creation of the scholar's study" (*Imagining Religion* xi). Tomoko Masuzawa traces the way that Europeans who travelled the world looking for religion always managed to find it. Having interpreted beliefs and customs of the most diverse kind as religion, they were able to declare religion a universal human trait. But such universality merely increased the pressure to distinguish, to discriminate, and ultimately to legitimate European Christian superiority in this area, as in the case of race and language. Max Müller exemplified this trend by combining the teleological historiography also seen in Lessing's own "Education of the Human Race" with the essentialism Lessing had even there evaded. In his 1870 lecture series "The Science of Religion," Müller confidently refurbishes the worn-out coin of truth as divine revelation:

> Like an old precious medal, the ancient religion, after the rust of ages has been removed, will come out in all its purity and brightness; and the image which it discloses will be the image of the Father, the Father of all the nations upon earth; and the superscription, when we can read it again, will be, not only in Judaea, but in the languages of all the races of the world, the Word of God, revealed, where alone it can be revealed – revealed in the heart of man. (121)

Turning away from Lessing's vision of many religions open to many truths, Müller believed comparative religion would establish the validity of a particular theological doctrine, and herald a to return to a single, revealed Father, a practice that would not only enshrine Christianity, but also participate in the larger project of constructing science as the legitimator of a hierarchy of culture.

NOTES

1 Herder, *Philosophical Writings* 160. In the later work, "culture" has moved up to the front of the list (288). See Michael Carhart and John Garber for discussions of the late-eighteenth-century development of a science of culture in Germany in the context of anthropology and ethnography. Peter Burke places this late-eighteenth-century development in a longer historical context.

2 See also Theodore Pietsch's fascinating book on the development of the tree image to represent the relationship between species. Pietsch, however, does not connect the trees to similar structures in use for other purposes, from family trees tracing lineage to linguistic trees.

3 This date is generally accepted as the beginning of the discipline. See also Molendijk, *Emergence of the Science of Religion* and Hjelde, "Science of

Religion." For accounts that move the origin back into the eighteenth and sixteenth centuries, respectively, see Baird, "How Religion Became Scientific" and Stroumsa, *A New Science*. In an excellent article, Peter Byrne delineates three ways to conceive the neutral, "scientific" approach to religion: naturalistically, phenomenologically, and through a cultural-symbolic approach. He traces the naturalistic approach back to David Hume. See also Hume, "Natural History of Religion" 33–87. Byrne attributes the phenomenological method – in which Christian doctrine is justified through comparison – to Rudolf Otto, and finds the origin of the cultural-symbolic approach in Herder and Hegel. I claim here, however, that in *Nathan the Wise*, Lessing applies Herder's cultural methodology more directly to religion, and that he provides a less hierarchical cultural approach than Hegel. I will end with a glance at the phenomenological method, which Max Müller exemplified far earlier than Otto.

4 See Alter, *Darwinism* for the influence of linguistics on Darwin's theory.

5 Lessing first published a less controversial segment of Reimarus's manuscript in 1774 without much public reaction, and then issued the five fragments which instigated the controversy in 1777 and a seventh fragment in 1778. For more, see Yasukata, *Lessing's Philosophy of Religion* 1–43 and Talbert, *Introduction to Fragments*.

6 For Schneider, however, the play also illustrates the inescapable material constraints that obstruct this self-creation.

7 Lessing, *Werke* 8: 888.

8 "Commentary on the Fragments of Reimarus" 63. It is precisely on these lines that Goeze focused his attack on Lessing.

9 While defending the Jews on the one hand as "dieses unendlich mehr verachtete als verächtliche Volk" (8: 321), "that infinitely more despised than despicable people" (69), Lessing here still conforms to a pervasive anti-Semitic prejudice that associates Jews with usury (8: 321; 69). All quotes from Lessing in the original are from the Deutscher Klassiker edition and will be cited by volume and page number parenthetically in the text.

10 Quotes from the Reimarus fragments are taken from Lessing, *Werke*. Translations of Reimarus are mine.

11 *Erziehung* is education or upbringing as in the title of Lessing's treatise "The Education of the Human Race."

12 English quotations of the play are taken from Ronald Schechter's translation. I will note when I have modified his translation or provided my own.

13 "Commentary on the Fragments," 70, trans. modified.

14 For a variety of perspectives, see Goetschel's "Lessing's 'Jewish' Question" and Adamo ("One True Ring or Many?"), who argue that Lessing presents a

respectful, multicultural perspective; and Oesmann ("Nathan der Weise") and Robertson ("'Dies hohe Lied der Duldung'?"), both of whom find Lessing's view of tolerance limited and limiting.

15 Karl Guthke notes that both Reimarus and Lessing focus on the monotheistic religions while acknowledging the much greater diversity around the world ("Die Geburt des Nathan" 17–18). As Guthke mentions, in Lessing's Jerusalem one encounters "'Franken,' Inder, 'Mohren,' Agypter, Araber, Parsen ('Gheber'), Juden und Mohammedaner, selbstverständlich, aber auch ein 'Wilder'" (24). The "savage" is, with Lessing's typical irony, a European Christian.

16 Al-Hafi is variously described as a Parsi, a Gheber, and a Dervish. The last of these designations conflicts with the first two, however. The Parsis are a Zoroastrian sect in India, which al-Hafi also mentions as his homeland (61). Gheber is a European word for a Zoroastrian, and there is evidence in the text that al-Hafi considers his religion to be other than the three monotheistic religions (51). On the other hand, Dervishes constitute a Muslim Sufi sect. Farquharson provides a convincing reading of Lessing's sources on Dervishes and Zoroastrians to suggest that he likely intended the character to be Zoroastrian rather than Muslim ("Lessing's Dervish" 47–67).

17 The fact that Nathan rejects the identification of individual and group does not constitute a rejection of each group. Nathan wears identifiably Jewish clothing or other outward indicators, as evidenced by the Templar's identification of him as Jewish as he approaches (54), and during his interview with the sultan he is determined not to convert. Moreover, while he points out that evidence of goodness that inspires the Christian lay brother to call a person a Christian simultaneously inspires *Nathan himself* to call that person a Jew (98), he does not reject either label in favour of a more universal designation. Nathan is committed to elucidating what religions share, and also to maintaining their distinctness. See Bennett for a related argument that *Nathan the Wise* promotes belonging to a tradition – which Bennett, however, equates with blood-relatedness – as "rationally arbitrary but realistically necessary" ("Reason, Error and the Shape of History" 70).

18 Since Peter Demetz's 1966 commentary on *Nathan the Wise*, which called the money metaphors the key to the ring story, the play, and Lessing's philosophical thought ("Lessing's 'Nathan der Weise'" 147), numerous reflections on money in the play have appeared, including examinations of generosity and gift-giving by Weidmann ("Ökonomie der 'Großmuth.'") and Librett ("How Does One Orient Oneself") and explorations of the ambiguous status of the power of the market economy by Lehrer ("Lessing's Economic Comedy") and Schönert ("Der Kaufmann von Jerusalem"). Demetz, Shell (*Money*,

Language, and Thought), Goetschel ("Negotiating Truth"), and Gray (*Money Matters*) have written on coin, representation, and truth. I will return to several of these readings.

19 Daniel Itzig was appointed Münzjude by Friedrich the Great and remained both Mintjew and court banker under Friedrich Wilhelm II (Breuer and Graetz, *Tradition and Enlightenment* 109–10, 148). Itzig's son Isaac Daniel Itzig and his son-in-law David Friedländer were leading figures in the Jewish Enlightenment, or Haskalah, along with Moses Mendelssohn. Lessing almost certainly knew several members of the family – one of Itzig's daughters who ran a Berlin salon, Sara Levy, recounted the acquaintance (Malino and Sorkin, *Profiles in Diversity* 193–4).

20 Coin was a common rhetorical player in debates about hermeneutics. See Gray and Shell.

21 While Nathan's "new currency" is therefore a step towards the logic of paper money, the two cannot be conflated, as Shell tends to do (159, 171).

22 As Goetschel notes, the worth of the old coin "is determined on the grounds of the custom and habit that present the framework of historical continuity"; "Negotiating Truth" 113.

23 Eva Knodt also reads Lessing as "proto-Nietzschean" in his views of truth. Lessing's intervention into the understanding of truth has been long noted by critics. In addition to Knodt ("Herder and Lessing on Truth"), see Schmitt, "'Die Wahrheit'"; Schneider, *Genealogie* 157–60; Goetschel, "Negotiating," 115; Leventhal and Fulda, *Schau-Spiele des Geldes* 4; and Schilson, "Dichtung und (religiöse) Wahrheit."

24 Robert Leventhal similarly points out the shift from the disregard for the "letter" or means of religious tradition in "Education" to the respect for historical specificity of traditions in *Nathan* ("Parable as Performance" 515, emphasis in original). Schneider attempts to reunite the two views by claiming the gulf between object and meaning sets both free by allowing the universal core to shine through the diverse particulars (169–70). I would add, however, that the particulars are not merely conduits to higher abstract universals, but instead that the sought-after meaning continues to integrate the bodily and particular with universal foundations.

25 Sara Eigen Figal complicates the picture still further by emphasizing the uncertainty surrounding the circumstances of Assad's relationships with women, and hence of the birth of the two children claimed to be his at the end of the play. The play's insistence on the allegiance associated with family bonds, while also recasting allegiance in the form of family bonds, unmasks the blood relation as a structuring idea rather than a material fact.

26 For a reading of Lessing's use of the word *Grund* as a critique of Enlightenment epistemology and hermeneutics, see Leventhal, "Parable as Performance" 506–7. Schneider comments on the double function of *Grund* as both the particular space we occupy and the universal foundation of our reason (170).

27 The convoluted nature of the interrelation between inside and out is revealed by the fact that Nathan makes this positive judgment based on observation of the Templar's external, i.e., bitter, features.

28 See Birus ("Das Rätsel der Namen") for the etymology of Recha's names.

29 The two rescues are also parallel in risk. While the jeopardy of rushing into a burning building is obvious, the patriarch renders the threat to Saladin explicit when he attempts to recruit Curd to assassinate his benefactor. It is Curd's special protected status that would make him the ideal choice for the job.

30 The formulation implies that the novel emotion caused by a visual impression could be something other than erotic love. Curd's life is after all intertwined with Recha's biologically and historically. We see here how even natural signs such as resemblance require the intervention of education before they can be properly understood.

31 As Katja Garloff has argued, "The integration of visual, aural, and tactile impressions" ("Sublimation and Its Discontents" 56) in the play distinguishes successful moments of cognitive intuition from less mature infatuations dependent on vision alone.

32 Saladin's explicit reference to tone of voice makes clear that Lessing here recognizes the material element even of verbal signs.

33 Elsewhere in this volume, Daniel Aureliano Newman describes a similar moment in a much later work by E.M. Foster, in which a character makes a significant life decision because the voice of his brother resonates with that of a lost parent. In that case, the siblings are half-brothers, and the voice explicitly connects the brothers to their common mother. While the timbre of the voice is materially inherited, the persuasive force of the voice comes from the experiential emotional attachment of the character to his mother.

34 British sibling incest narratives that involve Islam include Southey's *Thalaba the Destroyer*, Byron's *Bride of Abydos*, Coleridge's *Osorio*, Percy Shelley's *Revolt of Islam*, and Mary Shelley's *Frankenstein*, while Byron's *Manfred* appeals to Zoroastrian myths originating in a geographical area that had become Muslim. In German, Lessing's 1779 *Nathan the Wise* was joined by Schiller's *Braut von Messina* in 1803 and Günderode's *Udohla* in 1805. Until Thomas Mann's twentieth-century "Wälsungenblut," only Lessing's *Nathan*

also includes Jews, as far as I am aware. It is fascinating that critical responses to Lessing have overwhelmingly focused on Jewish–Christian relations to the exclusion of Islam. Exceptions are work by W. Daniel Wilson (*Humanität und Kreuzzugsideologie*), Karl-Joseph Kuschel (*"Jud, Christ und Muselmann"*), and David G. John ("Lessing, Islam and Nathan"). Performances of the play have initiated an engagement with Islam since the 2001 terrorist attacks in the United States and subsequent attacks in Europe, although an unfortunately biased one. See Kuschel, 9–32. For more on sibling incest narratives and cultural encounter, see Engelstein, "Sibling Incest and Cultural Voyeurism."

35 So that the point not be lost, the lay brother corrects the Templar's mistaken appellation of "father" to "brother" in their first encounter (37).

36 In one of few attempts to account for this oddity, Schneider sees the affirmation of the sibling over the lover as an attempt to sublimate erotic interest into a vision of universal brotherhood (197–9). Such a reading tells only half the story, however, overlooking the function served in an economy of group identity, rather than universal identity, by the structure of affective sibling relations. For more on the sibling in relation to both desire and civic affection see my "Sibling Logic; or, Antigone Again" and "Civic Attachments & Sibling Attractions: The Shadows of Fraternity."

37 See Foreman, "Lessing and the Quest" for Lessing's role in current theological debate.

WORKS CITED

Adamo, Christopher. "One True Ring or Many? Religious Pluralism in Lessing's Nathan the Wise." *Philosophy and Literature* 33 (2009): 139–49.

Adelung, Johann Christian. *Versuch einer Geschichte der Cultur des menschlichen Geschlechts.* Leipzig: Christian Gottlieb Hertel, 1782.

Alter, Stephen G. *Darwinism and the Linguistic Image: Language, Race, and Natural Theology in the Nineteenth Century.* Baltimore: Johns Hopkins UP, 1999.

Baird, Robert J. "How Religion Became Scientific." In *Religion in the Making.* Ed. Arie L. Molendijk and Peter Pels. Leiden, Boston, Köln: E.J. Brill, 1998. 205–30.

Bennet, Benjamin. "Reason, Error and the Shape of History: Lessing's Nathan and Lessing's God." *Lessing Yearbook/Jahrbuch* 9 (1977): 60–80.

Birus, Hendrik. "Das Rätsel der Namen in Lessings 'Nathan der Weise.'" In *Lessings "Nathan der Weise"*. Ed. Klaus Bohnen. Darmstadt: Wissenschaftliche Buchgesellschaft, 1984. 290–327.

Breuer, Mordechai, and Michael Graetz. *Tradition and Enlightenment 1600–1780: German-Jewish History in Modern Times.* Vol. 1. Ed. Michael A Meyer. New York: Columbia UP, 1996.

Burke, Peter. "Reflections on the Origins of Cultural History." In *Interpretation and Cultural History*. Ed. Joan H. Pittock and Andrew Wear. New York: St Martin's Press, 1991. 5–24.

Byrne, Peter. "The Study of Religion: Neutral, Scientific, or Neither?" *Method & Theory in the Study of Religion* 9.4 (1997): 339–51.

Carhart, Michael. *The Science of Culture in Enlightenment Germany*. Cambridge, MA: Harvard UP, 2007.

Demetz, Peter. "Lessing's 'Nathan der Weise': Wirklichkeiten und Wirklichkeit." In *Nathan der Weise.* By Gotthold Ephraim Lessing. Ed. Peter Demetz. Frankfurt am Main, Berlin: Ullstein Bücher, 1966.

Engelstein, Stefani. "Civic Attachments & Sibling Attractions: The Shadows of Fraternity." *Goethe Yearbook* 18 (2011): 205–21.

– "Sibling Incest and Cultural Voyeurism in Günderode's *Udohla* and Thomas Mann's *Wälsungenblut.*" *German Quarterly* 77.3 (July 2004): 278–99.

– "Sibling Logic; or, Antigone Again." *PMLA* 126.1 (January 2011): 38–54.

Farquharson, R.H. "Lessing's Dervish and the Mystery of the Dervish-Nachspiel." *Lessing Yearbook/Jahrbuch* 18 (1986): 47–67.

Figal, Sara Eigen. *Heredity, Race, and the Birth of the Modern.* New York, London: Routledge, 2008.

Foreman, Terry. "Lessing and the Quest for Religious Truth 200 Years On: His Role in the Current Anglophone Culture-War." *Lessing Yearbook/Jahrbuch* 32 (2000): 391–405.

Garber, John. "Von der Menschheitsgeschichte zur Kulturgeschichte: Zum geschichtstheoretischen Kulturbegriff der deutschen Spätaufklärung." In *Kultur zwischen Bürgertum und Volk*. Ed. Jutta Held. Berlin: Argument-Verlag, 1983. 76–97.

Garloff, Katja. "Sublimation and Its Discontents: Christian-Jewish Love in Lessing's Nathan der Weise." *Lessing Yearbook/Jahrbuch* 36 (2004/5): 51–68.

Goetschel, Willi. "Lessing's 'Jewish' Questions." *Germanic Review* 78.1 (2003): 62–73.

– "Negotiating Truth: On Nathan's Business." *Lessing Yearbook/Jahrbuch* 28 (1996): 105–23.

Gray, Richard T. *Money Matters: Economics and the German Cultural Imagination, 1770–1850*. Seattle, London: U of Washington P, 2008.

Guthke, Karl S. "Die Geburt des Nathan aus dem Geist der Reimarus-Fragmente." *Lessing Yearbook/Jahrbuch* 36 (2004/5): 13–49.

Herder, Johann Gottfried. *Philosophical Writings.* Trans. and ed. Michael N. Forster. Cambridge: U of Cambridge P, 2002.

Hjelde, Sigurd. "The Science of Religion and Theology: The Question of Their Interrelationship." In *Religion in the Making*. Ed. Arie L. Molendijk and Peter Pels. Leiden, Boston, Köln: Brill, 1998. 99–128.

Hume, David. "The Natural History of Religion." In *A Dissertation on the Passions and the Natural History of Religion*. Ed. Tom L. Beauchamp. Oxford: Clarendon Press, 2007.

John, David G. "Lessing, Islam and Nathan der Weise in Africa." *Lessing Yearbook/Jahrbuch* 32 (2000): 245–57.

Kittler, Friedrich A. "'Erziehung ist Offenbarung': Zur Struktur der Familie in Lessings Dramen." *Jahrbuch der Deutschen Schillergesellschaft* 21 (1977): 111–37.

Knodt, Eva M. "Herder and Lessing on Truth: Toward an Ethics of Incommunicability." *Lessing Yearbook/Jahrbuch* 28 (1996): 125–46.

Kuschel, Karl-Josef. *"Jud, Christ und Muselmann vereinigt"? Lessings "Nathan der Weise."* Düsseldorf: Patmos Verlag, 2004.

– *Vom Streit zum Wettstreit der Religion: Lessing und die Herausforderung des Islam*. Düsseldorf: Patmos Verlag, 1998.

Lacour, Claudia Brodsky. "'Is that Helen?' Contemporary Pictorialism, Lessing, and Kant." *Comparative Literature* 45.3 (1993): 230–57.

Lehrer, Mark. "Lessing's Economic Comedy." *Seminar* 20.2 (1984): 79–94.

Lessing, Gotthold Ephraim. "Commentary on the Fragments of Reimarus." In *Philosophical and Theological Writings*. Ed. and trans. H.B. Nisbet. Cambridge Texts in the History of Philosophy. Cambridge: Cambridge UP, 2005. 61–82.

– *Nathan the Wise*. Ed. and trans. Ronald Schechter. Boston, New York: Bedford / St Martin's Press, 2004.

– *Werke und Briefe*. Ed. Wilfried Barner. 12 vols. Frankfurt am Main: Deutscher Klassiker Verlag, 1989.

Leventhal, Robert S. "The Parable as Performance: Interpretation, Cultural Transmission and Political Strategy in Lessing's *Nathan der Weise*." *German Quarterly* 61.4 (1988): 502–27.

Leventhal, Robert S., and Daniel Fulda. *Schau-Spiele des Geldes: Die Komödie und die Entstehung der Marktgesellschaft von Shakespeare bis Lessing*. Tübingen: Niemeyer, 2005.

Librett, Jeffrey. "How Does One Orient Oneself in Giving? Cultural-Political and Theological Implications of Problematic Generosity in Lessing's *Nathan der Weise*." *Lessing Yearbook/Jahrbuch* 35 (2003): 35–60.

Malino, Frances, and David Jan Sorkin. *Profiles in Diversity: Jews in a Changing Europe, 1750–1870*. Detroit: Wayne State UP, 1991.

Masuzawa, Tomoko. *The Invention of World Religions: Or, How European Universalism Was Preserved in the Language of Pluralism*. Chicago, London: U of Chicago P, 2005.

Molendijk, Arie L. *The Emergence of the Science of Religion in the Netherlands*. Leiden, Boston: Brill, 2005.

Müller, Friedrich Max. *The Essential Max Müller: On Language, Mythology, and Religion*. Ed. Jon R. Stone. New York: Palgrave MacMillan, 2002.

Nietzsche, Friedrich. "On Truth and Lie in an Extra-Moral Sense." In *Writings from the Early Notebooks*. Ed. Raymond Geuss and Alexander Nehamas. Trans. Ladislaus Löb. Cambridge, New York: Cambridge UP, 2009.

Oesmann, Astrid. "Nathan der Weise: Suffering Lessing's 'Erziehung.'" *Germanic Review* 74.2 (1999): 131–45.

Pietsch, Theodore W. *Trees of Life: A Visual History of Evolution*. Baltimore: Johns Hopkins UP, 2012.

Robertson, Richie. "'Dies hohe Lied der Duldung'? The Ambiguities of Toleration in Lessing's Die Juden and Nathan der Weise." *Modern Language Review* 93.1 (1998): 105–20.

Rousseau, Jean-Jacques. "On Social Contract." In *Rousseau's Political Writings*. Ed. Alan Ritter and Julia Conaway Bondanella. Trans. Julia Conaway Bondanella. New York, London: W.W. Norton & Co, 1988.

Schilson, Arno. "Dichtung und (religiöse) Wahrheit: Überlegungen zu Art und Aussage von Lessings Drama *Nathan der Weise*." *Lessing Yearbook/Jahrbuch* 27 (1995): 1–18.

Schlegel, Friedrich. *Über die Sprache und die Weisheit der Indier: Ein Beitrag zur Begründung der Altertumskunde*. Vol. 8 of *Kritische Friedrich-Schlegel-Ausgabe*. Ed. Ernst Behler and Ursula Struc-Oppenberg. Munich, Paderborn, Vienna: Verlag Ferdinard Schöningh; Zurich: Thomas Verlag, 1975. 105–433.

Schmitt, Axel. "'Die Wahrheit ruht unter mehr als einer Gestalt': Versuch einer Deutung der Ringparabel in Lessings 'Nathan der Weise' 'more rabbinico.'" In *Neues zu Lessing Forschung*. Ed. Eva J. Engel and Claus Ritterhoff. Tübingen: Max Niemeyer Verlag, 1998. 69–104.

Schnapp, Alain. "Antiquarian Studies in Naples at the End of the Eighteenth Century: From Comparative Archaeology to Comparative Religion." *Naples in the Eighteenth Century: The Birth and Death of a Nation State*. Ed. Girolamo Imbroglia. Cambridge: Cambridge UP, 2000. 154–66.

Schneider, Helmut J. *Genealogie und Menschheitsfamilie. Dramaturgie der Humanität von Lessing bis Büchner*. Berlin: Berlin UP, 2011.

Schönert, Jörg. "Der Kaufmann von Jerusalem. Zum Handel mit Kapitalien und Ideen in Lessings Nathan der Weise." *Scientia Poetica: Jahrbuch für Geschichte der Literatur und der Wissenschaften* 12 (2008): 89–113.

Sharpe, Eric J. *Comparative Religion: A History*. New York: Charles Scribner's Sons, 1975.

Shell, Marc. *Money, Language, and Thought: Literary and Philosophical Economies from the Medieval to the Modern Era*. Berkeley: Los Angeles, London: U of California P, 1982.

Smith, Jonathan Z. *Imagining Religion: From Babylon to Jonestown*. Chicago: U of Chicago P, 1982.

Stroumsa, Guy G. *A New Science: The Discovery of Religion in the Age of Reason*. Cambridge, MA, London: Harvard UP, 2010.

Talbert, Charles H. *Introduction to Fragments by Hermann Samuel Reimarus*. Trans. Ralph S. Fraser. Philadelphia: Fortress Press, 1970.

Weidmann, Heiner. "Ökonomie der 'Großmuth.' Geldwirtschaft in Lessings *Minna von Barnhelm* und *Nathan der Weise*." *Deutsche Vierteljahrsschrift* 68.3 (1994): 447–61.

Weigel, Sigrid. *Genea-Logik: Generation, Tradition und Evolution zwischen Kultur- und Naturwissenschaften*. Munich: Wilhelm Fink Verlag, 2006.

Wellbery, David E. *Lessing's* Laocoon*: Semiotics and Aesthetics in the Age of Reason*. Cambridge, London: Cambridge UP, 1984.

Wilson, W. Daniel. *Humanität und Kreuzzugsideologie um 1780. Die "Türkenoper" im 18. Jahrhundert und das Rettungsmotiv in Wielands 'Oberon', Lessings 'Nathan' und Goethes 'Iphigenia.'* New York, Bern: Peter Lang, 1984.

Yasukata, Toshimasa. *Lessing's Philosophy of Religion and the German Enlightenment: Lessing on Christianity and Reason*. New York: Oxford UP, 2002.

10 Kin Selection, Mendel's "Salutary Principle," and the Fate of Characters in Forster's *The Longest Journey*

DANIEL AURELIANO NEWMAN

At the end of E.M. Forster's *The Longest Journey* (1907), Rickie Elliot is killed by a train as he saves his half-brother Stephen by pushing him off the rails. It is, John Colmer exclaims, an "extraordinary" ending ("*The Longest Journey*" 63), and it has been criticized for too neatly resolving a convoluted plot and for cavalierly disposing of its protagonist. Even queer theorists, who have so radically reread and contextualized the plot's apparent incoherencies, see Rickie's sacrifice as a betrayal of the text's queerness. Accepting these concerns, this chapter takes a new look at the novel, attending to its hitherto neglected engagement with genetics. *The Longest Journey* is obsessed, to quote one of its characters, with "hereditary business" (*Longest* 9). Examining Forster's thematic and structural use of heredity, I suggest a new, enlarged outlook on the novel's ethics, its treatment of character and its "overdetermined heroic ending" (Miracky, "Pursuing (a) Fantasy" 141).

To begin, a simple thought experiment. What can we learn about Rickie's death from J.B.S. Haldane's famous quip – that he would not risk his life to save his drowning brother, but would plunge in for two brothers or eight cousins (Marshall, "Ultimate Causes" 504)? In terms of evolutionary fitness, Haldane realized, the more closely related the rescuer and the drowner, the less it matters if the rescuer survives. Relatedness is, so to speak, overlap between individuals: identical twins overlap completely, being one genetic individual in two bodies; siblings overlap less (50%, on average), first cousins even less (12.5%, on average). Therefore, as Richard Dawkins updates Haldane, "the minimum requirement for a suicidal altruistic gene to be successful is that it should save more than two siblings ..., or more than four half-siblings ..., or more than eight first cousins, etc. Such a gene, on average, tends to live on in bodies of enough individuals saved by the altruist to compensate for the death of the altruist itself" (100). There is strangeness indeed in this view of life. According to Haldane's calculations, Rickie throws good genes after bad when he dies saving Stephen. It would take not one but "more than four half-siblings" to justify his sacrifice. Thus, Rickie's cynical aunt Emily Failing appears to be right to eulogize him "as 'one who has failed in everything he undertook'" (282). But then I have withheld some relevant details about Rickie and Stephen, details which complicate and reward a reading attuned to *The Longest Journey*'s particular genetic vision.

What follows is not, despite superficial resemblances, Literary Darwinism. I doubt this school of criticism can serve well outside its natural environment of social realism. A rigorous sociobiological reading would, I think, fail to register the modernist oddities that make *The Longest Journey* such a delightful read. My goal is neither to solve its "contradictions, gaps, and inconsistencies" (Miracky 130), nor to take these as indicators of aesthetic failure (see Carroll, *Literary Darwinism* 145). My reading is, in fact, continuous with the ongoing revisionist approach to Forster, here summarized by Alan Wilde: "In forgoing some of our assumptions about the novels' and stories' aesthetic coherence we will discover heretofore unrecognized levels of complexity, which make of the books, if less perfect and autonomous creations, at any rate a more authentic record of Forster's (and modernism's) struggles" (69).

Seeking "unrecognized levels of complexity," I pursue the analogy between Rickie and Haldane's drowning siblings and discover in *The Longest Journey* a relatively coherent hereditary logic, one sufficiently informed by contemporary genetics to bring into play some strange implications of post-Darwinian biology. Upholding a vision of identity Forster found – or would find – congenial with Mendelism, *The Longest Journey* lives up to its reputation as a modernist Bildungsroman, demanding that we see beyond human characters to the tiny particles, now called genes, that "swarm in huge colonies ... in you and in me" (Dawkins, *Selfish Gene* 21).[1] Thus, "the fate of characters" in my title plays on two planes of narrative action in *The Longest Journey*: on one, Rickie the developing human character; on the other, his inherited traits, or characters.

Such an estranging take on character confirms Forster's status as a modernist, as does, more broadly, the cosmopolitanism of his biological engagements. Throughout his novels, Forster enacts cultural encounters to reveal the poverty of nationalistic or ethnocentric views of human nature. English prejudices and national myths are challenged by Italy in *Where Angels Fear to Tread* (1905) and *A Room with a View* (1908) and by India in *A*

Passage to India (1924). While *The Longest Journey*, by contrast, seems wholly English, its apparent insularity is deceptive. A pervasive but subtle German influence emerges, especially when we read it alongside *Howards End* (1910), which, despite many differences, rewrites the earlier novel (I will return shortly to their affinities). That is, *Howards End* exposes an indebtedness to German culture that is only latent in its predecessor. It challenges an English nationalism Forster abhorred by naming its heroine Margaret Schlegel and making her neither "English to the backbone" nor "German to the backbone" (26) but, rather, a composite of "the two supreme nations, streams of whose life warmed her blood, but, mingling, had cooled her brain" (198). Less overt in *The Longest Journey*, German thought occasionally surfaces: Hegel looms large both thematically and structurally, and the novel's ethical centre, Ansell, is repeatedly associated with German aesthetics and philosophy.

For contemporary readers, moreover, the novel's focus on genetics would have evoked a science that was still dominated by German names like August Weismann, Carl Correns, and Richard Goldschmidt. By the 1890s, Haeckel was more popular in England than in Germany (Holland, "Walter Garstang" 248). Such figures were, if not household names, familiar enough in England to give public lectures (Hans Driesch delivered the 1913 Gifford Lectures) and to publish in high-brow English periodicals like *Fortnightly Review* (where, in the 1890s, Weismann and Spencer aired their differences). If *The Longest Journey* was engaging with estranging scientific ideas, these would have struck its audience as strangely foreign to boot.

My focus on genes does not deny traditional views on character or human interest. Certainly, Rickie's sacrifice is just that: an act of will and an expression of love, rather than a compulsion from his genes. And anyway, opposing human agency and genetic fitness is a bit of a straw man. Even Daniel Dennett, a most zealous neo-Darwinist, insists it is a mistake to think selfish genes survive because they cause us to act selfishly (*Darwin's Dangerous Idea* 422–7); it is more accurate to say that the genes that survive *appear to be* selfish (by virtue of their having survived), which says very little about the nature of our own human choices. My point is not that Rickie is thinking with his genes when he sacrifices himself. The selection in kin selection does not indicate agency but, rather, the retrospective appearance of agency. Rickie's choice in the moment makes sense to me only as a manifestation of agency, be it fully reasoned or partly instinctive.[2] Insofar as he can be said to act on behalf of his genes, he does so only in the future perfect: at the moment of his sacrifice, he *is not* acting selfishly, but, rather, *will have* acted selfishly when his action is analysed in hindsight. In any case, I am simply proposing that attending to a genetic logic that Forster was evidently interested in allows us to uncover an additional dimension to the twin narratological problems of character and plot development. This doubling of plot trajectories sheds new light on queer Forster criticism and suggests a crucial role for contemporary biology, particularly Mendelism and neo-Darwinism, in Forster's modernist ethics and aesthetics.

The great geneticist W.D. Hamilton, who formalized kin selection theory, believed an evolutionist must be endowed with "a fourth intellectual pigment of the retina capable of raising into clear sight patterns of nature and of the human future that are denied the majority of his fellows" (qtd. in Dugatkin, "Inclusive Fitness Theory" 1378). His theory certainly challenges received ideas, troubling conventional understandings of identity, family, altruism, heroism, and success – primary concerns of real life and fiction alike. Undoubtedly, any major scientific theory can, as Gillian Beer argues, "disturb assumed relationships and shift what has been substantial into metaphor" (*Darwin's Plots* 1). Quantum mechanics explodes our most fundamental ideas about reality – but then it hardly demands a revision of daily life, or of the narratives we spin to comprehend it. By contrast, a new genetic theory is always a new vision of human nature, of our individual and collective potential for improvement, of our past and destiny, of our very make-up and identity. Formalizing Haldane's anecdote of drowning kin (Dugatkin 1378), Hamilton opened up vistas as strange as Einstein's or Planck's. But his hit closer to home.

Hamilton's kin selection model inaugurated the now orthodox framework in evolutionary biology, Inclusive Fitness Theory. In this view, selection acts not on groups or individuals but on genes; individuals are mere vessels for selfish genes. This is certainly unsettling. A theory that reduces bodies into "survival machines" for genes (Dawkins 21) and behaviours into "apparent strategies" for optimizing fitness (Buss, "Mate Preference Mechanisms" 263) cannot but deliver an ontological shock. Even a champion of post-humanism like Donna Haraway shrinks from it, though she recognizes its potentially productive challenge to the myths of identity: "the pov [point of view] of the gene gives me a curious vertigo that I blame on the god-like perspective of my autotelic entity" (*Modest* 133).[3]

This "curious vertigo" distorts the stories we live by and those we produce as art. It has been exploited thematically in Ian McEwan's *Enduring Love* (1997) and David Lodge's *Thinks …* (2001). More pertinent here, it can shape narratives. Both Kurt Vonnegut's *Galápagos* (1985) and Zadie Smith's *White Teeth* (2001), for example, are structured by the randomness of survival and the discrepancies between individual merit and reproductive fitness (Vonnegut's Captain von Kleist is a total failure who, as a new Noah, fathers all future humans). That these two novels feature multiple generations and emphasize reproduction is not incidental: we should expect to find Inclusive Fitness Theory associated with certain literary genres (the family saga, the Bildungsroman, cyberpunk, Naturalism). The features that make these genres amenable to the logic of inclusive fitness predate by decades or centuries its formalization in the 1960s; the genres were, so to speak, pre-adapted to intersect with selfish genetics. For this reason, we can speak of inclusive fitness at work in novels as old as *The Longest Journey*.

Anachronistic as it may seem, my claim is supported by historical precedents. Indeed, the basic insights of inclusive fitness inhere in the work of Francis Galton (1822–1911) and Weismann (1834–1914), who both distinguished mortal bodies from potentially immortal genetic lines (Olby, *Origins of Mendelism* 57). Kin selection originates even earlier. In *The Origin of Species*, Darwin explains the puzzling existence of sterile worker-bees by proposing that "selection may be applied to the family, as well as to the individual, and may thus gain the desired end" (237). Aspects of inclusive fitness are therefore latent in Darwinism itself. If its precise articulation demands statistical and genetic knowledge unavailable before the 1920s, its implications could nevertheless emerge from earlier fictional treatments of heredity.

In the context of fiction, this emergence requires that the narratives meet specific conditions: a plot structured by genealogy; character relations stressing reproduction and kinship; and, crucially, a model of heredity sufficiently consistent with the modern notion of genes. The first two conditions are easily met; the limiting factor is the hereditary model, partly because most novels have concerns other than generating coherent genetic theories. Clearly, inclusive fitness would not obtain in a plot dictated by Lamarckian, or soft, inheritance. In soft inheritance, the genetic material changes as the body reacts to experience and environment; genetic identity is too closely aligned with personal identity for genes to act selfishly. The Lamarckian vision so intertwines the individual with the hereditary that Samuel Butler uses the word "personality" to speak of both (*Life and Habit* 78 ff.).

What is needed, then, is hard inheritance, "the essential constancy of the genetic material" (Mayr, *Growth of Biological Thought* 755). Hard inheritance decouples genetic from personal identity: the mother's blue-eyed gene continues in her son – even if his eyes are brown – and it could be traced back along her family tree for countless generations. Hard inheritance is exactly what we find in *The Longest Journey*, whose implicit genetic theory, stressing inherited traits, genetic determinism, and shared descent, demands readings that discriminate between the fate of characters and the fate of their genes.

A brief précis of *The Longest Journey* reveals a plot dictated by genealogical events – births, deaths, marriages, fertile couplings. Rickie has a hereditary clubfoot; marries Agnes Pembroke; and fathers a severely crippled daughter whose death convinces him "no child should ever be born to him again" (184). He learns that Stephen Wonham, a rustic drunk raised by Rickie's aunt Emily, is his illegitimate half-brother. More conventional than he would like to think, Rickie blames his hated father for the bastard and accordingly rejects Stephen; in reality, Stephen is the son of Rickie's beloved mother and Robert, a farmer. The revelation should surprise no one, for the kinship had to be maternal: all Elliots have a clubfoot, and Stephen has not. In any case, Rickie has a change of heart, leaves Agnes, moves to the country and dies under the train as inevitably as Anna Karenina. The novel closes idyllically with Stephen, now married and living off the royalties of Rickie's posthumously successful book, camping in the woods with a daughter named after his and Rickie's mother.

My crude summary strips the novel of its charm, but it suffices for demonstrating the narrative's structural reliance on genealogy. "We are expected always to bear the circumstances of [Rickie's] parentage in mind," as an early reviewer complained (qtd. in Gardner, *E.M. Forster*, 66). Like *Howards End*, *The Longest Journey* is shaped by genealogical events. Like *Howards End*, it enacts its drama and generates its values by having biological bloodlines overlap with and diverge from material or spiritual legacies. Like *Howards End*, it features the tortuously indirect inheritance of a country house and exploits the contrasts between legitimacy and bastardy, and between being "normal" and being cursed with "something congenital or hereditary" (*Howards* 285). Both novels resolve their notoriously complicated plots and give coherence to their unwieldy narrative structures by dividing the labour of inheritance between siblings.

Unlike his use of siblings, Forster's engagements with heredity enjoy little attention. Yet the two issues are inextricable. In *Howards End*, for example, Margaret Schlegel inherits Howards End but, choosing childlessness, bequeaths the house to her sister's illegitimate son. In "Tony and Ralph," the titular males find a way to live together through Ralph's marriage of convenience to Tony's sister. In *The Longest Journey*, the sibling relation is so important that the whole narrative hangs on the precise nature of Rickie and Stephen's kinship and on the actions their kinship inspires.

The Longest Journey heralds its genetic concerns early. We soon learn that Rickie is "rather lame" and that his lameness is "hereditary" (6, 9). His difficulties are then summarized as a predicament reminiscent of Hardy's Jude: "'He says he can't ever marry, owing to his foot. It wouldn't be fair to posterity. His grandfather was crocked, his father too, and he's as bad. He thinks that it's hereditary, and may get worse next generation … He daren't risk having any children'" (50). Consistent with such genetic determinism, Rickie frequently appears as a replica of his father. Even to his mother he is, unflatteringly, "the little boy who looked exactly like" her husband. At first glance, then, the novel seems to posit an inexorable hereditary curse, whereby '"the sins of the parents are visited on the children"' (*Longest* 261). Nowhere is Forster more clearly indebted to Naturalism and its assumption of "absolute determinism in all human phenomena" (Zola, "Roman" 324). The Elliot curse recalls the "thrust of [the] hereditary lesion" in Zola's *Germinal* (1885), which drives Étienne, "despite his communist theories" and "his moral education," to drink and "end up an assassin" (566, 423). Determinism hangs as inexorably, if less heavily, over Rickie. So he is understandably annoyed when Aunt Emily tells him, '"you are so like your father … It is curious – almost terrible – to see history repeating itself"' (*Longest* 92).

The Longest Journey's hereditary vision is, however, more nuanced, and its complexity rests partly on Forster's ability to use up-to-date theories of heredity. For historical if for no other reasons, Zola's novels are vague about the hereditary operations that shape his Rougon-Macquart cycle. In the preface to *La fortune des Rougon* (1871), the families he "studies" are victims of hereditary energies and inclinations, of "the slow succession of neurological and blood symptoms that arise in a race following an original organic lesion and determine in individuals of that race, according to the environment, the emotions, desires, passions, all those human manifestations whose products are called virtues or vices" ("Préface" 302). This view, typical of mid-nineteenth-century science, assigns family resemblances to contending ancestral forces, habits, or tendencies. In the decades leading up to Forster's novel, however, such models were being discredited by evidence for inheritance by material particles (Olby 63; Mayr 735). Galton's *particles*, Weismann's *biophores*, and Hugo de Vries's *pangens* all require, in various ways, "a transportation of material particles which are bearers of the individual hereditary characteristics" (Vries, *Intracellular Pangenesis* 7).

The genetic theory implicit in *The Longest Journey* is of the particulate variety. This may be unexpected: Forster is typically considered a disciple of Samuel Butler's theory of unconscious memory and progressive evolution (Heath, *Creator as Critic* 328). All the same, *The Longest Journey* contains a single explicit reference to genetics, and it foregrounds particulate inheritance, which is almost necessarily incompatible with Lamarckism. Thus, Emily mocks the pamphlets Stephen reads to support his evolutionism: '"One of those sixpenny books tells [him] that he's made of hard little black things, another that he's made of brown things, larger and squashy. There seems a discrepancy, but anything is better for a thoughtful youth than to be made in the Garden of Eden"' (103). Emily references contemporary debates about heredity, but both sides assume physical units – "little black" or "brown things." Her sarcasm could be read as a reliable indicator of the novel's genetic vision, but this reading is unsupported by the text: *The Longest Journey* always sides with Stephen against Emily. Moreover, she knows enough about how Stephen was "made" – in a real-life imitation of '"French comedy"' (236), complete with cuckoldry, elopement, and farcical hypocrisy – to raise the reader's suspicions about the sincerity of her appeal to the "Garden of Eden."

This passage must suffice, given the absence of Lamarckian or other such alternatives, to align the novel's genetic theory with particulate inheritance. Particles, unlike forces, are highly conserved across generations, retaining their molecular identity despite the vicissitudes of their carriers' lives. This conservatism has a weird corollary. Heredity is not about the person, or personal essence or identity, but about the particles housed within that person. Galton vividly illustrates this odd logic by likening the body to "a post office" and genetic particles to "heaps of letters" (qtd. in Olby, 63): the post office is just temporary storage space, and it is the letters and their movements that matter. If hereditary units are particles whose integrity and identity are conserved despite their carrier's environment and actions, their fate is at least partly distinct from that of the carrier. As Galton and later Weismann argued, the hereditary line (Galton's *stirp*, Weismann's *germ-plasm*) is fundamentally distinct from the body (Galton's person, Weismann's soma). In Weismann's words, "The cells of the organism are differentiated into two essentially different groups, the reproductive cells – ova or spermatozoa, and the somatic cells, or cells of the body … The immortality of the unicellular organism has only passed over to the former; the others must die, and since the body of the individual is chiefly composed of them, it must die also" (*Essays* 111). This model, as retrospect reveals, approximates the gene-centred view of evolution.

The germ-soma division allows us to reassess Rickie and Stephen's relation. They are, in this light, two somatic bodies whose germ lines overlap and whose genetic fates are therefore partially co-implicated. Rickie's change of heart about Stephen thus appears to be justified by the novel's genetic theory. When Rickie thinks Stephen is his paternal half-brother, he imagines they are competing for posterity. When his daughter dies, then, the outcome of the competition seems fixed: "There isn't any future," he tells Agnes, believing that "he, because his child had died, was dead" (190, 192). So he is rather upset by the prospect of healthy Stephen propagating the Elliot line. "As a final insult," Rickie muses, his father

> had brought into the world a man unlike all the rest of them, a man dowered with coarse kindliness and rustic strength, a kind of cynical ploughboy, against whom their own misery and weakness might stand more vividly relieved ... For that Stephen was bad inherently he never doubted for a moment *and he would have children: he, not Rickie, would contribute to the stream*; he, through his remote posterity, might be mingled with the unknown sea. (192, my emphasis)

The metaphorical equation of stream and lineage remains after Rickie discovers his maternal relation to Stephen. But its connotations change for the better:

> Something had changed ... On the banks of the gray torrent of life, love is the only flower. A little way up the stream and a little way down had Rickie glanced, and he knew that she whom he loved had risen from the dead, and might rise again. "Come away – let them die out – let them die out ... Let me die out. She will continue," he murmured, and in making plans for Stephen's happiness, fell asleep. (250–1)

Moments earlier, Rickie had saved his drunken half-brother from tipping over a banister, signalling his change of heart and foreshadowing his death. Knowing his true relation to Stephen, he finds his world transformed. Yet nothing structural has changed in the relation between them; according to the branches of a family tree they are still as closely related, half-brothers. The source of kinship matters more than its degree.

Significantly, Rickie, who resembles his father more than his mother, had already sensed fellow-feeling for Stephen '"down in what they call the subconscious self"' (191) – in, it could be said, the maternal elements lying latent in him. In any case, with the revelation of their maternal relation, what began as competition becomes what behavioural ecologists call reciprocal altruism. By facilitating Stephen's survival he ensures the survival of part of his own genetic makeup. Rickie believes himself "unfitted in body" and "in soul" (81), as he must remember every time he sings his school anthem, which begins, '"Perish each laggard!"' (158). This line, as implausible as it may seem, is lifted unchanged from Forster's own childhood school anthem, and Rickie probably sings it, as did Forster, thinking he will "be a prisoner throughout life's battle." The way out, writes Forster, is having "the courage to become a laggard" ("Literature" 89). In Stephen, Rickie finds the courage and a reason to let himself perish.

It is not pure selflessness that moves him to "gaz[e] at the pure stream to which he would never contribute" and sacrifice himself so that Stephen might contribute instead. It is, rather, an "apparent strateg[y]" (Buss 263) for transmitting the maternal traits he considers the best of him, happily divorced from any Elliot element. Rickie has found a way to survive genetically, to live on in the next generation without contributing directly to it. The situation recalls Darwin's early version of kin selection, designed to explain how traits in sterile individuals might nevertheless survive genealogically: "I have such faith in the powers of selection," writes Darwin, "that I do not doubt that a breed of cattle, always yielding oxen with extraordinarily long horns, could be slowly formed by carefully watching which individual bulls and cows, when matched, produced oxen with the longest horns; and yet no one ox could ever have propagated its kind" (238). Voluntarily sterile as an ox, Rickie may be "a stream that never reaches the ocean" (246). But "streams do divide" (272): a channel of his mother's stream is in him, combined with the Elliot line, but another channel, untouched by Elliot blood, has been diverted into Stephen. For Rickie, this makes his brother "the future of our race" (289).

The dividing streams offer Rickie a chance to correct a past mistake: his mother's naive '"marrying into the Elliot family"' (235) – a choice aptly described, given the novel's fluvial conceit, as "a plunge taken ... from the opposite bank" (22). By sacrificing himself for Stephen, he aborts the future of his paternal line without imperilling the maternal. This goal he cannot achieve as an individual; though he does symbolically manage to divorce his maternal and paternal selves when the train severs his (it is implied) crippled leg, the severance costs him his somatic life.

Instead, the effective division of streams occurs at the genetic level, in the future children that Rickie had previously begrudged his brother.

Helping Stephen now appears an interested act: Rickie saves Stephen so that Stephen can perpetuate the genetic particles they share. Reading Rickie's sacrifice as reciprocal altruism is supported by a draft of the previously quoted passage beginning "Something had changed" (250). Having discovered his true relation to Stephen, Rickie kisses his brother as "the portrait of their mother look[s] down upon them both" and prophesies:

> "She has risen from the dead ... Living in houses, as I must, we forget Nature. But at times ... she enters and makes her comment. She has commented on me. I daresay you have heard about my child ... I can bear to die out now ... I have seen just a little way up and down the generations, and I know there is a purpose in the tiny corner of the world that I have touched ... I stand with my face to the night[, but] it is not really darkness, for [those] I loved are handing the torches on ... *Nothing greater could happen to me – not even a child of my own.*" (376, my emphasis)

Rickie's survey of both past and future reveals the role he must play in order to extend, despite his refusal to have "a child of [his] own," his genetic existence. He must purge the Elliot from the extension of his mother's line. In Rickie the two lineages coexist, but Stephen is not so burdened (he inherits, however, his father Robert's alcoholism).

The determinism in *The Longest Journey* is less devastating than Zola's, but not because Forster's genetic theory is gentler. It is, instead, deterministic in ways that are neither simple nor linear. The Elliot curse is an irrevocable fact for Rickie, but it tells only half of his hereditary story; the other half is told by his mother. The genetic shuffling that accompanies reproduction belies any vulgar form of genetic determinism, by which we are copies of one of our parents. As we have seen, Rickie seems at first a copy of his father, who "resembled his son, being weakly and lame, with hollow little cheeks, a broad white band of forehead, and stiff impoverished hair" (22). His mother finds him to be "exactly like [his father] in disposition" (239). Yet the narrator insists they are not identical: Mr. Elliot's "voice, *which he did not transmit*, was very suave ... *Nor did he transmit his eyes*" (22, my emphases).

Rickie does not, in fact, exactly resemble his father in every trait; some traits, those the narrative deems desirable, descend from his mother. As in Weismann's theory, Rickie's inheritance involves recombination, the shuffling of genetic particles so necessary for introducing variation into procreation. Recombination on its own, however, does not allow Rickie's genetic survival in Stephen's daughter. As in most nineteenth-century genetic theories, including Darwin's and Galton's (as well as Butler's), Weismann's model assumes the fusion of parental characters, producing in the offspring an indivisible blend (see, e.g., *Germ-Plasm* 239). If inheritance is blending, Rickie and Stephen still share maternal genetic material; but the material is altered by the paternal elements with which it is mixed, and there is therefore no real genetic identity between the half-brothers. To put it schematically,

Mr Elliot	+	**Mrs Elliot**	→	**Rickie**
■	+	○	→	◘
Robert	+	**Mrs Elliot**	→	**Stephen**
×	+	○	→	⊗

The maternal element shared by Rickie and Stephen exists (○), to be sure, but its molecular identity has been modified. This blending model precludes the type of genetic survival I have outlined for Rickie, for in no sense would any part of him literally be preserved in Stephen and his daughter.

This outcome, which the novel appears to endorse, requires that maternal and paternal elements unite without fusing, retaining their integrity and independence:

Mr Elliot	+	**Mrs Elliot**	→	**Rickie**
■◊	+	○§	→	○■
Robert	+	**Mrs Elliot**	→	**Stephen**
Θ×	+	○§	→	○×

If inheritance is non-blending, odds are good Rickie and Stephen share ○, an atomistic genetic element unchanged by its combination with the complementary elements from different fathers.

The genetic theory in question must be Mendelism. Though formulated in the 1860s, Mendel's discoveries failed to reach a substantial audience before 1900, when they were rediscovered by de Vries, Carl Correns, and Erich von Tschermak and then, in England, championed by William Bateson and popularized by Reginald Punnett in *Mendelism* (1905). Mendel would also find a champion in Forster.

Mendelian inheritance involves genetic particles (now called genes), each coding for a specific trait. Each gene is transmitted independently from the genes coding for other traits. This is the Mendelian Law of Independent Assortment (the other is the Law of Segregation, which states that somatic cells contain two copies of each gene-variant, or allele, e.g., Rickie's ○■, but that each sex cell contains only one of the other, i.e., either ○ or ■) (Morgan, *Physical Basis* 15–16). The independence of each allele from the others allows offspring to inherit idiosyncratic mixes of their parents' genetic constitution.

Paternal inheritance is, in Rickie, the primary source of traits mentioned in the text, and it largely determines his development and life story. But the narrative clearly favours the maternal source, and from this valuation emerges a crucial system of narrative values. Knowing to consider what traits Rickie inherited from which parent, we find ourselves more attuned to the novel's norms. Because we know Rickie inherited his eyes from his mother and his club foot from his father, for example, we can deduce a lot from metaphors like Rickie "shut[ting] his eyes" to the failure of his marriage or dying from the amputation of his crippled foot.

Rickie's voice is especially significant. It is the special property and gift of his mother, "a girl whose voice was beautiful. There was no caress in it yet all who heard it were soothed, as though the world held some unexpected blessing" (22). Rickie even owes his existence to it, for it is what brought his parents together. We are never told explicitly that Rickie inherited his mother's voice, but this is strongly implied by the negation of paternal inheritance: Mr Elliot's "voice ... he did not transmit" (22). The maternal inheritance of voice is further supported in the metonymy that reduces Rickie to one of "the voices of boys who should call her mother" (240). The other boy, Stephen, does have her voice; when he asks Rickie to leave Agnes, Rickie has no real reason to accept, but he is persuaded by one crucial, hereditary reminder of his mother. Stephen's

> words were kind; yet it was not for their sake that Rickie plunged into the impalpable cloud. In the voice he had found a surer guarantee. Habits and sex may change with the new generation, features may alter with the play of a private passion, but a voice is apart from these. It lies nearer to the racial essence and perhaps to the divine; it can, at all events, overleap one grave. (257–8)

In Stephen's voice Rickie hears his mother and therefore, for the first time, can see Stephen as one of the "real brothers" he pined for when he was a boy (24).

Rickie's lameness and voice have different sources, and they therefore exert separate influences on our understanding of Rickie as a character. Each of his traits must be considered independently. Reading Rickie's fate and relation to Stephen, we must follow Bateson's Mendelian warning against seeing heredity at the individual level: instead, "the heredity of each character [trait] must be separately investigated" (*Mendel's* 8). This allows us to disentangle and decouple the genetic material combined in his soma and to look beyond the individual and "a little way up and down the generations" (*Longest* 376). Decoupling the inheritance of paternal lameness from maternal voice, Forster allows the genetic overlap between Rickie and Stephen to perform a material, as well as symbolic, role in Rickie's fate: genes identical to his, genes sharing a common history, literally survive in Stephen's daughter, a possibility inconceivable under blending inheritance. Thus, Forster proposes a genetic escape from genetic determinism. Realizing he embodies not one but two lineages, Rickie finds an escape from the genetic curse that, he thought, led only to his extinction. "The son of his mother had come back," the narrator says (*Longest* 249), referring to Stephen but using free indirect discourse and deictic shifters ("the son," "*his* mother") to include also Rickie. Agnes is right, though not in the way she imagines, to believe '"he'll come back in the end"' (261).

This Mendelian solution, easily accommodated into the Inclusive Fitness framework, is rather neat. Too neat – for it cannot quiet a lingering doubt, which I must detail before venturing on to suggest how Forster uses genetics strategically to further his ethical and political beliefs and construct his queer and modernist poetics.

The narrative solution of making Stephen a maternal brother may satisfy a gene-centred reading, but it lends a troubling triumphalism to Rickie's death. Some readers are, of course, untroubled and applaud Rickie's self-sacrifice. To Frieda Lawrence, for example, "Rickie of course isn't a bit dead, it's only one of those many healthsome deaths one dies" (qtd. in Gardner, 97). My own reading is not innocent of such abstraction. Also troubling, Forster's solution perhaps too starkly reduces the desire for one's own children to the genetic rewards of procreation, and thus risks endorsing Rickie's willingness to forgo the children he wanted. Unsettling is his realization of "the cruelty of Nature, to whom our refinement and piety are but as bubbles, hurrying downwards on the turbid waters. They break, and the stream continues" (192). At the human scale, the cost to him is too high and paid perhaps too readily. Is Rickie's death not a little too convenient, an easy way to eliminate an "unfitted" character (*Longest* 81)? Is not Stephen's inheritance of Rickie's posthumous royalties the novel's way of saying it '"can't stand unhealthiness"' (49)? Does it not endorse Rickie's self-loathing attempt to restore the status quo by offering his (monetary) inheritance to Agnes and her fiancé Gerald, thus harmonizing good income with good heredity?

Let us register these important concerns, but without repudiating the genetic reading above. Abandoning the genetic perspective would be to throw the baby out with the bathwater. Indeed, a biologically informed reading of *The Longest Journey* proves not at all inconsistent with Forster's career-long assault on prejudice or, for that matter, with recent queer interpretations of his work. In fact, by resolving Forster's seemingly paradoxical investment in both non-reproductive homoeroticism and procreation, the model by which Rickie survives genetically in Stephen's daughter grants the homosexual soma freedom from the genealogical imperative, without entirely closing off the genealogical future. It is telling that Edward Carpenter, whom Forster admired, would point to the "evolution of the worker-bee" from "two ordinary bee sexes" (*Intermediate* 11) – the very phenomenon that inspired Darwin to hypothesize kin selection – as a model of how homosexuals might contribute to a more harmonious future society.

Carpenter deplored the increasing differences between heterosexual men and women, a polarization he considered a symptom of unchecked progress. If individuals or societies are too forward-driven, he argues, their energies are dissipated and they become "woody" and "ossified" (*Angels* 244). The best hope for the future is, he suggests elsewhere, the mediating influence of "the intermediate sex or sexes" (*Intermediate* 12). Homosexuality thus contributes to Carpenter's notion of "the Return to Nature," "a reversionary process" or "counter-current" whereby "one ... feels back within oneself for another point of departure farther down" (*Angels* 219, 246–7). Carpenter defines the return to nature both as individual and society tonic and as evolutionary reversion, illuminating how Rickie, who tends to settle for a bad lot, is awoken by his true relation with the child of nature Stephen.

The boost Rickie feels from glancing "a little way up the stream and a little way down" (*Longest* 250) signals how his kinship with Stephen might serve his own interests. In a maternal half-brother, he finds a genetic alternative to having "a child of [his] own" without sacrificing what he inherited from his mother (*Longest* 376). He recognizes a way to *un*marry her from the Elliot family. Rickie's reversionary return to nature is not only the theme of his stories (all "harping on this ridiculous idea of getting into touch with Nature" [71]): it is the fate of his genes. At a moral and genealogical impasse, Rickie is saved by a sort of strategic atavism – an artistic return to myth, a literal move to the Wiltshire countryside, and a genetic step back that allows him to revive his mother's line and simultaneously shed his paternal inheritance. It is a boost because he can fulfil this goal without yielding to the reproductive imperative.

Forster's homosexual Maurice Hall finds happiness by accepting, despite his desire for children, '"the way of all sterility"' (*Maurice* 78). But in the formally if not substantively queerer *Longest Journey*, Rickie need not make such a choice, though he, too, resigns himself to childlessness. Nor must he follow Clive Durham and '"become normal"' in order to fulfil '"the need of an heir'" (*Maurice* 97). For Clive, procreation is the key to status and a conventionally good life, so he chooses to perpetuate the "visible work" of his forebears, who "handed on the torch their sons would tread out" (*Maurice* 78). Rickie, thanks to his partial genetic identity with Stephen, finds another means of "handing the torches on" (*Longest* 376), which demands not a pragmatic switch to heterosexuality and conventionality but a principled and deeply felt switch away from them. He must reject his loveless marriage and bleak suburban job and follow Stephen into the countryside. Clive compromises himself by accepting to let "Nature ca[tch] up this dropped stitch in order to continue her pattern" (*Maurice* 114), but Rickie, through Stephen, can remain a "dropped stitch" and yet still contribute materially to the genealogical "pattern."

My brief excursion into Carpenter's ideas suggests that Rickie's sacrifice might avail itself of queer interpretations not yet envisaged by queer theorists. Forster studies have been profoundly reinvigorated by queer theory, thanks largely to Judith Herz's identification of the "double nature of Forster's fiction" ("Double Nature" 254). In this model, Forster's fictions underlay the heterosexual surface-plot (darling of Merchant-Ivory productions) with a homosexual under-plot. This duality is often presented competitively, following Herz's argument that "one [plot] is true, the other a lie. Finally one or the other is displaced" (257). Of *The Longest Journey*, for instance, Scott Nelson bemoans Rickie and Stephen's kinship as a betrayal of the under-plot: "Forster displaces the homoerotic elements of the 'friendship' by making them half-brothers" (qtd. in Miracky, 141).

Herz's model has helped uncover in Forster's fiction a veritable wealth of ethical, ideological and aesthetic complexity. Yet such a powerful model inevitably brings its own blinders. An unfortunate consequence of focusing on the under-plot has therefore been the neglect of elements too easily attributed to the surface, heterosexual "lie." Illustrating this neglect, John Beer argues that "homosexuality gave [Forster] an 'outsider's' view of things, making him look at the world from a point of view which did not regard marriage or the procreation of children as central" (qtd. in

Martland, *E.M. Forster*, 20). Beer is not wrong, but his argument significantly underrates the importance, also noted by Elizabeth Heine ("Editor's Introduction" xxi), of reproduction throughout Forster's fiction. In *Where Angels Fear to Tread*, Gino and Lilia's baby is part of the heterosexual surface-plot, but he also energizes, by his parentage and death, the homoerotic under-plot linking Gino and Philip (Herz 255). Forster often thus distances reproduction from a simple heteronormative ideal: parents are of mixed race or rank (Lilia and Gino; Helen and Leonard; Mrs Elliot and Robert), and their offspring tend to catalyse same-sex dynamics (Gino and Philip; Helen and Margaret; Rickie and Stephen).

A reading sensitive to genetics disputes the view that Rickie's death is an aesthetic and political failure, on Forster's part, to let his plot endorse the homoerotic bond between Rickie and Stephen. Contemporary sexology had established that homosexuality was at least sometimes congenital, as Forster knew (Heine xxi–iv). It is therefore important to examine how *The Longest Journey* coordinates its queer poetics with its complex treatment of heredity. A key dynamic here is, I think, the favouring of horizontal over vertical genetic transmission, which Stefani Engelstein discusses in her contribution to this volume. A pertinent example here would be how kin selection has been invoked to explain the otherwise perplexing evolutionary survival of the "gay gene" (Ridley 279–80), and in Forster's novel it similarly bridges, tentatively, the apparently unbridgeable surface and under-plots. It allows different fates for the men and for their genes. On one level Rickie can follow Stephen "as a man" and "not as a brother" (257), thus preserving the homoeroticism some critics find incompatible with kinship (Miracky 141); on the other, genetic level the narrative exploits the precise nature of their kinship in order to further a seemingly contradictory set of interests.

This is not to say biology resolves everything. Indeed, *The Longest Journey*, like all Forster's novels, features an absolutely central system of non-genetic connections, which space prevents me from examining (these include, most notably, the affinities between Mr Failing and his "spiritual heir" Rickie (195) and between Rickie and Ansell). Even so, a genetic reading challenges the facile equation of the hetero/homosexual, reproductive/non-reproductive, and biological/cultural dichotomies.

A genetic perspective transcends these categories largely because it complicates and revises what it means to be an individual. Critics who deplore *The Longest Journey*'s incoherence as "a confused and inadequate vision of life" (Colmer 64) are, one might say, too narrowly focused on the human level in a narrative that defamiliarizes what it is to be a human. If, by contrast, we read Rickie as a bundle of independent traits with underlying genetic particles, a surprising parallel emerges between his self-inconsistency and those of the narrative itself. John Harvey might be writing about the character instead of the novel when he complains that "the disparate elements of which it is composed are never brought together into any kind of unity; at best they lie uneasily side by side" (qtd. in Colmer, 64). Sure, even the most post-humanist among us probably fails to be consoled by the view that our persons are evolutionarily disposable, and it is neither possible nor really desirable to be totally comfortable with Rickie's death. But the discomfort is instructive, because it not only highlights the undeniable aesthetic and political compromises in Forster's narrative solution, but also signals his attempt to reimagine character, and by extension humanness, in politically and ethically productive ways.

As a character, Rickie hardly coheres. He is, as Agnes tactfully ventures, "'a little – complicated"' (104). At least one contemporary reviewer agreed: "Rickie is drawn with too much care, his broader tendencies obscured by too many minor touches" (qtd. in Gardner, 66). The minor touches are so prominent that Rickie never becomes a character in the sense of "a repeatable integrity of form" (Abbott, "Character and Modernism" 393) or "a compendium of traits ... which gradually concatenate into a represented whole" (Levenson, *Modernism* 109). He has, as another early reviewer notes, "capacities for re-organizing himself" (Gardner 89) and even his name indicates his being "rickety" ("Mr. Elliot had dubbed him Rickie because he was rickety"; 23). To the end, he remains a more or less jumbled collection of physical features, ideas, attitudes, phrases, many of which survive, through genetic or other modes of transmission, his somatic death.

It is in this character incoherence that Forster carves out a future for Rickie – or rather for particles of Rickie. Recast as an archive of independent genes, Rickie avails himself of partial resurrection through what I have called strategic atavism, a biologically inflected development that is politically potent because atavism "punctures the modern idea of the self as individual and autonomous," and, as such, "open[s] up liberal notions of the privatized subject to the genealogical record" (Seitler, *Atavistic Tendencies* 2). Excluded by his disability and sexuality from so much of his world, Rickie is given some form of hope in the failure to cohere, a failure allowing Forster to reclaim, as did Carpenter, the "reversionary process" (Carpenter, *Angels'* 246) that was written off as pathology or perversion by contemporary racist, misogynistic, and homophobic pseudoscience.

Forster valued Mendel because his theory explained scientifically why humans, like peas, "keep throwing up recessive characteristics," atavisms ("Racial" 19). Mendelism, in Forster's view, confronts the human "desire to feel a hundred per cent" – the dangerous longing behind class-consciousness, nationalism and racism. From being "all of a piece" (ibid.), the self is reconstituted by Mendelism as a mosaic, each piece independent, some pieces lying latent until their reversion generations later.

Such atavisms participate rather subtly in *The Longest Journey*, in the genealogical structure of the narrative and under the cloak of symbolism worn by phrases like "risen from the dead" (*Longest* 251). But there is one intriguing hint of specifically Mendelian heredity: Robert, Stephen's father, woos Mrs Elliot with "an armful of sweet-peas" (235), his plant leitmotif. Sweet peas were also, of course, a favourite of early Mendelians, yielding some of the first major discoveries of twentieth-century experimental genetics. As Punnett writes in the preface to the 1907 edition of *Mendelism*, "the sweet pea and the stock have yielded up their secret, and we are at last able to form a clear conception of the meaning of 'reversion'" (vi). Later in the book, he notes that "the case of the sweet pea throws a flood of light upon a widespread phenomenon which has long puzzled the naturalist: the phenomenon of reversion on crossing," whereby white-flowered plants give plants with "red, or purple" flowers (Punnett 53). When Mrs Elliot elopes with Robert, her husband finds the drawing room "littered with sweet-peas. Their colour got on his nerves – magenta, crimson; magenta, crimson. He tried to pick them up, and they escaped. He trod them underfoot, and they multiplied and danced in the triumph of summer like a thousand butterflies" (236–7). It seems that in the union that will produce Stephen, reversion has bested Mr Elliot, '"a country man on the road to sterility"' (246).

The genetic vision behind such biological references is elucidated by more explicitly biological moments in Forster's other works. In *Arctic Summer*, Venetia Whitby, who understands heredity as "Mendelism" (148), outlines how the "desire to feel a hundred per cent" induces snobs to overlook the "recessive characteristics" that inconveniently pop up as atavistic reminders of their true, mixed pedigree ("Racial" 19). '"A genealogical tree that *is* genealogical would be valuable,"' she admits; "but … people are so apt to make a fuss about their eminent ancestors … and to hush up those who aren't. I know by my father. When he talks of 'family' he means only his grandmother's family. On the other sides he was nothing, and this gives a false view … There's no such thing as 'family' in England" (*Arctic* 151). A similar point appears in *Where Angels Fear to Tread.* Accused by Philip Herriton of misrepresenting her fiancé as "a member of the Italian nobility," Lilia strikes back: "'Well, we put it like that in the telegram so as not to shock dear Mrs. Herriton. But it is true. He is a younger branch. Of course families ramify – just as in yours there is your cousin Joseph.' She adroitly picked out the only undesirable member of the Herriton clan" (25). Forster probably did not have Mendel on the mind when he wrote Lilia's reply, though such an intention is plausible: his theories were much talked about in the early 1900s. But it hardly matters either way. More importantly, Forster would later find in Mendel a kindred spirit, a scientist whose theories shored up his own principles.

Over thirty years after *The Longest Journey*, Forster would reiterate and develop Lilia's and Venetia's genealogical arguments. A remarkable appeal to Mendel appears in a 1939 BBC broadcast aimed at "the ridiculous doctrine of Race Purity" ("Racial" 18). His target, given the imminent war, is obvious; but behind his urgent anti-Nazism lies a broader attack on snobbery and its links to genealogy – an attack familiar to readers of his novels. Scientific racism and family snobbery differ, he implies, only in degree; both draw on age-old myths of origins and blood purity. Forster challenges his audience: "Can you give the names of your eight great-grandparents?" Family pride, he implies, stems from the same stock ideas as Nazi race policy, and both are wrong – ethically and empirically – for they always conceal something "mortifying" ("Racial" 17):

> We can often get six or seven [great-grandparents], seldom the whole eight. And the human mind is so dishonest and so snobby, that we instinctively reject the eighth as not mattering, and as playing no part in our biological make-up. As each of us looks back into his or her past, doors open upon darkness ... On such a shady past as this – our common past – do we erect the ridiculous doctrine of Racial Purity. ("Racial" 18)

The doctrine is ridiculous because, "whether there ever was such an entity as a 'pure race,'" historical migrations and imperialism have ensured "there never can be a pure race in the future. Europe is mongrel for ever, and so is America" ("Racial" 18).

The doctrine is also ridiculous because it rests on "pseudo-science" ("Racial" 19), so Forster is canny to conclude his attack with an appeal to science. Freud and Einstein are mentioned – an oblique dig at the German state that demonized two of its own world-class scientists. But Forster's real praise is for yet another German-speaking scientist whose theories inconvenience Nazi "pseudo-science."

> Behind our problem of the eight great-grandparents stands the civilizing figure of Mendel ... He embodies a salutary principle, and even when we are superficial about him he helps to impress it in our minds. He suggests that no stock is pure, and that it may at any moment throw up forms which are unexpected, and which it inherits from the past ... He has unwittingly put a valuable weapon into the hands of civilized people. We don't know what our ancestors were like or what our descendants will be like. We only know that we are all of us mongrels, dark haired and light haired, who must learn not to bite one another. ("Racial" 19–20)

Forster may be simplifying Mendel's contribution to science and ethics in concluding that peas, like humans, "keep throwing up recessive characteristics, and cause us to question the creed of racial purity" ("Racial" 19), but he is hardly superficial. His views on Mendel and Nazism are directly informed by Julian Huxley and A.C. Haddon's *We Europeans* (Forster, *Commonplace* 301), and he clearly understands the Mendelian fact that "pure individuals may be bred from impure ones" (Bateson, *Naturalist* 183). In this remarkable phenomenon, Forster foresees the end of purity in any traditional sense of the word, and with it an end to scientific and genealogical apologies for prejudice. Insofar as purity survives after Mendelism, its applications have been evicted from blood or individual essence to single traits, where it bears the less catchy name of homozygosity. What looks like purity, moreover, often is not: seventy-five individuals that are pure for a given trait, writes Bateson, "are not all alike, but consist of twenty-five which are pure dominants and fifty which are really cross-breds" (*Naturalist* 176–7). As Forster would have read in *We Europeans*, "the picture of the hereditary constitution of human groups ... [is] very different from any which could be framed in the pre-Mendelian era": "Practically all human groups are of decidedly mixed origin" (103–4).

"The sense of purity is a puzzling, and at times a fearful thing," says the narrator of *The Longest Journey*. "It seems so noble, and it starts at one with morality. But it is a dangerous guide" (139). But if purity is displaced from human characters to "unit-characters" (Punnett 22ff.), Rickie's sacrifice appears not more justified but certainly more nuanced than previously recognized. Now, though combined with Mr Elliot's lineage in the person of Rickie, his mother's lineage is literally recoverable by future generations, in the granddaughter who aptly bears her name (289). As Walter Sutton explains Mendelism, "while in the organism, maternal and paternal potentialities are present in the field of each character, *the germ-cells in respect to each character are pure*" (231–2, original emphasis). Still, purity at the genetic level says nothing about the organism. As Forster observes, "too many factors are involved" in human heredity ("Racial" 19) to say anything quite conclusively.

I am under no illusion of having solved the difficulties that disappoint and delight readers of *The Longest Journey*. But I hope that, by investigating its treatment of genetics, my reading has opened a window among the "million ... possible windows" that Henry James imagined for "the house of fiction" (46). Other novels might offer similar views; but *The Longest Journey* is perhaps uniquely disposed to reveal that particularly strange implication of Mendelism, still relevant today in the age of selfish genes:

> The individual is an aggregate of unit-characters, and individuality is the expression of a particular aggregation of such characters. Though often reacting upon one another, the factors on which these characters are based behave as independent entities during the hereditary process, and heredity in consequence we may regard as a method of analysis, enabling us to judge of the number and condition of the unit-characters which go to make up the individual. The facts of heredity provide us with a series of reactions, which, if read aright, reveal to us the constitution of the living thing. And in the constitution of the living thing we have the key to its behaviour, to its potentialities and limitations, to what it can become, and what it can produce. (Punnett 74–5)

Mendelism offers no skeleton "key" to Rickie's "behaviour ..., potentialities and limitations." *The Longest Journey* permits no way to "connect up," to borrow from Forster's defence of homosexuality, "all the fragments [Rickie] was born with" (qtd. in Heine, xxiv). But the perspective of the gene reveals a different novel, shining new light on well-recognized patterns and opening the window on entirely new interpretations.

NOTES

I thank Stefani Engelstein for helpful comments on this essay, as well as Cannon Schmitt and Melba Cuddy-Keane for invaluable criticism of an earlier draft. For funding, I thank the Social Sciences and Humanities Council of Canada and the University of Toronto.

1 Throughout this essay, I favour general and anachronistic terms like "hereditary particle," "genetic line," and "genes" (in the colloquial sense) over, say, "biophores" and "alleles." Contemporary biologists used a dizzying array of terms, most since abandoned, some misleading. My reading would gain little from terminological fastidiousness, for its resolving power is limited by the novel's implicit genetic theory, which is, unsurprisingly, crude relative to its scientific counterparts.

2 As Haldane himself wryly notes, "On the two occasions when I have pulled possibly drowning people out of the water … I had no time to make such calculations" as the model would require (qtd. in Dawkins 103).

3 The genetic challenge to traditional notions of selfhood helps explain why I distance myself from Literary Darwinism, which assumes that readers share evolved "psychological dispositions" that "provide a common basis for understanding what is intelligible in … novels"; among these is "the idea of the self" (Carroll, *Literary Darwinism* xiv, 145, 126). But the very idea of the self is undermined by the genetic logic I find in Forster's novel – incidentally, a great example of an "unsatisfactory and confusing" novel about a "sociobiologically atypical" character (ibid. 145, 132).

WORKS CITED

Abbott, H. Porter. "Character and Modernism: Reading Woolf Writing Woolf." *New Literary History* 24.2 (1993): 393–405.

Bateson, William. *Mendel's Principles of Heredity*. New York: Putnam's, 1913.

– *William Bateson, Naturalist: His Essays and Addresses*. Ed. Beatrice Bateson. New York: Cambridge UP, 2009.

Beer, Gillian. *Darwin's Plots: Evolutionary Narrative in Darwin, George Eliot and Nineteenth-Century Fiction*. 2nd ed. New York: Cambridge UP, 2000.

Buss, David M. "Mate Preference Mechanisms: Consequences for Partner Choice and Intrasexual Competition." In *The Adapted Mind: Evolutionary Psychology and the Emergence of Culture*. Ed. Jerome Barkow, Leda Cosmides, and John Tooby. Toronto: Oxford UP, 1992. 249–66.

Butler, Samuel. *Life and Habit*. London: Fifield, 1910.

Carpenter, Edward. *Angels' Wings: A Series of Essays on Art and Its Relation to Life*. 6th ed. London: Allen & Unwin, 1920.

– *The Intermediate Sex: A Study of Some Transitional Types of Men and Women*. London: Allen & Unwin, 1921.

Carroll, Joseph. *Literary Darwinism: Evolution, Human Nature, and Literature*. New York: Routledge, 1995.

Colmer, John. "*The Longest Journey.*" In *E.M. Forster*. Ed. Harold Bloom. New York: Chelsea, 1987. 47–65.
Darwin, Charles. *On the Origin of Species: A Facsimile of the First Edition*. Cambridge, MA: Harvard UP, 1964.
Dawkins, Richard. *The Selfish Gene*. Rexdale, ON: Granada, 1983.
Dennett, Daniel. *Darwin's Dangerous Idea: Evolution and the Meanings of Life*. New York: Touchstone, 1996.
Dugatkin, Lee Alan. "Inclusive Fitness Theory from Darwin to Hamilton." *Genetics* 176 (2007): 1375–80.
Forster, E.M. *Arctic Summer and Other Fiction*. Ed. Elizabeth Heine and Oliver Stallybrass. London: Arnold, 1980.
– *Commonplace Book*. Ed. Philip Gardner. London: Scholar's Press, 1985.
– *Howards End*. Ed. Oliver Stallybrass. London: Arnold, 1973.
– "Literature or Life?" In *The Prince's Tale and Other Uncollected Writings*. Ed. P.N. Furbank. London: Deutsch, 1998. 89–93.
– *The Longest Journey*. Ed. Elizabeth Heine. London: Arnold, 1984.
– *Maurice*. Ed. Philip Gardner. London: Deutsch, 1999.
– "Racial Exercise." *Two Cheers for Democracy*. Ed. Oliver Stallybrass. London: Arnold, 1972. 17–20.
– *Where Angels Fear to Tread*. Ed. Oliver Stallybrass. London: Arnold, 1975.
Gardner, Philip, ed. *E. M. Forster: The Critical Heritage*. London: Routledge, 1973.
Haraway, Donna. *Modest_Witness@Second_Millennium.FemaleMan©_Meets_OncoMouse™: Feminism and Technoscience*. New York: Routledge, 1997.
Heath, Jeffrey M., ed. *The Creator as Critic and Other Writings by E. M. Forster*. Toronto: Dundurn, 2008.
Heine, Elizabeth. "Editor's Introduction." In *The Longest Journey*. By E.M. Forster. London: Arnold, 1984. vii–lxv.
Herz, Judith Scherer. "The Double Nature of Forster's Fiction: *A Room with a View* and *The Longest Journey*." *ELH* 21.4 (1978): 254–65.
Holland, Nicholas D. "Walter Garstang: A Retrospective." *Theory in Biosciences* 130 (2011): 247–58.
Huxley, Julian, and A.C. Haddon. *We Europeans: A Survey of "Racial" Problems*. London: Jonathan Cape, 1936.
James, Henry. *The Art of the Novel*. New York: Scribner's, 1962.
Levenson, Michael. *Modernism and the Fate of Individuality: Character and Novelistic Form from Conrad to Woolf*. New York: Cambridge, 1991.
Marshall, James A.R. "Ultimate Causes and the Evolution of Altruism." *Behavioral Ecology and Sociobiology* 65 (2011): 503–12.

Martland, Arthur. *E.M. Forster: Passion and Prose*. London: Gay Men's Press, 1999.
Mayr, Ernst. *The Growth of Biological Thought: Diversity, Evolution, and Inheritance*. Cambridge, MA: Harvard UP, 1982.
Miracky, James. "Pursuing (a) Fantasy: E. M. Forster's Queering of Realism in *The Longest Journey*." *Journal of Modern Literature* 26.2 (2003): 129–44.
Morgan, Thomas Hunt. *The Physical Basis of Heredity*. Philadelphia: Lippincott, 1919.
Olby, Robert. *Origins of Mendelism*. 2nd ed. Chicago: U of Chicago P, 1985.
Punnett, R.C. *Mendelism*. 2nd ed. Cambridge: Bowes & Bowes, 1907.
Ridley, Matt. *The Red Queen: Sex and the Evolution of Human Nature*. New York: HarperCollins, 1993.
Seitler, Dana. *Atavistic Tendencies: The Culture of Science in American Modernity*. Minneapolis: U of Minnesota P, 2008.
Sutton, Walter S. "The Chromosomes in Heredity." *Biological Bulletin* 4 (1903): 231–51.
Vries, Hugo de. *Intracellular Pangenesis*. Trans. Stuart Gager. Chicago: Open Court, 1910.
Weismann, August. *Essays upon Heredity*. Ed. Edward B. Poulton. Trans. A.E. Shipley et al. Oxford: Clarendon, 1889.
– *The Germ-Plasm: A Theory of Heredity*. Trans. W. Newton Parker and Harriet Rönnfeldt. New York: Scribner's, 1893.
Wilde, Alan. "Injunctions and Disjunctions." In *E. M. Forster*. Ed. Harold Bloom. New York: Chelsea House, 1987. 67–106.
Zola, Émile. *Germinal*. Paris: Charpentier, 1885.
– "Préface à *La Fortune des Rougon*." In *Anthologie des préfaces de romans français du XIXe siècle*. Ed. Herbert Gershman and Kerman Whitworth, Jr. Paris: Union Générale D'Éditions, 1971; Paris: Charpentier, 1885. 301–3.
– "Le Roman expérimental." In *Anthologie des préfaces de romans français du XIXe siècle*. Ed. Gershman & Whitworth. Paris: Union Générale D'Éditions, 1971. 307–61.

PART V

Displaying: Scientific Collections

11 Anatomy Collections in and of the Mind: Science, the Body, and Language in the Writings of Durs Grünbein and Thomas Hettche

PETER M. MCISAAC

This chapter is part of a larger set of episodic investigations I have been undertaking into the ways that anatomy exhibitions and medical collections have been deployed in German literary texts over the past 125 years. Insofar as these texts were penned by writers as diverse as Gustav Meyrinck and Gottfried Benn around 1900 to Durs Grünbein, Thomas Hettche, and Thor Kunkel in recent years, it is perhaps not surprising that they are not united by a single topos or references to a single institution or mode of display. It is all the more striking, then, that following the fall of the Berlin Wall, several prominent German literary texts sought to articulate concerns arising in the wake of German unification using the surviving anatomy specimens collected and displayed in institutions such as the Humboldt University and Berlin's Charité. As scholars have been quick to recognize, the long history and pre-eminent place of these institutions of Berlin's scientific and cultural landscape make them rich vehicles for probing how the contours and fault lines of today's thought, art, and culture are shaped by the complex legacies of the German past. The fact that the Charité itself underwent a thorough institutional reorganization in the 1990s – part of which saw its pathological collections reopened to the public with a good deal of sensation in 1998 – helped to make it a revealing (excavation) site in a city whose post-*Wende* transformations became a shorthand for so many effects of German unification. Perhaps not surprisingly, texts that deploy Berlin-based medical collections have been read by scholars such as Katharina Gerstenberger, Doerte Bischoff, and Birgit Dahlke primarily in terms of Berlin and its real and imagined contributions to a changing gendered German national identity.

Yet as crucial and productive as these readings are, framing texts narrowly in terms of Berlin's history and institutions threatens to obscure the nuanced engagement some of them make with a number of key issues connected to the creation and display of medical and science collections, on the one hand, and what their deployment in literary texts accomplishes, on the other. Where these issues become particularly acute is in the work of Durs Grünbein and Thomas Hettche. At a time when a turn to the medicalized and often dissected body manifested itself in a surprising number of high-profile texts by writers such as Reto Hänny, Ulrike Draesner, Ulrike Kolb, and Marcel Beyer (Magenau, "Der Körper" 12–20), Grünbein and Hettche stand out for their respective and highly revealing uses of historical medical collections and (in Hettche) the anatomical theatre in the Charité as privileged points of entry into the core aesthetic and medial parameters of their work and thought. As I will show, profound resonances exist between Grünbein's and Hettche's literary engagements with scientific display practices and their respective underlying conceptions of the body, language/thought, and science.

Exploring these resonances, as I will do in this essay first with Grünbein and then with Hettche, provides not merely deeper insight into what scholars such as Andrea Bachner have described as the development of a highly medicalized "wound aesthetic" specific to the past twenty years ("Hettche's Wound Ethics" 212–14). Rather, the resonances also help to recognize that material collections of medical specimens present unrivalled means of studying how past scientific conceptions and practices have impacted the body and the human sensory apparatus as a function of particular media, including literature and technological media such as film. If I may put it another way, with this approach I aim to show that the scientific and physiological discourses linked to the body represent not a mere borrowing of scientific and medical words and metaphors, but rather operate as an integral discursive and conceptual framework in which scientific ("fact") and linguistic-literary ("fiction") categories mutually contribute to an illumination of human thought and existence. What is perhaps most critical about the explication of this framework is not the generation of new literary interpretations in and of themselves, important though they may be. Rather, it is the realization that Grünbein's and Hettche's approaches to writing and conceptions of discourse allow them to create fictional medical museums whose operations transcend the capabilities of physical collections on their own. In other words, these fictional modes will be shown to represent indispensible ways of probing the place of science and scientific knowledge in our existence as biological beings at the turn of the third millennium.

Museums, Science, and Literature

Because my project introduces considerations of museums in addition to those of (scientific) fact and (literary) fiction, I will begin with some general remarks about how I am conceiving of literature, science, and museums. Museums, as I conceive of them, emerge as an integral product and driver of modernity in Western society. As such, museum operations involved in the preservation, categorization, and display of past objects are inseparable from modernity's generation of innovation, novelty, and obsolescence. At the same time, public museums' rise in political, social, and cultural importance from the nineteenth century on takes place at the same time as many modern disciplines such as the natural sciences, history, national literatures, and art history begin to the take the forms they will have for much of the nineteenth and twentieth centuries. Rather than exist side by side with each other temporally, museums, the sciences, and various forms of writing and image making are held to develop in dialectical relationship to each other.

As the modern arts and sciences differentiated over the nineteenth century, distinctions were increasingly made between the material repositories and material practices deemed relevant to a particular field and the particular imaginative aspects of those fields, be they narrative, historical, or theoretical. As they have become naturalized, these divisions have tended to obscure our sense of the contiguities that exist in thought and practices as they span the museum and the laboratory on the one side and the areas in which writing and imaginative processes take place on the other. This is particularly true for museums, which prior to 1800 tended to be understood, as Wolfgang Ernst argues, as a "cognitive field of ideas, words, and artifacts whose semiotic inventorying operations made the world readable" ("Archi(ve)textures" 18). In conceiving of the museum in this way, I therefore wish to construct a new optic through which I can examine complex exchanges of ideas and practices between fields and institutions that change dynamically over time, not only in relation to each other but also in response to the development of new media based on photographic, cinematic, or digital technologies.

Anatomical Collections in the Writing of Durs Grünbein

I want to argue that precisely these considerations permeate Durs Grünbein's analysis of scientific collections and displays. Indeed, awareness of

Berlin's anatomical collections entered public discussion in no small part due to an essay Grünbein wrote for the 1992 volume *Periphere Museen in Berlin* (Marginal Museums in Berlin), later republished under the title "In the Museum of Malformations." As Katharina Gerstenberger has shown, *Periphere Museen* was explicitly designed to draw attention to exhibitory institutions in Berlin with non-mainstream offerings, both as a means of increasing knowledge of Berlin's dizzyingly diverse cultural landscape and out of concern that the transformations affecting the city might cause these out-of-the-way museums to "fall victim to the unification process" ("'Only the Wall'" 130). Gerstenberger's global observation, that the essays in this volume sought "to preserve in writing the legacy of institutions that might not survive otherwise despite the fact that their primary mission is to protect their content against oblivion," is especially apt with respect to Grünbein's contribution, even if Gerstenberger portrays Grünbein's essay as effectively announcing the ultimate demise of the collections (130). As I will show, this perspective only partially unlocks the ways museums, science, and literature relate in his work.

In his essay "In the Museum of Malformations," Grünbein discusses two of the historically significant collections in Berlin's history: a collection founded by Friedrich the Great that was later known as the Gurlt Collection of Anatomical Malformations, and a separate collection founded at the Humboldt University. What is crucial is that Grünbein prefaces his discussion of Berlin's surviving anatomical displays with a framework that explicitly situates literature with respect to the uncertainties that collections of physical objects can face in modernity. To accomplish this, Grünbein sets the essay's key considerations with its first three sentences:

> How do you write about a museum that no longer exists? What kind of language is appropriate for something like this here, something so obviously wretched, damaged, deplorably neglected, a tiny pile of grotesque junk? Of a collection that was once unique in Europe, that burned in an air raid in the Second World War and whose better surviving pieces were then scattered to the winds, what remains is only a chimera. (221)[1]

Faced with a collection largely in ruins and a need to work in largely imaginary registers, Grünbein frames his project as an act of literary recovery, reconstruction, and preservation. Key to this project, I want to suggest, is a choice of discourse capable of achieving at least two things at once: it must be able to evoke the material specimens themselves in all their complexity at the same time as it enables a precise historicizing of the collection in its socio-political disciplinary contexts from its moments of creation, its transformations, and its ultimate demise, as Grünbein already begins to sketch out here. Though the notion of a "chimera" clearly has resonances reaching back to Greek mythology, the kind of chimera Grünbein has in mind is in fact a specifically scientific one. As Grünbein immediately explains about his discourse in a crucial aside, "(biology imposes itself on the discussion of its own accord. Aren't *chimeras* living beings whose bodies possess cells with divergent chromosomal structures; organisms built out of genetically separate cells?)" (221; original emphasis). As a writer with extensive training in medicine and biology (Ryan, "Das Motiv" 301–15), Grünbein's invocation of a biological idiom as the best way to recover and preserve this anatomy collection is highly meditated and a key to unlocking his writing and thought.

What deserves immediate attention are the registers this deliberate choice of discourse makes available for thinking about science, literature, and museums in the destructive flow of modernity. Grünbein's turn to biological discourse serves as a way of plotting the functions of the anatomical and zoological collections with respect to the categories and methodologies variously prevailing in the modern life sciences. With a thick history-of-science perspective, Grünbein demonstrates that the collecting of biological specimens formed the living backbone of the nineteenth-century life sciences. "It is no wonder," he writes, that the collection grows rapidly around 1800. It is at this time that Europeans "are starting to amass great osteological archives, obeying a mania that sees the skulls of primitive man placed next to those of Greek statuettes, cat skeletons placed next to torsos in the display vitrines. The age of the taxonomies and bloodlines has begun" (221–2). As science moves from Goethe, Lavater, Gall, and various late-eighteenth-century projects of morphology, comparative anatomy, and teratology to phylogenetic, Darwinian, and anthropological perspectives many decades later, the collections expand, shift, and recombine in what Grünbein portrays as a living part of life science research. "Soon," he writes, "the collections will massively branch out, indent like joints (*Gelenkteile*) or fuse organically to support phylogenies, Darwinism, anthropology" (222). As Grünbein explains, life-science research programs depend on collections so deeply at this time because collecting's core operations work to make biological phenomena visible and thus comprehensible:[2] "But before all this can happen, people collect, prepare specimens, make inventories, a provisional sense of order comes into being" (222). Insofar as the processes of collecting and exhibiting feed knowledge production, the collection's ability to create order relative to prevailing research programs lends the collections their scientific vitality and viability.

Worth emphasizing about the museum qua life form that Grünbein sketches out is that he connects the collections and their disciplinary formations to a substrate of select but revealing political and cultural impulses. Thus, it is not some abstract quest for knowledge in the life sciences that propels the founding of the veterinary institute and its collection, but rather a specific recommendation of Friedrich the Great. Though Friedrich saw fit to clad the school and museum in grand architecture created by the designer of the Brandenburg Gate, Carl Gotthard Langhans ("Im Museum" 222), Friedrich's motivation for pushing veterinary and biological research was openly instrumental, if not militaristic: namely, to improve breeding and treatment of the animals used by the Prussian cavalry (224). But if this legacy is still brought to mind by the fact that the skeleton of Friedrich the Great's horse Condé has managed to survive the tribulations that have befallen so much of the other objects in the Gurlt collection, most of the political impacts in Grünbein's account relate to moments of complete loss and destruction. Of the two main branches of the life science collections Grünbein discusses, one was decimated by an air raid in the Second World War (223), while the other fell victim to the "Marxist-Leninist" priorities of the GDR regime (225). In the long view, then, the upheavals wrought by German unification would appear to present only the latest round of disciplinary and professional processes whose end effect would seem to be the inevitability of the specimens' ultimate destruction.

Paradoxically, it is the palpable and highly specific obsolescence of these anatomical collections that directly bears on their contemporary value. One thing the Berlin collections can hardly avoid is a kind of historical reflexivity that demands to be noticed.[3] So scarred and miserable are the collections today that they obtain a kind of meta-significance and self-referentiality, as Grünbein indicates when he says today's "collection of malformations is simultaneously a malformation of what such a collection could be. And what it once was, at its high point in the age of inventorying and classifying! *That this age has passed is something one grasps at one stroke, perhaps only now and in this space*" (224; my emphasis). As the last sentence makes clear, the apprehension of historical rupture available in this exhibition space involves much more than a realization that this particular collection has seen better days or even that the life sciences have in many ways abandoned collections-based research inquiry. At stake in the experience of this exhibition space is, rather, the awareness that an entire age has passed, precisely due to the disruption of the historically appropriate mode of display. It is precisely what Grünbein calls the "diorama" that is violated through the East German remaking of the display space. As a result of the destruction, "theological disputation took the place of the direct examination of nature and illustrated research. It is as if they wanted to replace the diorama with official regulations and the display vitrines with a wall newspaper of unfocused *Heimatfotos*" (225). The offence caused by Marxist-Leninist ideological interference is not merely that it destroyed accumulations of evidence and impeded research based on scientific principles, but that its sense of "progress" entailed the destruction of the antiquated modes of exhibition Grünbein regards as so characteristic of natural history collections, display vitrines and the diorama, terms with particular valence in Grünbein's writing.

The preservation of these antiquated modes of display is crucial to Grünbein for the way they structure personal and collective memory in the larger crush of modern media and historical processes. As he writes in the essay "Childhood in the Diorama," his ecstatic experiences gazing at the animal dioramas in Dresden's Natural History Museum represent core moments in how he learned to view and organize his knowledge of the world. Looking back at the museum epiphanies he had as a child, he writes,

> Today it seems to me that in such moments, my entire childhood entered the diorama. Like the Chinese painter of whom legend has it that he was absorbed into his finished landscapes, the child's imago slipped into those fantastic middle realms of near and far, its ideal place to be. As if a magic word had been uttered, everything that was there, the exotic and strange and the familiar objects from home, was intermingled with the fragments of lived experience (*Erlebnisfragmente*) from my early years … Here in the museum they were inventoried as archetypal dream images, and it had to be possible to call them back up when their time came. The diorama was the "open sesame" [realm] in which my memories lie stored as primal geographical motifs. (122–3)

Elsewhere I have worked with the Benjaminian resonances in this passage in order to reveal that for Grünbein, the diorama operates as a key site for the intermingling of personal and collective memory as Benjamin describes them in his essay "On Some Motifs in Baudelaire" (Benjamin 159; McIsaac, *Museums of the Mind* 37–8). Important about this argument for this discussion are two related sets of considerations. The first, which

I will return to as I turn to Thomas Hettche's uses of anatomy collections, involves showing how the diorama becomes a shorthand for the way that memory, language, science, and museums relate in Grünbein's thought and what they might suggest about the relationship of science and literature, fact and fiction. The second set involves the recognition that Grünbein's Benjaminian conception of the diorama can help to articulate the stakes of maintaining and encountering antiquated modes of knowledge production such as natural history displays. From this perspective, and in accordance with my analysis of Grünbein's writing above, natural history displays represent an occasion, to use Benjamin words, to "awaken … the world from the dream about itself" (*Arcades Project* 456). That is, the continuing existence of the diorama presents the opportunity to recognize that many of the worn-out forms of the nineteenth century – in this case, antiquated forms of natural history display – continue to structure our thinking without our full awareness and without their corresponding in a productive way to the dynamics of modernity as they exist today.[4]

Seen this way, the highly damaged form of natural history display as it exists at the Humboldt University's veterinary faculty is valuable for the way it resituates the past in relation to the present. Thus, while the displays manifest once prevailing organizing principles and modernity's destructive effects, their mode of presentation puts them at a remove from the dynamics of the present day. As a result, a distanced perspective is enabled on forces whose workings otherwise remain imminent and thus difficult to apprehend.

Just such a perspective is what Grünbein is looking to develop when he situates the collection's "historical examples" of biological malformation relative to their "modern variants" ("Im Museum" 227). If, as Grünbein writes, today's malformations "for good reasons are never shown" in museums like their historical counterparts, this is not because the malformations themselves have ceased appearing. Indeed, when Grünbein writes that what separates the historical examples from today's variants is "the statistical magnitude of mutations today," he sees malformation as an increasing tendency (227). But in explaining the differences between past and present using notions of statistics and mutation, Grünbein also points to shifts that have taken place in biology and medicine, as morphological typology has given way to population biology and genetics. In the context of the Humboldt museum, the absence of modern specimens in museums would seem to be justified scientifically speaking, with the collections' obsolescence figuring them as a kind of dead-end in the evolution of those disciplinary practices. Yet what is easily overlooked, and what Grünbein's rich discourse strives to recover, is the sense that the earlier specimens fulfilled functions in the realms of "myth, religion and science" (226). Unwilling to grant that advances in science mean the end of myth and religion, Grünbein tracks their movement into institutions and media such as film whose aesthetic functions work to assuage the anxiety presented by "the evolutionary horror vacui" (226, 227). Without collapsing categories of evolution and culture, Grünbein's biological-Benjaminian discourse likewise pushes the conclusion that whatever progress science and medicine may make in preventing the malformations that once ended up in the Humboldt's collections, natural means of generating evolutionary variation and thus malformation will be massively accelerated in modern human culture. In Grünbein's polemical horror vision, these trends will outpace contemporary habitual norms of life and ethics to such an extent that genetic manipulation will soon permit people to follow the dictates of fashion, spinning out ghastly visions that will become consumable in ways that make today's collections of "ever new phenotypes" resemble "Paris' semi-annual fashion shows," and making contemporary horror film look quaint in the process (228). A key point about this logic is the notion that unlike old-fashioned collections, prevailing mainstream media such as film and digital special effects offer less and less distance from the phenomena they are depicting, leaving precious little in the way of media that enable deep reflection on what makes us human. Seen this way, film and other technological media exert pressure on collections, but not in a straightforward way.

In my reading, Grünbein's concern is therefore not so much that film will simply displace collections, as Katharina Gerstenberger has argued, but that emerging media configurations promise fewer and fewer opportunities to gain perspective on modernity's flow (133). The seeming obsolescence of physical life-science collections such as the Humboldt's – and here it is worth mentioning that Grünbein makes similar arguments about obsolescence in zoos and natural history museums generally (for instance, in the essay "Before Mankind Is Alone with Itself") – is thus something to be highly prized, particularly when they are probed and engaged by literary means. At stake in this notion is more than just a validation of Grünbein's practice of writing about collections; there is also a recognition of the physiological bases of what links and valorizes material collections and literary and other modes of writing. A brief discussion of this point will help to explicate the place of the diorama in Grünbein's conception of fact, fiction, and human thought.

One of the fascinating things about Grünbein's notion of the diorama is that it manages to place personal and collective recollections into a kind of mental inventory. In Grünbein's thinking, the capacity of museum displays to organize thought stands in direct relationship to the neurological underpinnings of all human cognition. As critics as diverse as Wolfgang Riedel, Amir Eshel, and Andrea Bachner have respectively argued, human thought works in a kind of post-post-structuralist way for Grünbein.[5] In contrast to notions such as the Derridian "hors-texte," which recognize no ontological reality outside language, Grünbein's theorization insists that the *only* reality that exists for us is generated by the brain situated in the body. The result is an ascription of a biological reality to all cognitive activity – what Grünbein calls imagination – that precedes the generation of images and language. The implications of this "neurological realism" are not merely that "the body determines what the method is. Behind the semantic order stands the anatomical," as Grünbein once put it in the essay "My Babylonian Brain" (33). Rather, human mental activity, and especially image production and memory, tend to work in terms of spatial images that are then transformed into forms appropriate to specific media and discourse such as painting, film, or poetry. Thus, while each medium retains particularities in Grünbein's thought, each shares a fundamental basis in psychic acts whose neuro-physiological bases allow them to intersect and draw on each other's techniques. Crucial is that spatial-representational layouts such as museum displays figure again and again as key paradigms for Grünbein's exploration of the organization of the human psyche and how it makes sense of the world with all the tools at its disposal. For this reason, Grünbein states in interviews, "In museums you can see without interference how the battles of memory have been fought (*Schlachten der Erinnerungsarbeit*). Where else could I, in the briefest amount of time, learn more about the way my brain works?" (68).

It follows from Grünbein's conceptions that language and literature are capable of intervening profoundly in the neurological responses related both to the experience of museum space and to its imagining. This, I would argue, is precisely what makes his project of "writing about a museum that does not exist" more than a documentary or nostalgic exercise. Indeed, it is only when literary techniques invest museum remnants with knowledge that that which is old, forgotten, damaged, and destroyed can best be explored in the mind's eye. But more than this: Grünbein's selection of biologized discourse for his discussion of the Humboldt's life science collections deserves particular attention if neuro-physiological acts are posited as the basis of all human thought. For in addition to the functions I have tried to illuminate, this discourse also works to signal that scientific modes of thought can be thought of as integral to every human psychic act – including those that are artistic – without collapsing differences between individual media and discourses. Grünbein's ability to deploy this biologized discourse to multiple ends points not only to his skill as a writer and thinker, but to the key role science and literature, fact and fiction can play together in order to illuminate deep questions about ourselves and our place in the world.

Medicalized Bodies and Anatomy in Thomas Hettche's Prose

Though anatomical media and related commentary surface at many points in Thomas Hettche's texts, his 1995 *Wenderoman Nox* is probably the one best known for the prominence of its anatomical collections. Yet perhaps because the malformed bodies and organs in the pathological museum and the eerie trappings of the adjoining anatomical theatre seem to provide an almost too perfect backdrop for a novel that stages a graphic murder, violent sado-masochistic sex acts, and a casting of recent German history in terms of wounds, pain, and scars, key features of Hettche's literary museum have escaped critical notice.[6] When read with an understanding of how literary techniques can intervene in and exploit museum practices, these features can be shown to illuminate many of Hettche's core aesthetic and ethical concerns. These, as I will review in a moment, include the way the interaction of science, language, and visual media in modernity structure and maintain a problematic mind-body split. If these have been productively analysed in terms of what Andrea Bachner has called a "wound aesthetic," some of the functions of the museum in *Nox* are to depict, in performative terms, chief conflicts that accompany humanity's attempts to grasp itself and where it is ultimately going as a species in terms of science, language, and culture.

As *Nox* is a novel whose investment in anatomy cannot be separated from its basic narrative premises, it will be helpful to say a few words about that relationship before analysing the anatomical collection's functions in the text. Taking place on 9 November 1989, *Nox*'s peculiar anatomizing of the text turns on the brutal killing of the narrator. Following the murder, the narrating mind is radically separated from the body, which, the text is careful to stress, becomes solely a disembodied object. This conceit allows the narrator not only to describe his decaying body using biochemically and medically precise terminology (79), but also to move omnisciently through the city and relate four interlocking narrative strands: the actions of his murderess, an escaped guard dog from the East German border, the director of the Charité medical collections, and several other protagonists whose stories intertwine via the fall of the Berlin Wall. At the same time, the separation of narrativizing mind and body qua object breaks the bonds of post-Cartesian subjectivity. As the narrator remarks once death has set in,

> The body in which we exist only acts as if it obeys our minds. It alone, however, actually decides at what we gaze, and we do not notice that the things we glimpse are what the body wants to see, through eyes indifferent [to our will]. Only when one is dead does one hear how everything eats away at the stone in a city. [With my body] now a thing among things, the city opened itself into my head, and my body reflected its noise. (31)

No longer (mis)perceived as an object to be controlled, the body's dominance becomes a force to be reckoned with and reimagined in relation to subsequent acts of seeing, naming, and narrating in the text.

With the body posited as a key determinant in this narrative logic, anatomical "facts" can be shown to be a, if not the, key register in which the text attempts to depict the consequences of disrupting the traditional mind-body split. A major consequence of death opening the narrator's body to the movements of the city is that, as several critics have noted, the city becomes assimilable in bodily terms. Accordingly, areas around the Berlin Wall, for instance, develop as skin adapts to a wound, producing "new layers of skin" and "scar tissue" (89–90) in response to the Wall's erection, and then pain when the breach of the Wall reopens the wound (96–7). That the female protagonist wanders the city without a name, coherent memories, and the ability to close herself off to the bodies and experiences and also the anatomized city, signals a peculiar kind of crisis in identity. Yet as Andrea Bachner and Doerte Bischoff have both noted, this crisis can be read in terms of narrative perspective that is in the process of being renegotiated (Bachner 214–20; Bischoff 134). Conceived with an awareness that it is impossible to simply erase the long history of the medialized and medicalized body, the renegotiation also moves to the anatomized body in an underappreciated form: the novel's harnessing of the Charité's medical collections.

Key to grasping the "work" the medical collections perform with respect to this renegotiation is the registering of the parameters with which the collections are subtly deployed in the text. Though critics focusing on bottled, stillborn fetuses and malformed organs have tended to overlook it, the collection first appears in the text through interaction with its fictional director, Professor Matern of the Berlin Charité. When the reader first meets him, Matern is immersed in the active augmentation of the collection, interestingly enough not through human specimens, but rather medical technology. Having just received an advanced Japanese pacemaker, Matern's immediate response is to position it within the medical collections: "In the morning, Matern had had the pacemakers brought from the display cases, where they were normally exhibited next to the internal prostheses and the artificial organ implants. For today, after extended correspondence and great difficulties with bureaucratic approvals, the little package Matern had been awaiting for over a year had come in the mail" (17). As this passage reveals, Hettche's text takes great pains to situate the Charité's collections with respect to prevailing cultural and technological developments. Confirming the text's preceding identification of him as the "Director of the Institute for Pathological Anatomy of the Berlin Charité, Capital of the GDR" (17), the text places Matern in the privileged position of being able to have historical artefacts taken off display for his own personal use. Matern has managed to obtain his prized, foreign-manufactured display piece after pushing his request through channels that, as a post-*Wende* reader might suspect, would have required compelling rationales for the use of precious hard currency. This marker of his perseverance testifies to his embeddedness in GDR power structures as they are linked to a manifest relationship to the objects on display.

A notable aspect of this situation is that a presumably fully operational, cutting-edge pacemaker goes not into medical use (where it could save or prolong a life), but straight into a museum collection.[7] A strong driver of this logic is a particular mode of display that, when rendered in textual form, helps to delineate what museum dynamics contribute to the aesthetic argument Hettche mounts in the novel. To see this, it is helpful to start with the literary strategies. "Professor Matern," the text reads as it registers the unfolding museum scene, "pushed the small cardboard boxes laid out with surgical cotton on his imitation walnut desktop. Pacemakers from twenty years of medical engineering (*Medizintechnik*), its progress legible in the diminishing size of the apparatus. Tiny stickers noted the years of their introduction into the marketplace" (17). Only after establishing the presence of the display context in the mind's eye does the text shift attention to the set of pacemakers, with their sense of existence as a grouping of undistinguished elements reinforced by descriptive equivalency (they all hail from the past twenty years) and the lack of a verb that imparts a sense of synchronous stasis. What the pacemakers represent – the progress of medical technology – emerges only upon the introduction of ordering criteria that, in spite of appearing to inhere in the objects themselves, rely on both a particular sequential sweep (big to small) and the temporal vector (1969–89) established by the tiny labels to valorize and ascribe meaning to the arrayed objects. Through its use of grammar and sequence, the text translates display techniques into linguistic equivalents that invite one to notice the operations that work to generate object-based narratives not as pre-existing entities, but in the performative moment of reading. One result of this literary strategy is to reveal the idea of technologically driven medical progress to be a powerful museum effect simultaneously reflected and illuminated by the text.

The development of the strategy reveals that the desire to make an even more compelling display of technological progress underwrites Matern's acquisition of the foreign pacemaker. After arraying the museum's extant collection, Matern

> carefully took the device made by the MATSUSHITA ELECTRIC INDUSTRIAL CO LTD OSAKA JAPAN from the tiny, polyethylene-lined box no larger than a box of matches. According to what he had read, the device used the patient's body warmth [as an energy source] and so for the first time no longer required the batteries that had prevented further miniaturization of pacemakers up until that point. (17–18)

The latest in pacemaker technology in terms of size and performance, Matern's new model dramatically expands the argument made by the "front room" display: medical technology continues to beat back limits of man and nature. An instantiation of a general Enlightenment trope, this narrative of progress resonates in particular with prevailing GDR valorizations of science, technology, and medicine, insofar as they, in the hands of socialism, were purported to deliver mankind from myth and the fickleness of nature (Assheuer).[8]

But if one point of relating the arrival of Matern's acquisition is to mark it as being capable of substantiating a particular GDR narrative, a crucial aspect of this scene is how it works to show that Matern's museum manifests the contours of contemporary medicine, economy, and culture in ways potentially at odds with the prevailing ideological dictates of the day. By introducing the collections via Matern's "behind the scenes" perspective, the text constructs a display in which the identity of the most advanced model figures prominently ("the MATSUSHITA ELECTRIC INDUSTRIAL CO LTD OSAKA JAPAN"). If placed on an exhibit label, this information might well shift the pacemakers' narrative about "humanity's inexorable march towards progress" to one in which capitalist entities play an important, if not the leading, role. Yet in the "front room" version of this narrative as it is depicted on display labels, the centrality of capitalism as a driver of late-twentieth-century modernity is literally made small, appearing on tiny labels showing devices' "year of introduction *into the marketplace*" (17; my emphasis). It is in the margins, Hettche's text guides the reader to see, and not in the main display, that this GDR museum has its finger on the pulse of modernity, a modernity whose ubiquitous, market-driven realities cannot be denied, only pushed into the background. But only for so long: for, in a kind of dramatic irony the post-*Wende* reader can readily grasp, that very modernity is about to render the "front room" version of things prevailing on 9 November 1989 itself a kind of museum piece.[9] With dynamics captured in textually unique ways, *Nox*'s museum is made to show itself as an assemblage of specimens and artefacts dialectically indexing the conditions that have promoted its making and use, as well as its destruction and abuse, throughout its existence.

Yet what enables Hettche's narrative to harness the revelatory capacities of the museum (and later also the anatomical theatre) for its own intellectual and aesthetic purposes is its sustained attention to Matern's interactions with those environments. Taking a variety of forms, these interactions repeatedly showcase the ability of exhibitory environments to generate narratives shaped by the minds and knowledge of those who engage them. In the case of the pacemaker display, the information that clinches the new device's seamless fit into the extant array originates in Matern's head ("according to what he had read").[10] Once revealed as an essential element in the textual display's construction of sequence and meaning, cognitive acts become possible and in fact highly flexible sources of components and information, creating a form of composite discourse capable of referencing subjective and objective registers at the same time.[11] This double-voiced quality is precisely what is manifested when, for instance, Matern leads students through the Charité's historical collection. By keeping signals that Matern is moving and speaking with an audience to a minimum (an exception is the "you can see" reported on p. 25), long passages become indistinguishable from interior monologues (23–4; also 83–8). While not strictly necessary in terms of plot – the routine and nature of guided tours means readers would otherwise probably grasp them as containing a subjective dimension – this strategy of inscribing an interior dimension accomplishes three interrelated things. First, in showing Matern in a position of recognized authority, it demonstrates his extensive knowledge of the collections and their functions in a textually economic way. Second, this dimension foregrounds Matern's thorough personal identification with the collections (including his obsession with anatomy and museum icon Rudolf Virchow). Together, these help to naturalize several passages in which Matern is in effect interpreting and activating the collection for the reader when no audience is involved. In important ways, Matern is thus the conduit through which the collection is activated and passed into the present in the text, with the text also working to make the pathological collection and anatomical theatre museums of his mind.

Such a condition is important in no small part because it is through Matern that the novel spells out many of the historical features that help connect the plotlines of 1989 to the fault lines of (malformed) body and (wounded) city reaching back to the early nineteenth century. But if these emphases make the Charité, as Katharina Gerstenberger aptly puts it, into "a center of monstrous exchanges" that describes the ways in which humanity's darker tendencies will anything but disappear in the present day (138), it is crucial to recognize that Matern's comments often refer, in self-reflexive fashion, to important functions the museum has in the text. When, for instance, Matern explains the museum's value as "a piece of cultural history of humanity" (25), he articulates the premise that I have shown underwrites the museum's operation from the moment it appears in the novel. Along similar lines, after showing Matern in the act of expanding the collection, the text explains that his pet project consisted of "the reconstruction of Rudolf Virchow's collection, which had been nearly completely destroyed in the war" (23). But more than confirm these aspects of the museum's function in the text, *Nox* has Matern perform and also comment on acts related to dissection and reanimation of organic tissue that, when understood in terms of the performative process, yield fresh insight into the place of anatomy in Hettche's approach to science, narrative, and media.

Crucial scenes involve a dog skeleton that Matern keeps next to the desk in his office. Symbolically rich, the skeleton carries particular significance because it connects to the core topoi in the text. The remains of a German shepherd that had once guarded the Wall, the skeleton references both the topic of German-German division as well as the living animal that follows the murderess through the city of Berlin. More crucial still is that the skeleton became a specimen as part of Matern's only partially successful plan to reconstitute the museum as it was maintained by its founding pathologist, Rudolf Virchow. As the text recalls,

> There was too little room for the human skeleton that can be seen in the old photos of Rudolf Virchow's offices ... and that stood next to the high window as if it were looking out into the summer light. But Matern had a new

> dog specimen prepared like the one that had sat on Virchow's desk for some thirty years. He had thought of a small dog, a terrier perhaps, that would not be too large for the desk. When a dead German shepherd was brought to him, he had to put it on the floor. (18)

Bowing to what the space and situation will allow, Matern's attempt to emulate Virchow is significant for how, in museal terms, it works as a metaphor for the impossibility of achieving anything like seamless restoration of a lost condition. For what Matern (or anyone familiar with these canonical photos) must see in entering his office are the gaps left by the missing skeleton and the almost farcical reincarnation of Virchow's dog. A synecdoche for the near total loss of Virchow's legacy, these gaps function as a kind of museal scar that testifies to the forever altered state of tissue marked by a cut or wound. Though no doubt also meant to represent Matern's outsized and malformed ego, the distorted reinstallation of Virchow's office works to capture the contours of his larger museal ambition in ways that perfectly align with what Andrea Bachner has called Hettche's "wound aesthetic" (212–14). For no matter what Matern does, his restorative project cannot but express that he is working on terrain – both literally the Charité collections, buildings, and grounds the text depicts as ruins (124–6) and the state of German culture, figuratively – that will carry the marks of what has come before even as it is reworked as an embodiment of the present. A metaphor that captures the thrust of the wound aesthetic in the physical and spatial registers of the museum as a dialectical index of its day, the dead guard dog shows its difference vis-à-vis Virchow's day not only in size and location, but also in being the deadly by-product of the Berlin Wall.

Especially striking in this context is Hettche's focus on Matern's cognitive responses to the dog:

> Matern did not know that when it came to the cadaver, it was that of a dead guard dog from the border that one had taken to the rendering facility near the sewage fields in the north-eastern part of the city. When Matern looked down at the dog skeleton, he always involuntarily completed its form with muscles, fat, coat, ears, eyes and flews. And there was always a moment of uncertainty in the process, when it also seemed possible that he was constituting a completely different animal in his head. (18–19)

Highly significant as a general comment on how meaning is made in museums, Matern's mental restoration of the dog to full form inflects several of Hettche's core concerns. The covering over of an object whose origins are imperfectly known can be read in one register as an allegory of the fate of the past transmitted in museum contexts.[12] Crucial, too, is the seemingly irresistible propensity to seek wholeness out of parts. In this sense, this museum scene resonates with a variety of related subtexts, most prominently the Platonian "one out of two" myth of sexual origins retold by none other than the living counterpart of Matern's specimen, the escaped guard dog that follows the murderess as she wanders the city (158–9).[13]

Yet in being unable to avoid feeling like he might come up with the wrong animal altogether, Matern, in his mental animation of the dead canine, does more than urge caution with respect to the "fictionality" of cognitively produced wholeness in historical or sexual registers. Animation and its discontents, rather, tie directly into Hettche's larger diagnoses of what ails modern society and culture in terms of media, thought, and knowledge. As explored in Hettche's correspondingly titled 1999 book *Animationen* (Animations), the idea of "animation" serves as a way of referencing the socio-scientific problems posed by embodiment in representation and media, particularly in the aftermath of the Cartesian mind-body and subject-object splits (94–5). Whereas in *Nox* these splits are explored in the topography of a divided Berlin as I began to describe above, in *Animationen* they are excavated in the context of Venice, a terrain marked by not only divides such as between land and sea (43–51) but also by a long, intertwining history of publishing and medicine (82–101). Read in terms of how gaze, word, and image work to disentangle the problem posed by a body whose inner workings cannot be grasped without destructive dissection (88–9), Hettche's Venetian-centred genealogy seizes on the innovations of Andreas Vesalius's *De humani corporis fabrica* and early-modern anatomy theatres as the first instances when the dissecting, scientific gaze seemed to evade the aporias of the dead body (98). Marking not just what Hettche considers to be "*the beginning of modern science*" (83; original emphasis to show quote from O'Malley and Saunders, *Illustrations* 19), in this account the schooling of the gaze offered by scientific anatomy decisively set the coordinates of modern word, image, and media. Insofar as media "following the anatomical theatre" are tasked with "supplanting the opened dead body" (98),[14] the history of media involves not ways of producing "fictions," as Hettche goes on to write, but rather "feats of engineering" that align representations (*Abbilder*) so as to defeat awareness of the dead or dissected body (98).

Seen this way, acts of animation as Matern performs them on the dead guard dog need to be regarded not as departures into falsehood, as commonsense understandings of fiction might have it. Rather, such acts stand in relation to techniques of medial representation whose practice will be historically conditioned. As a repository of specimens preserved according to prevailing conventions and practices, the medical museum thus emerges as a paradigmatic site for plumbing the past and present techniques of "animation." As was the case with Grünbein, however, museum techniques' ability to generate insights of this kind get significant boosts when translated into literary registers, revealing the processes of exposing and hiding (Hettche's "feats of engineering") that enable objects and bodies to signify in comfortable or scientifically appropriate fashion. It is in literary discourse, that is, as fiction, that Hettche mobilizes the museum as dialectical index of modernity.

At the same time, it might be too simple just to ignore literature's complicity in the violence and suffering it clearly works to explore. As if to drive home the point that the production of image and narrative in the present day and age remains tethered to the ongoing cutting and fragmenting of bodies, *Nox* stages a second animation scene. Set in the middle of a long interior monologue in which Matern reconstructs in his mind the forces that brought Virchow and countless bodies from the east to Berlin until being stopped by the Wall (86–7), Matern again turns to the dog on the floor:

> Standing at the door, he looked as always once more at the dog skeleton on the floor and tried to stretch skin over the bones. And in fact saw for a moment coat and ears and snout and how the animal panted and moved and looked up at him. It has yellow eyes Matern thought as they gazed at him. He hastened over to the anatomical theatre, as the dissection lecture rooms used to be called. (87)

Though similar to the act of animation in the opening pages, this instance works to introduce the anatomical theatre not only as physically proximate to the medical collection, but also as conceptually part of the same scientific-medial complex. Though standing in the tradition of the old theatres in "Bologna, Amsterdam or Cracow" (87), *Nox*'s anatomical theatre functions in medial terms the text likens to those of cinema. Outfitted with penetrating lights and a finely wrought stainless steel table so as to become the equivalent of a giant, mechanical eye (87–8), the theatre also works such that Matern believes that "the soundtrack (*Synchronisation*) in the theatre of anatomy is the scream" (88). One reason for this association might be that, as an institution always in dialogue with the dominant media of the day, *Nox*'s theatre might be expected to generate images in line with today's dominant media, film, television, and digital imaging.

That these media are no less implicated in the production of pain than earlier media is perhaps one point of making the anatomical theatre the site not just of a cinematic sado-masochistic orgy, but also of the transfer of Charité footage of decaying bodies that most critics take to be of Nazi human experimentation (87, 102–3, 128; Gerstenberger 138).

What literature might achieve through this kind of gesture is a reversal of what Hettche calls the "feats of engineering," the medial adjustments that render the suffering intrinsically wrought by representation imperceptible. Seen that way, the deployment of museum and anatomical theatres as self-reflexive indices of modern science and media might be regarded as showing that the inclusion of cuts and wounds and pain represents the only ethical way to produce images and narratives. That critics until now have yet to fully grasp the self-reflexive and media-critical work done by medical collections in *Nox* perhaps reveals the limits of such a strategy, if the key question is whether a text can be made less complicit in the images it produces by its demand that readers notice its self-reflexivity. However that question of complicity is answered, what cannot be overlooked is that Hettche's writing, like that of Grünbein, shows that literary techniques remain uniquely capable of showing why fiction matters, precisely in the context of biology and medicine.

NOTES

1 Unless otherwise indicated, all translations are mine.
2 Precisely these developments inform the phenomena Dana Weber, in her chapter in this volume, explores with respect to the ethnographic uses of mannequins in the nineteenth century.
3 Dana Weber's reading of nineteenth-century mannequins picks up on this dynamic, in which death, absence, and memory are involved in a complex interplay that becomes more apparent with changing historical conditions (see Weber, chapter 12, below).
4 On the mimetic conventions and mechanisms that accompany this kind of display using human figures, see Dana Weber's chapter in this volume.
5 The argument in this paragraph rehearses points I have made on p. 31 in *Museums of the Mind.*
6 Most treatments of the museum and anatomical theatre in *Nox*, while thoughtful, nonetheless focus on thematic and plot-related resonances. See Magenau 18; Dahlke, "Sexing Berlin" 89–90; Gerstenberger 137–8; Bischoff, "Berlin Cuts" 134; Bachner 226–7.

7 Though often theorized as institutions that obtain objects whose usefulness has expired, the Pathological Museum defies this expectation.

8 This subtext resonates with Matern's belief that the Charité collection had been swept into the city by two centuries of superstition.

9 The text's rendering of small but telling details in the construction of the displays also contributes to this irony. Though appropriate on some level to the idea of surgical intervention, a notable contrast nonetheless exists between the use of cheap surgical gauze to present the pacemakers and the device's increasing technological sophistication (17). Similarly, the text draws attention to the use of tiny nails and fishing line to construct a display of historical surgical instruments in the space behind Matern (17). However functional, these approaches belie a museum left to scrap and scrimp as it struggles to do justice to the historical and monetary value of the artefacts and possessions in its collections.

10 The original German ("Das Gerät, wie er gelesen hatte, nutze ...") implies Matern had read this information before his unpacking of the device, but a cognitive dimension would still be in operation, even if the scene were taken to refer to an act of reading commensurate with the opening of the box.

11 It is worth observing that cognitive registers are not limited by material constraints in the way that exhibit labels are (which often cannot exceed more than a few hundred words), even as they are capable of supplying context in comparable ways. In other ways, cognitive registers can be used to represent information the museum visitor takes in or associates with a display but whose multivalence is not fully grasped, creating contexts that suggest unconscious and other complex cognitive operations.

12 These processes are nicely unpacked in the context of past and present displays of human mannequins in Dana Weber's chapter in this volume.

13 Through this doubling, Hettche also seems to shows an awareness of the enlivening dimension involved in his own act of storytelling.

14 In the original, "ersetzen" carries a range of meanings including "displace," "restore," "replace," and "compensate for," all of which shade Hettche's point in different ways. "Und alle Medien in der Nachfolge des anatomischen Theaters suchen wesentlich, diesen geöffneten Leib zu ersetzen."

WORKS CITED

Assheuer, Thomas. "Die Olympiade der Leichen. Der Tabubruch erreicht eine neue Qualität: Gunther von Hagens' Körperwelten ziehen in ein

Hamburger Erotik-Museum. " *Die Zeit* 35 (21 August 2003). http://www.zeit.de/2003/35/K_9arperwelten.

Bachner, Andrea. "Thomas Hettche's Wound Ethics." *German Quarterly* 82.2 (2009): 212–30.

Benjamin, Walter. *The Arcades Project* (Cambridge, MA: Harvard UP, 1999).

– "Charles Baudelaire: Ein Lyriker im Zeitalter des Hochkapitalismus." In *Gesammelte Schriften*. Ed. Rolf Tiedemann et al. Frankfurt am Main: Suhrkamp, 1974.

– "On Some Motifs in Baudelaire." In *Illuminations.* Ed. Hannah Arendt. New York: Schocken, 1968.

Bischoff, Doerte. "Berlin Cuts: Stadt und Körper in Romanen von Nooteboom, Parei und Hettche." *GegenwartsLiteratur: A German Studies Yearbook* 4 (2005): 111–42.

Dahlke, Birgit. "Sexing Berlin." *German Life and Letters* 64.1 (2011): 83–94.

Ernst, Wolfgang. "Archi(ve)textures of Museology." In *Museums and Memory.* Ed. Susan A. Crane. Stanford: Stanford UP, 2000. 18–34.

Eshel, Amir. "Diverging Memories? Durs Grünbein's Mnemonic Topographies and the Future of the German Past." *German Quarterly* 74.4 (2001): 407–16.

Gerstenberger, Katharina. "'Only the Wall Put a Stop to the Inflow of Monsters': Bodies and Borders in Post-Wall Berlin." *Studies in 20th and 21st Century Literature* 28.1 (2004): 126–51.

Grünbein, Durs. "Im Museum der Mißbildungen." In *Galilei vermißt Dantes Hölle und bleibt an den Massen hängen: Aufsätze 1989–1995.* Frankfurt am Main: Suhrkamp, 1996. 221–8.

– "Kindheit im Diorama." In *Galilei vermißt Dantes Hölle und bleibt an den Massen hängen: Aufsätze 1989–1995.* Frankfurt am Main: Suhrkamp, 1996. 117–28.

– "Mein babylonisches Gehirn." In *Galilei vermißt Dantes Hölle und bleibt an den Massen hängen.* 18–33.

Grünbein, Durs, and Heinz-Norbert Jocks. *Durs Grünbein im Gespräch mit Heinz-Norbert Jocks.* Cologne: Dumont, 2001.

Hettche, Thomas. *Animationen.* Cologne: Dumont, 1999.

– *Nox.* Frankfurt am Main: Surhkamp, 1995.

Magenau, Jörg. "Der Körper als Schnittfläche." In *Wespennest. Zeitschrift für brauchbare texte und bilder* 102 (1996): 12–20.

McIsaac, Peter. *Museums of the Mind: German Modernity and the Dynamics of Collecting.* University Park: Pennsylvania State UP, 2007.

O'Malley, Charles, and J.B. Dec. M. Saunders. *The Illustrations from the Works of Andreas Vesalius of Brussels.* New York: World Publishing Co., 1950.

Riedel, Wolfgang. "Poetik der Präsenz: Idee der Dichtung bei Durs Grünbein." *Internationales Archiv für Sozialgeschichte der deutschen Literatur* 24.1 (1999): 82–105.

Ryan, Judith. "Das Motiv der Schädelnähte bei Durs Grünbein." In *Schreiben nach der Wende. Ein Jahrzehnt deutscher Literatur: 1989–1999*. Ed. Gerhard Fischer and David Roberts. Tübingen: Stauffenberg, 2001. 305–15.

12 Vivifying the Uncanny: Ethnographic Mannequins and Exotic Performers in Nineteenth-century German Exhibition Culture

A. DANA WEBER

The use of mannequins in ethnographic displays is common in German museums and exhibitions of all kinds. Although regarded as a problematic, even obsolete, display form,[1] mannequins continue a lively existence as media of ethnic and cultural representation. Such objects pose a major paradox: their three-dimensional human appearance occasionally overshadows their designated function as display aid for original ethnographic objects, so that audiences might only too easily mistake them for the display goals instead. In other words, the human likeness and tangibility of the mannequin inadvertently complicates its exhibition purpose, calling for an accurate circumscription of its ontological condition with significant consequences for the interplay between fact and fiction in the production and reception of these museum displays.

This chapter theorizes the ethnographic mannequin's medial condition as situated between the lifeless, albeit life-like, and therefore uncanny object used in the service of cultural representation, and the cultural performer who often served as its model.[2] The claim is that, in terms of audience reception, the mannequin's potential uncanniness emerges as the imaginary reverse of the delight caused by its inspiration and flip side, the living human performer.

I read these contradictory yet related reactions through the lenses of Sigmund Freud's concept of the "uncanny" and Eric Ames's "vivification," which conceptualize receptive imagination with the help of literary fiction as paradigm for interpreting the facts of external reality. The theoretical focus on these two "domain[s], emotional movement[s], concept[s]"[3] helps account for the reasons why the mannequin has survived to this day as a means of mediating cultural information. Beyond their literary foundation, both concepts coincide in their performative spin: just as scientific and aesthetic interpretations of external facts (at least in these two theories) follow an analytical dynamic that deconstructs the scrutinized object, one can conceptualize theatrical roles as the fragmentation of human behaviour and its subsequent reconstruction on stage.

By following this line of argument, the chapter complements Peter McIsaac's incisive analysis of the effect of museum techniques on the creation of literary fictions which are guided by equally transgressive and fragmenting strategies. While McIsaac explores how display ideologies and methods have informed the German literary imagination in the last decades, this analysis is interested in how, a century earlier, audience perceptions of tangible museal and entertainment displays of human-shaped objects and human beings were influenced by the literary fiction as guiding principle for engaging with the culturally unfamiliar. At this time, when numerous new media technologies appeared and the market for print products increased dramatically, fiction texts offered accessible and ubiquitous models for imagining ontological and cultural Others. Although in time this mode of conceptualizing imagination changed under the impact of audiovisual media,[4] it still (and famously) came into play in numerous of Freud's writings – not least in his seminal essay "The Uncanny" (1919). In theorizing "vivification," Ames also acknowledges literary fictions as crucial element for the reception of turn-of-the-century exotic shows. Read together, McIsaac's and the current essay reveal that, at least in the last two centuries, the processes of imagination that shape aesthetic creation and reception have relied on the indissoluble bind between literary fictions and scientific and performed facts.

1. Turn-of-the-Century Technologies of Human Representation

One finds mannequins in exhibitions worldwide. This article focuses on such exhibits in German locations because the theories used to describe them were designed in or in reference to German-speaking cultures. Certainly, this correspondence is not obligatory and one could just as easily select other examples to discuss naturalistic museum figures. Nonetheless, drawing from German contexts ensures not only the cultural cohesiveness of the argument, but also integrates the article into the cultural framework of this collection.

Ethnographic mannequins range from hyper-realistic and lifelike to abstract and stylized ones. They were and continue to be used to display ethnographic items and artefacts and to illustrate scenes from the lives of distant cultures. I am interested particularly in those that represent individual human beings with a high degree of realism. Not coincidentally, the heyday of these objects was in the last decades of the nineteenth and the first of the twentieth centuries, that is, in a period of rapid technological innovation that brought forth audiovisual recording media such as photography, film, and the phonograph. These technologies made possible the precise recording of human bodies and significantly affected their hyper-exact reproduction with various materials. During the same era, the emergence of modern scientific disciplines such as anthropology, ethnology, and ethnomusicology (which, in their turn, profited from this media development) impacted the foundation and design of Germany's imperial museums and exhibitions.[5] Not least, as this was also a time of innovations in entertainment technologies and genres, the boundaries between fact and fiction, scientific display and spectacle were not always drawn clearly.

Unlike other media and exhibition modes of this era that soon became obsolete, the ethnographic mannequin has not disappeared for reasons that this argument hopes to illuminate with the help of two examples: the figure of a Piegan Blackfoot woman exhibited in the Native American exhibition at the Karl-May-Museum in Radebeul near Dresden[6] (*figure 12.1*) and the figure of an Australian Aboriginal dancer from the Tiwi islands displayed at the Grassi Museum of Ethnology in Leipzig (Grassi Museum für Völkerkunde zu Leipzig) (*figure 12.2*). While controversial, the Karl-May-Museum's Native American exhibition[7] is one of the significant German collections of Indian arts and artefacts.[8] Modelled by artists Vittorio Güttner (1869–1937) and Ernst Grämer (1899–1966), its mannequins, busts, and sculptures depict major indigenous groups from the North American continent (Hoffmann, "Zur Geschichte" 109–10).[9] Nevertheless, their main function is that of display structures for the museum's original ethnographic objects. Most of the figures look static, according to the taste of the time when they were created, the first decades of the twentieth century. Only their flexed legs or bent elbows suggest some movement. Among them, the "costume figure" of a young Piegan woman[10] stands out. Portrayed in an upright position, "she" serves to present a spectacular dress of mountain sheep leather richly decorated with the teeth of a Wapity stag (Dräger and Krusche, "Ausstellung" 78). The figure holds a bag and wears exquisite beaded accessories as well as indigenous jewellery of silver and bone. Its relaxed appearance invites immediate fantasizing: one can easily imagine that "she" has stopped during a leisurely stroll, perhaps because "she" encountered a friend or the viewer. The Piegan mannequin's almost impishly smiling lifelike countenance attracts the attention of less adept visitors (such as the author)

Figure 12.1 Piegan woman, Karl-May-Museum Radebeul, near Dresden (1928). Copyright by Karl-May-Museum Radebeul. Photos courtesy of Karl-May-Museum.

Figure 12.2 Aboriginal from the Tiwi Islands, Australia. Grassi Museum für Völkerkunde zu Leipzig, Staatliche Ethnographische Sammlungen Sachsen (2009). (Photograph by Birgit Scheps-Bretschneider.)

immediately, just a moment *before* they become aware of its superb original attire.

Nearly one hundred kilometres away, at the Grassi Museum of Ethnology in Leipzig, a diorama features the figure of a middle-aged Aboriginal dancer whose process of creation and exhibition is far better documented than that of the Piegan woman.[11] This figure's composite portrait of a father and a son was created on the basis of photographs. By collaborating with the figure's two Aboriginal models, their families, and cultural community, the makers of the exhibit took pains to ensure that the mannequin offers both an accurate and a dignified depiction of an imaginary yet lifelike figure and a specific culture. The mannequin shows the dancer in the final moment of a Pukumani burial ritual. On such occasions, dances can last for days to honour and please the souls of the deceased so that they return to reincarnate. Visibly exhausted, the dancer steps forward. Far from having a static appearance, the figure lifts arms and hands that hold two ornamented spear-tips called tungaliti and tungatini. These prestige objects reveal their owner's respected position in the community. The dancer's gesture indicates that the satisfied soul has finally departed, and the community is allowed to restart its everyday life. The figure's facial expression is calm and kindly but, to a sensitive and empathetic observer, "his" eyes may appear moist from effort and rapture.

Oftentimes, visitors who encounter objects such as the Piegan and the Aboriginal mannequins experience the "peculiar emotional effect of the thing" (Freud, "Uncanny" 227) as a "disquieting strangeness" (Cixous 525) or even disgust. Others are fascinated by them and wish to learn more about the cultures they represent.[12] Thus, although they are meant to render cultural information in the most accessible and – in the absence of living individuals – in the most realistic three-dimensional manner, mannequins usually elicit reactions that are difficult to pinpoint and describe. They are caused by the viewer's imaginative engagement with the object that subtly complements, even overrides, the pragmatic and scientific facts these figures are called upon to convey. In other words, such exhibits may inadvertently evoke spontaneous fantasizing although they are designed to render facts. As facts and fictions intermingle in them, mannequins have the potential to puzzle us with their tangible and life-sized human form and to confront us with an ontological and hermeneutic conundrum.

Theorizing the ontological status of three-dimensional objects made to portray human beings – from statues, dolls, and robots to waxworks figures and ethnographic mannequins – cannot dispense with the Freudian concept of the uncanny that approaches them via their fundamental ontological ambiguity: although they are inanimate things, they often appear eerily alive to their viewers. Theories of the uncanny such as Freud's and Ernst Jentsch's (to whom Freud was responding) tend to focus on the lifelessness of the human-like object and its effect on the viewer's psyche without paying much attention to the living person who may have served as its model. The role of imagination in such perceptions can be extended if mannequins used for cultural representation are theorized in conjunction with their models, some of whom performed in turn-of-the-century exotic shows (*Völkerschauen* in germanophone countries).[13]

This association makes sense especially in the case of hyper-exact ethnographic mannequins like the two described earlier. The stress here is on the hyper-exactness of the depiction, although the identity of the represented person may be uncertain as in the case of the Piegan woman or factually inexistent as in the case of the Tiwi dancer. The high degree of accuracy of such human portraits, produced industrially since the last decades of the nineteenth century, resulted from the fact that they were created either from three-dimensional plaster imprints or from model sittings and photographs of living individuals. As performances of "commercial ethnography" (Bruckner 233), exotic shows corresponded to museum exhibits insofar as they too presented foreign artefacts and cultural aliens, albeit in a live theatrical context. Such performances animated what stood frozen in ethnographic mannequins and dioramas, making possible

> what museum exhibitions could not: they presented the foreign humans in the original – living, moving, speaking bodies ... The *Völkerschau* represented what was [regarded as] typical for a specific ethnicity. Its performers presented traditional clothing, instruments, and objects, and they performed mundane activities that were considered as characteristic [for the represented groups, as well as] profane, and religious ceremonies. (Lange 57–9)[14]

In short, the *Völkerschau* breathed life into the exhibits of ethnographic and anthropological museums. The doubling of the living person by his or her objectification in display allows the discussion of these two forms of ethnic and ethnographic display as opposite poles of a spectrum of representation and medialization that depends on modes of spectating and problematizes the relationship between scientific facts and the fictions emerging in their contemplation.

One might claim that, in principle, any medium is at once an effigy and a replica: Technological media purport to convey information about a segment or aspect of transient life, yet can potentially replicate it indefinitely. The recorded information is, however, not the life it purports to present and therefore always calls attention to something that is missing ontologically. In this sense, all media constitute effigies because – even in live broadcasting – they always mark the absence of tangible presences. The tension between external reality and medial effigy is particularly pronounced when the medium's external form does not reveal its ontological condition immediately, for example, when it adopts the shape of a human being. (In contrast, neither the writing on the page or the screen nor audiovisually recorded information can be touched as self-standing physical entity or even remotely resemble the outer appearance of any living being, so that the difference between medium and the existential status of the human receiver always remains clear.) Mark B. Sandberg's concept of the effigy includes the mannequin as only one "tangible manifestation of a wider array of circulating corporeal traces and effects" that, in the last decades of the nineteenth century, aimed to fill in the places of absent persons while offering "new possibilities for imagining space and time" (*Living Pictures* 5). Wax figures, Sandberg's object of investigation, and ethnographic mannequins are such replacements. Like photography or film, they implicitly convey to their viewers that the represented individuals and their cultural contexts are absent temporally, spatially, or both. By one and the same gesture, ethnographic dioramas and exhibits serve as records of geographic, cultural, and personal information as well as evidence of its physical absence. Britta Lange therefore identifies such objects as symptoms of the fundamental paradox of ethnology: the attempt to depict absent cultures while claiming their immediacy (140–1). This paradoxical relationship between presence and the lack thereof has the potential to confuse viewers' perceptions of the objects that imply it, triggering the reaction of imagining them as uncanny. And yet, as will become apparent later, imagination also has the power to rescue the mannequin if the latter contains a certain amount of representational inexactitude: precisely by giving some leeway to imagination, an inaccurate human representation in fact makes possible a quicker and more exact ontological ascription and therefore opens space for delight.

Like the naturalistic life-size statues, late-nineteenth-century ethnographic figures also occupy "the same volume as the real body" they portray (Flynn, *Body in Three Dimensions* 21). Although the wax figures of panopticons or cabinets of curiosities are identical with them in this regard, they were usually designed to be unique and perishable and to represent celebrities and well-known historical, spectacular, or fictional scenes. Instead, museum mannequins were created to be reproducible and durable, and to represent anonymous individuals in mundane or extraordinary scenes from the lives of "exotic" cultures (Lange 69). The actual information they conveyed through original objects and accurate cultural contexts was (ideally) obtained by direct scientific, cultural, and personal interactions of Europeans with the represented groups. Since this specific information was ultimately presented by means of generic, homogenized human types, however, an abundance of scientific facts was transmitted on the basis of their shortage on an individual level. Precisely the lack of personal information in the mannequin constitutes a major point of critique for this medium because such a depersonalized mode of representation is not only guided by but also invites an objectifying, oftentimes colonial, and levelling perspective in contemplation.

The anonymity of mannequins also stands in contrast to their high degree of aesthetic realism. Long before the advent of the museum figure, the tendency towards an idealized naturalism in European sculpture already manifested itself in "objects which directly mimic the body – dolls, waxworks, automata, robots – [that] have been present as sculpture's *doppelgänger*, or double, since time immemorial" (Flynn 7). Whereas naturalistic sculpture and body mimicry share the same quest for accurate representation, however, waxworks models, death masks, or plaster effigies – many of them produced as direct imprints of human body parts – do not serve primarily as means of aesthetic expression but oftentimes as *memento mori* of deceased individuals (16–17). Such objects fulfil a recording function comparable to that of photography, yet they conserve human features also for tangible memory. As three-dimensional, exact-scale records of past persons that broadcast from the ever-absent netherworld, such objects potentially become "uncanny presence[s] for the spectator" (21), and therefore fully deserve the designation of "media" in its entire ambivalence.

A person's absence owing to death complicates the effect of ethnographic mannequins further. Although the individuals who serve as models for such figures are usually alive at the moment when their likeness is taken, their personal historicity inevitably associates them with death sooner or later. For example, if the model for the Piegan woman was still alive in the 1920s,[15] she cannot possibly be alive anymore today. Similarly, the Aboriginal's portrait conflates the likenesses of a father and a son because the initial model, the father, passed away during the lengthy production process of the figure.[16] Even if they were modelled from living humans, the ontological condition of such objects gradually and inevitably shifts to that of memorabilia of the deceased as they outlive their models and makers. The ethnographic mannequin accrues its function as a *memento mori* only inadvertently, given that it is designed specifically to transmit scientifically ratified, not personal information. And yet, this function resonates permanently beyond its purportedly objective, naturalistic surface.

Both the mannequin and the body souvenir were created by technological methods that served to replace earlier and even eerier forms of human representation, such as taxidermied human bodies. In them, the human epidermis generated another type of *memento mori* of individuals who were paradoxically present and absent at once thanks to the tangible presence of their skins. This proved to be also the most problematic aspect of such specimens. Not only did human skin cause problems for mounting and preservation, but it also had an eerie effect on viewers because it highlighted the person's genuine dead-ness and thus the object's artificiality (Lange 111). A classical example for such an exhibit is that of Angelo Soliman's body, the "Moor of Vienna" (Mohr von Wien), an African-born Freemason, valet, and tutor at the court of Liechtenstein. In 1796, his mortal remains were preserved and displayed without his or his family's consent in a private imperial Viennese collection. Although, during his lifetime, Soliman had been an educated, cosmopolitan, and politically engaged man, his remains were used to portray him as a clichéd noble savage wearing a feather headdress and belt, porcelain beads, and a shell necklace ("Angelo Soliman"). The racial stereotyping that Soliman may have evaded in life became literally affixed to his skin after death, raising questions about the limits of personal agency and the respectful treatment of human remains. Regrettably, this mode of human representation was accepted until the end of the twentieth century.[17]

Although techniques for producing death masks were not new when they were adopted by the natural sciences in the nineteenth century, they now offered a welcome alternative to human taxidermy. As they were put in the service of novel scientific goals such as the precise registration and cataloguing of human physical features, mask- and body-casting techniques benefited from the development of accurate anthropological measurement techniques and innovations in visual recording (photography and, later, film). Scientists took natural casts of living humans ("Naturabgüsse") while on expeditions, or from the performers of the exotic shows that toured Europe in this period (Lange 78). In effect, this was a print method: not only were the created moulds called clichés or stereotypes according to terms from print vocabulary, but the objects created with their help were often made of papier-mâché (a mix of paper pieces, glue, and water) and thus, technically, paper prints. Paradoxically, paper gave a better impression of human skin than preserved skin itself, so that figures created in this manner were described as "naturgetreu" (true to nature), "natürlich" (natural), "streng nach Natur" (strictly from nature), and "lebensecht" or "lebenswahr" (true to life), indicating that the mannequins were considered adequate plastic representations of human bodies, but not identical to them (72).

However, neither were all ethnographic figures produced in this manner nor were the body casts restricted to the natural sciences: sculptors

Figure 12.3 Édouard Joseph Dantan, *A Casting from Life* [Un moulage sur la nature] (1887). Photo courtesy of the Gothenburg Museum of Art, Hossein Sehatlou.

and plastic artists used them too. Édouard Joseph Dantan's naturalistic painting *A Casting from Life* (1887), for example, depicts the moment when a painter and his assistant remove the plaster negative from the leg of a female nude (*figure 12.3*). Adolph Menzel's oil study *Atelierwand* (1872)[18] represents a wall, to which casts of human body parts (the front of a female and a male torso, death masks including those of children) have been attached next to measuring tools (*figure 12.4*). Significantly for the current argument, Dantan's and Menzel's artworks illustrate the contradictory hermeneutic potential of three-dimensional body prints. Dantan's painting thematizes the technological creation of a perfect human representation according to a classical aesthetic of elegance and beauty.[19] Not without blatant gender implications, it narrates the positive story of a media negative, the plaster cast. However, this snapshot from an artist's studio ultimately withholds the final aesthetic product for which the cast was made (if it is not the female nude or the painting itself), so that the story that the painting tells offers viewers the hope but not the certainty that the technological process glorified by the image will eventually generate an exceptionally beautiful naturalistic artwork.

Contrary to Dantan's affirmative interpretation of the sculptural negative, Menzel's study offers a dissenting vision of the casting technology as a process of fragmentation. It agrees with aesthetic practice, however, in that a complete body imprint cannot be taken in one sitting but only through partial castings. Accordingly, in Menzel's grim still life, positives created from the moulds of body parts hang desolately from walls, testifying to disintegration and lifelessness in the service of art. Like Dantan's, his image also denies viewers insights into a finalized artistic product. However, unlike Dantan's well-lit, wholesome, and hopeful scene that represents (male) artists evidently working at something remarkable, Menzel's pessimistic and literally dark vision focuses on how technological replicas of the human body in fact dismantle life in the service of portraying it accurately. Only dimly illuminated here and there by a flickering glow, Menzel's suspended copies of human parts hover in an expressionistic twilight between life and death, between organic being and its life-less objectification, withholding rather than promising aesthetic wholeness. And yet, as viewers might well imagine while contemplating these images, artworks will be created with the help of the methods and means depicted by both painters, artworks whose graceful appearances will obfuscate their fragmented origins. Although it might exist, so far I have not found evidence

Figure 12.4 Adolph Menzel, *Atelierwand* (1872). Copyright by Hamburger Kunsthalle/bpk. (Photography by Elke Walford.)

of an aesthetic or ethic meditation about the production of ethnographic mannequins by their makers, so that Dantan's and Menzel's painterly comments on methods of accurate human representation must serve here as contiguous reflections. The two painters' diverging engagement with techniques of body copying do not only illuminate how technical facts come into play in the creation of visual fictions, but also illustrate the major concepts at stake in this argument, the uncanny and fragmentation, as precursors and preconditions to the ideal aesthetic reconstitution of the human body into an imaginary, even living and breathing artwork (in performance).

A conjoint discussion of the visual arts, physical anthropology, and ethnology as fields of the mannequin is not so far-fetched as it might seem, considering that modern European aesthetic and scientific explorations of the human body have employed biometrics at least since the second half of the eighteenth century to uncover what were considered typical features of ethnic and cultural groups and individuals.[20] At this time, anthropological theories were often influenced by aesthetic thought such as Johann Joachim Winckelmann's reconstructivist idea that the ideal human body did not exist in reality but could only be assembled from the most beautiful parts of multiple bodies (Kaufmann 108–10). Further developed in the following decades, the purportedly scientific assessment of the mental and psychological capacities of individuals and groups through biometric measurements eventually contributed to the virulent American and European racisms of the nineteenth and twentieth centuries and peaked in Arthur de Gobineau's Aryan theory and its appropriation by the Nazis (Burke 270–1). The interplay between the European aesthetic and scientific interests in the human body ultimately imagined race as purportedly empirical, measurable, but also aesthetic fact, and one that was literally printed in 3D in the ethnographic mannequin.

While this history renders this medium as extremely problematic from a contemporary viewpoint, at their heyday in the late nineteenth century, the greatest problem that such objects posed to their makers and audiences was their representational authenticity, that is, their medial capacity to broadcast measurable ethnic and cultural information as accurately as possible. The highest degree of natural faithfulness or realism was ascribed to mannequins made from body casts because they contained indexes of original human bodies that Dantan's and Menzel's paintings of *figures 12.3* and *12.4* scrutinize with such contrasting results. Another category of ethnographic mannequins consisted of those created in portrait sittings or from photographs. Their value was considered merely iconic, however.

Interposed media, such as brochures with explanatory texts and images, had to vouch for the scientific and informational accuracy of these objects (Lange 80).[21] Ironically, in spite of the considerable artistic skill required to create an ethnographic figure by modelling rather than casting, the technically produced imprint of a person's external appearance was ascribed more scientific and economic value, indicating (at least in the case of museum mannequins) that factual information was assessed higher than creative imagination and artistic ingenuity.

And yet, regardless of the methods by which they were produced, all mannequins inherited some of the problems reaching back to taxidermied human bodies, first and foremost their unsettling effect on viewers. Thus, in 1902, ethnographic figures representing a group of Australian Aboriginals at the Grassi Museum were touched by visitors, who also pilfered some of the objects they were supporting (Lange 153). This audience response does not only reflect the questionable morals of some visitors, but also suggests that, in the new media-scapes at the turn to the twentieth century, visual and acoustic criteria no longer sufficed for the ontological classification of naturalistic three-dimensional human-like figures. Unlike the three-dimensional digital technologies of our time that usually cannot be touched, however, the mannequin's condition as a 3D medium was not a visually created illusion, and palpation proved to be the only certain method of establishing its identity or non-identity with a human body.

2. The "Uncanny" and "Vivification" in Human Exhibits and Performances

The reactions to ontological uncertainty that the Leipzig case illustrates also account for the uncanny feelings theorized by psychoanalysts. In his article "Zur Psychologie des Unheimlichen" (1906), Jentsch asserts that uncanny feelings are caused by uncertainties regarding the familiar, for example, when the aliveness of a supposedly living being is doubted or, vice versa, when supposedly inanimate beings appear to show signs of organic life (197). He observes this phenomenon particularly in relation to the life-like figures of wax museums, panopticons, and dioramas, which elicit "half-conscious secondary doubts that are caused automatically by renewed contemplation and the perception of fine details" (198). In other words, what is most uncanny about such objects is not what they represent, but the precision of their execution. Indexical body prints can be subsumed under this definition too, considering that their hyper-exact rendering of a person's physique might easily elicit doubts, as it did in the Leipzig case.

Freud's response to Jentsch's argument in "The Uncanny" adapts this concept to his own psychoanalytical thought. For Freud, the familiar subsumes the home and with it the intimate and the sexual, which have to be concealed. It is not the exactness of representation that causes the uncanny feeling, but the resurfacing of an all-too-familiar which "ought to have remained secret and hidden but has come to life" (225) to confront the viewer.[22] According to Freud's logic, the uncanny effect of an object thus has to do with virtually dead, that is, repressed sexuality. This means that automatons, mannequins, dolls, or waxwork figures frighten us because their absence of life and thus of the capacity to reproduce themselves organically signifies an evolutionary danger to the human species. For Freud, life – and with it successful procreation – is indicated by the eyes (240), whose removal elicits the fear of castration in his reading of E.T.A. Hoffmann's novella *Der Sandmann* (1816), the centrepiece of his reflections on the uncanny.[23] Indeed, the most conspicuous and emotionally most troubling part of the replicated human body is the face, whose eyes are the first checking points for life. Both in death masks and in the face casts taken from living individuals they are shut, suggesting death. By the same token, the colourful and shining glass or painted eyes of ethnographic mannequins have the potential to unsettle us in line with Jentsch's argument, because they are lifeless objects that nevertheless suggest life. Indeed, a look at the faces of the Piegan woman or the Australian dancer might constitute a viewer's first reality check for these figures. If the response is positive, we are tempted to give back the jovial smile of the Piegan woman and be moved by the raptness that we sympathetically believe to detect but, in fact, imagine, in the glossy eyes of the Aboriginal dancer. By causing either uncanny fear or eager fascination,[24] however, both reactions confuse the museal reality of the object with that of an imagined person.

One can infer from here that the hyper-realistic ethnographic mannequin is a faulty medium because its physical form interferes with its scientific message so that an unintended and individually fantasized meaning overrides what it has been designed to transmit. Thus, be they indexical or iconic, such objects broadcast first and foremost that they are both copies and proxies of human beings. The fact that ethnographic mannequins do not represent persons with readily recognizable personal identities adds to this effect because viewers might easily believe that they are encountering unfamiliar individuals, which is a mundane and realistic situation for anyone. (In contrast, when wax figures portray celebrities, their purported identities themselves account for the viewers' disbelief in the possibility of personal presence, allowing observers to delight in the objects' false or effigial one.)[25] The anonymous individuals depicted by ethnographic mannequins thus have more potential to cause disturbances in reception precisely because of their familiar unfamiliarity.

Both wax figures and ethnographic mannequins enthral or disconcert and disgust us not least because they mimic human figures so well that they double, that is, repeat them. Not coincidentally, repetition is a crucial element in both Freud's and Jentsch's theories of the uncanny. Jentsch remarks that eerie feelings re-emerge in the repeated contemplation of an object even after its actual nature has been identified (198). For Freud, the "constant recurrence of the same thing" causes uncertainty not least because it alludes to the "doubling, dividing and interchanging of the self" ("Uncanny" 234),[26] in other words to a threat to the self's integrity that might end with its undoing. Fragmentation begins with the separation between the concepts of the soul and the body of a human being that generates not only the idea of the body's first abstract double but also that of denying death (235). When the "evolutionary universalist" Freud (Zilcosky, "Uncanny Encounters" 149) moreover equalizes the early mental states of childhood with those of primitivism that have supposedly been surmounted by adulthood and European civilization ("Uncanny" 249, 251), he adds another layer to this double: the "savage" (242) who, like the ghost, uncannily returns to confront and haunt contemporary humans with their repressed cultural past (Zilcosky 139, 149). Precisely these "savages" that Freud had in mind may have served as models for ethnographic mannequins and also appeared in *Völkerschauen*. Yet, they did not always frighten their viewers.

Instead, the same selves and psyches that were subject to fragmentation in Freud's and Jentsch's views of the uncanny, often "persuaded ordinary observers [of non-Europeans] to blur the line between the self and the other, the familiar and the exotic" (Zilcosky 151–2) in *Völkerschauen*. The fact that spectators bridged the divide postulated by psychoanalysts when they searched for affinities and commonalities in the encounters with performers of exotic shows suggests the possibility of a positive approach to the double. Hillel Schwartz notes, for example, that "our skill at the creation of likenesses of ourselves, our world, our times" (*Culture of the Copy* 11) generates the "impostors, 'evil' twins, puppets, 'apes,' tricksters, fakes, and plagiarists" of our pervasive "culture of the copy" (17). Instead of fearing them, however, we can use them to restore a more coherent sense of ourselves through compassion by reaching out and thus learning intellectually and emotionally. Schwartz's optimistic take on the copy is theatrical rather than technical in that it assumes a person's doubling not in an art or science object but in a *role* whose performance provokes positive changes in the self. An industrially reproduced inanimate medium, the ethnographic mannequin had foils and counterparts in living humans, who often performed themselves culturally, theatrically, or both. The future mannequin and the potential performer became connected indirectly, for example, in the awkward situations wherein anthropologists created face casts of indigenous people. As their body parts were copied, the living models also *acted* (in the sense of taking independent action). One such instance was reported by Otto Schellong (1858–1945), a doctor from Leipzig, who travelled on an expedition to the German colonial territories in Papua New Guinea in 1885 (Friederici, "Lebensmasken" D2 5). There, he took the face negatives of thirty-nine individuals (D2 6).[27] Schellong, who spent extended periods of time among the indigenous people and learned their language, reports that the Papuans were suspicious about the casting process.[28] This comes as no surprise if one considers what it consisted of: The model's face was covered with grease so that the plaster could easily be removed, and two rolls of paper were inserted into the person's nostrils to allow him or her breathe. A sturdy ribbon wound around the model's face prevented the cast's still fluid plaster from flowing off. "Of course," Schellong declares, "sometimes funny scenes happen, when the Papuan does not hold still, for example when he squints so that plaster gets into his eyes or when he suddenly becomes afraid under the pressure of the mask; then he is up and gone at once and if he [turns around and] looks back, he looks like chocolate with whipped cream" (qtd. ibid. D2 7).

While the reasons for the model's fear become more than understandable from the way Schellong describes the casting process, his report is formulated like a slapstick scene featuring the notorious pie-in-the-face gag from vaudeville and early film. Not only are racial innuendos easily detectable behind the visually and ideologically telling "chocolate and whipped cream" remark, but those involved in the situation are portrayed according to clichéd roles. Schellong, the omniscient first-person narrator and a German doctor, obviously plays the part of the well-informed, rational, and composed protagonist. In contrast, the indigenous character is staged as an innocent fool whose lack of familiarity with scientific procedures causes his irrational fear and his making a spectacle of himself – "he" standing generically for all Papuans. Beyond testifying to a condescending colonial attitude, Schellong's scene illustrates an anthropological method in the terms of a theatrical performance. Other than in the doctor's interpretation, role-play in fact translates here into emancipatory action on the side of the Papuan, who disrupts the casting process.

Casting connects theatre and anthropology. Not unlike creating a collection of anthropological masks through plaster casting, *performance* casting also constitutes a preliminary procedure for assembling acting ensembles. Here the process refers to the choice of physical markers (faces, bodies) and theatrical skills, whose interplay will render the most substantial part of the show. Like plaster casting, role casting also assembles a group (a collection) of individuals intended to be displayed before an audience. One can easily imagine how, in the last decades of the nineteenth century, indigenous individuals such as Schellong's Papuan (whose face cast became part of a German museum collection) may have been *cast* for participation in the exotic shows of commercial ethnography. Here, the selection also focused on the individuals' physical markers (ethnic and physical features) and on their displayable skills (cultural expertise and the ability to present it appealingly to a foreign audience). For example, Native American performers who appeared in Wild West shows not only had to match the visual clichés of American "Indians," but also to possess skills such as riding or sharp shooting alongside sufficient histrionic talent to fit typified ethnic roles that were already well established in European theatre (e.g., the noble "Indian" chief or prince, the villain, or the maiden or princess).[29]

Paradoxically, individuals with such capabilities earned a living in popular spectacles that claimed to meet the newest ethnographic standards although they were enhanced by fictional and theatrical elements.[30] Scientists like Schellong often collected the physical and cultural information of such performers through technological methods ranging from voice recording to body measurements and plaster casting. For example, a show presented by twenty Omaha at Castan's Panopticon in Berlin in 1884 included dancing, singing, and shooting tricks. After the group left, Castan's catalogue of masks featuring diverse "ethnic types" (Völkertypen) contained thirteen made from members of this group[31] (Friederici, "Völker der Welt" D3 6–7). Their example underscores the overlaps between anthropological plaster and artistic performance casting and reveals the ontological and medial relation between ethnographic masks and figures and *Völkerschau* performers, all of which were regarded as vehicles for presenting ethnic features and cultural information.

Beyond their entanglements with anthropological and ethnographic research, ethnographic shows were always also entertainments that responded to the centuries-old European curiosity about exotic aliens. In

Wilhelminian Germany, the degree of this curiosity was remarkable. Scholars' estimates about the numbers of exotic shows that toured the country until the first decades of the twentieth century range from 120 between 1874 and 1931 (Thode-Arora, *Für fünfzig Pfennig* 168–78)[32] to 400 between 1875 and 1930 (Dreesbach, *Gezähmte Wilde* 79). While these numbers are likely not complete, they nevertheless suggest how strong the presence of non-European individuals was in Germany at this time and how heavily it was not only researched, but also marketed. A remarkable example of such a touring troupe is that of nine male Bella Coolas who performed in numerous cities, enthused the scientific community in 1885, and also presented a significant collection of ethnographic artefacts. They inspired the work of German anthropologists and ethnomusicologists (Ames, *Hagenbeck's Empire* 107–8; Lange 60–1; Penny, *Kindred by Choice*).[33] The Ethnology Museum in Leipzig alone bought five hundred of the group's ethnographic objects, thus acquiring the largest individual sub-collection of its North America inventory (Friederici, D3 12). However, the Bella Coolas failed to attract the attention of a wider public that favoured competing groups from the Plains such as Frank Harvey's "Sitting Bull Sioux Indians" (Ames, *Hagenbeck's Empire* 108) or Chief Spotted Tail's Sioux troupe from the Rosebud reservation,[34] because they fitted their publics' stereotyped expectations about "Indians" better (109).

The Bella Coolas' example illustrates once again how scientific activities, exotic entertainments, and the production of ethnographic figures overlapped. Scientific facts and performed fictions intersected not least because the individuals involved in them acted in several cultural fields at once. For instance, the Bella Coolas' impresario, Adrian Jacobsen, worked for Carl Hagenbeck's company of animal trade that also managed ethnographic shows (Ames, *Hagenbeck's Empire* 103). Hagenbeck, as it happens, was Johann Friedrich Gustav Umlauff's brother-in-law (Lange 59), and thus privately connected to the leading producer of ethnographic mannequins in turn-of-the-century Germany. In turn, Umlauff's company hosted and managed ethnographic shows on its own premises or in collaboration with museums.

The cultural and theatrical self-performances of individuals who appeared in the arenas of exotic shows constitute effigies in their own right. The protagonists of these entertainments were persons with their own biographies and cultural identities who were understood to act out generic scenes from their indigenous lifeworlds – and even did so, to a degree. However, what they also suggested was the spatial and even temporal absence[35] of precisely the cultures that they aimed to represent. The effigial status of such performers serves, in other words, as the flip side of the uncanny mannequin on one and the same ontological and imaginary coin.

While the ethnographic objects selected according to the scientific standards of the time and exhibited on mannequins may have compensated, to a degree, for the cultural knowledge and self-representation of *Völkerschau* entertainers, they were arranged in inanimate exhibits. Such displays could be easily interpreted negatively as uncanny (in the sense discussed earlier) and associated with the (lifeless) information of science rather than with lived cultures. And yet, they were often staged according to theatrical parameters.[36] Exotic shows also purported to present replicas of scenes from alien cultures, but they did so live. Thus, these popular performances had no overt negative connotations for their audiences because their first condition (even when representing allegedly doomed Native Americans) was incarnate life, not the dead soullessness of the inorganic mannequin. Precisely this liveliness opened *Völkerschauen* up to an imaginary process that Ames calls "vivification" and theorizes in the example of exotic shows featuring American indigenous performers.

Shows representing indigenous groups from the American Plains – first and foremost William Cody's "Wild West" – enjoyed an immense success in Germany.[37] To account for their popularity, Ames explains that, unlike the scientists who treated ethnographic performers as literal bodies of data, spectators perceived them as embodiments of the fictional figures they already knew from adventure literature (*Hagenbeck's Empire* 105). Far from being an "ontological error," this "dramatic reinterpretation of ethnographic performances as fantasy" constituted the principle of "vivification" that governed the reception of exotic shows by Wilhelminian audiences (105–6). Spectators thus appropriated the performances not as means of education and self-cultivation, like the mannequins of anthropological museums, but as incarnations of their fantasy dreams of the Wild West: "Rather than preserve the traces of people who were supposedly either dead or on the verge of dying, as ethnographic museums and folk museums would claim to do, the shows were seen as giving 'life' to [fictional, literary] figures that never existed" (114).

A comparison of the angst of the "uncanny" and the enjoyment of "vivification" reveals that both are caused by the interplay between sensory perception and imagination in contemplation and spectating. However, whereas uncanny reactions relate ontological uncertainty to the fear of death, "vivification" ties factual and ontological certainty to life, so that "the very idea of vivification ... at once surprised and delighted viewers, almost as if the practice of spectatorship had become a form of magical thinking" (ibid. 113) that could bring to life cherished fictions. It is in its recourse to magical thinking that "vivification" coincides with Freud's "uncanny." According to Freud, magic is a technique of animism that establishes imaginary relations in external reality where there are none in order to ward off the fear of death. As it thus at least assumes the possibility of immortality ("Totem and Taboo" 865–7), such thinking in fact relies on a "narcissistic overvaluation of [the subject's] own mental processes" ("Uncanny" 240) and generates erroneous perceptions about one's "omnipotence of thought" ("Totem and Taboo" 873). Animist magical thinking turns against itself in the uncanny quality of ethnographic figures because, out of a fear of their suspected dead-ness and all it entails in Freud's vision (as noted earlier), it imagines anxiously that it could bring to life the inanimate human depiction. By a similar token, in *Völkerschauen* flesh-and-blood human beings with personal and cultural identities are magically animated into fictional, now tangible figures that had hitherto populated only the imagination of fiction writers and their readers. Assessing such individuals by the parameters of literary fiction does not rule out the awareness of their non-fictional personal and ethnic identities, however, and so maintains the ambivalent thought needed for the enjoyment of "vivification."

Eugenio Barba's theory of theatrical roles helps cement the analogies between the uncanny and vivifying performance that this argument has carved out so far. As Barba describes it, acting consists of comporting oneself according to elaborate behaviour systems, which are not those of everyday conduct, yet are still determined culturally and acquired by conditioning and training. They are based on body techniques created through the dismantling of functional and unconscious mundane behaviours and gestures and their performative reconstruction in ways that are entirely non-habitual and practically inefficient (*Paper Canoe* 15–16), yet theatrically effective. The physical body that is recreated in this process only shows actions, but does not necessarily relive them (32). In short, the presence created in theatrical acting "means *to remove* what is obviously the body's daily aspect in order to avoid it being only a human body condemned to resemble itself" (32, Barba's italics). Such a concept of play acting transforms a mundane into an extraordinary body through fragmentation and reconstitution. Likewise, it entails a double effigy as it gestures at both the absence of the fictional persona in mundane reality and that of the private person on stage. And yet, unlike the factual absences hinted at by the ethnographic mannequin, those evoked by human performers remain simultaneously present in the performance as mutual doppelgängers (of the person or the persona), demanding from spectators to decide on only one as the focus of their contemplation. (Ideally, of course, the goal of conventional European acting styles is the suspension of disbelief, i.e., voluntarily ignoring the mundane parameters of the event, for example, the private identities of the cast or the artificiality of the sets. The audience must imagine the ever-present everyday backdrop of the performance as absent in order to immerse itself in the theatrical illusion.)

Conceptualizing performance in this manner complicates this argument's reading of Ames's "vivification" by identifying it too as a kind of effigy. Considering that *Völkerschau* performers were seen as enacting their private selves and habitual cultural roles (which may or may not have been the case), the fictional identities with which at least their German audiences endowed them compensated for their lack of conventional theatrical acting and fictional identities. As Ames's concept of "vivification" reveals, audiences collectively drew from the era's leading provider of fantasy, literature, to fictionalize these real individuals (*Seeing the Imaginary* 214; *Hagenbeck's Empire* 105–6, 133). Moreover, in Barba's definition, acting techniques are primarily physical activities that deconstruct the body in uncomfortable ways before reconstituting it counter-intuitively in performance. This means that, similarly to the ethnographic figures that are created by way of physical fragmentation, as noted earlier, and therefore always imply its organic consequence, death, the enacted human body is also generated from behavioural fragments, that is, the death of mundane behaviours in the service of suggesting life. In "vivification," not the actors but the spectators *joyfully* performed this reconstitution as a result of their cultural habituation as theatre viewers and fiction readers, when they complemented the supposedly authentic exotic performances with their own fantasies that overrode the initial anthropological and ethnographic intentions of the exotic spectacles.

Just as literary or theatrical fantasy hinges on life in "vivification," the narcissistic fantasies of magic thinking described by Freud fancy themselves powerful enough to maintain life without death, however with the caveat that they might generate potentially threatening ghostly or savage revenants. In both cases, the amount of leeway that is left to the spectator's imagination ultimately dictates his or her visceral response to the representation. Both Freud's and Ames's concepts utilize literary fictions as reference points for conceptualizing these workings of the (European) imagination. Commenting on Freud's psychoanalysis, Hélène Cixous and Lionel Trilling agree that it is "a science standing upon the shoulders of a literature" (Trilling, "Freud and Literature" 35), with fiction authors serving as its "precursors and coadjustors" (42).[38] Given that specifically Freud's "uncanny" aims to bring forth a definition of uncertainty and hesitation, it becomes a metaphor for the undefinable it aims to define as it itself oscillates between "figures of science" and "some type of fiction" (Cixous 526). Moreover, as Cixous reveals, Freud does not hesitate to adapt Hoffmann's *Sandmann* to his psycho-sexual analysis by deliberately obfuscating the significance of the doll Olympia (532–3).[39] Not only does Freud thus fictionalize fiction in the service of his scientific analysis, but he does so in a theatrical manner: "What unfolds without fail before the reader's eyes is a kind of puppet theater in which real dolls or fake dolls, real and simulated life, are manipulated by a sovereign but capricious stage-setter" (525): the psychoanalyst himself. As the text thus stages its own argument in a dramatic manner, it posits fragmentation at the centre stage of a theory of the uncanny, in which the original triggers of this reaction, objects that might somehow appear as lifelike, are suppressed in the service of a psychoanalytical fiction of castration. This intra-textual performance highlights the dynamic relationship between scientific truth and the mechanics of fiction in Freud's prose (531), which aims to design a scientific theory about the human perception of external facts.

With less intra-textual artifice, Ames uncovers the model for the collective fictionalization of performers meant to convey ethnographic and anthropological information in adventure writing which, in the era of Darwinism and colonialism, was dominated by a plethora of exoticist writings, from pulp fiction and serial novels to the works of popular authors.[40] Although Barba does not specifically refer to textual fictions, for him too, the success of the fictional presence that the actor creates from fragments depends to a large degree on the viewer's investment of imagination.

Taken together, Freud's (alongside Jentsch's), Ames's, and Barba's theories reveal that, if the form is human, it indeed affects the message. The cases discussed in this chapter suggest that representations of human beings must maintain sufficient non-identity with a person for their audiences to remain certain about what they are invited *not* to believe: namely, that museum mannequins are living individuals and that *Völkerschau* performers are ethnographic exhibits. Owing to the fact that these theories conceptualize both human bodies and human-looking objects in theatrical performances or exhibitions through fragmentation, reconstitution, and technological or histrionic reproduction, they posit the "uncanny" and "vivification" as polar opposites on the continuum of our imaginary engagement with external facts, especially when these facts have to do with the human form. One can infer from here that a successful reception of such individuals and objects requires space for contemplative imagination: the signals that the body and its copies broadcast have to be calibrated in such a manner, that they unambiguously convey their intended message: ethnographic information or a performed role. If this message is not perfectly adjusted, perturbations such as the uncanny emerge or the performance is perceived as wanting in some way. If the respective representations allow for enough engagement of the imagination in perception, however, then facts and fictions collude in a successful media message about human beings, the life form with which we are most familiar.

3. Postscript: Successful or Unsuccessful Human Simulations Today

In recent years, a related dilemma has been particularly felt in another domain that aims to create replicas of the world and its humans: three-dimensional computer-generated digital animation (3D CGI). As designers strove to represent human life ever more accurately, they soon came to learn that excessive mimetic photorealism elicits disturbed, morbid reactions in the viewers of digital animations. Echoing Jentsch, digital designer Saint John Walker explains this effect by noting that "our brains seemingly magnify the slightest imperfections. We note the soul-less eyes, the rigid lips. Our empathy with the character is curtailed, and in some cases we feel a form of revulsion" ("A Quick Walk" 32). Already in 1978, Japanese roboticist Masahiro Mori had coined the term "uncanny valley" to describe this reaction (ibid. 31–2). To avoid triggering it, Walker suggests that, instead of "cloning [the] world" (34), digital designers ought to strive for emotional – not representational – plausibility, even if "the temptation to describe the human form and physical objects with oppressive levels of detail will always be there" (38). Currently, 3D digital representations mature aesthetically when they fuse human acting with digitally designed fantasy settings and when they limit themselves to stylized or cartoon portrayals of human beings.

The predecessors of the "uncanny valley" were certainly at work in late-nineteenth-century media, in ethnographic mannequins, and – to a degree – even in the obsolete *Völkerschauen*. As museums and exhibitions aimed for an ever-higher accuracy of representation by charging their displays with too much factual information, their exhibits curtailed the viewer's imagination and lost their attention. The Bella Coolas are a case in point, not only because they were culturally too different from the glorified Plains Nations, but perhaps also because their enactment of their own lives was not staged enough for European tastes. Before becoming unacceptable owing to their racial and colonial implications, those exotic shows that catered to their audiences' imaginary reinterpretations of cultural difference prevailed at least for some time.[41] Less ostentatiously, museum mannequins created by artistic means, not as imprints of human bodies, such as the Australian Aboriginal and the Piegan woman, remain successful as museum exhibits to this day.

The Tiwi man's devotion and exhaustion, for example, move us because they suggest the emotional depth of the ceremony that this exhibit represents in the first place. As Birgit Scheps-Bretschneider, the curator of the Aboriginal figure, explained to me, the choice to create and exhibit a museum mannequin in 2009 was not easy, given the medium's colonial history. Nevertheless, the museum decided to continue its exhibition tradition (comparable to that governing the Native American displays of the Karl-May-Museum), while actualizing it in line with contemporary sensibilities. Thus, what distinguishes the new figure both in its process of creation and its display, according to Scheps-Bretschneider, is the respect for the portrayed culture. No body measuring or cast taking affronted an individual's physique for the creation of this exhibit. The same care was devoted to creating an appropriate arrangement of the diorama. Such factors were rarely taken into consideration in the past, when exhibits were considered accumulations of data and arranged in purely pragmatic and culturally insensitive ways, to often inappropriate effects.

Today, a critical yet optimistic perspective on ethnographic mannequins at least suggests that they are understood not as mere objects, but as both informative and expressive artistic creations. In the case of the Leipzig exhibit, the adequate depiction of an event of great significance for Aboriginal cultures is achieved by presenting a composite portrait during a ceremony that speaks of emotional and cultural legacies. Coincidentally, the represented event informs about a specific cultural view on an existential issue that also lingers at the core of the uncanny and, why not, of performance: the immortal soul. The goal of the Tiwi islanders' ritual, however, is not the Western medial one of summoning an absent spirit, but rather the ontological one of inviting reincarnation. This cultural logic excludes the uncanny, because it conceptualizes the life of the soul through organic, not technical reproduction. The museum exhibit depicting this belief permits sufficient distance between these ethnographic, religious, and ontological facts and us observers to allow us to perceive this message in an empathetic and imaginative way through the ethnographic figure.

The Piegan figure also looks real and appeals to us because "she" smiles, but we will ultimately not mistake "her" for a human being. The bright eyes and beaming face suggest an origin in artistic sculpture rather than anthropological face casting and the mannequin appears as charming to us not least because its facial expression opens a window in time, allowing us to imagine how mischievously and yet warmly the model may have smiled at the artist while posing. Just as a Piegan woman might have done, too.

NOTES

1 Britta Lange calls the mannequins used in German colonial exhibitions from the 1920s already "anachronistic" (*Echt* 265).

2 I am grateful to the independent researcher Hartmut Rietschel (Dresden) and Dr Birgit Scheps-Bretschneider, curator of the Australian exhibition at the Grassi Museum of Ethnology (Leipzig), for generously sharing their materials and expertise with me while I was researching this article.

3 In these words, Cixous circumscribes Freud's concept of the uncanny as realm of uncertainty and strangeness ("Fiction and Its Phantoms" 525). As I discuss in the course of this argument, "vivification" has affinities with Freud's concept, so that these terms can be applied to it as well.

4 Today one might even argue that the relationship is inverted, with literature borrowing many of its themes and aesthetic methods from media (e.g., film).

5 For discussions of new modes of scientific and entertainment displays in Wilhelminian Germany see, for example, Ames (*Seeing the Imaginary*, *Hagenbeck's Empire*), Bruckner ("Tingle-Tangle of Modernity"), Lange (*Echt. Unecht. Lebensecht*), Penny (*Objects of Culture*), and Zimmerman (*Anthropology and Antihumanism*).

6 Karl May (1842–1912) was one of the most significant German authors of adventure fiction. Located in his former residence, the Karl-May-Museum is dedicated mainly to his biography and works.

7 For example, in 2014, the exhibition of supposedly Ojibway scalps caused a widely publicized public debate and an agreement between the Karl-May-Museum and representatives of the Ojibway nation. See, for example, media reporting by Liebschner ("Die Kopfhaut"), Oltermann ("German Museum"). For belated accounts, see Eddy ("Lost in Translation") and Pitzke ("Der Streit"). Leipold ("Über die Rückforderung") complements them with a curatorial approach.

8 The Karl-May-Museum's Native American exhibition is located in a separate building called "Villa Bärenfett" (Villa Bear Fat, a name evoking May's

Wild West fictions). This log cabin was erected in 1926 for Patty Frank (1876–1959), a circus performer, ethnographic collector, and the museum's later administrator, as an exhibition space and private residence. The quality of today's collection owes much to Frank's expertise and connections as a collector. Still, as his memoir reflects, Frank's attitude towards Native Americans was replete with racism and clichés (*Ein Leben im Banne Karl May's*).

9 To this author, Güttner's portraits appear more artfully executed than Grämer's. His most prominent mannequin exhibit is a diorama depicting the family of a Plains Chief that welcomes home victorious warriors. The painted backdrop representing these warriors was created by controversial artist Elk Eber (1892–1941), who is best known for his depictions of German soldiers during the Third Reich. On Eber's relationship to the Karl-May-Museum and Native Americans, see Penny, *Kindred by Choice*, chap. 4, "Modern Germans and Indians." I am grateful to Hartmut Rietschel for the historical details about the mannequins of the Karl-May-Museum.

10 While its actual production year is unknown, the figure was first mentioned in 1928, the year of the museum's opening (Hoffmann, "Zur Geschichte" 102).

11 All information about this exhibit is courtesy of Birgit Scheps-Bretschneider. Personal communication, 18 June 2012.

12 Observation by Scheps-Bretschneider.

13 Other models were selected from indigenous groups visited by anthropologists.

14 Unless stated otherwise, all translations from German are mine.

15 I did not find detailed information about the sources and production process of the mannequins created by Güttner. However, Rietschel's private document collection of the historical Wild West scene in Saxony contains a photograph depicting the artist and his wife, as an inscription on the photograph explains. Both were members of the renowned and still existing Munich cowboy club (Cowboy-Club-München 1913 e.V.). In the image, Güttner is dressed as a cowboy and his spouse as a Native American Plains woman. A close comparison between her face and the Radebeul mannequin's suggested at least to this viewer that the figure might be an idealized and younger depiction of Güttner's wife whose ethnicity remains to be identified. (Undated photograph by Franz Xaver Lehner, presumably from the 1920s; reference and information courtesy of Hartmut Rietschel.)

16 Personal communication with Scheps-Bretschneider.

17 In 1916, a natural history collection donated to the Spanish village Banyoles still contained the taxidermied body of a Bushman, who was removed from the exhibition only in 1992 and returned to Botswana another eight years later (Moyano, "'Nègre de Banyoles'" 145).

18 Under the same title, Menzel painted a predecessor to this study in 1852. This image depicts the casts of two arms hung from a wall between a shelf and a window. One arm is bent, the other holds an elongated object (possibly a carving or drawing tool). Both are suspended above a mummified human hand and a skull. The mood of this painting is similar to that of its 1872 complement: dark and foreboding, it is created by sparse light that illuminates the depicted objects from below. The 1852 painting also suggests morbidity and an ominous sense that technological and organic replication and preservation may (literally) go *hand in hand* with physical and aesthetic de-composition.

19 Although the subject is clear, this image lends itself to an even more positive reading if the negative's function is inverted. Thus, the depicted moment could be interpreted not as the taking of a cast but as that when male makers free their flawless creation from its mould, the last trace of its technological origin. Dantan's painting may suggest that the two artists have *created* such a naturalistic representation of a lovely woman – "sur la nature," i.e., from life – and that "she," the visual focus of the canvas, has come to life just as in the Pygmalion myth.

20 Johann Friedrich Blumenbach's and Samuel Thomas Soemmering's proto-racial theories, for example, aimed to establish morphological classifications of "nationalities" or to derive the psychological features of human groups on the basis of biometric and cranial measurements. (Burke, "Wild Man's Pedigree" 268–70, Kaufmann, "Vom Zeichen" 108–12). See also Zimmerman's excellent discussion of German methods of anthropological measurement at the heyday of Wilhelminian imperialism (Zimmerman 86–171).

21 Authenticity was defined not least economically. One of Umlauff's product catalogues from 1909 not only lists the various nationalities depicted by mannequins, but also indicates the price distinction between the more expensive full-body figures made of durable papier-mâché and the cheaper ones with doll bodies and wax or papier-mâché heads, hands, and feet. All figures, however, came with "original and authentic" clothes, jewellery, and weapons (Lange 267–9).

22 As he notes himself, Freud borrows this idea from Schelling ("Uncanny" 225).

23 Freud also observes that our organs of sight are often connoted negatively, for example, as the ominous and potentially deadly evil eyes of popular beliefs.

24 Freud notes that uncanny reactions vary from person to person. Scheps-Bretschneider also reported that many visitors encountering the Tiwi man's portrait feel enthralled, not repelled by it.

25 Or would anyone be easily convinced that the actual Angela Merkel, John F. Kennedy, or Barack Obama gather in the same building of Madame Tussaud's Berlin branch? ("Wen möchten Sie treffen?")

26 Freud notes that he draws from Otto Rank's theory of the double ("Uncanny" 235).
27 The casts were meant to complement Otto Finsch's collection in Berlin that consisted of 164 life masks.
28 The fact that they were suspicious because they did not comprehend the procedure calls into question Schellong's degree of transparency towards his collaborators.
29 Warren's *Buffalo Bill's America* (2005) and Sagala's *Buffalo Bill on Stage* (2008) offer insightful examples and analyses of such staple-fare ethnic characters in the context of the theatrical performances of William Cody (a.k.a. Buffalo Bill).
30 For example, at the time when it toured Germany, Buffalo Bill's "Wild West" was regarded as the latest trend in ethnographic exhibits (Ames, *Seeing the Imaginary* 213).
31 They were incorrectly listed as "Sioux." Coloured reproductions of the face masks were commercially available at the price of 15 marks (Friederici, D3 7).
32 Of these, Carl Hagenbeck's animal trade company alone managed 69.
33 For a detailed and current transnational analysis of the Bella Coolas' tours and impact on their German audiences, see particularly the subsections "The Showmen and the Sioux" (chap. 1), "German Audiences" (chap. 3), and "Diffusion and Cultural Traits" (chap. 8) in Penny, *Kindred by Choice*.
34 Like the Omaha, this troupe performed at Castan's Panopticon in Berlin in 1898–9. It was the last one of five Native American troupes that had appeared in this location since 1882 (Friederici, D3 16).
35 Usually, performers presented scenes from the lives of contemporary colonized and European cultures. However, because Native Americans were considered a vanishing race in line with the ideology of Manifest Destiny, their performances portrayed – at least in the understanding of their turn-of-the-century audiences – cultures on the verge of extinction.
36 Presenting mannequins in so-called life groups was one of the most popular modes to exhibit them. Such arrangements were governed by principles of staging borrowed from theatre and spectacle. For example, in his instructions regarding such a display, anthropologist Franz Boas (1858–1942) wrote: "In order to set off such a group to advantage it must be seen from one side only, the view must be through a kind of frame which shuts out the line where the scene ends, the visitor must be in a comparatively dark place while there must be a certain light on the objects and on the background" (qtd. in Lange 163). Not only through its vocabulary ("view," "frame," "scene," "background"), but also its practical suggestions about how the figures should be positioned and illuminated for best effect, this remark reflects the anthropologist's familiarity with the aesthetics of conventional theatre and the fact that he aimed to

transpose this aesthetics into the museum. Boas, one of the most significant figures of modern American anthropology, had been a curator of the Royal Museum of Ethnology in Berlin before he moved to New York. He too had seen the Bella Coolas. He also made gypsum casts of Kwakiutls and used photographs of Umlauff mannequins in his work in New York (ibid.).

37 Buffalo Bill's "Wild West" toured Germany in 1890 and 1906, where it performed in over sixty cities and towns (Kort and Hollein, *I Like America* 230). This and other Wild West shows were so successful that, after the North American groups left, German show producers such as Hagenbeck and Hans-Stosch Sarrasani hired Native American performers for their own Wild West shows in the first decades of the twentieth century. For a recent analysis of these entertainments see Penny, *Kindred by Choice*.

38 A similar point is made by Josef Rattner and Gerhard Danzer (*Literatur und Psychoanalyse* 27–43).

39 Olympia's function in the text as lifelike albeit lifeless figure would have kept the definition of the uncanny too close to Jentsch's. Cixous further observes that Freud sets up a confrontation between the sandman and the neurotic Nathaniel that is more sustained and obsessive than Hoffmann narrates it. He thus literally reinvents his source text by pruning it of any elements that did not serve his reading (533), i.e., by fragmenting and reconstructing it to serve his own goals.

40 Ames refers specifically to James Fenimore Cooper, Friedrich Gerstäcker, and Karl May (*Seeing the Imaginary* 214; *Hagenbeck's Empire* 109, 131).

41 As it offered its spectators ethnically marked human bodies in acting, on which they could project their German literary fantasies of America, a spectacle such as William Cody's "Wild West," for example, left an indelible mark on popular culture whose reverberations are felt to this day in German western films and events, Native American and other American re-enactments, and Karl May festivals.

WORKS CITED

Ames, Eric. *Carl Hagenbeck's Empire of Entertainments*. Seattle: U of Washington P, 2008.

– "Seeing the Imaginary: On the Popular Reception of Wild West Shows in Germany, 1885–1910." In *I Like America: Fictions of the Wild West*. Ed. Pamela Kort and Max Hollein. Munich: Prestel, 2006. 212–29.

"Angelo Soliman." At http://www.sadocc.at/angelo-soliman.shtml. N.d.

Barba, Eugenio. *The Paper Canoe: A Guide to Theatre Anthropology*. Trans. Richard Fowler. London: Routledge, 1995.

Bruckner, Sierra Anne. "The Tingle-Tangle of Modernity: Popular Anthropology and the Cultural Politics of Identity in Imperial Germany." Diss., University of Iowa, 1999.

Burke, John G. "The Wild Man's Pedigree: Scientific Method and Racial Anthropology." In *The Wild Man Within: An Image in Western Thought from the Renaissance to Romanticism*. Ed. Edward Dudley and Maximilian E. Novak. Pittsburgh: U of Pittsburgh P, 1972. 259–80.

Cixous, Hélène. "Fiction and Its Phantoms: A Reading of Freud's Das Unheimliche (The 'Uncanny')." *New Literary History* 7.3 (1976): 525-48.

Dräger, Lothar, and Rolf Krusche. "Ausstellung 'Indianer Nordamerikas.'" In *Indianer Nordamerikas: Ausstellung im Blockhaus "Villa Bärenfett" des Karl-May-Museums*. Ed. Lothar Dräger, Rolf Krusche, and Klaus Hoffmann. Radebeul: Karl-May-Stiftung, 1992. 5–88.

Dreesbach, Anne. *Gezähmte Wilde: Die Zurschaustellung "exotischer" Menschen in Deutschland 1870–1940*. Frankfurt: Campus Verlag, 2005.

Eddy, Melissa. "Lost in Translation: Germany's Fascination with the American Old West." *New York Times*, 17 August 2014. http://www.nytimes.com/2014/08/18/world/europe/germanys-fascination-with-american-old-west-native-american-scalps-human-remains.html?_r=0.

Frank, Patty. *Ein Leben im Banne Karl May's und kleine Erzählungen*. Radebeul bei Dresden: Karl-May-Verlag, 1942.

Flynn, Tom. *The Body in Three Dimensions*. New York: Harry N. Abrams, 1998.

Freud, Sigmund. "Totem and Taboo." In *The Basic Writings of Sigmund Freud*. New York: Modern Library, 1938. 807–930.

– "The Uncanny." In *The Standard Edition of the Complete Psychological Works of Sigmund Freud*. Ed. James Strachey. Vol. 17. London: The Hogarth Press, 1957. 218–56.

Friederici, Angelika. "Lebensmasken aus Papua-Neuguinea." In *Castans Panopticum: Ein Medium wird besichtigt*. Vol. 6. Berlin: Verlag Carl-Robert Schütze, 2009. D2, 1–23.

– "Völker der Welt auf Castans Bühnen."In *Castans Panopticum*. Vol. 10. Berlin: Verlag Carl-Robert Schütze, 2011. D3, 1–24.

Hoffmann, Klaus. "Zur Geschichte des Karl-May-Museums, seiner indianischen Sammlungsobjekte und deren Präsentation." In *Indianer Nordamerikas: Ausstellung im Blockhaus "Villa Bärenfett" des Karl-May-Museums*. Ed. Lothar Dräger, Rolf Krusche, and Klaus Hoffmann. Radebeul: Karl-May-Stiftung, 1992. 89–114.

Jentsch, Ernst. "Zur Psychologie des Unheimlichen." *Psychiatrisch-Neurologische Wochenschrift* 8.22, 25 August 1906. Halle: Carl Marhold Verlag, 195–8.

Karl-May-Museum Radebeul. Ed. Karl-May-Museum. Reichenbach: Verlag Bild und Heimat, n.d. Print.

Kaufmann Stefan. "Vom Zeichen zur Ursache einer kulturellen Differenz. Die Körper der Wilden in der Anthropologie des 18. Jahrhunderts." In *Der Alteritätsdiskurs des Edlen Wilden: Exotismus, Anthropologie und Zivilisationskritik am Beispiel eines europäischen Topos.* Ed. Monika Fludernik, Peter Haslinger, and Stefan Kaufmann. Würzburg: Ergon Verlag, 2002. 95–120.

Kort, Pamela, Max Hollein, eds. *I Like America: Fictions of the Wild West.* Munich: Prestel, 2006.

Lange, Britta. *Echt. Unecht. Lebensecht. Menschenbilder im Umlauff.* Berlin: Kulturverlag Kadmos, 2006.

Leipold, Robin. "Über die Rückforderung eines Skalps aus der Sammlung des Karl-May-Museums in Radebeul: Eine Chance zur Provenienzforschung." *Amerindian Research. Zeitschrift für indianische Kulturen von Alaska bis Feuerland* 9.3 (2014): 156–61. Print.

Liebschner, Wolf Dieter. "Die Kopfhaut der Begierde." *sz-online.de*, 19. March 2014. At http://www.sz-online.de/sachsen/die-kopfhaut-der-begierde-2799241.html.

Moyano, Neus. "Le 'Nègre de Banyoles.'" In *Exhibitions: L'invention du sauvage.* Ed. Pascal Blanchard, Gilles Boëtsch, and Nanette Jacomijn Snoep. Arles: Actes Sud Éditions, 2011. 145.

Oltermann, Philip. "German Museum in Row with US Activists over Tribal Scalps." *The Guardian*, 10 March 2014. http://www.theguardian.com/world/2014/mar/10/german-museum-karl-may-native-american-scalps.

Penny, Glenn H. *Kindred by Choice: Germans and American Indians since 1800.* Chapel Hill: U of North Carolina P, 2013.

– *Objects of Culture: Ethnology and Ethnographic Museums in Imperial Germany.* Chapel Hill: U of North Carolina P, 2002.

Pitzke, Marc. "Der Streit um die Skalpe von Radebeul." *Spiegel online*, 18 August 2014. http://www.spiegel.de/panorama/gesellschaft/karl-may-museum-in-radbeul-us-ureinwohner-fordern-skalpe-zurueck-a-986608.html.

Rattner, Josef, and Gerhard Danzer. *Literatur und Psychoanalyse.* Würzburg: Königshausen & Neumann, 2010.

Sagala, Sandra K. *Buffalo Bill on Stage.* Albuquerque: U of New Mexico P, 2008.

Sandberg, Mark B. *Living Pictures, Missing Persons.* Princeton: Princeton UP, 2003.

Schwartz, Hillel. *The Culture of the Copy: Striking Likenesses, Unreasonable Facsimiles.* New York: Zone Books, 1996.

Thode-Arora, Hilke. *Für fünfzig Pfennig um die Welt: Die Hagenbeckschen Völkerschauen*. Frankfurt: Campus Verlag, 1989.

Trilling, Lionel. "Freud and Literature." In *The Liberal Imagination: Essays on Literature and Society*. Viking Press: New York, 1950. 34–57.

Walker, Saint John. "A Quick Walk through 'Uncanny Valley.'" In *Modes of Spectating*. Ed. Alison Oddey and Christine White. Bristol: Intellect, 2009. 29–40.

Warren, Louis S. *Buffalo Bill's America: William Cody and the Wild West Show*. New York: Vintage Books, 2005.

"Wen möchten Sie treffen?" N.d. At http://www.madametussauds.com/Berlin/UnsereFiguren/Default.aspx.

Zilcosky, John. "Uncanny Encounters: Adventure Literature, Psychoanalysis, and Ethnographic Exhibitions." In *Literature and Science. Literatur und Wissenschaft*. Ed. Monika Schmitz-Emans. Würzburg: Königshausen & Neumann, 2008. 139–58.

Zimmerman, Andrew. *Anthropology and Antihumanism in Imperial Germany*. Chicago: U of Chicago P, 2001.

Contributors

Tina Young Choi is associate professor of English and a member of the Graduate Faculty in Science and Technology Studies at York University in Toronto. Her research and teaching interests include nineteenth-century literary and scientific writing, and the histories of the city and of the body. She is the author of *Anonymous Connections* (U Michigan P, 2015) and the editor of *Medicine and Sanitary Science* (Pickering and Chatto, 2012).

Stefani Engelstein is associate research professor of German at Duke University and associate professor of German at the University of Missouri. She is author of *Anxious Anatomy: The Conception of the Human Form in Literary and Naturalist Discourse* (SUNY, 2008) and co-editor of *Contemplating Violence: Critical Studies in Modern German Culture* (Rodopi, 2011). Her work has also appeared in such journals as the *PMLA* and *Critical Inquiry*. She is currently completing a manuscript entitled *Sibling Action: The Genealogical Structure of Modernity*.

Jocelyn Holland received her PhD from Johns Hopkins in 2003 and is currently associate professor of German at the University of California, Santa Barbara. Her publications include *German Romanticism and Science: The Procreative Poetics of Goethe, Novalis, and Ritter* (Routledge, 2009), *Key Texts by Johann Wilhelm Ritter (1776–1810) on the Science and Art of Nature* (Brill, 2010) as well as special editions of *Configurations* on *The Aesthetics of the Tool* (co-edited with Susanne Strätling) and *Sub-Stance* on *The Archimedean Point: From Fixed Positions to the Limits of Theory* (co-edited with Edgar Landgraf). Her current project is on the mechanical lever as a figure of thought in the eighteenth and nineteenth centuries.

Michael House (PhD, Princeton, 2009) is an assistant professor of German in the Department of Languages, Literatures and Cultures at the University of South Carolina. Before joining the faculty, he was an assistant professor at Dalhousie University and an Andrew Mellon postdoctoral fellow at the Jackman Humanities Institute (2009–10) at the University of Toronto. His research explores the intersections of literature, epistemology, and human sciences around 1800. He has recently published articles on this theme, including "Beyond the Brain: Skeptical and Satirical Reactions to Gall's *Organologie*," in *Neurology and Modernity* (2010), and "Kant's Uncertain Mariner," in *Schiffbrüche und Idyllen* (2014). He is currently completing a manuscript, tentatively titled *Grounding Fictions: Skepticism, Idealism and the Modern Individual.*

Alice Kuzniar has been professor of German and English at the University of Waterloo since 2008, after teaching 25 years at the University of North Carolina at Chapel Hill, with guest professorships at Princeton, Rutgers, and the University of Minnesota. Her books include *The Queer German Cinema* (Stanford University Press, 2000) and *Melancholia's Dog: Reflections On Our Animal Kinship* (University of Chicago Press, 2006). She has just completed a book entitled *The Romantic Art of Homeopathy.*

Christine Lehleiter is an associate professor of German at the University of Toronto. Her research focuses on the intersection between literature and the life sciences. Among her publications are the monograph *Romanticism, Origins, and the History of Heredity* (Bucknell University Press, 2014) and articles on eighteenth-century notions of generation and gender.

Peter McIsaac is associate professor of German Studies and Museum Studies at the University of Michigan. He works at the intersections of German literary culture and museums; on popular anatomy exhibitions (Body Worlds and its predecessors); uses of digital devices in museum galleries; and with digital humanities approaches to mainstream nineteenth-century German periodicals. His publications include the book *Museums of the Mind: German Modernity and the Dynamics of Collecting* and articles that have appeared in *The German Quarterly*; *Seminar*, *Monatshefte*, *Literatur für Leser*, *German Life and Letters*, and *The International Journal of Cultural Policy*. With Gabriele Mueller, he co-edited *Exhibiting the German Past: Museums, Film, and Musealization* (University of Toronto Press, 2015).

John K. Noyes is professor of German at the University of Toronto since 2001. He has written on the cultural history of colonialism, postcolonial theory, and the history of sexuality. His books include *Colonial Space* (1992), *The Mastery of Submission* (1997), and most recently *Goethe's Faust: Theatre of Modernity*, edited with Hans Schulte and Pia Kleber (2010). His book *Herder: Aesthetics against Imperialism* will appear with University of Toronto Press in September 2015.

Daniel Aureliano Newman is an associate at the Institute for the History and Philosophy of Science and Technology (University of Toronto). His research focuses on the two-way traffic of narrative structures between innovative fiction and scientific theories and models. He has essays published or forthcoming in *Style* and *James Joyce Quarterly*, as well as in the *American Journal of Botany* and *Oikos*. His other research interests include the Bildungsroman, unnatural narratology, strange narrators in Irish fiction, and selfish-gene theory.

Ann Shteir is professor emerita at York University in humanities and the graduate program in gender, feminist, and women's studies. She is author of *Cultivating Women, Cultivating Science: Flora's Daughters and Botany in England 1760 to 1860* (1996), which won the Joan G. Kelly Prize in Women's History. She co-edited *Natural Eloquence: Women Reinscribe Science* (1997) with Barbara T. Gates, and *Figuring It Out: Science, Gender, and Visual Culture* (2006) with Bernard Lightman. Current projects are women and botany in early-nineteenth-century British North America, and mythography and science.

Christian P. Weber is associate professor of German studies at Florida State University, Tallahassee. His research aims for a comprehensive phenomenological and critical investigation of the human imagination by examining its various manifestations in literature (especially Goethe and the Romantics), the sciences, and the history of nationalism. He is the author of *Die Logik der Lyrik: Goethes Phänomenologie des Geistes in Gedichten* (Rombach, 2013).

A. Dana Weber is an assistant professor of German in the Department of Modern Languages and Linguistics at Florida State University. She is currently completing a monograph on the intersections of literature, folklore, and performance in German Wild West festivals. Dana's published articles explore legends in media, cultural transfers in German festivals and performances, Native American theatrical representations, and the transcultural dynamics of fraternity bonds in Quentin Tarantino's *Django Unchained* (2012).

Tobias Wilke, PhD and Dr. phil., is assistant professor in the Department of Germanic Languages at Columbia University, New York. His work focuses primarily on the history of German literature and culture from the mid-nineteenth century onwards, with a particular emphasis on the broader contexts of European modernism, the history of media and media theory, and the interrelations between aesthetics and empirical psychology. He is the author of two books: *Medien der Unmittelbarkeit: Dingkonzepte und Wahrnehmungstechniken 1918–1939* (Fink, 2010), and *Einführung in die Literatur der Jahrhundertwende* (Wissenschaftliche Buchgesellschaft, 2nd ed., 2011), co-authored with Dorothee Kimmich. He is also the co-editor of a special issue of *Grey Room*, "Walter Benjamin's Media Tactics" (Spring 2010), and the co-editor of the volume *Gefühl und Genauigkeit: Empirische Ästhetik um 1900* (Fink, 2014). His articles have appeared in such journals as *DVjs*, *MLN*, *Scientia Poetica*, *Monatshefte*, *Grey Room*, and *Zeitschrift für deutsche Philologie*.

Index

www.ingramcontent.com/pod-product-compliance
Lightning Source LLC
LaVergne TN
LVHW090148080826
844660LV00013B/716/J

* 9 7 8 1 4 4 2 6 4 5 9 8 1 *